MONTEREY & CARMEL

STUART THORNTON

Contents

MONTEREY
& CARMEL

DISCOVER
Monterey & Carmel

Monterey Bay is California in microcosm. Here, you can experience the best the Golden State has to offer—without the big-city crowds and complications.

The best days in Monterey are spent in the water. Dive into a kelp forest. Explore the scenic coastline on a kayak or stand-up paddleboard. Scout for migrating whales passing near the shores.

The idyllic village of Carmel possesses seaside charm. From white-sand beaches to luxurious hotels, it promises a refined, high-class vacation bursting with art galleries and tasting rooms. Nearby Pebble Beach offers world-class golfing and stunning scenery.

Not far away, excursions range from quirky beach town Santa Cruz to opulent Hearst Castle. Big Sur is the region's most dramatic stretch of coastline, and the perfect geography for an unforgettable road trip.

Monterey Bay is not just a collision of land and sea, but also a juxtaposition of jarring colors and symbiotic ecosystems. From world-class wines and fine foods to a wonderland of marine life, Monterey encapsulates the California dream.

Clockwise from top left: Casa Palmero in Pebble Beach; coastline along Highway 1 in Big Sur; sea lion in Monterey; Point Lobos; Pacific Grove Monarch Butterfly Sanctuary; golf course at The Lodge at Pebble Beach.

10 TOP EXPERIENCES

1 **Explore the Monterey Bay Aquarium:** See the marine habitats and sea creatures that make up the local aquatic ecosystem at this artful aquarium (page 40).

2 **Spot Whales.** Hop on a boat tour to spy humpbacks, blue whales, and gray whales as they migrate through Monterey Bay (page 55).

3 **Go Wine-Tasting: Carmel-by-the-Sea** (page 107) has more than a dozen tasting rooms within a few-block radius, while **Carmel Valley** (page 126) and the **River Road Wine Trail** (page 141) near Salinas offer a more laid-back experience and charming tasting rooms.

>>>

4 **Kayak the Coast:** Rent a kayak or stand-up paddleboard or book a tour to explore Monterey Bay up close (page 54).

^
^
^

5 **Catch Your Thrills on the Santa Cruz Beach Boardwalk:** This throwback amusement park set right on the beach delights summer lovers with its wooden roller coaster, rides, and arcades (page 162).

6 **Surf Santa Cruz:** Try out your skills at superb surf breaks like **Steamer Lane** and **Cowell's Beach** (page 168).

7 **Gaze Up in Awe at the Spires of Pinnacles National Park:** Full of castle-like rock formations, canyons, and caves created by volcanic activity, this wonderland in the Salinas Valley is best explored on foot (page 148).

8 **Cruise the Big Sur Coast Highway:** This twisty, two-lane highway offers a scrapbook's worth of postcard-perfect views (page 205).

9 **Hike in Big Sur:** Big Sur has some of the state's best and most varied hiking. Walk through coast redwood forests, hike to stunning waterfalls, and discover pristine seashores (page 216).

10 **Tour Hearst Castle:** Explore the opulence of another era with a guided tour of the hilltop estate of William Randolph Hearst (page 246).

Planning Your Trip

Where to Go

Monterey

Visit the **Monterey Bay Aquarium** to learn about the area's fascinating marine life, and then head out on a **kayak, stand-up paddleboard,** or on a **whale-watching trip** to view sea otters, harbor seals, and migrating whales. Afterward, explore **downtown Monterey** and dig deep into the scenic town's rich history at the adobe buildings of **Monterey State Historic Park.** Take in the silence in **San Carlos Cathedral,** which was built as a place of worship for the Spanish military in 1794.

Carmel

Wander around in the art galleries of **Carmel-by-the-Sea,** and then stroll along **Ocean Avenue** to the scenic sands of **Carmel Beach.** If you are a wine lover, be sure to hit the **wineries** downtown or head out to **Carmel Valley** to taste some of the area's best varietals. Or go for a hike in one of Carmel's beautiful **regional parks.**

Salinas

Stroll around **Oldtown Salinas** before a visit to the **National Steinbeck Center,** a museum devoted to famed writer and Salinas native John Steinbeck. Follow that with lunch at **The Steinbeck House,** where the writer was born. Head south down Salinas Valley to spend some time in **Pinnacles National Park** and gawk at the amazing rock formations.

Santa Cruz

Have some throwback fun on the Giant Dipper roller coaster at the **Santa Cruz Beach Boardwalk** then grab a board and **surf** one of Santa Cruz's many waves. Be sure to experience the town's vibrant downtown with a walk along **Pacific Avenue,** stopping for lunch in one of its many restaurants. Drive into the **Santa Cruz Mountains** for the coast redwoods at **Henry Cowell Redwoods State Park,** or see a colony of elephant seals at **Año Nuevo State Park.**

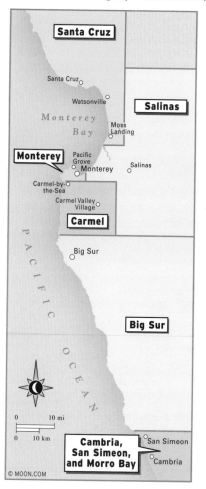

Big Sur

Some of the most beautiful coastline in the world is along this section of the **Pacific Coast Highway.** Make sure your camera or phone has lots of room for photos of **Pfeiffer Beach** and **McWay Falls.** Slip on your hiking boots for a longer day hike at **Julia Pfeiffer Burns State Park** or **Andrew Molera State Park.** Since Big Sur is a particularly volatile region prone to fires, floods, and mudslides, check trail conditions and closures on the **California State Parks website** (www.parks.ca.gov) before making hiking plans.

Cambria, San Simeon, and Morro Bay

Tour grandiose **Hearst Castle** in San Simeon. Take time to visit the area's unique natural features, such as Cambria's **Moonstone Beach** or **Montaña de Oro State Park,** outside of Morro Bay.

Know Before You Go

When to Go

The Monterey region's best feature is its **all-season** appeal. In **summer,** expect significant crowds at popular attractions, wineries, beaches, and campgrounds. In **fall,** the area is a bit less crowded, but the weather is still warm. It's also when some of the best surfing waves occur along the coast. Note that late summer-early fall is also **wildfire season,** during which access to affected areas and air quality can be severely impacted. **Winter** is the rainy season, although the days between storms are often clear with mild temperatures. The crowds are lightest at this time, except on holiday weekends. During **spring,** the land is green and colored with wildflowers. The winds can really kick up in the afternoon along the coast.

Summer fog is likely along the coast. Bring

a rock formation at Pfeiffer Beach

seagull in Monterey

layered clothing. Also bring sunscreen; that coastal fog doesn't stop UV rays.

Reservations

It is essential to make advance reservations for lodging and camping in Big Sur, Monterey, Carmel, and Santa Cruz, especially during summer. It's necessary to reserve a spot in a Hearst Castle tour before arriving. Expect the Monterey Bay Aquarium to have significant crowds during the summer (visit 2pm-6pm Tues.-Thurs. when there are fewer people.) Finally, an advance reservation is the only way you'll be able to play on Pebble Beach's famed golf courses.

Transportation

If you're road-tripping through the region, visit the California Department of Transportation website (www.dot.ca.gov) for current road conditions. It is especially important to know about road conditions in the Big Sur and Santa Cruz Mountains given frequent road closures due to the mudslides and rockslides that often occur in these two regions.

The Best of Monterey and Carmel

The major attractions of the Monterey Bay region can be explored in a long weekend, but taking up to five days will allow for a more immersive experience. The two best approaches to exploring the area are to choose a home base (like Monterey or Pacific Grove) and plan day trips; or to take a road trip through the region, beginning in Santa Cruz, continuing into Monterey, Carmel, and Big Sur, and ending in Cambria or Morro Bay.

Monterey: Maritime Escape

Time in Monterey should be spent exploring the bay itself, whether by visiting the world-renowned Monterey Bay Aquarium or heading out on the water on a kayak, stand-up paddleboard, or whale-watching vessel.

Day 1

After an early arrival in Monterey, take a leisurely walk around the Monterey Harbor on the Monterey Bay Coastal Recreation Trail. Be sure to head out on the Coast Guard Pier if you want to view some harbor seals and sea lions up close.

Grab a seafood lunch with a harbor view at The Sandbar & Grill or an artfully done sandwich, salad, or pizza at Alta Bakery & Cafe before heading over to Cannery Row to spend the afternoon taking in furry sea otters and swirling

Monterey Bay

Monterey's popular Cannery Row

jellyfish at the **Monterey Bay Aquarium.** Head back to downtown Monterey for a beer at the popular **Alvarado Street Brewery** or enjoy a stellar cocktail and snack at **Montrio.** Stay there for dinner or head to **Monterey's Fish House** for oak-grilled seafood.

The **Portola Hotel & Spa** in downtown Monterey has an ideal location near Alvarado Street and Monterey's Fisherman's Wharf, while **Monterey Bay Inn** is perched right over the bay just walking distance from Cannery Row. Budget travelers can bed down at **Lone Oak Lodge** off North Fremont Street.

Day 2

It's time to experience Monterey's amazing marine life firsthand. Mornings are the best time to hit the water, before the winds start. Rent a **kayak** or **stand-up paddleboard** from **Monterey Bay Kayaks** and paddle out into the bay from nearby **Monterey State Beach.** Or, head underwater by **scuba diving** or **snorkeling** off Monterey's **Breakwater Cove,** one of the best beginner dive spots in the state.

Another way to experience the bay is to secure a seat on a **whale-watching** tour that leaves from Monterey Harbor. During the winter and spring migrations, gray whales swim right along Monterey's coast.

For dinner head to Wave Street, one block from Cannery Row. Have a drink at **The Sardine Factory,** a longtime Monterey landmark. Enjoy a steak dinner next door at the **Whaling Station,** or walk up Lighthouse Avenue for island fare and fun at **Hula's Island Grill & Tiki Room.**

Day 3

Begin the day with a coffee and a snack in downtown Monterey at **Captain + Stoker,** or take a short trip to **The Butter House** in Seaside for one of the area's best breakfasts, with options like lemon curd pancakes and chicken-and-waffles.

Return to Monterey and explore its historic buildings. The **Monterey State Historic Park** has historic adobes and old government buildings scattered around downtown that are well worth visiting. The **Custom House** and **Pacific House Museum** located around Custom House

Plaza are good places to start. Take an hour-long **guided walking tour** of the park for an overview of the area's history.

Fans of old Victorian buildings should spend time in **Pacific Grove** and take in its quaint downtown along **Lighthouse Avenue.** Be sure to detour down to **Lovers Point Park** for its views of the curving bay.

Stay in Pacific Grove for dinner. **Passionfish** is known for serving tasty and sustainable seafood, while **Poppy Hall** serves California rustic cuisine—superb seafood, veggie, and meat dishes.

Day Trip to Salinas

Break a sweat and then crack open a bottle of wine on a day trip around inland Monterey County. Start by embarking on the hour-long drive to one of the country's newest national parks: **Pinnacles National Park,** a wonderland of rock spires, sheer walls, steep canyons, and caves. The park's west end, the closest entrance from Monterey, provides access to a handful of trails. One recommended hike is the **Juniper Canyon Loop,** which goes up to the impressive High Peaks.

Cool off afterward by crossing the Salinas Valley to reach the **River Road Wine Trail,** a string of wineries in the Santa Lucia Highlands. Post up on the outdoor deck at **Hahn Winery Tasting Room** for views of Pinnacles rising in the distance as you sample pinot noir and chardonnay.

Head to **Salinas** for dinner. Choose between upscale European fare at **Patria,** hearty Italian food at family-friendly **Gino's,** or tasty tri-tip at **Salinas City Barbeque.**

Pacific Grove in spring

Carmel: Art, Wine, and Beaches

Carmel-by-the-Sea has one of the state's best beaches, along with a downtown full of art galleries and tasting rooms. Carmel Valley is home to an up-and-coming wine industry.

Day 1

Start your time in Carmel with a superb breakfast at Stationaery; the menu rotates frequently, but maybe you'll luck out with the chilaquiles or potato pancake with salmon. Then stroll along Ocean Avenue, taking time to peer into the art galleries and upscale boutiques. Make your way west as the road starts its descent to Carmel Beach, one of the finest beaches in the entire state. Once on the sugar-white sands, take off your shoes and let your dog run on the beach. Save some energy for the walk back up Ocean Avenue.

After returning to your vehicle, head 3 miles (4.8 km) south on CA-1 to reach Point Lobos State Natural Reserve, which is rumored to have inspired Robert Louis Stevenson's *Treasure Island*. There, the Cypress Grove Trail boasts twisted Monterey cypress trees and stunning coastline views.

Return to Carmel-by-the-Sea for a drink and snack on the rooftop bar at Vesuvio, or sample some high-end mescal and Mexican food at Cultura Comida y Bebida.

Spend the night with the sounds of the nearby sea at La Playa Carmel or stay in the Far East-inspired Tradewinds Carmel. Traveling with a furry friend? Consider the pro-pup Cypress Inn, formerly co-owned by the late actress and animal-rights activist Doris Day.

Day 2

Get a hearty breakfast at the Little Swiss Café or grab a coffee and pastry at Carmel Valley Coffee Roasting Co. Then take a tour of the

Carmel

Play in the Bay

Monterey Bay features coastline directly in the impact zone of ocean swells, as well as tranquil, protected areas uncommon to most of the California coast. These conditions make the region suitable for lots of different water-based recreation.

SURFING

Santa Cruz is the surf capital of this region. Steamer Lane has surfers from around the world drooling with anticipation, while many beginners have caught their first waves at Cowell's Beach. Pleasure Point is another great place for long, peeling waves.

In Monterey County, Carmel Beach and Asilomar State Beach are consistent beach breaks worth checking out.

KAYAKING AND STAND-UP PADDLEBOARDING

Monterey is one of the best places along the California coast to kayak or stand-up paddleboard. The relatively protected waters from Monterey's Municipal Wharf to the Monterey Bay Aquarium make for a great paddle. If the swell or winds kick up, duck into Monterey Harbor for protection.

Although known for its golf courses, Pebble Beach also has Stillwater Cove, a superb paddling spot. Moss Landing's Elkhorn Slough provides a place to see otters and seals without being exposed to ocean swells.

One of the highlights of Morro Bay is getting out in the bay on a kayak or stand-up paddleboard, where you might spot some local wildlife like sea otters.

SCUBA DIVING AND SNORKELING

The best way to see the multitude of sea life, kelp forests, and reefs off the Monterey shoreline is to put on some snorkeling or scuba gear and get underwater. People come from all over California to dive in Monterey. Breakwater Cove is a popular, easy-to-access spot where lots of people have completed their certification dives. Nearby, Pacific Grove's Lovers Point Park has a protected cove and kelp forest for snorkelers and scuba divers.

Carmel's Monastery Beach is for advanced divers and features a steep drop-off into a deep underwater canyon. Point Lobos State Natural Reserve has underwater attractions in addition to terrestrial sights. Make reservations in advance to dive the park's Whaler's Cove and the deeper Bluefish Cove.

Tor House, a fascinating castle-like structure on Carmel Point constructed by nature poet Robinson Jeffers. Tours are only offered on Fridays and Saturdays.

It's afternoon by now, and you deserve some wine. Carmel-by-the-Sea has a handful of tasting rooms downtown, including the popular Scheid Vineyards Carmel-by-the-Sea Tasting Room.

For dinner, enjoy Asian fusion fare at the chic Pangaea Grill or get some of the freshest sushi around at the hole-in-the-wall Akaoni.

Day 3

For your third day in this area, head inland to Carmel Valley. Save your appetite for a hearty down-home breakfast at the Wagon Wheel Restaurant or a more creative egg dish at Jeffrey's Grill & Catering.

Work off those calories with a hike at Garland Ranch Regional Park, an expansive parcel of land with steep hikes, ridges, and fine views of the valley. One option is the Mesa Trail. Head to Refuge Spa to soak your sore legs in its warm waters.

Carmel Valley is a burgeoning but unassuming wine region, so be sure to head to the Carmel Valley Village for some wine-tasting. Seven tasting rooms are located in a small strip mall, while several more are a short walk away. Some

artful nigiri at Carmel Valley's Mika Sushi

recommendations include **I. Brand & Family Winery** and **Boekenoogen Vineyard & Winery.**

Enjoy dinner at **Café Rustica,** with its superb pizzas and entrées, or enjoy raw seafood and sake at **Mika Sushi.** If you are still standing, visit the **Running Iron Restaurant and Saloon** and take in its Old West decor with a nightcap.

Santa Cruz: Coast and Mountains

Visit Santa Cruz to experience an eclectic California surf town, explore redwood-cloaked mountains, and take in the lightly developed north coast.

Day 1

Getting to **Santa Cruz** is an easy 50-minute (44-mi/71 km)) drive up CA-1 from the Monterey Peninsula. The eclectic beach city is an ideal place to try and catch a wave, whether you are a novice or an accomplished wave rider. **Cowell's Beach** is great for learning, while both **Pleasure Point** and **Steamer Lane** have larger waves. Afterward, visit the one-room **Santa Cruz Surfing Museum,** just above Steamer Lane.

Walk along **West Cliff Drive** and stop into **The Picnic Basket** for a sandwich or salad. Wander across the street to the **Santa Cruz Beach Boardwalk** to ride the wooden Big Dipper roller coaster.

Head to downtown Santa Cruz's lively **Pacific Avenue** and check out local shops like the wonderful **Bookshop Santa Cruz.** For dinner, stop at the **Abbott Square Market,** a food court with options that range from vegetarian to seafood to Neapolitan pizza. Or, head south of downtown to eat sushi amid skateboard-art at **Akira.**

To hear some live music, make for the **Kuumbwa Jazz Center,** an intimate venue that hosts jazz and acoustic performances, or

Roaring Camp Railroads

The Catalyst, the place for indie, rap, and reggae bands.

Now it's sleepy time. The **Seaway Inn** has basic motel rooms in a location that can't be beat, while the adjacent **West Cliff Inn** offers an upscale bed-and-breakfast experience in a gleaming white mansion. Across the street, the **Santa Cruz Dream Inn** reflects the playfulness of the nearby boardwalk and has a view of Cowell's Beach.

Day 2

To see the big trees, drive 8 miles (12.9 km) to the Santa Cruz Mountains town of **Felton.** Experience the impressive coast redwoods by taking a ride on the **Roaring Camp Railroads.** Hop on the **Redwood Forest Steam Train** and chug up a small mountain or take the **Santa Cruz Beach Train** down through the redwood-cloaked San Lorenzo River Canyon to the Santa Cruz Beach Boardwalk.

Stay in Felton for lunch. The **Cowboy Bar & Grill** serves creative comfort food. After lunch, head to nearby **Henry Cowell Redwoods State Park** for a walk in its grove of old-growth redwoods.

For dinner, enjoy tacos and margaritas at **El Palomar** in Santa Cruz, or head just east out of town for roasted chicken at **Café Cruz.**

Day 3

The coastline just west and north of Santa Cruz is worth your time if you have an extra day. On the way out of town, stop in for a Brazilian breakfast at **Cafe Brasil.** Continue on CA-1, where buildings cede to farmland, marine terraces, and secluded beaches. Two miles (3.2 km) west of the city boundary is **Wilder Ranch State Park,** a great place to get a feel for this landscape. The **Old Cove Landing Trail** walks along the coast's edge.

Six miles (9.7 km) farther up CA-1, **Davenport** is a small community perched on coastal bluffs. If it's migration season, keep your eyes opened here for whales traveling offshore. One of the region's best beaches is **Davenport Landing Beach.** Make sure to take a swing on the beachside swing set, whether you're a kid or an adult.

Continue north about 8 miles (12.9 km) on

CA-1 to reach **Año Nuevo State Park,** where up to 10,000 elephant seals can be found on the beach. Make sure to get a reservation for the guided tour before heading up to the park.

Return south on CA-1 to Davenport. Get a burger or sandwich at the **Whale City Bakery Bar & Grill.**

Big Sur to Cambria Road Trip

Big Sur is the 90-mile (145-km) stretch of stunning coastline that spans Carmel to San Simeon, the coastal town best known for being the home of Hearst Castle. The drive along CA-1 can be done in less than three hours, but you'll want to set aside more time, as you'll be driving past some of the state's best parks, beaches, and trails.

Day 1

Steer your vehicle down the **Big Sur Coast Highway** (CA-1) for a stunningly scenic drive. Make sure to stop 15 miles (24 km) south of Carmel to photograph the **Bixby Bridge,** an architectural marvel spanning a deep canyon with the Pacific Ocean in the background. Drive mindfully around here as this is a very popular photo-op.

For breakfast, opt for one of two worthy restaurants: the **Ripplewood Café,** which does home-style breakfasts, and the **Big Sur River Inn Restaurant,** where you can dine on an outdoor deck near the Big Sur River.

Big Sur has superb hiking options. To take in the coastal bluffs and beaches, cruise the **Ridge Trail and Panorama Trail Loop** at **Andrew Molera State Park.** Want to pass through a tunnel blasted through rock that leads to a secluded cove? Then **Partington Cove Trail** at **Julia Pfeiffer Burns State Park** is for you. Afterward, drive 2 miles (3.2 km) south to the

coastline near Big Sur

Catch of the Day

The Monterey Bay region is known for its seafood and abounds with superb seafood restaurants.

MONTEREY

- The Sandbar & Grill (page 64) has some of Monterey's best golden-fried calamari. Its location hanging over Monterey Harbor means you may be able to watch sea otters do the backstroke during your meal.

- Get a taste of local Sicilian recipes like squid pasta at Monterey's Fish House (page 64).

- Prefer your seafood raw? Crystal Fish (page 69) serves fresh fish in sushi rolls bestowed with tasty sauces and unique ingredients.

PACIFIC GROVE

- One of Monterey Peninsula's most popular seafood restaurants is Passionfish (page 83), which is known for its commitment to sustainable seafood and its staff's extensive knowledge of coastal cuisine.

- Wild Fish (page 83) showcases locally sourced seafood from all over the California coast.

MOSS LANDING

- Tucked between the harbor and the ocean in Moss Landing, Phil's Fish Market (page 96) serves up hearty and tasty cioppino and sea scallops.

CARMEL

- Japanese cooking methods meet California cuisine in the seafood entrées at the Flying Fish Grill (page 113).

- A hole-in-the-wall sushi restaurant in Carmel, Akaoni (page 113) does some of the area's freshest and tastiest rolls and nigiri.

The chef at Akaoni prepares some amazing sushi.

- Slightly larger than Akaoni, Toro Sushi (page 113) has fresh sushi and a range of sakes.

SAN SIMEON, CAMBRIA, AND MORRO BAY

- The Sea Chest Oyster Bar (page 254), in a cottage across from Moonstone Beach, wows seafood lovers with everything from calamari strips to cioppino.

- Just off Cayucos Beach, Rudell's Smokehouse (page 262) serves seafood tacos with big flavors, including smoked salmon and smoked albacore, along with an unexpected topping: chopped apples.

- Right on Morro Bay's Embarcadero, Tognazzini's Dockside Restaurant (page 272) is the place for fresh barbecued oysters in garlic butter.

Morro Rock

park's main entrance and take the short walk out to see **McWay Falls,** an 80-foot (24.4-m) waterfall that plummets into the Pacific.

Catch sunset at **Pfeiffer Beach** and snap a selfie with the offshore rocks as a backdrop. Head south again to **Nepenthe** for a late dinner of an Ambrosia burger and a terrific view. If there's a line at Nepenthe, head 1.5 miles (2.4 km) north to the **Big Sur Taphouse** for a craft beer and tacos with the locals.

Check if the **Henry Miller Memorial Library,** just 0.25-mile (0.4-km) south of Nepenthe, has an evening event, like a film screening or music performance. Otherwise, head to the **Fernwood Tavern** to mingle with locals and tourists from around the world.

Fall asleep in a tent within the **Pfeiffer Big Sur State Park Campground** or in an artfully decorated room at **Glen Oaks Big Sur.** For a splurge, have a once-in-a-lifetime overnight experience at the luxury **Post Ranch Inn.**

Day 2

Fuel up for a drive at Big Sur's **Deetjen's,** known for its cozy atmosphere and eggs Benedicts. For something quicker, swing into the **Big Sur Bakery** for a pastry and coffee.

Big Sur's south coast has two worthy stops for travelers headed toward San Simeon and Cambria. **Sand Dollar Beach** is 60 miles (97 km) south of Carmel and one of Big Sur's best beaches. **Salmon Creek Falls** is an impressive roadside waterfall located 8 miles (12.9km) south of Gorda.

Drive past **San Simeon** to **Cambria,** where you'll stroll on scenic **Moonstone Beach.** When hunger hits, head back to Cambria for dinner. The **Main Street Grill** is a casual eatery with a tasty tri-tip sandwich, while **Robin's** has an eclectic international menu.

Get a full night's sleep at **Sand Pebbles Inn** across from Moonstone Beach.

Day 3

Drive to opulent **Hearst Castle.** Tours of this ranch, built for newspaper magnate William Randolph Hearst, offer insight into the lifestyle of the rich and infamous. Be sure to make a tour reservation in advance!

Drive a half hour south to the scenic town of **Morro Bay** and stare up at **Morro Rock,** a 576-foot (176-m) volcanic plug looming over the active harbor area. Then walk along the **Embarcadero** to check out **The Shell Shop** and stop in for a craft beer at **The Libertine Pub.**

Dine on seafood for dinner with fish tacos at **Taco Temple** or barbecued oysters at **Tognazzini's Dockside Restaurant.** Spend the evening at the **Masterpiece Hotel** or enjoy the **Beach Bungalow Inn & Suites,** just two blocks up from the bustling Embarcadero.

Best Beaches

The Monterey Bay region has an impressive range of beaches, from sweeping expanses of sand to pocket beaches crammed between towering headlands. Many of these beaches provide access to the area's myriad ocean-based recreation opportunities, from sea kayaking and surfing to scuba diving and snorkeling.

Monterey
MONTEREY STATE BEACH
Best for Long Strolls, Kayaking, SUP
This large strand of beach begins just north of the Monterey Harbor and stretches to the neighboring city of Seaside. Head out for a long walk or paddle out from the wharf in a kayak or stand-up paddleboard (page 52).

SAN CARLOS BEACH PARK
Best for Scuba Diving, Picnicking
This sliver of sand is located right in Monterey, south of Monterey Harbor. It's a superb place to picnic and take in the curving bay or don scuba equipment and head offshore to one of the area's most popular dive spots (page 53).

LOVERS POINT PARK
Best for Families, Snorkeling, Wading
The small, protected beach here allows a spot for kids to dip their feet into the cool Pacific, while the waters offshore feature a kelp forest that provides snorkelers and beginning divers with an introduction to the region's underwater features (page 78).

ASILOMAR STATE BEACH
Best for Strolling
Take a walk south toward Pebble Beach on this scenic, mile-long beach. Return on the wooden boardwalk above the sand (page 79).

MOSS LANDING STATE BEACH
Best for Fishing, Birding
A long stretch of beach with frequently powerful waves offshore, this state beach draws both anglers and birders for its substantial wildlife (page 96).

Carmel
CARMEL BEACH
Best for Scenery, Sunsets, Dog Lovers
With its pale sand and contrasting blue-green ocean water, Carmel Beach is a jewel of Monterey Bay. It's also one of the state's friendliest beaches for dogs (page 107).

Santa Cruz
SANTA CRUZ BEACH BOARDWALK
Best for Families, Mild Thrill Seekers
Just feet away from Cowell's, the Santa Cruz Beach Boardwalk makes families happy with its rides, games, and entertainment. The Boardwalk's Giant Dipper roller coaster has been thrilling folks since 1924 (page 162).

COWELL'S BEACH
Best for Beginning Surfing
Santa Cruz's Cowell's Beach has slow, rolling

waves perfect for beginners. Even though it gets crowded, the surfers here are usually friendly (page 168).

SEACLIFF STATE BEACH
Best for Shipwreck Lovers, Fishing
How many beaches in California have their own hulking shipwreck right offshore? The pier offers the best views of the concrete vessel and is also a preferred spot for local anglers (page 185).

DAVENPORT LANDING BEACH
Best for Beachcombing, Kitesurfing
The northern coast of Santa Cruz County has a handful of scenic, rugged beaches. Davenport Landing Beach is one of the best and easiest to access. The beach has two rocky headlands on either end (page 194).

AÑO NUEVO STATE PARK
Best for Wildlife, Scenery
At Año Nuevo, gigantic elephant seals turn the beach into a battleground. You can also catch a glimpse of an eerie, abandoned light station right offshore (page 196).

Big Sur

ANDREW MOLERA STATE PARK
Best for Scenery, Views
See the Big Sur River spilling into the sea and a beach decorated with driftwood huts (page 208).

PFEIFFER BEACH
Best for Photo Ops, Sunsets
Make sure that your camera (or phone) has fully charged batteries for a trip to Big Sur's windswept Pfeiffer Beach, with picture-perfect rock formations offshore (page 209).

SAND DOLLAR BEACH
Best for Picnics, Long Walks
Protected by cliffs on windy days, crescent-shaped Sand Dollar Beach is a great spot for a picnic or a long walk (page 213).

Carmel Beach

Lovers Point Park

San Simeon, Cambria, and Morro Bay

MOONSTONE BEACH
Best for Beachcombing

Hunt for the eponymous moonstones on this Cambria beach. Its impressive driftwood structures are also worthy discoveries (page 249).

CAYUCOS STATE BEACH
Best for Sunbathing, Lounging

The primary attraction of Cayucos is this protected beach and its pier, perfect for a day of lazing in the sun (page 260).

SPOONER'S COVE
Best for Scenery, Picnics

Soak up the natural beauty of Spooner's Cove, in Montaña de Oro State Park. A scenic arch decorates the bluffs on the south end of the cove (page 268).

MORRO ROCK BEACH
Best for Photo Ops, Surfing

Take a photo in front of 576-foot-high (176-m) Morro Rock. The beach to its south is popular with surfers of all skill levels (page 269).

Wine Time

Monterey

After a day of sightseeing, stay in the seaside city and sample its tasting rooms (page 50). The **Pierce Ranch Vineyards Tasting Room** is housed in a cozy cottage and occasionally hosts live music. **A Taste of Monterey** pours wine from more than 95 local wineries in a stunning Cannery Row location with views of the bay. Also in Monterey, **Sovino Wine Bar & Merchant** has a great selection of wines, fun events, and a great location near Custom House Plaza.

Carmel

Tasting rooms are popping up all over downtown **Carmel-by-the-Sea** (page 107). One of the best is the **Scheid Vineyards Carmel-by-the-Sea Tasting Room,** a social spot where you can sample wines, including the popular claret. **Caraccioli Cellars Tasting Room** pours smooth brut and brut rose that are a perfect fit for the sleek, upscale tasting room.

Make a day of exploring the many wineries of **Carmel Valley** (page 126). **Boekenoogen Vineyard & Winery** does great pinot noirs, zinfandels, and Syrahs, while **I. Brand & Family Winery** serves three different labels (at three different price points) in a hip tasting room where vinyl records soundtrack your visit. Keep drinking into the evening hours at **The Wine House.** Its great outdoor area has fire pits and games, including a bocce ball court.

Salinas

The **River Road Wine Trail** has a string of wineries known for their valley views, fine chardonnays, and exemplary pinot noirs (page 141). **Hahn Winery Tasting Room** has a superb outdoor deck for wine sampling.

Santa Cruz

On the Santa Cruz coast is the town of Davenport, where the **Beauregard Wine Bar** is an ideal

The Wine House

Best Hikes

The Monterey and Carmel region contains outstanding hiking trails for all levels of hikers. Options include everything from an easy leg-stretching hike to a strenuous multiday backpacking adventure.

EASY HIKES

- One of Monterey's best hikes is also its easiest. The **Monterey Bay Coastal Recreation Trail** (18 mi/29 km total) follows a former railroad track to Pacific Grove. The 2-mile (3.2 km) walk one-way from Fisherman's Wharf to Lovers Point Park is highly recommended (page 57).

- The **Skyline Trail** (0.8 mi/1.3 km round-trip) in Jack's Peak County Park offers a view of Monterey from the peninsula's highest point (page 58).

- Point Lobos State Natural Reserve has plenty of easy hikes that pay impressive dividends with stunning scenery, abundant wildlife, and unique natural features. The **Cypress Grove Trail** (0.8 mi/1.3 km round-trip) is one of the best, with its twisty cypress trees and vantage points of the sea (page 109).

- Most visitors to Big Sur want to view the 80-foot (24.4-m) waterfall that drops precipitously into the ocean. It can be seen from the **Overlook Trail to McWay Falls** (0.6 mi/1 km round-trip) in Julia Pfeiffer Burns State Park (page 211).

- Andrew Molera State Park occupies a big parcel of Big Sur's spectacular coastline. At the end of the **Creamery Meadow Trail** (2 mi/3.2 km round-trip) hikers are rewarded with a wild beach where the Big Sur River spills into the sea (page 216).

- Also in Julia Pfeiffer Burns State Park is the **Partington Cove Trail** (1 mi/1.6 km round-trip), which ventures out from the highway, over a bridge, and through a tunnel to a rocky cove (page 219).

INTERMEDIATE HIKES

- For a view of the Carmel coast from above, take Palo Corona Regional Park's **Inspiration Point Hike** (1.3 mi/2.1 km round-trip) to a bench where the shoreline spreads out below.

Julia Pfeiffer Burns State Park

Be sure to first secure a permit to hike in the park (page 109).

- Pinnacles National Park has rock formations that seem to be nature's take on castles and towers. The **Juniper Canyon Loop** (4.3 mi/6.9 km round-trip) travels up to some fine examples, especially on the steep and narrow portion of the trail (page 150).

- Also in Pinnacles National Park, the **Moses Spring-Rim Trail Loop** (2.2 mi/3.5 km round-trip) takes in both Bear Gulch Cave—a cavern with a stream running through it—and Bear Gulch Reservoir, which was built by the Civilian Conservation Corps (page 150).

- Take the **Ridge Trail-Panorama Trail Loop** (8 mi/12.9 km round-trip), also known as **Eight-Mile Loop,** in Andrew Molera State Park for views of the Big Sur coast (page 217).

- Towering above the south coast of Big Sur, Cone Peak in the Ventana Wilderness is a giant, rocky mountaintop with fantastic 360-degree views. The **Cone Peak Trail** (5 mi/8 km round-trip) is a doable day hike to the summit of Big Sur's second-highest peak (page 220).

Monterey's Pierce Ranch Vineyards Tasting Room

place to taste the products of the nearby Santa Cruz Mountains (page 194).

San Simeon, Cambria, and Morro Bay

The Central Coast has a few worthy tasting rooms (page 252). The San Simeon-based **Hearst Ranch Winery** pours wines down the hill from Hearst Castle.

Morro Bay's **Stax Wine Bar & Bistro** is a fine place to taste local varietals while gazing out at imposing Morro Rock (page 271).

Monterey

Monterey has roots as a fishing town. Native

Americans were the first to harvest from the sea, augmenting their diet of acorns with shellfish. Later, whaling and then fishing became an economic driver with the arrival of European settlers.

Author John Steinbeck immortalized this unglamorous industry in his 1945 novel *Cannery Row*. The city's blue-collar past is still evident in its architecture, even if the cannery workers have been replaced by tourists.

This coastal city has one of California's oldest and richest histories. Spanish explorer Sebastián Vizcaíno noted that the bay and harbor would make for a great port way back in 1602. In 1770, the Spanish constructed the Presidio of Monterey to protect the port. After that,

Highlights

Look for ★ to find recommended sights, activities, dining, and lodging.

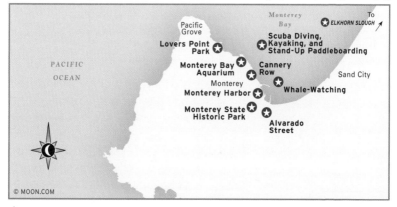

★ **Cannery Row:** Made famous by John Steinbeck's novel, this was once a working neighborhood lined with fish canneries. Today it's been reinvented as a tourist destination overlooking a scenic strip of Monterey Bay (page 40).

★ **Monterey Bay Aquarium:** This mammoth aquarium astonishes with a vast array of sea life and exhibits on the local ecosystem (page 40).

★ **Monterey State Historic Park:** This park preserves the old adobes dotting Monterey's downtown and allows people to imagine what life was like here in the 1800s (page 44).

★ **Alvarado Street:** Monterey's downtown thoroughfare is lined with historic adobes, modern restaurants, and thriving bars (page 44).

★ **Monterey Harbor:** The best way to see one of the most scenic harbors on the Central Coast is by strolling along the **Monterey Bay Coastal Recreation Trail** (page 47).

★ **Scuba Diving, Kayaking, and Stand-Up Paddleboarding:** Experience Monterey Bay's calm water and unique wildlife by getting into the water (pages 53 and 54).

★ **Whale-Watching:** Monterey's whale-watching vessels offer easy and amazing opportunities to view gray, humpback, blue, and killer whales in the bay (page 55).

★ **Lovers Point Park:** This Pacific Grove park is located on a scenic peninsula that juts out into the bay, offering a protected beach and great views (page 78).

★ **Elkhorn Slough:** Get some of the best views of the bay's marine mammals at this estuary in Moss Landing (page 95).

Monterey became the capital of the Spanish territory of Alta California; later, it would be the capital of California under Mexican and U.S. military rule. When California composed the documents to apply for U.S. statehood in 1849, it did so in Monterey.

Today, Monterey is the "big city" on the well-populated southern tip of the wide-mouthed bay. There are two main sections of Monterey: the old downtown area and "New Monterey," which includes Cannery Row and the Monterey Bay Aquarium. The old downtown is situated around Alvarado Street and includes the historic adobes that make up Monterey State Historic Park. New Monterey bustles with tourists during the summer. The canneries are long gone, and today the Row is packed with businesses, including the must-see Monterey Bay Aquarium, seafood restaurants, shops, galleries, and tasting rooms. The aquarium is constantly packed with visitors, especially on summer weekends. One way to get from one section of town to the other is to walk the Monterey Bay Coastal Recreation Trail, a paved path that runs right along a stretch of beautiful coastline.

PLANNING YOUR TIME

Monterey and its immediate surroundings can be explored over 2-3 days. The communities of the Monterey Peninsula have distinct characters, so you can stay in the town that best suits your needs. To be near the aquarium, opt for lodging in Cannery Row. If you're a history buff, stay next to some of the state's oldest buildings in downtown Monterey. If you love old Victorians and bed-and-breakfasts, stay in Pacific Grove. To experience a Central Coast harbor community, overnight in Moss Landing. No matter where you stay, you'll be able to easily explore the nearby towns.

The Monterey Bay Aquarium is the area's most popular attraction. While it is expensive—adult admission is $50—the aquarium's artfulness makes it worth a visit. Cannery Row, the area surrounding the aquarium, has a few sights, most notably Ed Ricketts's laboratory, but otherwise it's mainly a lot of gift shops and restaurants.

History buffs should not miss Monterey State Historic Park, a collection of historic government buildings and residences in downtown Monterey. Water enthusiasts should get out in the calm waters off Monterey, whether it is to kayak, stand-up paddleboard, or scuba dive.

Pacific Grove is worth a visit for its unique Victorian residences and fine stretch of coastline, including Lovers Point Park. Seaside has some of the best inexpensive eateries in the area, while Marina has Fort Ord Dunes State Park, one of the California coast's newest state parks. Head up to Moss Landing to explore Elkhorn Slough, a tidal marsh that's home to abundant wildlife.

ORIENTATION

Alvarado Street is the main street of **downtown Monterey,** while **Lighthouse Avenue** is lined with a lot of New Monterey's businesses and restaurants. **Cannery Row** is a touristy street by the bay, three blocks from Lighthouse Avenue; it's where Monterey Bay Aquarium is located.

Pacific Grove is west of Monterey. Its main street is **Lighthouse Avenue,** which connects the two towns. Upon entering Pacific Grove, Lighthouse Avenue becomes Central Avenue, while Lighthouse Avenue moves two blocks up from the bay.

Highway 1 connects Monterey with the northern Monterey County cities of **Seaside, Marina,** and **Moss Landing.**

Previous: Asilomar Coast Trail; a humpback whale in Monterey Bay; street sign for Monterey's Cannery Row.

Monterey Peninsula

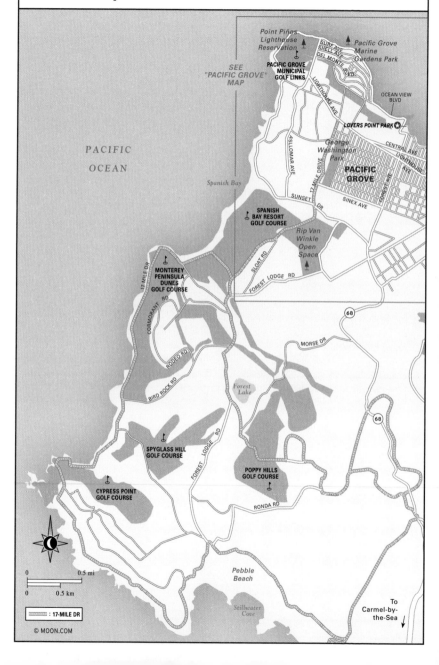

PACIFIC OCEAN

Point Piños Lighthouse Reservation

Pacific Grove Marine Gardens Park

SURF AVE
SHELL AVE
DEL MONTE BLVD

SEE "PACIFIC GROVE" MAP

PACIFIC GROVE MUNICIPAL GOLF LINKS

OCEAN VIEW BLVD

LIGHTHOUSE AVE

LOVERS POINT PARK

ASILOMAR AVE

George Washington Park

PACIFIC GROVE

CENTRAL AVE

FOREST AVE

LIGHTHOUSE AVE

Spanish Bay

17-MILE DRIVE

SUNSET DR

SINEX AVE

SPANISH BAY RESORT GOLF COURSE

Rip Van Winkle Open Space

SLOAT RD

FOREST LODGE RD

MONTEREY PENINSULA DUNES GOLF COURSE

17-MILE DR

CORMORANT RD

68

MORSE DR

RODEO RD

BIRD ROCK RD

Forest Lake

68

SPYGLASS HILL GOLF COURSE

FOREST LODGE RD

POPPY HILLS GOLF COURSE

CYPRESS POINT GOLF COURSE

RONDA RD

Pebble Beach

0   0.5 mi
0   0.5 km

Stillwater Cove

To Carmel-by-the-Sea

: 17-MILE DR

© MOON.COM

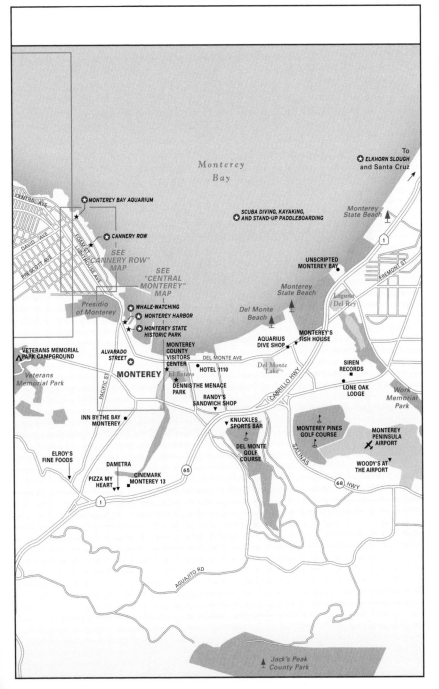

Sights

★ CANNERY ROW

Cannery Row (www.canneryrow.com) did once look and feel as John Steinbeck described it in his famed novel of the same name. In the 1930s and 1940s, fishing boats offloaded their catches straight into the huge warehouse-like cannery buildings. Low-wage workers processed the fish and put it into cans, ready to ship across the country and around the world. During World War II, Monterey became known as the "Sardine Capital of the World." But overfishing took its toll, and by the late 1950s Cannery Row was deserted; some buildings even fell into the ocean.

A slow renaissance began in the 1960s, driven by new interest in preserving the historic integrity of the area, as well as a few savvy entrepreneurs who understood the value of beachfront property. Today, what was once a workingman's wharf is now an enclave of boutique hotels, big seafood restaurants, and souvenir stores selling T-shirts adorned with sea otters. Cannery Row is anchored at one end by the aquarium and runs for several blocks that include a beach; it then leads to the Monterey Harbor area.

The Monterey Bay Aquarium is the best attraction around, but the **Monterey Mirror Maze and Highway 1 Golf** (751 Cannery Row, 831/649-6293, http://montereymirrormaze.com, hours vary, mirror maze adults $12, children 4-6 $8, mini golf adults $12, children 4-6 $8) offers touristy family fun. Navigate the mirror maze with its disorienting lights and music or putt 9 to 18 holes of mini-golf on a glow-in-the-dark course with attractions inspired by California's Highway 1.

Thankfully, a few remnants of Cannery Row's past remain in the shadows of the area's touristy shops. The most important is a battered little shack located between the Monterey Bay Aquarium and the InterContinental luxury hotel. The **Pacific Biological Laboratories** (800 Cannery Row, 831/646-1569, www.monterey.org) was the workplace and home of famed marine biologist Ed Ricketts, a good friend of Steinbeck's who appeared as "Doc" in Steinbeck's classic novel *Cannery Row*. Following Ricketts's death in 1948, the building hosted a men's club where ideas were batted around over drinks and card games. One of the ideas to make it out of the lab was Jimmy Lyon's concept of putting on an annual music festival in Monterey, an event that would eventually become the long-running Monterey Jazz Festival. The club still meets to this day. Now owned by the city, the lab is open for free tours one day a month and for group tours by reservation. The shack's interior has not changed much since Ricketts's time. It's essentially decorated with books and bottles. That said, the old building provides a fascinating look at the old Monterey immortalized in Steinbeck's writing.

TOP EXPERIENCE

★ MONTEREY BAY AQUARIUM

The first aquarium of its kind in the country, the **Monterey Bay Aquarium** (886 Cannery Row, 831/648-4800, www.montereybayaquarium.org, daily hours vary, adults $50, students and seniors $40, children 5-12 $35) is still unique in many ways. From the very beginning, the aquarium's mission has been conservation, and it's not shy about it. Many of the animals in the aquarium's tanks were rescued, and those that survive may eventually be returned to the wild. All the exhibits you'll see in this mammoth complex contain only local sea life.

The aquarium displays a dazzling array of species. When you come to visit, a good first step is to look up the feeding schedules for the tanks that most interest you. It's smart to

Central Monterey

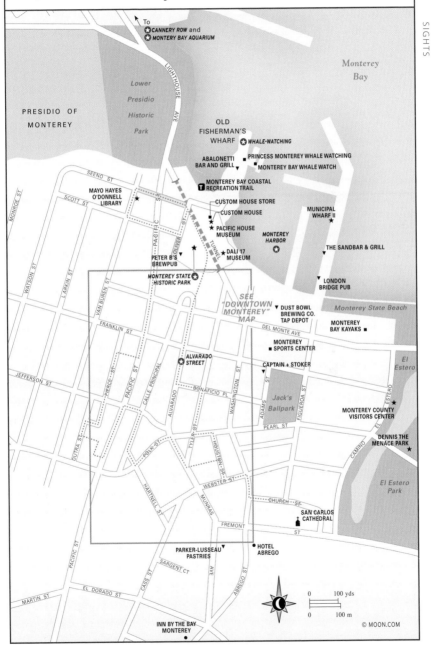

To
CANNERY ROW and
MONTEREY BAY AQUARIUM

Monterey Bay

PRESIDIO OF MONTEREY

Lower Presidio Historic Park

LIGHTHOUSE AVE

OLD FISHERMAN'S WHARF ★ WHALE-WATCHING

SEENO ST

MAYO HAYES O'DONNELL LIBRARY ★

SCOTT ST

MONROE ST

ABALONETTI BAR AND GRILL ▼
PRINCESS MONTEREY WHALE WATCHING ■
MONTEREY BAY WHALE WATCH ■

MONTEREY BAY COASTAL RECREATION TRAIL

CUSTOM HOUSE STORE
CUSTOM HOUSE
★ PACIFIC HOUSE MUSEUM

MUNICIPAL WHARF II ★

PACIFIC ST
OLIVER ST

PETER B'S BREWPUB ▼

★ DALI 17 MUSEUM

MONTEREY HARBOR

Monterey Harbor

THE SANDBAR & GRILL ▼

MONTEREY STATE HISTORIC PARK

TUNNEL

SEE "DOWNTOWN MONTEREY" MAP

LONDON BRIDGE PUB ▼

WATSON ST
LARKIN ST

VAN BUREN ST

Monterey State Beach

FRANKLIN ST

DUST BOWL BREWING CO. TAP DEPOT ▼

DEL MONTE AVE

MONTEREY BAY KAYAKS ■

PIERCE ST
PACIFIC ST
CALLE PRINCIPAL

ALVARADO STREET

MONTEREY SPORTS CENTER ■

JEFFERSON ST

CAPTAIN + STOKER ▼

El Estero

ALVARADO ST
BONIFACIO PL
WASHINGTON ST

ADAMS ST

Jack's Ballpark

FIGUEROA ST
ESTERO ST

MONTEREY COUNTY VISITORS CENTER ★

DUTRA ST

PEARL ST

POLK ST

DENNIS THE MENACE PARK ★

CAMINO

TYLER ST
WEBSTER ST
HOUSTON ST

WEBSTER ST

MUNRAS AVE

El Estero Park

HARTNELL ST

CHURCH ST

SAN CARLOS CATHEDRAL ✝

PACIFIC ST

FREMONT ST

CASS ST

PARKER-LUSSEAU PASTRIES ▼

● HOTEL ABREGO

SARGENT CT

ABREGO ST

MARTIN ST
EL DORADO ST

0   100 yds
0   100 m

INN BY THE BAY MONTEREY
●

© MOON.COM

Cannery Row

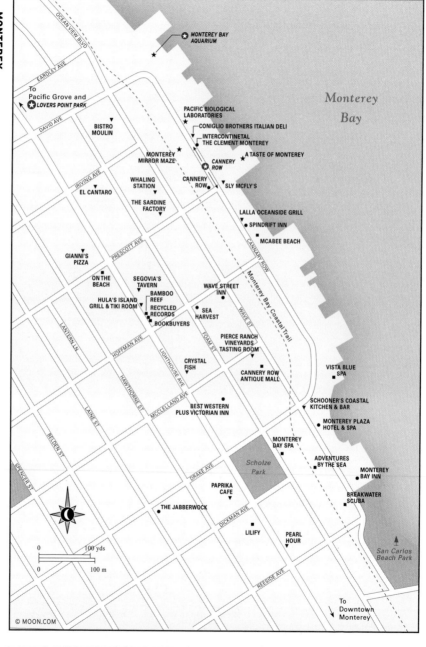

MONTEREY BAY AQUARIUM

Monterey Bay

OCEAN VIEW BLVD

EARDLEY AVE

To Pacific Grove and
LOVERS POINT PARK

DAVID AVE

BISTRO MOULIN

PACIFIC BIOLOGICAL LABORATORIES

CONIGLIO BROTHERS ITALIAN DELI

INTERCONTINETAL THE CLEMENT MONTEREY

IRVING AVE

MONTEREY MIRROR MAZE

A TASTE OF MONTEREY

CANNERY ROW

EL CANTARO

WHALING STATION

CANNERY ROW

SLY MCFLY'S

THE SARDINE FACTORY

LALLA OCEANSIDE GRILL

SPINDRIFT INN

PRESCOTT AVE

MCABEE BEACH

GIANNI'S PIZZA

CANNERY ROW

ON THE BEACH

SEGOVIA'S TAVERN

WAVE STREET INN

Monterey Bay Coastal Trail

BAMBOO REEF

HULA'S ISLAND GRILL & TIKI ROOM

RECYCLED RECORDS

SEA HARVEST

WAVE ST

LANTERN LN

BOOKBUYERS

FOAM ST

PIERCE RANCH VINEYARDS TASTING ROOM

HOFFMAN AVE

LIGHTHOUSE AVE

CRYSTAL FISH

VISTA BLUE SPA

HAWTHORNE ST

MCCLELLAND AVE

CANNERY ROW ANTIQUE MALL

SCHOONER'S COASTAL KITCHEN & BAR

LAINE ST

BEST WESTERN PLUS VICTORIAN INN

MONTEREY PLAZA HOTEL & SPA

MONTEREY DAY SPA

BELDEN ST

DRAKE AVE

Scholze Park

ADVENTURES BY THE SEA

SPENCER ST

PAPRIKA CAFE

MONTEREY BAY INN

THE JABBERWOCK

BREAKWATER SCUBA

DICKMAN AVE

LILIFY

PEARL HOUR

San Carlos Beach Park

REESIDE AVE

0   100 yds
0   100 m

To Downtown Monterey

© MOON.COM

The Steinbeck Effect

John Ernst Steinbeck was born in Salinas, then a tiny, isolated agricultural community, in 1902. He somehow managed to escape life as a farmer, a sardine fisherman, or a fish canner and ended up living the glamorous life of a writer for his too-short 66 years.

Steinbeck's experiences in the Salinas Valley farming community and in the fishing town of Monterey informed many of his novels. The best known of these is *Cannery Row*, but *Tortilla Flat* is also set in working-class Monterey (though no one knows exactly where the fictional Tortilla Flat neighborhood was supposed to be). His family epic *East of Eden* mostly takes place in the Salinas Valley, while Pulitzer Prize-winning *The Grapes of Wrath* takes some of its inspiration from the same region. Steinbeck used the valley as a model for farming in the Dust Bowl during the Great Depression.

Steinbeck was fascinated by the plight of the worker; his novels and stories depict ordinary folks going through tough and terrible times. Steinbeck lived and worked through the Great Depression, and thus it's not surprising that many of his stories don't feature Hollywood happy endings. He was a realist in almost all of his novels, portraying the good, the bad, and the ugly of human life and society. His work gained almost immediate respect: In addition to his Pulitzer Prize, Steinbeck also won the Nobel Prize for Literature in 1962. Almost every U.S. high school student since the 1950s has read at least one of Steinbeck's novels or short stories, and his body of work forms part of the country's literary canon.

As the birthplace of California's most illustrious literary son, Salinas became famous for inspiring his work. Steinbeck's name is taken in vain all over now-commercial Cannery Row, where even the cheesy wax museum tries to draw customers in by claiming kinship with the legendary author. More serious Steinbeck fans prefer the **National Steinbeck Center** (page 139) and **The Steinbeck House** (page 140), both in the still-agricultural town of Salinas. And if the museums aren't enough, plan to be in Monterey County in early August for the annual **Steinbeck Festival** (page 143), a big shindig put on by the Steinbeck Center in order to celebrate the great man's life and works in fine style. The writer is buried at **Garden of Memories Memorial Park** (850 Abbott St.) in Salinas; staff can help you locate his gravestone, which is usually covered in tributes. Seek out Susan Shillinglaw's book, *A Journey Into Steinbeck's California*, to find Monterey County sites referenced in the author's works.

arrive several minutes in advance to get a good spot near the glass. Current feeding times are also listed on the aquarium's website.

In the living, breathing **Kelp Forest**, leopard sharks glide through the swaying strands, anchovies coalesce in silver clouds, and warty sea cucumbers and starfish adorn rocks.

The deep water tank in the **Open Sea** exhibit area always draws a crowd. Inside its depths, hammerhead sharks sweep the bottom like vacuum cleaners, while giant bluefin tuna cruise by. Although infrequent, the aquarium sometimes hosts one of the ocean's most notorious predators in this tank: the great white shark; if one is on display, it's definitely worth spending time with this sleek and amazing fish up close.

The **Wild About Otters** exhibit gives

visitors a close view of rescued otters. These adorable, furry marine mammals come right up to the glass to interact with curious children and enchanted adults. They may be the true stars of the aquarium. Another of the aquarium's most popular exhibits is the **Jellies Experience,** which illuminates delicate crystal jellies and the comet-like lion's mane jellyfish.

The aquarium is a wildly popular weekend destination, especially in the peak summer season when the crowds can be forbidding. Time your visit for Tuesday-Thursday (especially 2pm-6pm) or plan to come in fall and winter when it's less crowded. Download a map online and check the daily feeding times before arrival so that you can maximize your time.

★ MONTEREY STATE HISTORIC PARK

Monterey State Historic Park (park office 20 Custom House Plaza, 831/649-2907, www. parks.ca.gov) pays homage to the long and colorful history of the city of Monterey. This busy port town acted as the capital of California when it was under Spanish and then Mexican rule. It seemed poised to become the capital once again until the Gold Rush shifted the focus of the state farther north. Today, the park comprises a collection of historic buildings, scattered about downtown Monterey, that provides a peek into the city as it was in the middle of the 19th century.

Built in 1827, the **Custom House** (east of Fisherman's Wharf, 10am-4pm daily, free) is the oldest government building still standing in the state. Wander about the adobe building and check out the artifacts on display, meant to resemble the goods within the building when it was under Mexican rule. Nearby is the **Pacific House Museum** (20 Custom House Plaza, hours vary seasonally, free). The first floor shows a range of Monterey's history, from the Native Californians to the American Period. The second floor has a plethora of Native American artifacts.

The other buildings that compose the park were built mostly with adobe and/or brick between 1834 and 1847. These include the **Casa del Oro** (210 Oliver St., closed to the public until further notice); **Larkin House** (464 Calle Principal, 831/649-7172, private tours $80 for up to 12 people); **Sherman Quarters** (on the grounds of the Larkin House, closed to the public); **Old Whaling Station** (391 Decatur St., 831/375-5356, 10am-2pm Tues.-Fri., free); **First Brick House** (next to the Old Whaling Station, 10am-4pm daily, free); **Casa Soberanes** (336 Pacific St., 831/649-7172, private tours $80 for up to 12 people); **First Theater** (intersection of Pacific St. and Scott St.); and **Stevenson House** (530 Houston St., 831/649-7172, private tours $80 for up to 12 people), once a temporary residence of Robert Louis Stevenson.

Behind almost every historic structure are well-maintained gardens. Some of the finest include the **Memory Garden** (behind the Pacific House Museum), **Stevenson House Garden**, and **Casa Soberanes Garden.** Opening hours for the gardens are typically 9am-5pm in summer and 9am-4pm in winter, depending on staffing.

For a great introduction to the park and its history, take the hour-long **guided walking tour** (meets at the Custom House, hours vary seasonally, $10). A **cell phone tour** (831/998-9458) offers a two-minute rundown on each building.

★ ALVARADO STREET

Named after Juan Bautista Alvarado, the governor of the Mexican territory of Alta California from 1836 to 1842, **Alvarado Street** (831/655-8070, www.oldmonterey. org) has always been Monterey's main street, despite the fact that Cannery Row draws more visitors. Along its three blocks, the one-way road is lined with historic landmarks as well as some of the city's best restaurants and bars, such as Alvarado Street Brewery, Rosine's, and Old Monterey Café.

Stroll the walkable sidewalks, stopping to admire the **Golden State Theatre** and the historic adobe that Alvarado called home. **Hellam's Tobacco Shop** (423 Alvarado St., 831/373-2816, www. hellamstobaccoandwineshop.com, 10am-10pm Mon.-Sat.) is both California's oldest tobacco shop and Monterey's oldest continually operating business.

COLTON HALL

The grand white-stone building of **Colton Hall** (580 Pacific St., www.monterey.org) is where the state of California was born, when 48 delegates met for a month-and-a-half in the fall of 1849 to draft California's first constitution. Among the subjects that were debated were the state's eastern boundary and

---

1: Casa Soberanes in Monterey State Historic Park
2: Fisherman's Wharf

Downtown Monterey

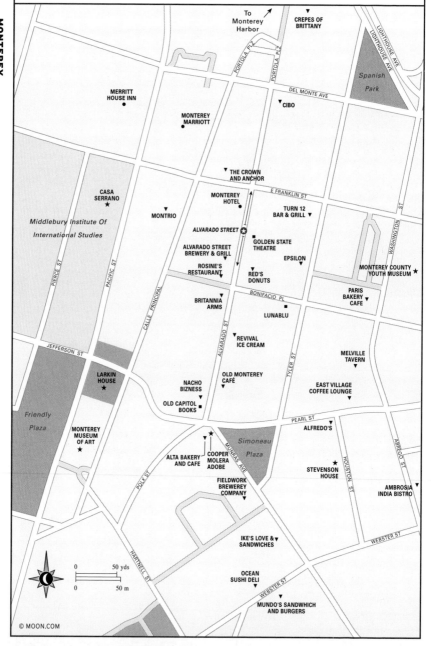

To Monterey Harbor

CREPES OF BRITTANY

LIGHTHOUSE AVE

Spanish Park

MERRITT HOUSE INN

DEL MONTE AVE

CIBO

MONTEREY MARRIOTT

THE CROWN AND ANCHOR

E FRANKLIN ST

CASA SERRANO ★

MONTEREY HOTEL

MONTRIO

TURN 12 BAR & GRILL ▼

WASHINGTON ST

Middlebury Institute Of International Studies

ALVARADO STREET

GOLDEN STATE THEATRE

ALVARADO STREET BREWERY & GRILL ▼

EPSILON

MONTEREY COUNTY YOUTH MUSEUM ★

ROSINE'S RESTAURANT ▼

RED'S DONUTS ▼

PIERCE ST

PACIFIC ST

CALLE PRINCIPAL

BONIFACIO PL

PARIS BAKERY CAFE ▼

BRITANNIA ARMS ▼

LUNABLU

ALVARADO ST

REVIVAL ICE CREAM ▼

JEFFERSON ST

MELVILLE TAVERN ▼

TYLER ST

LARKIN HOUSE ★

NACHO BIZNESS ▼

OLD MONTEREY CAFÉ ▼

EAST VILLAGE COFFEE LOUNGE ▼

Friendly Plaza

OLD CAPITOL BOOKS ■

MONTEREY MUSEUM OF ART ★

PEARL ST

ALFREDO'S ▼

ABREGO ST

Simoneau Plaza

COOPER MOLERA ADOBE ★

ALTA BAKERY AND CAFE ▼

MUNRAS AVE

STEVENSON HOUSE ★

HOUSTON ST

AMBROSIA INDIA BISTRO ▼

FIELDWORK BREWEREY COMPANY ▼

POLK ST

WEBSTER ST

IKE'S LOVE & ▼ SANDWICHES

HARTNELL ST

OCEAN SUSHI DELI

WEBSTER ST

MUNDO'S SANDWICH AND BURGERS ▼

0   50 yds
0   50 m

© MOON.COM

whether California would allow its citizens to own slaves.

Upstairs is the **Colton Hall Museum** (831/646-5640, www.monterey.org, 10am-4pm daily), housed in the long, wood-floored room where the constitution was drafted. The constitution itself is now in Sacramento, but there are other documents from the convention under glass, including a piece of paper where the delegates practiced their signatures. A large portion of the building still houses the working offices of Monterey's City Hall.

The rear of Colton Hall is the location of the **Old Monterey Jail** (831/646-5640, www.monterey.org, 10am-4pm daily, free), which makes an appearance in John Steinbeck's 1935 novel *Tortilla Flat*. Wander into the granite jailhouse that hosted Monterey's malcontents from 1854 to 1956 and peer into its cells.

One final aspect of Colton Hall worth mentioning is the **Moon Tree,** which can be found in front of the building in Friendly Plaza. This towering coast redwood has the unique distinction of growing from a seed that traveled to the moon in 1971 before it was planted here in 1976.

The **Monterey Harbor** (Del Monte Ave., www.monterey.org) has always been an important part of Monterey, from its fishing past to its tourism-focused present. Sailboats creak and clank in the Municipal Marina, while fishing boats head out in search of squid and other seafood. A superb way to survey the scene is to walk the 1-mile (1.6-km) section of the **Monterey Bay Coastal Recreation Trail** (831/646-3866, www.monterey.org) along the harbor's edge.

Three piers jut out into the water and provide nice views of the harbor. The most popular is **Fisherman's Wharf** (1 Old Fisherman's Wharf, www.montereywharf.com, hours vary daily), which resembles a smaller version of San Francisco's popular tourist attraction of the same name. Where tons of sardines were once shipped out of Monterey Harbor, you'll now find a collection of seafood restaurants, touristy gift shops, and whale-watching boats. (Most of the wharf's seafood restaurants offer free shots of their competing clam chowders to those walking by. It may be enough to stave off your hunger until the next meal.) The wharf has also been featured in the HBO series *Big Little Lies*.

Colton Hall

Abalone Underfoot

Visitors walking out onto Municipal Wharf II might be surprised to learn that there is a hidden farming operation right under their feet. The **Monterey Abalone Company** (160 Municipal Wharf II, 831/646-0350, www.montereyabalone.com, 8am-4:30pm Mon.-Fri., 8am-3pm Sat.) grows abalones in cages that dangle down from the wharf's underside. Due to the destruction of the mollusk's wild populations, farmed abalones are the only ones available for retail sale. You can stop by the storefront to purchase your own abalone. The kind folks at the Monterey Abalone Company can also provide you with some recipe ideas.

The **Coast Guard Pier** is a 1,700-foot-long (518-m) breakwater on the south end of the harbor. It is one of Monterey's best wildlife-viewing areas, and it's a guarantee that you'll be able to see some sea lions and harbor seals if you walk out on the structure.

Municipal Wharf II is located on the eastern edge of the harbor. It still has working fishing operations along with a few wholesale fish companies, a couple restaurants, an abalone farm underneath its deck, and fine views of the harbor and nearby Del Monte Beach.

SAN CARLOS CATHEDRAL

The **San Carlos Cathedral** (500 Church St., 831/373-2628, www.sancarloscathedral.org) is integral to Monterey and early California's history. It has the distinction of being the oldest building in Monterey, the oldest continuously operating church on the West Coast, and California's first cathedral. The first chapel on the site was a wood hut constructed in 1771, a year before Carmel Mission was built. The current Spanish Colonial-style building dates back to 1794.

It is best to visit the cathedral, which is also known as the Royal Presidio Chapel, when the **Heritage Center** (1:15pm-3:15pm 2nd and 4th Mon. of the month, 10am-noon Wed., 10am-2pm Fri.-Sun.) is open. The two-room museum displays artifacts that were discovered during the cathedral's renovation, along with fascinating artifacts like sections of the cathedral's old whalebone sidewalk and a Spanish coin from 1779. The most impressive item might be a piece of oak tree known as the

Serra-Vizcaíno Oak, once an important landmark for the early Spanish explorers.

The T-shaped chapel has a handful of interesting features. The niche at the top of the cathedral's façade holds a statue of Our Lady of Guadalupe that is the oldest non-indigenous sculpture in California. Inside the long, narrow building are a few exposed sections that showcase old friezes and panels. Another fascinating aspect is a crypt for a local Monterey family that is buried under a slab right in front of the altar.

COOPER-MOLERA ADOBE

Surrounded by a historic adobe wall, the **Cooper-Molera Adobe** (525 Polk St., 831/223-0171, http://coopermolera.org, 10am-4pm Wed.-Sun.) is a 2.5-acre (1-ha) shared-use facility and an oasis for contemplating Monterey's rich history right in the city's downtown. Originally built in 1827, the on-site adobe buildings include two homes, with one that housed early resident John Bautista Rogers Cooper, who came to live in Monterey when it was under Mexican rule. The house museum features rooms decorated with Victorian-era decor and exhibits on the adobe's residents and visitors along with a rotating collection of local art.

The renovated complex of historic buildings and gardens includes the museum, a day-use garden, the Barns at Cooper-Molera event space, the Alta Bakery & Café, and the Cella Restaurant, which serves fresh California fare in an outdoor garden setting.

Monterey's Pillaging Pirate

The only pirate in California history did most of his plundering and pillaging in Monterey. Born in France, **Hippolyte Bouchard** moved to Argentina and was granted Argentine citizenship in 1813. In 1817, he embarked on a campaign by ship to torment the ships and settlements of Argentina's foe, Spain.

In 1818, Bouchard and his men sailed into the small coastal California port of Monterey, then the capital of the Spanish territory of Alta California, to wreak a bit of havoc. They were initially met with a volley of cannon fire from the Spanish military posted at the current site of the Lower Presidio Historic Park in Monterey. This incident is the only land and sea battle in California history.

Bouchard and his crew eventually made it to shore. Once on land, they raised the Argentine flag and burned the Spanish Presidio (fort) among other buildings. They captured Monterey for six days before Spanish reinforcements were notified, causing Bouchard and his men to flee.

It is worth visiting Monterey's **Lower Presidio Historic Park** to view the informative panels on the pirate's takeover. The park has a small Argentine flag that still flies today in honor of this piece of little-known history.

MONTEREY MUSEUM OF ART

The **Monterey Museum of Art** (559 Pacific St., 831/372-5477, www.montereyart.org, 11am-5pm Thurs.-Mon., adults $10, students, military personnel, and children free) is a three-story building across the street from historic Colton Hall. Its eight galleries showcase works from paintings to photographic art with a focus on works created by California artists.

Less than a mile away, the Monterey Museum of Art's **La Mirada location** (720 Via Mirada, 831/372-3689) is only open for special museum events and programs. The building was once an adobe in the Mexican period and later a private estate where Richard Burton and Elizabeth Taylor stayed while filming their 1965 film *The Sandpiper* in nearby Big Sur.

MY MUSEUM

The goal of **MY Museum** (425 Washington St., 831/649-6444, www.mymuseum.org, 10am-5pm Tues.-Sat., noon-5pm Sun., adults and children $8, children under two free) is to entertain the youngest members of your family. Touting itself as a "playground for the mind," this downtown kids' museum aims to show wee ones what makes Monterey special.

It does this with exhibits including a beach area where children can make sand castles from sand blocks and a mini putting green where budding golfers can work on their technique. The museum also maintains a regular schedule of children's classes, concerts, and craft-making sessions.

LOWER PRESIDIO HISTORIC PARK

Located on a hillside above Monterey Harbor, 25-acre (10.1-ha) **Lower Presidio Historic Park** (Artillery St. and Private Bolio, www.monterey.org) is one of the city's richest historical sites. Local Native Americans congregated here before Spanish explorer Sebastián Vizcaíno visited the spot in 1602, when he claimed California for the Spanish crown. The Spanish later used the site to build El Castillo, a fort then overtaken by the Mexican government. During the Civil War, it became a U.S. military installation that was visited by the Buffalo Soldiers, the famed African-American cavalry regiment.

Today, wheelchair-accessible trails lined with interpretive panels lead to the park's features, which all share a superb view of Monterey Harbor below. On the hillside are cannons and a large monument to U.S. commodore John Drake Sloat that is topped with a concrete eagle. (Sloat is the officer whose men raised the U.S. flag in Monterey, effectively transferring the territory of California from Mexican to American rule.) Close to the harbor is a stone statue of Father Junípero Serra.

One section of the park is devoted to the tale of Hippolyte Bouchard, a pirate who, for six days in 1818, took control of Monterey from the Spanish. Bouchard engaged in the only land-sea battle to occur on the Pacific coast; his story is told through two interpretive panels. A stone monument and Argentine flag were erected here by Argentina.

The park is also home to the **Presidio of Monterey Museum** (Corporal Ewing Rd., Bldg. 113, 831/646-3456, www.monterey.org, 10am-1pm Mon., 10am-4pm Thurs.-Sat., 1pm-4pm Sun., donations appreciated). The one-room museum is located in an old military administrative and storage building. It interprets the history of Monterey through a military lens, with exhibits and artifacts, including cannonballs from El Castillo, field uniforms, and more.

DENNIS THE MENACE PARK

The brainchild of Hank Ketcham, the creator of the *Dennis the Menace* comic strip,

Dennis the Menace Park (777 Pearl St., 831/646-3860, 10am-dusk daily) opened in 1956. Ketcham was heavily involved in the design process; he moved to the area after World War II, and lived here until his death in 2001. There's a 9-foot (2.7-m) climbing wall, suspension bridge, curvy slides, brightly colored jungle gyms, a (fenced in, non-working) locomotive, and a whole lot more, as well as a bronze sculpture of the little menace near the entrance.

WINE-TASTING

On Cannery Row, **A Taste of Monterey** (700 Cannery Row, Ste. KK, 831/646-5446, www.atasteofmonterey.com, 11am-8pm Fri.-Sat., 11am-6pm Sun.-Thurs., tasting $15) provides an unbeatable view of the bay while you sample wines from 95 Monterey County wineries. The tasting room, in a renovated sardine cannery building, also has a bistro that makes small plates, sliders, and nachos to pair with the fine wines. Right up from Cannery Row is the **Pierce Ranch Vineyards Tasting Room** (499 Wave St., 831/372-8900, www.piercevineyards.com, noon-7pm Mon.-Thurs., noon-8pm Fri.-Sat., noon-6pm Sun., tasting $5), which looks like a small family home. Inside, they pour glasses

Dennis the Menace Park

of cabernet sauvignon, petite sirah, and zinfandel made from grapes grown on their southern Monterey County vineyard.

The team behind Pessagno Winery and Puma Road Winery on the River Road Wine Trail in the Santa Lucia Highlands also runs **Puma Road Portola Plaza** (281 Alvarado St., 831/747-1911, 1pm-6pm Thurs.-Sun., tasting $15) in downtown Monterey.

Tucked along a pedestrian walkway between Alvarado Street and Custom House Plaza, **Sovino Wine Bar & Merchant** (241 Alvarado St., 831/641-9463, www.sovinowinebar.com, 11am-11pm Fri.-Sun., 3pm-10pm Mon.-Thurs.) provides several reasons to stop for a glass of wine. One is their offering of around 12 local and regional reds and whites by the glass at fair prices; another is their great happy hour (4pm-6pm Sun.-Thurs.), when offerings are half-off. The wine bar also pours glasses of craft beer and serves food from charcuterie plates to paninis.

SIGHTSEEING TOURS

More than 215 movies have been filmed in Monterey County, from Clint Eastwood's directorial debut *Play Misty for Me* to the goofy Tom Hanks comedy *Turner & Hooch*. **Monterey Movie Tours** (800/343-6437, www.montereymovietours.com, adults $60, seniors $55, children $40) provides a three-hour bus tour that visits film locations on the Monterey Peninsula. The tour bus pulls up to Monterey sights like the historic Colton Hall, where you'll see a clip from 1959's *A Summer Place* on the video screen mounted in the bus. Then, at the Monterey Bay Aquarium, you'll watch footage from *Star Trek 4: The Journey Home*, where scenes from the movie were filmed. The scenic tour also heads into Pebble Beach and stops at the Lone Cypress and The Lodge at Pebble Beach. Owner and operator Doug Lumsden uses the tour to impart impressive knowledge about the peninsula's history and notable attractions, including anecdotes about legendary Carmel resident Clint Eastwood.

Let the knowledgeable locals of **Dream Tours By-the-Sea** (200 Clock Tower Pl., Ste. D206, Carmel, 831/888-7555) shuttle you to the area's best sights in a small passenger van. One of their specialties is a customized winetasting and vineyard tour.

Some tourists zip around and see the sights in bright yellow, convertible scooter cars that resemble souped-up golf carts. Rent one yourself at **Sea Car Tours** (230 Alvarado St., 831/884-6807, www.seacartours.com, 10am-6pm daily, one-hour tour $60-160). There is a one-hour tour of Monterey, a two-hour tour that covers Monterey and Pacific Grove, and a three-hour tour that lets you do your own thing.

Monterey Bay Food Tours (831/204-2211, www.montereybayfoodtours.com, $150) specializes in showcasing the bounty of the county, from food purveyors to local wineries and craft breweries. This walking tour also includes introductory information about downtown Monterey.

Monterey's Hidden History

Explore this trio of lesser-known, yet historic buildings that sit just a few blocks away from Alvarado Street in downtown Monterey.

MAYO HAYES O'DONNELL RESEARCH LIBRARY

The **Mayo Hayes O'Donnell Research Library** (155 Van Buren St., 831/747-1027, www.mayohayeslibrary.org, 1:30pm-3:45pm Wed. and Fri.-Sun.) is a striking red structure that stands out on this little-visited block. Constructed in 1876, the building was the first protestant church erected in Monterey and was where John Steinbeck's son Thomas was baptized. Today, it's a non-circulating research library run by the Monterey History and Art Association. Collections include maps, periodicals, historic art, and books, some of which date to the 1800s.

CASA SERRANO

Casa Serrano (412 Pacific St., 831/372-2608, http://montereyhistory.org, 2pm-4pm Sat., donations appreciated) is truly one of Monterey's hidden treasures. Built in 1843, this four-room adobe was one of Monterey's earliest schools; it is now home to an outstanding collection of art. On display are works by early California painters like Armin Hansen and Evelyn McCormack, along with a room devoted to artist Jo Mora's sculptures, lithographs, oil paintings, and pen-and-ink renderings.

LARA SOTO ADOBE

Built in the 1830s, the **Lara Soto Adobe** (460 Pierce St.) is now an administration building for the Middlebury Institute of International Studies at Monterey, a graduate school. But for fans of the author John Steinbeck, this is where he lived in 1944-1945, the pivotal years when he wrote *The Pearl* and when his novel *Cannery Row* was published. Though closed to the general public, visitors can view the building's renovated exterior. A plaque out front details Steinbeck's connection.

Recreation

Monterey Bay is the premier Northern California locale for a number of water sports, especially scuba diving. It's also one of the best areas on the California coast for kayaking and stand-up paddleboarding due to its protection from the open ocean and its vibrant marine life.

BEACHES

Monterey State Beach

Monterey State Beach (Del Monte Ave., 831/649-2836, www.parks.ca.gov, dawn-sunset daily) is a fee-free beach stretching from the Monterey Municipal Wharf II to Seaside. The relatively flat state beach is good for walks or beach runs, while the protected waters offshore are usually nice places to paddle out into the bay in a kayak or on a stand-up paddleboard. Access points include the Monterey Municipal Wharf II and the end of Canyon del Rey Boulevard in Seaside. You can access a popular locals' section by turning left onto Casa Verde Way off Del Monte Avenue while heading toward Seaside from downtown Monterey. The street then turns into the one-way Surf Way, which dead-ends into Tide Avenue; that street offers parking right along the beach. A section of the state beach is known as Del Monte Beach, which can be a bit confusing.

Between the state beach and El Estero Park is the city's **Window on the Bay** (831/646-3860, http://monterey.org, 6am-10pm daily), which has volleyball courts, picnic tables, and barbecue pits.

San Carlos Beach Park

One of the most popular places for scuba divers to access the bay, the **San Carlos Beach Park** (Cannery Row at Reeside Ave., 831/646-3860, www.monterey.org, 6am-10pm daily) is south of the Coast Guard Pier and Monterey Harbor. This small spit of beach is backed by a grassy lawn, and there's also a lighted outdoor basketball court near the Recreation Trail.

McAbee Beach

To get some sand in your shoes while walking around Cannery Row, check out **McAbee Beach** (Cannery Row and Hoffman Ave., 831/646-3860, www.monterey.org, 6am-10pm daily), a pocket beach tucked between the Spindrift Inn and El Torito Restaurant. This sliver of sand still has a few ruins from Cannery Row's fishing heyday. The little beach boasts a vibrant history: It was once a launching spot for Portuguese whalers and the site of a small Chinese fishing village. Learn more by reading the interpretive panels above the beach.

★ SCUBA DIVING

Any native Northern Californian knows that there's only one really great place in the region to get certified in scuba diving: Monterey Bay. Even if you go to a dive school in the Bay Area, they'll take you down to Monterey for your open-water dive. Accordingly, dozens of dive schools cluster in and around the city of Monterey.

One of the best places for novices and more experienced divers is in **Breakwater Cove** (novice to advanced, 10-60 ft/3-18.3 m) off San Carlos Beach. It's easy to access with lots of parking and a beach entry. Breakwater's accessibility results in busloads of folks from Bakersfield to Berkeley coming to the spot to do their checkout dives. Despite this, it rarely feels crowded in the water. You can spot fish, Dungeness crab, and harbor seals along the rocks of the cove's namesake breakwater. To

the west is a reef with a kelp bed. It's shallow enough that even snorkelers can see their fill of sea life.

A more advanced dive off San Carlos Beach is on the **Metridium Field** (advanced, 35-60 ft/10.7-18.3 m), which involves a swim out into the bay. Once there, you'll be treated to reefs covered in Metridium anemones, which look like white underwater mushrooms. To reach the site, swim 50-60 feet (15.2-18.3 m) out from the beach pump house. Look for a large pipe and follow it to the end. Then swim north for another 30 feet (9.1 m).

An easy-access dive spot is off Cannery Row's **McAbee Beach** (novice to advanced, 10-50 ft/3-15.2 m). Swim out from the beach 30-40 feet (9.1-12.2 m) to reach a kelp forest colored with invertebrates.

Cannery Row Aquatics (225 Cannery Row, Ste. M, 831/717-4546, http://canneryrowaquatics.com, 9am-6pm Mon.-Tues. and Thurs.-Fri., 7am-6pm Sat.-Sun., lessons $200-600, gear rental $65/day) occupies an enviable spot close to the Breakwater Cove diving spots. It rents equipment, teach classes, and conduct tours of the Breakwater Cove area.

A locals' favorite, **Bamboo Reef** (614 Lighthouse Ave., 831/372-1685, www.bambooreef.com, 9am-6pm Mon.-Fri., 7am-6pm Sat.-Sun. summer, lessons $175-470, gear rental $70/day) offers scuba lessons and rents equipment just a few blocks from popular dive spots, including Breakwater Cove. The aquamarine storefront on Lighthouse Avenue has been helping people get underwater since 1980.

Aquarius Dive Shop (2040 Del Monte Ave., 831/375-1933, http://aquariusdivers.com, 9am-6pm Mon.-Thurs., 9am-7pm Fri., 7am-7pm Sat., 7am-6pm Sun., lessons $125-294, gear rental $65-75/day) offers everything you need to go diving in Monterey Bay, including air and nitrox fills, equipment rental, certification courses, and help booking a trip on a local dive boat. Aquarius works with five boats to create great trips for divers of all interests and ability levels.

Sea Sanctuary

Monterey Bay is in a federally protected marine area known as the **Monterey Bay National Marine Sanctuary** (MBNMS, http://montereybay.noaa.gov). Designated a sanctuary in 1992, the protected waters stretch far past the confines of Monterey Bay to a northern boundary 7 miles (11.3 km) north of the Golden Gate Bridge and a southern boundary at Cambria in San Luis Obispo County. The sanctuary was created for resource protection, education, public use, and research. The MBNMS is the reason so many marine research facilities, including the Long Marine Laboratory, the Monterey Bay Marine Laboratory, and the Moss Landing Marine Laboratories, dot the Monterey Bay's shoreline.

MBNMS holds many marine treasures, including the Monterey Bay Submarine Canyon, which is right offshore of the fishing village of Moss Landing. The canyon is similar in size to the Grand Canyon and has a rim-to-floor depth of 5,577 feet (1,700 m). In 2009, MBNMS expanded to include another fascinating underwater geographical feature: the Davidson Seamount. Located 80 miles (129 km) southwest of Monterey, the undersea mountain rises an impressive 7,480 feet (2,280 m), yet its summit is still 4,101 feet (1,250 m) below the ocean's surface.

TOP EXPERIENCE

★ KAYAKING AND STAND-UP PADDLEBOARDING

With all the focus on sustainable tourism in Monterey, coupled with the lovely recreation area formed by Monterey Bay, it's no wonder that sea kayaking is popular here. Monterey's coastline is as scenic a spot as any to learn to kayak or stand-up paddleboard (SUP). Whether you want to try paddling for the first time or you're an expert who hasn't brought your own gear out to California, you'll find a local outfit ready and willing to hook you up.

The coast off Monterey is an ideal place for paddling. It is less exposed than other spots along the California coast. If the swells are big, duck into Monterey Harbor, where you can paddle past moored boats and harbor seal colonies. When the surf is manageable, the paddle from San Carlos Beach to the aquarium and back (1.2 mi/1.9 km round-trip) pretty much guarantees that you will see an otter or a harbor seal in the water near you. The Monterey Bay National Marine Sanctuary regulations require all paddlers to stay 150 feet (45.7 m) from all sea otters, sea lions, and harbor seals.

Adventures by the Sea (299 Cannery Row, 831/372-1807, www.adventuresbythesea.

com, 9am-sunset daily, kayak tours $60-85 pp, kayak rentals $35-60/day, SUP rentals $50/day) rents kayaks by the day to let you choose your own route around the magnificent Monterey Bay kelp forest. If you're not confident enough to go off on your own, Adventures offers tours from Cannery Row. Your guide can tell you all about the wildlife you're seeing: harbor seals, sea otters, pelicans, seagulls—and maybe even a whale in the winter. The tour lasts about 2.5 hours and the tandem sit-on-top kayaks make it a great experience for school-age children. Adventures by the Sea also runs a tour of Stillwater Cove at Pebble Beach. Reservations are recommended for all tours, but during the summer the Cannery Row tour leaves regularly at 10am and 2pm, so you can stop by and see if there's a spot available. There are several other locations in Monterey (685 Cannery Row and 210 Alvarado St.).

Rent a kayak or SUP from **Monterey Bay Kayaks** (693 Del Monte Ave., 831/373-5357, www.montereybaykayaks.com, 9am-5pm daily, kayak tours $45-100, kayak rentals $30-45 pp, SUP rentals $45/two hours) and paddle into the bay from the beach just south of the Municipal Wharf. (There's also a branch in Moss Landing on the Elkhorn Slough.) You can also choose to paddle out with an experienced guide. The tours include kayak fishing,

Sunday sunrise excursions, and a Point Lobos paddle. If you really get into it, you can also sign up for closed-deck sea kayaking classes to learn about safety, rescue techniques, tides, currents, and paddling techniques.

SURFING

Monterey is not the best place on the Monterey Peninsula to surf. (That would be Carmel Beach and Pacific Grove's Asilomar Beach.) That said, occasionally the break off Monterey State Beach's Casa Verde stretch has waves. When the swells get big, an easy beginner wave sometimes forms off Monterey's Municipal Wharf.

On the Beach (693 Lighthouse Ave., 831/646-9283, http://onthebeachsurfshop. com, 10am-6pm Mon.-Thurs., 10am-7pm Fri.-Sat., surfboard rental $30-35/day, wetsuit rental $20/day) is on the same street a few blocks away and rents boards. It is a large, organized shop with lots of gear.

TOP EXPERIENCE

★ WHALE-WATCHING

Whales pass quite near the shores of Monterey year-round. While you can sometimes even see them from the beaches, any number of boats can take you out for a closer look at the great beasts as they travel along their own special routes north and south. The area hosts many humpbacks, blue whales, and gray whales, plus the occasional killer whale, minke whale, fin whale, and pod of dolphins. Bring your own binoculars for a better view, but the experienced boat captains will do all they can to get you as close as possible to the whales and dolphins. Most tours last 2-3 hours and leave from Fisherman's Wharf, which is easy to get to and has ample parking. This is an easy and highly recommended way to take in the Monterey Bay's amazing marine life.

Monterey Bay Whale Watch (84 Fisherman's Wharf, 831/375-4658, www. montereybaywhalewatch.com, adults $65-79, children 4-12 $53-67, children 3 and under $15) leaves from an easy-to-find red building

on Fisherman's Wharf and runs tours in every season. You must make a reservation in advance, even for regularly scheduled tours. Afternoon tours are available.

Princess Monterey Whale Watching (96 Fisherman's Wharf, 831/372-2203, www. montereywhalewatching.com, adults $60-80, children 3-11 $40-60) prides itself on its knowledgeable guides/marine biologists and its comfortable, spacious cruising vessels. The *Princess Monterey* offers morning and afternoon tours, and you can buy tickets online or by phone.

Fast Raft Ocean Safaris (Monterey Harbor and Moss Landing Harbor, 408/659-3900, www.fastraft.com, $150-295/pp) offers an intimate way to see the Monterey coastline and the wildlife of Monterey Bay. The "fast raft" is a 33-foot-long (10.1-m) inflatable boat with a rigid hull that accommodates just six passengers. The raft does whale-watching trips out of Moss Landing and coastal safaris that depart from Monterey and head south to Pebble Beach's Stillwater Cove and Point Lobos when the weather cooperates. The vessel has a few advantages over the other larger whale-watching ships for those who want to see marine mammals up close and personal. It is low to the water and open, which makes any nearby whale that is surfacing, spouting, or breaching an even more incredible experience to behold. The engine is also quieter, and the captain doesn't use amplified speakers to address the passengers, making it easy to hear the exhalations of surfacing and diving whales. Although the six shock-absorbing straddle seats look like something you'd find on an amusement park roller coaster, they provide a surprisingly comfortable sit even in bumpy ocean conditions. It's worth noting that the fast raft does not have a restroom, and it doesn't allow passengers under 12 years old.

FISHING

J&M Sport Fishing (66 Fisherman's Wharf, 831/372-7440, http://jmsportfishing.com, $70-175) took over the longtime Randy's Fishing fleet. The operation leaves shore for salmon,

rock cod, halibut, and a fishing/crabbing combo trip.

To catch your own seafood, head out with **Westwind Charter Sport Fishing & Excursions** (66 Fisherman's Wharf, 831/392-7867, http://montereysportfishing.com, salmon $650/up to four people, rock cod, lingcod, or halibut $550/up to four people). Depending on what's in season, you can catch salmon, rock cod, lingcod, or halibut.

SAILING

A good way to see the bay is by sailboat. **Monterey Bay Sailing** (78 Old Fisherman's Wharf, 831/372-7245, www.montereysailing.com, bay cruises adults $55-85, children $45, boat rentals $250-475/day) offers daytime cruises, sunset cruises, sailboat rentals—and even sailing lessons. **Carrera Sailing** (Municipal Wharf II, A-Tier, 831/375-0648, www.sailmontereybay.com, 1.5-hour cruises $38-50 pp) can also get you out on the water, whether it's a nature excursion, romantic sunset cruise, or sailing lessons.

PARKS

Monterey State Historic Park (20 Custom House Plaza, 831/649-2907, www.parks.ca.gov, 9am-5pm daily May-Sept., 10am-4pm daily Oct.-Apr., free) has three bocce ball courts. Stop in at the Pacific House Museum to borrow a free set of bocce balls.

El Estero Park

El Estero Park (bordered by Del Monte Ave., Camino Aquajito, Fremont Blvd., and Camino El Estero, 831/646-3866, www.monterey.org, 6am-10pm daily) is 45 acres (18.2 ha) and hosts a variety of facilities, including the very popular **Dennis the Menace Park** (777 Pearl St., 831/646-3860, 10am-dusk daily May-Sept., 10am-dusk Wed.-Mon. Sept.-May), a playground park that came to be in part due to the efforts of *Dennis the Menace* cartoonist Hank Ketchum.

Rent a paddleboat (some are designed to look like giant swans) at **El Estero Boating** (corner of Camino El Estero and Del Monte Ave., 831/375-1484, 10am-5pm Mon.-Fri., 10am-6pm Sat.-Sun. summer, 10am-4pm daily winter; regular paddleboats $30/hr, swan paddleboats $40/half hour) and cruise around the goose-laden waters. Or walk the path around the lake, where you can utilize the park's physical fitness equipment (parallel bars, balance beam) if you need a workout. The park's other features include a nice group barbecue area, a baseball diamond, a youth center, a dog park, and the **Monterey Skate Park** (9am-dusk daily), which has obstacles like stairs and rails.

Veterans Memorial Park

Veterans Memorial Park (Skyline Dr. and Jefferson St., 831/646-3860, www.monterey.org, 6am-10pm daily) is uphill from downtown Monterey and has fine views of the bay. With a large lawn and barbecue facilities, it's a good place for a picnic. There are also hiking trails and a basketball court. It's the access point for **Huckleberry Hill Nature Preserve,** with 81 acres (32.8 ha) of open space webbed with hiking trails.

Jack's Peak County Park

Jack's Peak in **Jack's Peak County Park** (25020 Jacks Peak Park Rd., 831/755-4895, www.co.monterey.ca.us, 8am-close daily year-round, vehicles Mon.-Fri. $4, Sat.-Sun. and holidays $5) is the Monterey Peninsula's highest point at 1,068 feet (326 m). The park is located a few miles east of downtown Monterey and has some nice views of the city and its harbor. There are 8.5 miles (13.7 km) of trail here, including a self-guided nature trail that shows off some fossils from the Miocene epoch. The park also has picnic areas and bathrooms.

HIKING

If you want to explore Monterey's coastline without getting wet, head out on the **Monterey Bay Coastal Recreation Trail**

1: humpback whale in Monterey Bay 2: stand-up paddleboarding 3: kayaking in Monterey Bay

(831/646-3866, www.monterey.org). The 18-mile (29-km) paved path stretches from Pacific Grove in the south all the way to the Monterey County town of Castroville in the north, following the former tracks of the Southern Pacific Railroad. The most scenic section is from Monterey Harbor down to Pacific Grove's Lovers Point Park. On busy weekends, start in Seaside and head north for fewer crowds.

Jack's Peak County Park (25020 Jacks Peak Park Rd., 831/755-4895, www.co.monterey.ca.us, 8am-close daily, vehicles Mon.-Fri. $4, Sat.-Sun. and holidays $5) is home to the highest point on the Monterey Peninsula. Its **Skyline Trail** (0.8-mile/1.3 km, easy) passes through a rare Monterey pine forest and offers glimpses of fossils from the Miocene epoch before reaching the summit, which offers an overview of the whole peninsula.

An interesting little hike in **Veterans Memorial Park** (Skyline Dr. and Jefferson St., 831/646-3860, www.monterey.org, 6am-10pm daily) leads to a former quarry. The **Quarry Park Trail** (1.3 mi/2.1 km round-trip, easy) can be found northeast of the park's large, grassy lawn. It traverses a hillside before winding down into the former quarry, where it is said rocks were taken to build Monterey Harbor's breakwater. Now the quarry feels like a tranquil box canyon.

Accessible from Veterans Memorial Park, **Huckleberry Hill Nature Preserve** has an intact Monterey pine forest. The **Huckleberry Hill Loop Trail** (1.8 mi/2.9 km round-trip, moderate) gains 300 feet (91.4 m) as it makes a loop around the perimeter of the preserve.

BIKING

A terrific way to see Monterey's coastline is to hop on a bike and hit the **Monterey Bay Coastal Recreation Trail** (831/646-3866, www.monterey.org), which allows you to bike past Monterey Harbor and Cannery Row and out to Pacific Grove's Lovers Point Park. **Adventures by the Sea** (299 Cannery Row,

831/372-1807, www.adventuresbythesea.com, 9am-8pm daily summer, 9am-6pm daily winter, bike rentals $30-125, electric bikes $50-75) rents bikes in various locations (685 Cannery Row, 210 Alvarado St.) along the Rec Trail. Try your team-building skills by renting a two- to six-person surrey bike ($90-240).

GYM

If you have been indulging in the Monterey Peninsula's excellent dining scene, work off some of your added pounds at the **Monterey Sports Center** (301 E. Franklin St., 831/646-3730, www.monterey.org, 5:30am-9:30pm Mon.-Fri., 7am-6pm Sat., 8:30am-6pm Sun., adults $9, seniors $6.50, 6-17 years old $5.50, under 5 $3.75). This clean city-run facility has a weight-training center, a cardio fitness room, two indoor pools, a sauna facility, and a waterslide. They also offer more than 100 group exercise options every week, from aqua Zumba to Pilates, for an added fee.

GOLF

The **Monterey Pines Golf Course** (Fairground Rd. and Garden Rd., 831/656-2167, www.montereypeninsulagolf.com, Mon.-Fri. $18-34, Sat.-Sun. $20-37) might boost your confidence after a lousy day playing on Pebble Beach's challenging greens. The course is a beginner-friendly 18 holes next to the Monterey County Fairgrounds.

The Pebble Beach Company manages the **Del Monte Golf Course** (1300 Sylvan Rd., 800/877-0597, www.pebblebeach.com, $110). It opened as a nine-hole course way back in 1897 as a place for guests of the Hotel Del Monte to play. Now expanded to 18 holes, it claims to be the oldest continuously operating course west of the Mississippi.

CAR RACING

If you're feeling the need for speed, you can get lots of it at the **WeatherTech Raceway Laguna Seca** (1021 Monterey-Salinas Hwy., 831/242-8201, www.co.monterey.ca.us), one of the country's premier road-racing venues.

Here you can see historic auto races, super-bikes, speed festivals, and an array of Grand Prix events. The major racing season runs May-October. In addition to the big events, Laguna Seca hosts innumerable auto clubs and small sports car and stock car races. Be sure to check the website for parking directions specific to the event you plan to attend—this is a big facility. There is even a campground here known as the **Laguna Seca Recreation Area** (831/242-8200, www.co.monterey.ca.us, RV sites $40, tent sites $35) that is run by the Monterey County Parks Department.

SPAS

Monterey is as good a place as any on the California coast to spoil yourself. One of the best places to so is at the **Vista Blue Spa** (Monterey Plaza Hotel & Spa, 400 Cannery Row, 831/920-6710, http://montereyplazahotel.com, treatments 10am-6pm Wed.-Mon., sundeck 9am-8pm daily, massages $130-360), high above the bay in the Monterey Plaza Hotel & Spa. Make sure to spend some time before or after your treatment on the outdoor sundeck with fabulous bay views.

The **Monterey Day Spa** (380 Foam St., Ste. A, 831/373-2273, www.montereydayspa.com, 9am-7pm Mon.-Sat., 9am-5pm Sun., massages $90-260) will freshen you up with massages, facials, waxing, nail care, and more. The spa packages range from a "Girlfriend Getaway" to a "Couples Sanctuary." You can also throw a sparty (spa party) at Monterey Day Spa to celebrate a wedding, a birthday, or any other important life event.

"Elysium" is an ancient Greek word for perfect happiness. **Elysium** (700 Cass St., Ste. 112, 831/375-1976, www.elysiumtotalbliss.com, 9am-5:30pm Mon.-Fri., 9am-5pm Sat.-Sun. by appointment, massages $45-130) does massages, body treatments, and cosmetic work (teeth whitening, hair removal) to help you get to your happy place.

Entertainment

BARS AND CLUBS

Descending into **The Crown & Anchor** (150 W. Franklin St., 831/649-6496, www.crownandanchor.net, 11am-1:30am daily) feels a bit like entering a ship's hold. Along with the maritime theme, The Crown & Anchor serves 20 different international beers on tap. Sip indoors or on the popular outdoor patio. They also have good pub fare, including cottage pies and curries; the curry fries are a local favorite. Lively but not a pickup joint, The Crown & Anchor is a go-to place for locals and tourists.

Britannia Arms (444 Alvarado St., 831/656-9543, www.britanniaarmsofmonterey.com, 11am-1:30am daily) is a British pub right on Alvarado Street owned by an actual Brit. The "Brit," as it's known to locals, is usually packed with a younger crowd on Friday and Saturday nights, when there's a DJ spinning. There's also karaoke four times a week (Tues.-Thurs. and Sun.). At less crowded times, the Brit is a good place to watch sports, and if you are an English Premier League soccer fan, this pub has you covered. Choose between 24 beers on tap and a full bar.

The location of the **London Bridge Pub** (256 Figueroa St., Wharf II, 831/372-0581, http://lbpmonterey.com, 11:30am-11pm Fri.-Sat., 11:30am-10pm Thurs.-Mon.) sets it apart from Monterey's other drinking establishments. Situated right beside the Monterey Harbor, and adjacent to the Municipal Wharf, the pub takes advantage of the setting with an outdoor heated patio that has views of the boats docked in the harbor.

The best place in Monterey to watch your favorite sports team is **Knuckles Sports Bar** (1 Old Golf Course Rd., 831/372-1234, http://monterey.regency.hyatt.com, 4pm-midnight daily). Its 24 flat-screen TVs have individual detached speakers that you can bring to your table so you can actually hear the commentators. There are free peanuts and popcorn, along with a better-than-average bar menu including a burger of the month.

The **Turn 12 Bar & Grill** (400 Tyler St., 831/372-8876, www.turn12barandgrill.com, 11:30am-1am daily) pays tribute to nearby Laguna Seca Raceway with vintage motorbikes and framed images of racecars and motorcycles. The large space includes a 50-foot-long (15.2-m) pewter bar ideal for watching sporting events (there are flat-screen TVs behind the bar) while enjoying a bite from the solid food menu of salads, pizzas, pastas, meat, and seafood. The chili verde skillet is one of the highlights. It's a great place to go when downtown Monterey is crowded.

Pearl Hour (214 Lighthouse Ave., www.pearlhour.com, 5pm-midnight Thurs.-Mon.) takes its name from a line in Steinbeck book *Cannery Row* about the magic of dusk. The author would probably have found himself at home in this speakeasy and on its rambling back deck, where creative cocktails utilizing seasonal ingredients and mostly small-batch spirits are the star. Led by longtime local mixologist Katie Blandin, Pearl Hour has also become a magnet for some of Monterey's cooler events including performances by local musicians, thespians, DJs, and dancers.

A true dive bar, **Segovia's** (650 Lighthouse Ave., 831/718-8932, 3pm-2am Mon.-Fri., 2pm-2am Sat.-Sun., cash only) doesn't have windows, draft beer, or a cash register that takes credit cards. It does have cheap drinks, a jukebox, a fireplace, a smoking patio, and some interesting matador decor.

A distinct stone building just a couple blocks off Alvarado Street, **Alfredo's** (266 Pearl St., 831/375-0655, 10am-2am daily, cash only) is a cozy dive bar for the downtown Monterey crowd. This comfortable drinking establishment has dim lighting, a gas fireplace, cheap drinks, and a good jukebox. It's a fine place for a drink if you actually want to hear what your companion is saying. Ask for dice to play a round of Liar's Dice.

BREWERIES

Microbrew fans should make time for **Alvarado Street Brewery** (426 Alvarado St., 831/655-2337, www.alvaradostreetbrewery.com, 11:30am-11pm Fri.-Sat., 11:30am-10pm Sun.-Thurs.). Occupying a boisterous, modern space, it has more than 20 beers on tap,

Alvarado Street Brewery

including its own sours, ales, and a Mai Tai PA—which won a gold medal at the Great American Beer Festival—not to mention one-offs, collaborations, and more. Sip the tasty brews on the sidewalk patio in front or in the beer garden out back.

Peter B's Brewpub (2 Portola Plaza, behind Portola Hotel & Spa, 831/649-2699, www.portolahotel.com, 4pm-11pm Mon.-Thurs., 4pm-midnight Fri., 11am-midnight Sat., 11am-11pm Sun.) opened in 1996 as the area's first craft brewery. The selection includes five house beers along with four or five seasonal offerings, and some experimental brews. The menu includes salads, burgers, pizzas, and entrées along with worthwhile appetizers like crispy cheese curds and tempura cauliflower in a tangy buffalo sauce. There's also a pet-friendly patio with four fire pit tables, and 18 flat-screen TVs are inside so that you can catch whatever game is on when you arrive.

Fieldwork (560 Munras Ave., 831/324-0658, http://fieldworkbrewing.com, noon-10pm Fri.-Sat., noon-9pm Sun.-Thurs.) is a Berkeley-based craft brewery with a satellite taproom in Monterey. This is a stripped-down operation: The taps are in shipping containers and seating is outside in a beer garden. Folks come here for creative brews that include a Churro Cream Ale (inspired by the Mexican dessert) and Galaxy Juice, a hazy IPA.

Turlock-based craft brewery **Dust Bowl Brewing Company Tap Depot** (290 Figueroa St., 831/641-7002, http://dustbowlbrewing.com, 3pm-8pm Mon.-Thurs., noon-8pm Fri.-Sun.) has a Monterey outpost that's a local favorite due to its abundant outdoor seating, breadth of beer styles, and superb location beside the Rec Trail and near Monterey Harbor. It keeps a diverse array of more than 20 beers on tap, including the flagship Hops of Wrath IPA, lagers, fruit beers, and stouts. The large patio area has fire pits, corn hole, and a food truck that serves killer tacos. On a sunny day, this is the place to enjoy a beer outdoors.

LIVE MUSIC

Downtown Monterey's historic **Golden State Theatre** (417 Alvarado St., 831/649-1070, www.goldenstatetheatre.com) hosts live music, a speaker series, and dance, comedy, and theater productions. The theater dates back to 1926 and was designed to look like a Moorish castle. Performers in its ornate main room have included music legends from Arlo Guthrie to "Weird Al" Yankovic along with more contemporary acts like Fleet Foxes. The current owners also run the Fox Theatre in Redwood City.

Cibo (301 Alvarado St., 831/649-8151, www.cibo.com, 4pm-close daily) has live music six nights a week and draws a mostly middle-aged crowd. It hosts mellow jazz on Sundays, Tuesdays, Wednesdays, and Thursdays before heating up with funk, soul, and more upbeat genres on Friday and Saturday.

Sly McFly's (700 Cannery Row, Ste. A, 831/649-8050, www.slymcflys.com, 11am-2am Fri.-Sat., 11am-1am Sun.-Thurs.) is one of the few places in the area that guarantee live music seven days a week. On weekends, a middle-aged crowd spins and dips on the wooden dance floor in front of the stage. There are also lots of TVs for catching sporting events.

For old-school cool, stop into **The Sardine Factory** (701 Wave St., 831/373-3775, www.sardinefactory.com, 5pm-10:30pm Sun.-Thurs., 5pm-11pm Fri.-Sat.) any night from Tuesday to Saturday between 7:30pm and 10:30pm to see local musician David Conley play piano in the restaurant's lounge. He takes requests, and it's a kick hearing piano bar versions of modern songs.

THEATER

In Cannery Row you'll find Monterey's off-beat playhouse, the **Paper Wing Theatre and Supper Club** (711 Cannery Row, 831/905-5684, www.paperwing.com), which does a very popular take on *The Rocky Horror Picture Show* leading up to Halloween. It's also a supper club and hosts a large range of other

Monterey Pop Festival

The 1967 Monterey Pop Festival changed popular music forever. It launched the careers of icons including Jimi Hendrix, Janis Joplin, and Otis Redding, while basically creating the blueprint for the current multi-act music festival. It all began as an idea hatched by a small group of music industry heavyweights including producer Lou Adler and John Phillips of the folk act The Mamas & the Papas.

During their show at the Monterey County Fairgrounds, The Who wowed the audience by smashing their instruments onstage. This was the same event where Hendrix set his guitar on fire during his performance, and the same place where Otis Redding made inroads into mainstream music due to a well-received set he played with Booker T. & the MGs as a backing band.

The Monterey Pop Festival is immortalized in D. A. Pennebaker's legendary concert film *Monterey Pop*.

events, including magic shows, drag brunches, and comedy nights.

FESTIVALS AND EVENTS

The Monterey region hosts numerous festivals and special events each year. Whether your pleasure is fine food or funky music, you'll probably be able to plan a trip around some sort of multiday festival. There are dozens of events and performances scheduled during Monterey's busy year.

Hordes of spandex-clad cyclists take over the WeatherTech Raceway Laguna Seca and beyond for the **Sea Otter Classic** (1021 Monterey-Salinas Hwy., 800/218-8411, www. seaotterclassic.com, May), which is touted as the largest cycling festival on the continent. This "celebration of cycling" includes everyone from amateurs to Olympians competing in mountain bike and road bike races.

Since debuting in 2010, the three-day **California Roots Music & Art Festival** (Monterey County Fairgrounds, 2004 Fairground Rd., http://californiarootsfestival. com, late May) has become the world's largest reggae-rock festival. Previous acts have included Rebelution, Slightly Stoopid, and reggae royalty from the Marley family.

Gearheads love **Monterey Car Week** (peninsula-wide, Aug.), when classic cars clog up the area's motorways. There are also high-dollar car auctions, vintage car races, and the accompanying **Concours d'Elegance** (Pebble Beach, http://pebblebeachconcours. net). The event with the best sense of humor is the **Concours d'Lemons** (Seaside City Hall, 440 Harcourt Ave., Seaside, http://24hoursoflemons.com), which showcases battered junkers and strange, limited-edition automobiles.

The Monterey County Fairgrounds is known nationally for events like the Monterey Jazz Festival, but it's also the place where the **Monterey County Fair** (Monterey County Fairgrounds, 2004 Fairground Rd., 831/372-5863, www.montereycountyfair.com, Aug.) occurs every year. Enjoy deep-fried foods, amusement park rides, 4-H animals, and live concerts.

Monterey's Italian heritage is honored in early September every year during the **Festa Italia** (Custom House Plaza, 831/625-9623, www.festaitaliamonterey.org, Sept.). The three-day fest showcases music, a bocce tournament, and plenty of terrific Italian food. Don't miss the *arancini* (Italian stuffed-rice balls).

One of the biggest music festivals in California is the **Monterey Jazz Festival** (Monterey County Fairgrounds, 2004 Fairground Rd., 831/373-3366, www. montereyjazzfestival.org, Sept.). As the site of the longest-running jazz festival on earth, Monterey attracts 500 artists from around the world to play on the fest's eight stages. Held each September at the Monterey County Fairgrounds, this long weekend of amazing music can leave you happy for the whole year. Recent acts to grace the Monterey Jazz Festival's stages include Herbie Hancock, Chick Corea, and rapper Common.

One way to get into the holiday spirit and explore Monterey's historic buildings is to secure a ticket to **Christmas in the Adobes** (downtown Monterey, www.mshpa.org, Dec.). This popular event allows ticketholders to explore Monterey's oldest buildings, including those in Monterey State Historic Park and other private adobes that are only open to the public for this event. The event includes people in period dress, dancers, and music performances.

Shopping

CANNERY ROW

Cannery Row is mostly home to shops selling touristy T-shirts, candy, and refrigerator magnets. One of the best shops in Cannery Row is the **Monterey Bay Aquarium's Gift & Bookstore** (886 Cannery Row, 877/665-2665, http://shop.montereybayaquarium.org, 10am-5pm daily late May-early Sept., 9:30am-6pm daily early Sept.-late May). There are field guides, children's books, Monterey Bay-inspired art, and squishy stuffed sea otters. It has also started a run of retro apparel featuring aquarium animals. If you are not buying a pass to the aquarium, you can ask an aquarium manager to escort you into the shop by calling 877/665-2665 on weekdays from 10am to 4pm.

Lighthouse Avenue, a couple of blocks away from Cannery Row, is the place to find locally owned shops. Between Cannery Row and Lighthouse Avenue is the **Cannery Row Antique Mall** (471 Wave St., 831/655-0264, www.canneryrowantiquemall.com, 10am-5:30pm Mon.-Fri., 10am-6pm Sat., 10am-5pm Sun.), which is located in a former cannery building. It boasts 100 antiques dealers selling all sorts of items, from jewelry to sports memorabilia.

If a visit to Monterey is inspiring you to re-read some of John Steinbeck's classic works (or read them for the first time), stop into **BookBuyers** (600 Lighthouse Ave., 831/375-4208, 11am-5pm Sun.-Thurs., 11am-8pm Fri.-Sat.), a used bookshop that almost always has some Steinbeck titles as well as other books about the Monterey Bay area.

Lilify (281 Lighthouse Ave., 831/207-1380, www.lilify.com, 10am-5pm Mon.-Sat., noon-5pm Sun.) sells hipster-approved gifts, housewares, and jewelry.

DOWNTOWN MONTEREY

Downtown Monterey is dominated by restaurants and bars, but there are a few local shops worth seeking out as well. The **Old Monterey Business Association** (831/655-8070, www.oldmonterey.org) has a directory of downtown businesses on their website.

Lunablu (176 Bonifacio Pl., 831/641-0616, 11am-5pm Sun.-Mon., 11am-8pm Tues., 11am-7pm Wed.-Sat.) is a thrift store that deals in gently used designer clothes and unique housewares.

Located in Monterey State Historic Park's Custom House, the aptly named **Custom House Store** (1 Custom House Plaza, 831/649-7111, www.mshpa.org, 10am-4pm daily) carries unique items, from old-fashioned toys to Mexican hot-chocolate mixes to a great selection of books on local history. One booklet worth picking up is "The Old Pacific Capital," an essay penned by Robert Louis Stevenson about what Monterey was like in 1879.

Siren Records (527 Ramona Ave., 831/920-2801, www.sirendisc.com, 10am-4pm Mon.-Thurs., 10am-6pm Fri., noon-4pm Sat.-Sun.) has a great selection of new vinyl, including rare releases and imports. For used records, head over to New Monterey's **Recycled Records** (604 Lighthouse Ave., 831/375-5454, www.recycledrecordsmonterey.com, 10am-5pm daily), where the "New Arrivals" section is always worth thumbing through.

A hub for ideas in downtown Monterey, **Old Capitol Books** (482 Alvarado St., Level M, http://oldcapitolbooks.com, noon-6pm Thurs.-Sun.) sells new, antiquarian, and many used books from a small space on the second floor of an Alvarado Street business complex. Its books tend to focus on LGBTQ, feminism, black history, and ethnic studies issues. Old Capitol also hosts a wide range of events including readings, live music, open mics, discussion groups, and more.

DEL MONTE SHOPPING CENTER

Del Monte Shopping Center (1410 Del Monte Center, 831/373-2705, www.delmontecenter.com, shop hours vary) is an open-air shopping mall just off the Munras exit of Highway 1. The mall is home to usual suspects like the Apple Store, Vans, and The Gap, but there are also some local gems as well, including Green's Camera World and worthwhile dining options like Pizza My Heart and Lalla Grill. It's also the place to go to see the latest blockbusters at **Century Theatres** (1700 Del Monte Ave., 831/373-8051, www.cinemark.com).

Food

The organic and sustainable food movements have caught hold on the Central Coast. The Monterey Bay Seafood Watch program (www.seafoodwatch.org) is the definitive resource for sustainable seafood, while the Salinas Valley inland hosts a number of organic farms.

DOWNTOWN
Seafood

One seafood dish that is on almost all of the menus around Monterey is fried calamari. But ★ **The Sandbar & Grill** (Municipal Wharf II, 831/373-2818, http://sandbarandgrillmonterey.com, 11am-9pm Mon.-Sat., 10:30am-9pm Sun., $12-30) has the best fried squid appetizer around: a plate of tender, flat pieces of calamari golden fried in a seasoned batter. It's also known for its fresh sand dabs and Dungeness crab sandwich with bacon. The restaurant hangs off the Municipal Wharf over Monterey Harbor, which means you might be able to catch a sea otter stroking by as you dine.

On weekends, there is typically a line out the door at ★ **Monterey's Fish House** (2114 Del Monte Ave., 831/373-4647, http://

montereyfishhouse.com, 11:30am-2:30pm and 5pm-9:30pm Mon.-Fri., 5pm-9:30pm Sat.-Sun., $11-30), one of the peninsula's most popular seafood restaurants. Once you get inside, you can expect attentive service and fresh seafood including snapper, albacore tuna, and calamari fished right out of the nearby bay. Nods to Monterey's Italian anglers include Sicilian calamari and seafood pastas.

Out on Fisherman's Wharf, **Abalonetti** (57 Fisherman's Wharf, 831/373-1851, www.abalonettimonterey.com, 11:30am-9pm daily, $13-43) serves up fresh Monterey Bay calamari in the standard fried variety and the surprisingly good buffalo style, with tentacles and rings drenched in the tangy sauce usually reserved for chicken wings. More substantial and pricier options include cioppino and grilled Monterey abalone. Dine with a fine view of Monterey Harbor.

Sushi

Ocean Sushi Deli (165 Webster St., 831/645-9888, www.oceansushi.com, 11am-8pm Sun.-Wed., 11am-9pm Thurs.-Sat., $7-16) has a dizzying menu of 194 items. Chilly? Try the udon, ramen, or miso soup. In the mood for seafood? Opt for some very fair-priced sushi or sashimi. Really hungry? The teriyaki donburi bowls are a hearty mix of your choice of meat cooked in teriyaki sauce and vegetables over a bed of rice. Less expensive than other area sushi restaurants, Ocean Sushi Deli is set up like a café where you place your order at the counter.

New American

Considered one of the best restaurants in Monterey, ★ **Montrio** (414 Calle Principal, 831/648-8880, www.montrio.com, 4:30pm-8:30pm Wed.-Sun., $21-42) is an elegantly casual eatery located inside an old brick firehouse. The ever-changing menu includes meat and seafood entrées, but Montrio is also an ideal place for a lighter dinner, with its nice small bites and appetizer offerings.

★ **Woody's at the Airport** (Monterey Regional Airport, 200 Fred Kane Rd., 831/373-1232, www.woodysattheairport.com, 11am-7pm Mon.-Fri., 10am-7pm Sat.-Sun., $15-34) takes airport dining to new heights; even if you aren't catching a flight out of town, this is a fine place for a meal, with the added entertainment of planes soaring out over the bay. Chef Tim Wood, formerly of Carmel Valley Ranch and Bernardus Lodge, crafts elevated comfort food. The menu includes salads and sandwiches—including a superb patty melt—and entrées like sautéed sand dabs and a fried calamari steak. Look out for daily specials like the Saturday prime rib French dip sandwich.

Four miles (6.4 km) out of downtown Monterey on the way to Salinas is long-running restaurant **Tarpy's Roadhouse** (2999 Monterey-Salinas Hwy., 831/647-1444, www.tarpys.com, 11:30am-10pm daily, $14-40). A complex of patios, gardens, and a unique stone building, Tarpy's does creative comfort food. The superb appetizers and cocktails are ideal for a social outing, while the heartier entrées include steak, brisket, ribs, meatloaf, and chili-crusted chicken.

Classic American

Rosine's Restaurant (434 Alvarado St., 831/375-1400, www.rosinesmonterey.com, 11am-8pm Mon.-Fri., 9am-8pm Sat.-Sun., $12-26) is a longtime family-run restaurant that is very popular with families. This Alvarado Street institution serves hearty breakfasts, lunches, and dinners. It's known for its homemade lasagna, meatloaf, and slabs of cake that tower over a foot high. Rosine's became even more popular when it was featured in an episode of the Food Network's *Diners, Drive-Ins and Dives.*

A cozy locals' spot in a brick building off Alvarado Street, **Melville Tavern** (484 Washington St., 831/643-9525, www.melvilletav.com, 11:30am-8pm Mon.-Wed., 11:30am-9pm Thurs., 11:30am-10pm Fri., 10am-10pm Sat., 10am-8pm Sun., $11-30) nods to its namesake author with some books on shelves and a quote on the wall that reads "If you can get nothing better out of the world, get a good dinner out of it at least." The straightforward, well-executed menu of sandwiches, salads, wood-fired pizzas, and pastas will hit the spot. The restaurant also has a nicely curated mix of 10 beers on tap and wine by the glass or bottle.

Mexican

If you are the kind of person who orders nachos for dinner, then **Nacho Bizness** (470 Alvarado St., www.nachobiz.biz, 11am-10pm Tues.-Sat., 11am-7pm Sun., $10-18) is your place. The homemade cheese sauce and toppings are slathered on top of chips from nearby San Luis Obispo. Go big with "The Phife"—all the meats, all the cheeses, all the toppings—or try one of the specials, which might be pulled pork, butter chicken, or mac-and-cheese nachos.

French

Popular **Crepes of Brittany** (211 Alvarado St., 831/649-1930, www.crepesofbrittany.com, 7am-4pm daily, $4-10) brings northwest France to the Monterey Bay with tasty organic buckwheat flour crêpes. These flat, wide packets of goodness hold sweet or savory options, like brie and caramelized onion. The

"Complete," with ham, eggs, and cheese, is a winner for breakfast or lunch. The eatery also has salads and sandwiches for the less crêpe inclined.

Greek

The best place for Greek food in the area is ★ **Epsilon** (422 Tyler St., 831/655-8108, www.epsilonrestaurant.com, 11am-2pm and 4pm-7:30pm Tues.-Fri., 4pm-7:30pm Sat., $19-28). Attentive black-vested waiters deliver upscale dishes to tables draped in white tablecloths. Walls showcase a mishmash of Greek art, while the menu highlight a range of Greek staples including gyros, spanakopita, and shish kebabs. There's a nod to seafood as well, with a whole grilled boneless trout and flash-grilled octopus. The salads, which can be topped with grilled meats, are the best around.

Pizza

Located in the Del Monte Shopping Center, **Pizza My Heart** (660 Del Monte Center, 831/656-9400, http://pizzamyheart.com, 11am-10pm Sun.-Thurs., 11am-11pm Fri.-Sat., $3.50-4.25) is a great place to grab a slice of pizza. Go for a traditional cheese or choose a specialty like the chicken-and-bacon pie made with a white sauce. Dine inside among surfing photos.

Michael Foley opened **Heirloom Pizza** (700 Cass St., #102, 831/717-4363, http://heirloompizzapie.com, 5pm-8pm Wed.-Mon., $14-27) after working for the Woodstock's Pizza chain and at San Francisco's Little Star Pizza. At Heirloom, he serves deep-dish pizza, including the delicious namesake pie with spinach, bacon, mushrooms, onions, garlic, ricotta, and gorgonzola.

Sandwiches

Ike's Love & Sandwiches (570 Munras Ave., Ste. 70, 831/643-0900, www.loveand sandwiches.com, 10am-7pm daily, $9-13) is

part of a Bay Area chain of sandwich shops that has made its way down into Monterey Bay. People are quite excited by the giant, creatively made sandwiches that include the "Jaymee Sirewich," a delectable fried chicken creation, and the "Joe Montana," which combines halal chicken, bacon, avocado, and jack cheese under a dripping of sesame dressing. There's also the "Robert Louis Stevenson," a Monterey exclusive with turkey, bacon, red pepper pesto, and havarti cheese.

Monterey locals swear by **Randy's Sandwich Shop** (1193-D 10th St., 831/375-9161, 6:30am-2pm Mon.-Fri., $4.50-6, cash only), a tiny spot that serves large breakfast and lunch sandwiches to go. The "Jaws 2" is an impressive pile of meats and cheeses. The shop also offer some specials, like a calamari sandwich on Fridays. Bring cash because they don't accept debit or credit cards.

Mundo's Café (170 Webster St., 831/920-1400, www.mundoscafemonterey.com, 10am-5pm daily, $6.50-9) impresses with giant sandwiches. The best of the bunch is the Argentinean beef brisket with a chimichurri sauce. They also have burgers, including a beef/chorizo hybrid. Their original location is at 2233 Fremont Street (831/656-9244, 10am-5pm daily).

Breakfast

Old Monterey Café (489 Alvarado St., 831/646-1021, http://oldmontereycafeca. com, 7am-2:30pm daily, $7-14) is a local favorite for hearty eggs Benedict, egg scrambles, and pancake dishes. The interior is cramped, and there is frequently a line out the door on weekends.

Red's Donuts (433 Alvarado St., 831/372-9761, www.redsdonutsinc.com, 6am-12:30pm Sun.-Mon., 6am-1pm Tues.-Sat., $1-6) has been serving up sugary breakfast treats since 1950. Enjoy your glazed, coconut, maple, or chocolate donut at the counter with other locals. There's also a Seaside location (1646 Fremont Blvd., 831/394-3444, 4am-3pm daily).

1: Woody's at the Airport 2: Nacho Bizness
3: Captain + Stoker 4: Alta Bakery & Cafe

Hotel Del Monte

Monterey's reputation as a travel destination began with one massive resort: the Hotel Del Monte. The sprawling 20,000-acre (8,093-ha) resort was built by railway tycoon Charles Crocker in 1880. In 1919, developer Samuel F. B. Morse—a distant relative of the inventor of the same name—and his company Del Monte Properties acquired the hotel and began to highlight the resort's recreation facilities, including an auto racetrack, polo fields, a horse-racing track, and a Roman plunge pool. Pebble Beach's popular 17-Mile Drive was developed as an attraction for the Hotel Del Monte's guests (though its route has since changed). During its heyday, the resort hosted an impressive range of notable guests, including President Theodore Roosevelt, actor Charlie Chaplin, actress Marlene Dietrich, surreal artist Salvador Dalí, aviation pioneer Amelia Earhart, and author Ernest Hemingway.

The U.S. Navy bought the resort in 1947, and it is now home to the Naval Postgraduate School. Visitors can experience the beauty of this fabled resort during **Champagne Sunday Brunches** (11am, last Sun. of the month and some holidays, 831/656-7512, http://monterey. navylifesw.com, adults $35, children 5-10 $13). To gain access, submit your name as it appears on a government-issued ID, date of birth, and a cell phone number at least two weeks before the event.

Bakeries and Coffee Shops

Named after the two riding positions on a tandem bike, ★ **Captain + Stoker** (398 E. Franklin, www.captainandstoker.com, 6:30am-4pm Mon.-Fri., 7:30am-4pm Sat.-Sun.) roasts and brews coffee in a converted garage across from the Monterey Sports Center. The coffee is good, the atmosphere is hip, and bike enthusiasts will enjoy staring at the vintage cycles hanging from the ceiling. Look for the rotating coffee specials, like a transcendent peach affogato.

The **East Village Café** (498 Washington St., 831/747-1387, 7am-3:30pm daily) occupies a cool stone building with a tower. It serves café fare like coffees, expressos, and teas, but there's also a focus on chais, which are made daily from a traditional recipe. A Nepalese tuk-tuk decorates the interior of the building and nods to owner Ryan Lama's heritage.

Many Monterey businesses are housed in historic adobes. Among them is **Parker-Lusseau Pastries & Café** (539 Hartnell St., www.parkerlusseau.com, 831/641-9188, 7:30am-4pm Mon.-Fri., 7:30am-3pm Sat.), which occupies a charming adobe that was built in 1847. Inside, the café feels like Paris, where colorful macarons, tarts, baked goods, and quiches are displayed. There are also breakfast croissants and small but tasty

lunch sandwiches available. Part of the historic Cooper-Molera Adobe complex, **Alta Bakery & Cafe** (502 Munras Ave., 831/920-1018, www.altamonterey.com, 7am-4pm daily, $7-17) showcases Chef Ben Spungin's creative and playful pastry skills. On the counter, behind glass, are piles of cookies, croissants, scones, and a donut of the day. For lunch, Alta serves pizzas, soups, salads, and sandwiches. Keep an eye out for the rotating specials, including a popular fried chicken sandwich and Reuben croissant sandwich.

It's difficult to resist the baked temptations on display behind glass at the **Paris Bakery** (271 Bonifacio Pl., 831/646-1620, www.parisbakery.us, 6am-4pm daily). These include pastries, cakes, breads, and cookies. They also serve coffee, soup, salads, and sandwiches.

Desserts

Pricey but delicious, **Revival Ice Cream** (463 Alvarado St., 831/747-2113, www.revivalicecream.com, noon-10pm Mon.-Thurs., noon-11pm Fri.-Sat. May-Sept., noon-9pm Mon.-Thurs., noon-10pm Fri.-Sat. Oct.-Apr.) utilizes locally sourced, organic ingredients in its frozen dairy treats. There are some pretty creative scoops served here (apple horseradish! kelp milk jam and waffle?), but a popular offering is the Bee's Knees with burnt honey, beeswax, bee pollen, and honeycomb candy in an organic custard.

Markets

The primary farmers market in the county, the **Old Monterey Farmers Market** (Alvarado St. between Del Monte and Pearl, 831/655-2607, www.oldmonterey.org, 4pm-7pm Tues. Oct.-Apr., 4pm-8pm Tues. May-Sept.) fills more than 3.5 blocks of downtown Monterey with fresh produce vendors, restaurant stalls, jewelry booths, and live music every Tuesday afternoon. If you miss the Tuesday farmers market downtown, the local community college hosts the **Monterey Farmers Market at Del Monte Shopping Center** (1410 Del Monte Center, in front of Chipotle and Starbucks, www.montereybayfarmers.org, 9am-2pm Fri.) on Fridays.

A locally owned alternative to Whole Foods, **Elroy's Fine Foods** (15 Soledad Dr., 831/373-3737, www.elroysfinefoods.com, 8am-8pm Mon.-Sat., 9am-7pm Sun.) is a community market with curated groceries and produce from local farmers. The extensive prepared foods counter is a great place to stock up for a picnic.

CANNERY ROW
Seafood

For a South Pacific spin on seafood, head to ★ **Hula's Island Grill & Tiki Room** (622 Lighthouse Ave., 831/655-4852, www. hulastiki.com, 4pm-9:30pm Mon., 11:30am-9:30pm Tues.-Thurs., 11:30am-10pm Fri.-Sat., 4pm-9pm Sun., $12-23). With surfing movies playing on the TVs and tasty tiki drinks, Hula's is Monterey's most fun and casual restaurant. It serves tasty and sometimes imaginative food, including fresh fish dishes, a range of tacos, and land-based fare like Jamaican jerk chicken. If you're on a budget, Hula's has seriously long happy hours (4pm-6pm Sun.-Mon., all day Tues., 2pm-6pm Wed.-Sat.), when you can score tiki drinks and pupus (appetizers) for just six bucks a pop.

Opened in 1968 before Monterey's tourism boom, ★ **The Sardine Factory** (701 Wave St., 831/373-3775, 5pm-10:30pm Sun.-Thurs., 5pm-11pm Fri.-Sat., $26-63) is the area's iconic seafood and steakhouse. Its abalone bisque was served at one of President Ronald Reagan's inaugural dinners, and part of Clint Eastwood's 1971 directorial debut *Play Misty for Me* was filmed in the restaurant. This place oozes old-school cool, from the piano player tickling the ivories by the bar to the formal Captain's Room. The menu has pasta, steak, and seafood including wild abalone medallions, an item not found in many area restaurants. The friendly staff will happily show off the restaurant's impressive rooms, including its stunning glass-domed conservancy and the fascinating wine cellar.

Dine on seafood while staring at the sea within **Schooners Coastal Kitchen & Bar** (400 Cannery Row, 831/372-2628, www. schoonersmonterey.com, 8am-8pm Sun.-Tues., 8am-9pm Fri.-Sat., $25-52). Suspended off the Monterey Plaza Hotel & Spa over the bay, dishes at Schooners include cioppino and Morro Bay sablefish. On a sunny day, the deck is a great place for a sip and a snack.

For an informal seafood meal in the Cannery Row area, walk up a couple of blocks to the **Sea Harvest Fish Market & Restaurant** (598 Foam St., 831/646-0547, http://seaharvestmonterey.com, 8am-8pm Sun.-Thurs., 8am-9pm Fri.-Sat., $10-21). Purchase raw seafood to cook at home or let them cook up some for you. The grilled salmon sandwich with fries or coleslaw is $17, and worth it.

Sushi

Fresh seafood and creative rolls make ★ **Crystal Fish** (514 Lighthouse Ave., 831/649-3474, http://crystalfishmonterey. com, 11:30am-2pm and 5pm-9:30pm Mon.-Thurs., 11:30am-2pm and 5pm-10pm Fri.-Sat., 1pm-10pm Sat., 1pm-10:30pm Sun., entrées $14-27, rolls $4-13) the Monterey go-to for sushi. There's not a lot of ambience, but there are a lot of rolls, including fresh salmon, tuna, eel, octopus, and calamari, accentuated by sauces like creamy avocado, mango, wasabi, and miso. Unusual ingredients include lemon slices, asparagus, and eggplant.

American

★ **Lalla Oceanside Grill** (654 Cannery Row, 831/324-0891, www.lallaoceansidegrill. com, 11am-10pm Sun.-Wed., 11am-11pm Thurs.-Sat., $10-34) is the sort of drink-and-dinner spot that satisfies a wide range of diners, with something for everyone—from stellar salads to tasty tacos to large steak and seafood entrées. The movie-screen-sized windows over the bay add to the experience.

French

After putting Carmel's Casanova Restaurant on the map as their chef, Didier Dutertre opened his own restaurant a block up from Cannery Row: **Bistro Moulin** (867 Wave St., 831/333-1200, www.bistromoulin.com, 5pm-10pm daily, $19-42). The menu is classic European through and through with items including escargot, moules frites (steamed mussels and fries), and osso buco. If it's a weekend, you will want to make a reservation; Bistro Moulin is a small restaurant with limited seating.

Mediterranean

The owner of the small **Paprika Café** (309 Lighthouse Ave., 831/375-7452, www. paprikacafe-monterey.com, 11am-7pm Mon.-Sat., noon-6pm Sun., $7-13) will take your order, cook your food, ring you up, and then do the dishes. This one-man operation whips up tasty falafels, kebabs, hummus, and gyros. The recommended item is the unique and flavorful garlic chicken pita wrap; just make sure you have some breath mints after the meal.

Steakhouse

Monterey is definitely a seafood town, but there is a place to get a tasty cut of beef in Cannery Row. Located next to The Sardine Factory, the ★ **Whaling Station** (763 Wave St., 831/373-3778, http://thewhalingstation. com, 4:30pm-9pm Sun.-Thurs., 4:30pm-10pm Fri.-Sat., $26-99), a Monterey institution since 1970, is that place. Before you order, you can beef up on your beef knowledge as the waiters show off different cuts of meat on a tray and answer questions about the best qualities of each piece. Start off with the decadent prime rib egg rolls if you are hungry or a Caesar salad tossed at your table for something lighter. This is an unabashedly decadent establishment where the steamed broccoli

sandwich at Coniglio Brothers Italian Deli

comes with hollandaise sauce and the spinach sides come studded with chunks of bacon. Not in the mood for a full meal amid the white tablecloths in the dining room? Cozy up to the bar, where you can order a steak sandwich or a burger made with ground filet mignon from the moderately priced bar menu.

Vegetarian

An inspired concept done well, El Cantaro (791 Foam St., 831/646-5465, www.elcantaro. us, 10am-9pm Sun.-Thurs., 10am-3:30pm Fri., $4-12) serves vegan Mexican food. Vegetables and vegan imitation meat (including a vegan tuna fish) fill out tortas, burritos, mole dishes, and chilaquiles. It's good stuff, but a tad bit pricier than other local taquerias.

Pizza

Gianni's Pizza (725 Lighthouse Ave., 831/649-1500, www.giannispizzamonterey. com, 11am-11pm Fri.-Sat., 11am-10pm Sun., $6-25) is a classic, old-school pizza joint with giant pies delivered to tables draped in red-and-white-checkered tablecloths. Begin with breadsticks and a side of ranch or marinara sauce for dipping. Then move on to pizza pies the size of small tires. Their Big Wheel (a few pepperoni slices, a few Hawaiian slices, a few veggie slices, and a few slices of cheese) is the call for a table that can't agree on toppings. They serve sodas with free refills and pitchers of beer to wash it all down.

Deli

An inspired alternative to Cannery Row's overpriced restaurants is the casual Coniglio Brothers Italian Deli (750 Cannery Row, Ste. 108, 831/901-3175, http://conigliodeli. com, 10am-5pm daily, $9-13). The house sandwiches rely heavily on classic Italian meats and cheeses, with the popular Uncle Philly being a tasty, tangy combo of dry coppa, provolone, lettuce, pepperoncini, and a zippy house spread on a seeded roll. Other options include charcuterie plates and a daily special that actually changes weekly.

Breakfast

First Awakenings (300 David Ave., http:// firstawakenings.net, 7am-2pm daily, $6-12) serves up oversized versions of classic breakfast fare, including huevos rancheros, eggs Benedict, crepes, and omelets. Locals are fond of this spot, frequently voting it the county's top breakfast spot.

Accommodations

DOWNTOWN
Under $150

Located near the Monterey Fairgrounds, the ★ Lone Oak Lodge (2221 N. Fremont St., 831/372-4924, www.loneoaklodge.com, $119-229) has unexpected amenities for what seems like a typical motel complex. Every room, from the standard queen to the king room with fireplace and giant soaking tub, has cable TVs, free Internet, a mini-fridge, microwave, and fresh flowers (a nice touch!). The on-site cottages with two bedrooms and a fully equipped kitchen can accommodate six people. The grounds include an area to wash scuba diving equipment, an outdoor courtyard with barbecue grills, and a wood-walled spa room with a hot tub and sauna. The thoughtfulness of the staff leads many visitors to return.

The section of Munras Avenue between the Highway 1 exit and downtown Monterey has a string of hotels and motels including chains like Days Inn and Best Western. One of the most popular inexpensive options on this stretch is the Inn By the Bay Monterey (936 Munras Ave., 831/372-5409, http://innbythebaymonterey.com, $99-399). The rooms come with basic amenities including Wi-Fi and flat-screen TVs with cable.

$150-250

The **Casa Munras Hotel & Spa** (700 Munras Ave., 831/375-2411, www.hotelcasamunras. com, $139-329) is named after a former residence that was built in the same spot back in 1824. A portion of the original adobe walls can still be viewed within the modern hotel's Marbella Meeting Room. The 170 rooms of the Casa Munras are designed to recall Monterey's old style. The comfortable but somewhat basic rooms provide a great base for exploring downtown Monterey's adobes, including some that are just a few hundred yards away. Amenities include a heated kidney-shaped pool, a fitness center, and a complimentary DVD library that provides guests an eclectic mix of films. The hotel grounds also include the terrific tapas restaurant **Esteban Restaurant** and a **spa.** All of the rooms are pet friendly except for the suites.

Hotel 1110 (1110 Del Monte Ave., 831/655-0515, www.hotel1110.com, $150-285) feels like the kind of boutique hotel you'd find in a big city. The common areas range from artful to borderline extravagant, and there's a rooftop deck to take in views of the small city, including a glimpse of Monterey's Municipal Wharf jutting out into the bay. Every room is different but most have electric fireplaces, bamboo flooring, and comfortable beds. Fourteen of the rooms also include jetted soaking tubs. Hotel 1110 also offers budget rooms on the first floor sans breakfast (which is included for other rooms). The hotel is located just 0.5 mile (0.8 km) from downtown's Alvarado Street and right across the street from Del Monte Beach. There are a few quirks here, but there are also some unexpected amenities for such a moderately priced hotel.

Built in 1904, the **Monterey Hotel** (406 Alvarado St., 831/375-3184 or 800/966-6490, www.montereyhotel.com, $209-264) was once called "the finest European hotel west of Chicago." With its red awnings shading Alvarado Street's sidewalk, it still has a striking presence downtown. All of its 45 rooms have Victorian furnishings and fireplaces for a comfy stay that recalls an earlier time.

The Merritt House is an adobe built in 1830 and where Monterey County's first judge resided. Now it is part of the **Merritt House Inn** (386 Pacific St., 831/646-9686, www. merritthouseinn.com, $140-250), which is conveniently located a block up from downtown Monterey and the harbor area. The old adobe is now split into three suites, each one with a fireplace and a parlor. The inn also has 22 rooms with fireplaces, fridges, and coffeemakers. Enjoy the expanded continental breakfast in the morning.

The greatest asset of **Monterey Tides** (2600 Sand Dunes Rd., reservations 800/242-8627, hotel 831/394-3321, http:// montereytides.com, $200-400) is its proximity to the sand and surf. The four-story building sits overlooking Monterey State Beach, with 102 of the 196 rooms facing out toward Monterey Bay. At night, take in the tapered triangle of lights of the Monterey peninsula from your room or on the wooden patios on the hotel lobby level. The on-site pool is heated year-round with a spa tucked into a corner. The lobby bar, **Bayside Bar & Lounge,** and the top-floor restaurant, **Tides Waterfront,** have stellar views to accompany meals and drinks. Rent a bike to explore the Monterey Bay Coastal Recreation Trail or skim over the bay on a rented stand-up paddleboard.

The **Monterey Marriott** (350 Calle Principal, 831/649-4234, www.marriott.com, $229-499) has one of the best locations of any downtown Monterey lodging option. It's also where the folks behind the TV show *Mad Men* stayed when filming the finale in the area. It's connected to the Monterey Conference Center by a sky bridge and has 319 rooms and 22 suites. In addition to its location, other pluses include an outdoor heated pool, a fitness center, and the on-site **Fin & Field,** which serves grilled-cheese sandwiches and grilled New York steaks.

1: Casa Munras Hotel & Spa 2: the rooftop deck of Hotel 1110

Over $250

Connected to the Monterey Conference Center, the ★ **Portola Hotel & Spa** (2 Portola Plaza, 831/649-4511, www.portolahotel.com, $229-379) occupies prime real estate between the west end of Alvarado Street and Monterey State Historic Park's Custom House Plaza. The large hotel complex has 379 comfortable rooms decorated in a red and blue motif; many have full or Juliet balconies or patios with views of the harbor or downtown Monterey. Guests can relax in the lobby, where live ficus trees (watered by a natural stream under the hotel!) reach up toward the glass skylights, dine at the on-site **Jack's** restaurant, or grab a pint at **Peter B's** brewery. Though there are many sights to explore nearby, the hotel's spa, larger-than-average fitness center, pool, and hot tub can make one reluctant to leave.

A boutique hotel just a few blocks from downtown, the **Hotel Abrego** (755 Abrego St., 831/372-7551, www.hotelabrego.com, $269-400) has 93 rooms; most have a balcony or patio and a fireplace. Amenities include complimentary Wi-Fi, free parking, an exercise studio, an outdoor heated pool, and a hot tub.

CANNERY ROW
$150-250

Tucked into a residential street within New Monterey, the ★ **Jabberwock Inn** (598 Laine St., 831/372-4777, www.jabberwockinn.com, $209-599) is named after a nonsense poem written by Lewis Carroll that is contained in his 1871 novel *Through the Looking Glass*. Despite its name, the amenities and pluses of this comfortable former convent turned eight-room bed-and-breakfast are no-nonsense. The common area includes a covered wraparound sun porch with views of the Monterey Bay and two fireplaces to warm up by during the winter months. The morning breakfasts are tasty and filling, while the innkeepers are warm and knowledgeable. There are also nice little perks including free

parking and late-afternoon wine and appetizers along with evening milk and cookies. In addition, the B&B is just a short walk to Cannery Row, the aquarium, and the businesses on Lighthouse Avenue. The lowest-priced room has a private detached bathroom down the hall, while the Borogrove Room has a long list of worthwhile features that includes a large hot tub, gas fireplace, and sitting area with a coastal view. There are no TVs or telephones here, but there are books, including a few by Steinbeck, and, of course, a number by Carroll.

The ★ **Monterey Bay Inn** (242 Cannery Row, 831/373-6242 or 800/424-6242, www.montereybayinn.com, $199-675) has a generic name, but the setting is anything but. Located between San Carlos Beach and the start of Cannery Row, the boutique hotel's oceanfront rooms have private balconies that allow guests to peer right down into the clear waters of Monterey Bay. In-room binoculars are handy for spotting diving cormorants, bobbing harbor seals, and playful otters. The rooftop hot tub offers another vantage point to take in the marine action offshore. Enjoy a continental breakfast delivered to your room in the morning and some tasty cookies in the evening.

Hear the barks of seals and the squawks of seagulls at the ★ **Spindrift Inn** (652 Cannery Row, 831/646-8900, www.spindriftinn.com, $170-750), a boutique hotel towering above the golden sand and clear green waters of scenic McAbee Beach. This 45-room establishment has been called the country's most romantic hotel, and with good reason. Most of the hardwood-floored rooms have gas fireplaces that burn real wood, and full or half canopy beds. Stare out of your window after dark as the lights of Monterey and its surrounding cities ring the bay. The very friendly staff serves up a wine-and-cheese reception (4:30pm-6pm daily) and delivers a complimentary continental breakfast to your room in the morning.

1: Jabberwock Inn 2: Monterey Bay Inn 3: Spindrift Inn

The only problem with staying at the Spindrift is that you'll never want to leave.

Wave Street Inn (571 Wave St., 831/375-2299, www.wavestreetinnmonterey.com, $180-499) has a great location just a block from Cannery Row. The rooms are modern and comfortable with Keurig coffeemakers and 50-inch (127-cm) TVs. The family suites can accommodate larger groups with two beds in one room and a pullout couch in the living room. A stay here saves you some money compared to a bayside establishment—especially when the friendly staff hands you a snack bag at check-in.

A locally operated hotel under an international chain umbrella, the **Best Western Plus Victorian Inn** (487 Foam St., 831/373-8000 or 800/232-4141, www.victorianinn.com, $192-580) is just two blocks up from Cannery Row. Rooms have marble fireplaces, and guests are treated to a deluxe continental breakfast in the morning. The inn has two family suites that sleep up to six guests.

Over $250

Luxury hotel **InterContinental The Clement Monterey** (750 Cannery Row, 831/375-4500, www.ictheclementmonterey.com, $250-1,100) has a can't-be-beat location just a splash away from the bay and feet from the Monterey Aquarium. The hotel has 208 rooms and 12 luxury suites that are decorated with tasteful Asian elements, including a bonsai tree, a book-sized Zen garden, and some live white orchids. Most of the marble-floored bathrooms have a separate soaking tub and walk-in shower. The oceanside rooms have views of the bay, while the units on the other side of Cannery Row all have fireplaces. There are a lot of amenities and features outside the comfortable rooms, including a fitness room, an outdoor whirlpool, **The Spa, The C Restaurant & Bar,** a sliver of an outdoor pool long enough to swim laps in, and an artsy jellyfish-inspired staircase connecting the first and second floors.

Want to stay right on Cannery Row in a room overlooking the bay? You'll pay handsomely at the **Monterey Plaza Hotel & Spa** (400 Cannery Row, 831/646-1700, www.montereyplazahotel.com, $289-1,000). This on-the-water luxury hotel has it all: restaurant, coffee shop, spa, private beach, room service, and upscale guest room goodies. Rooms range from "budget" garden and Cannery Row-facing accommodations to oceanview rooms with private balconies and huge suites that mimic posh private apartments.

CAMPING

A mile up a hill from downtown Monterey, the 50-acre (20.2-ha) **Veterans Memorial Park** (Via Del Rey and Veterans Dr., 831/646-3865, www.monterey.org, $40/single vehicle, $50/two vehicles) has 40 first-come, first-served campsites with views of the Monterey Bay below.

There's also a campground at Laguna Seca, known as the **Laguna Seca Recreation Area** (831/242-8201, www.co.monterey.ca.us, RV sites $40, tent sites $35) and run by the Monterey County Parks Department. The year-round RV campsites have water and electricity, while the 70 tent-camping sites are only available from April to October.

Transportation and Services

CAR

Most visitors drive into Monterey via scenic Highway 1. Inland, US-101 allows access into Salinas from the north and south. From Salinas, Highway 68 travels west into Monterey.

AIR

Monterey has its own airport: the **Monterey Regional Airport** (MRY, 200 Fred Kane Dr., 831/648-7000, www.montereyairport. com). The airport connects the city to San Francisco, San Diego, Los Angeles, Phoenix, Las Vegas, Denver, Dallas, and Seattle with 40 flights a day. Downtown Monterey and Cannery Row are just a 5-mile (8-km) taxi ride away.

A lot of visitors to Monterey fly into Bay Area airports. The **San Francisco International Airport** (SFO, US-101, San Francisco, 800/435-9736 or 650/821-8211, www.flysfo.com) can be just two hours away if traffic cooperates. **Mineta San José Airport** (SJC, 1701 Airport Blvd., San Jose, 408/392-3600, www.flysanjose.com) is an hour and 15 minutes to an hour and a half away from Monterey. The **Monterey Airbus** (831/373-7777, www.montereyairbus.com, one way $35-50 pp) provides bus transportation from San Francisco and San Jose airports to downtown Monterey and the nearby city of Marina.

TRAIN

For a leisurely ride, **Amtrak's Coast Starlight train** (11 Station Place, Salinas, www.amtrak.com, station waiting room 11am-7:30pm Mon.-Fri.) travels through Salinas. **Greyhound** (3 Station Pl., Salinas, 800/231-2222, www.greyhound.com, 24 hours daily) offers service into Monterey from Salinas.

PUBLIC TRANSIT AND RIDE SHARES

Once in Monterey, take advantage of the free **WAVE** bus (Waterfront Area Visitor Express, 831/899-2555, www.monterey.org, 10am-7pm daily late May-late June, 10am-7pm Sun.-Fri., 10am-8pm Sat. July-early Sept., 10am-7pm Sat.-Sun. weekend after Labor Day-Memorial Day weekend), an old-fashioned trolley that runs on electricity and loops between downtown Monterey and the aquarium. **Monterey-Salinas Transit** (888/678-2871, www.mst.org, $1.50-3.50) has routes through Monterey.

Monterey and the Monterey Peninsula have drivers for users of the ride-sharing apps **Uber** (www.uber.com) and **Lyft** (www.lyft.com).

SERVICES

A recommended first stop in Monterey is the **Monterey Visitors Center** (401 Camino El Estero, 888/221-1010, www.seemonterey.com, 10am-5pm daily). They have an array of pamphlets and a staffed information desk.

The local daily newspaper is the *Monterey County Herald* (www.montereyherald.com). The *Monterey County Weekly* (www.montereycountyweekly.com) is a popular free weekly with a comprehensive listing of the area's arts and entertainment events.

The Monterey **post office** (565 Hartnell St., 800/275-8777, www.usps.com, 8:30am-5pm Mon.-Fri., 10am-2pm Sat.) is conveniently located a couple blocks east of downtown Monterey.

For medical needs, the **Community Hospital of the Monterey Peninsula** (CHOMP, 23625 Holman Hwy., 831/624-5311 or 888/452-4667, www.chomp.org) provides emergency services to the area.

Pacific Grove

Sandwiched between historic Monterey and exclusive Pebble Beach, and close to major attractions like the Monterey Bay Aquarium, Pacific Grove makes a fine base for exploring the peninsula. It's also worth a visit for its colorful turn-of-the-20th-century Victorian homes and its striking strand of coastline. The town has chosen "America's Last Hometown" as its nickname; it may make you nostalgic for small-town living. Founded in 1875 as a Methodist summer retreat, this quiet city is not the place to go for a night of carousing. But Pacific Grove's downtown is perfect for a relaxing afternoon of strolling among the yellow, purple, and green Victorian homes and cottages on **Lighthouse Avenue.** (It's worth noting that there's a different Lighthouse Avenue in adjacent Monterey.)

For those who don't want to pay the entrance fee to drive Pebble Beach's 17-Mile Drive, Pacific Grove's "Poor Man's 17-Mile Drive" winds around a piece of coastal real estate between Lovers Point Park and Asilomar Beach that's almost as striking. Start on Ocean View Boulevard by Lovers Point and continue onto Sunset Drive to get the full experience. In the springtime, flowering ice plant right along the road adds a riot of color to the landscape.

SIGHTS
★ Lovers Point Park

It is no surprise that the aptly named **Lovers Point Park** (Ocean View Blvd. and 17th St., 831/648-3100, www.cityofpacificgrove.org) is one of the area's most popular wedding sites. A finger of land with a jumble of rocks at its northernmost point, Lovers Point offers expansive views of the interior section of Monterey Bay.

The scenic spit of land is home to a large lawn, a shallow children's pool, a picnic area, restrooms, a beach volleyball court, and the Beach House Restaurant, which is perched on an envious spot with a fine bay view. The

park also has a sheltered pocket beach that is ideal for a dip or wading on Pacific Grove's infrequent hot days. A kelp forest right offshore offers a superb spot for snorkelers to get a feel for Monterey Bay's impressive underwater ecosystem.

During summer months, there is an old-fashioned hamburger stand above the beach and a vendor that rents kayaks, bikes, and snorkeling equipment.

Point Pinos Lighthouse

Surrounded by a golf course, **Point Pinos Lighthouse** (80 Asilomar Ave. between Lighthouse Ave. and Del Monte Ave., 831/648-3176, www.pointpinoslighthouse.org, 1pm-4pm Thurs.-Mon., adults $4, children $2) has the distinction of being the oldest continuously operating lighthouse on the West Coast. It was one of the first eight lighthouses built on the West Coast, starting operations in 1855. Point Pinos is also notable for the two female lighthouse keepers who served there during its long history. The light was automated in 1975, but it is still an active aid to local marine navigation. Lighthouse lovers and appreciators of the past will enjoy walking through the building's two floors and cellar, where they can take in an eight-minute introductory film, peruse displays on the lighthouse keepers, and climb a spiral staircase to a point right under the light.

Monarch Butterfly Sanctuary

Pacific Grove is also known as "Butterfly Town U.S.A." The small **Monarch Butterfly Sanctuary** (250 Ridge Rd. between Lighthouse Ave. and Short St., 831/648-5716 ext. 20, www.cityofpacificgrove.org, free) has stands of eucalyptus and pine trees that attract the colorful insects during the migration period (Nov.-Feb.). An impressive migration of monarch butterflies used to descend on the town each year, but, in recent years, the

Pacific Grove

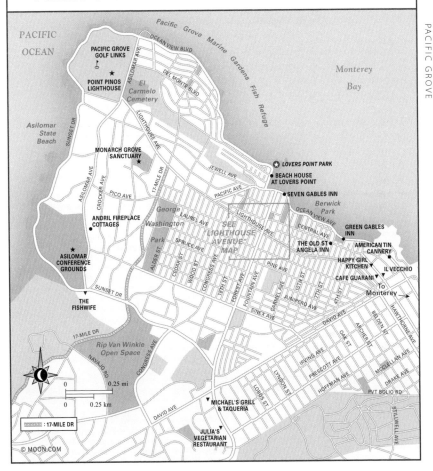

number of winged visitors has unfortunately plummeted.

The best time to visit the sanctuary is in the early afternoon, when sunlight illuminates the butterflies on the trees and docents are around to answer your questions. Just don't get too close to any of our flying friends, because anyone who molests a butterfly will be slapped with a hefty $1,000 fine.

Asilomar State Beach

One of the Monterey Peninsula's most popular beaches, **Asilomar State Beach** (Sunset Dr., 831/646-6440, www.parks.ca.gov, 8am-8pm daily) draws beachgoers, walkers, and surfers. The beach itself is a narrow mile-long strip of coastline with a boardwalk trail on the dunes behind it. You can keep walking on the trail into nearby Pebble Beach, an easy, cost-free way to get a taste of that exclusive community.

Right across Sunset Drive, visitors can explore the **Asilomar Dunes Natural Preserve** and the **Asilomar Conference Grounds** (800 Asilomar Ave., 888/635-5310, www.visitasilomar.com). The dunes preserve is 25 acres (10.1 ha) of restored sand dune ecosystem that can be accessed via an 0.25-mile-long (0.4-km) boardwalk. The conference grounds are shaded by Monterey pines and studded with Arts and Crafts-style structures designed by Hearst Castle architect Julia Morgan. Even if you are not staying overnight on the grounds or participating in a conference, you can enjoy the facilities, including the Phoebe A. Hearst Social Hall, which has pool tables, a fireplace, and some comfy seats.

Guided state park tours (831/646-6443, www.parks.ca.gov, check Asilomar State Beach/State Park Tours) of the grounds are available and include information on architecture and the state park's natural resources, including the many bird species that pass through the area.

To reach Asilomar, take the Route 68 West exit off Highway 1 and turn left on Sunset Drive.

Pacific Grove Museum of Natural History

Nature enthusiasts visiting the area should stop into the **Pacific Grove Museum of Natural History** (165 Forest Ave., 831/648-5716, www.pgmuseum.org, 10am-5pm Tues.-Sun., adults $9, children, students, and military $6), which will help them identify the animal and plant species they encounter while on the Monterey Peninsula. The museum feels of a past era, with its mounted and stuffed animals, but it does provide a fairly comprehensive overview of the region's biodiversity. One room is dedicated to our feathered friends and includes 300 mounted birds found around the county, including the gigantic California condor. Other rooms highlight large terrestrial mammals (mountain lions, bears) and whales. With this being Butterfly Town U.S.A., there's a space devoted to the monarch butterfly. Out front is a life-sized gray whale statue, and out back is a native plant garden that includes an impressive jade boulder that was found on the Big Sur coast.

RECREATION
Scuba Diving and Snorkeling

Some of the best scuba diving and snorkeling spots on the Monterey Peninsula lie off Pacific Grove. **Lovers Point Park** (Ocean View Blvd. and 17th St., novice to advanced, 10-40 ft/3-12.2 m) has a protected cove and kelp forest right off its shores. The cove's protected sandy beach makes an easy entry point for scuba divers and snorkelers who want to explore the

the Monarch Butterfly Sanctuary

Lighthouse Avenue

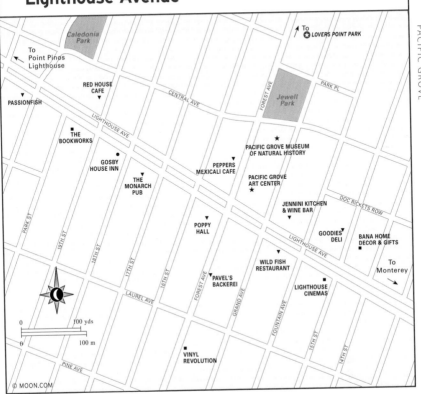

Caledonia Park

To
Point Pinos
Lighthouse

To
LOVERS POINT PARK

PASSIONFISH

RED HOUSE CAFE

CENTRAL AVE

PARK PL

FOREST AVE

Jewell Park

LIGHTHOUSE AVE

THE BOOKWORKS

GOSBY HOUSE INN

PACIFIC GROVE MUSEUM OF NATURAL HISTORY

THE MONARCH PUB

PEPPERS MEXICALI CAFE

PACIFIC GROVE ART CENTER

JENNINI KITCHEN & WINE BAR

DOC RICKETS ROW

PARK ST

18TH ST

18TH ST

17TH ST

POPPY HALL

LIGHTHOUSE AVE

GOODIES DELI

BANA HOME DECOR & GIFTS

To
Monterey

WILD FISH RESTAURANT

16TH ST

FOREST AVE

PAVEL'S BACKEREI

GRAND AVE

LIGHTHOUSE CINEMAS

LAUREL AVE

FOUNTAIN AVE

15TH ST

14TH ST

0   100 yds

0   100 m

VINYL REVOLUTION

PINE AVE

© MOON.COM

kelp forest. Just a few blocks away is **Otter Cove** (Ocean View Blvd. and Sea Palm Ave., novice to advanced, 10-60 ft/3-18.3 m) at the intersection of Ocean View Boulevard and Sea Palm Avenue. It's a dive spot that is best during days of calm seas. One of the highlights is an underwater pinnacle that rises from 50 feet (15.2 m) to just 18 feet (5.5 m) below the surface. A notable site is the nearby **Coral Street Cove** (Coral St. and Ocean View Blvd., advanced, 20-50 ft/6.1-15.2 m), which is known for its fish populations.

If you need equipment, visit **Bamboo Reef** (614 Lighthouse Ave., 831/372-1685, www.bambooreef.com, 9am-6pm Mon.-Fri., 7am-6pm Sat.-Sun. summer, lessons $175-470, gear rental $70/day, **Aquarius**

Dive Shop (2040 Del Monte Ave., 831/375-1933, http://aquariusdivers.com, 9am-6pm Mon.-Thurs., 9am-7pm Fri., 7am-7pm Sat., 7am-6pm Sun., lessons $125-294, gear rental $65-75/day) or **Cannery Row Aquatics** (225 Cannery Row, Ste. M, 831/717-4546, http://canneryrowaquatics.com, 9am-6pm Mon.-Tues. and Thurs.-Fri., 7am-6pm Sat.-Sun., lessons $200-600, gear rental $65/day) in nearby Monterey.

Surfing

During the summer and fall, clean swells produce fun waves at **Asilomar State Beach** (Sunset Dr., 831/646-6440, www.parks.ca.gov), making it one of the peninsula's most popular surf spots. Winter produces big, often dangerous swells, so stay out of the water during that time of the year. To get there, take the Route 68 West exit off Highway 1 and turn left on Sunset Drive.

During big swells, **Lovers Point** (Ocean View Blvd. and 17th St.) turns into a nice left. There are some rocks in the lineup so it is probably best to go out with someone who knows the break on your first outing.

On the Beach (693 Lighthouse Ave., 831/646-9283, http://onthebeachsurfshop. com, 10am-6pm Mon.-Thurs., 10am-7pm Fri.-Sat., surfboard rental $30-35/day, wetsuit rental $20/day) rents boards and wetsuits in nearby Monterey.

Hiking

A superb way to experience the rugged coastline of the Monterey Peninsula is to hike the **Asilomar Coast Trail** (2 mi/3.2 km roundtrip, easy). The trail extends from the north end of Asilomar State Beach and continues north toward Point Pinos. Flat but with fine views of the crashing surf, the trail offers access to sandy beaches, rocky headlands, and extensive tidepools on its way to the park's northern boundary, a gazebo perched atop the headlands.

Golf

Pacific Grove Golf Links (77 Asilomar Blvd., 831/648-5775, www.playpacificgrove. com, sunrise-sunset daily, Mon.-Thurs. $53, Fri.-Sun. and holidays $58) doesn't have the acclaim of the nearby Pebble Beach courses, but it's located on a similarly gorgeous length of coastline just a few miles away.

ENTERTAINMENT

Bars

Pacific Grove didn't have a proper bar until **The Monarch Pub** (617 Lighthouse Ave., 831/324-4987, 11am-11pm daily). Prohibition laws were kept in effect in the quiet city until 1968. This simple drinking establishment has six beers on tap and serves cocktails along with pub grub like fish-and-chips. The real coup here—besides getting a pub opened in

P.G.—is the heated outdoor patio overlooking Lighthouse Avenue.

Art Galleries

For more than four decades, the **Pacific Grove Art Center** (568 Lighthouse Ave., 831/375-2208, www.pgartcenter.org, noon-5pm Wed.-Sat., noon-4pm Sun.) has showcased the work of emerging artists in four galleries, including paintings, photos, sculptures, mixed media, and other artistic endeavors.

Cinema

Downtown Pacific Grove has its own small-town movie theater: the **Lighthouse Cinemas** (525 Lighthouse Ave., 831/643-1333, www.sregmovies.com), with four screens showing first-run movies.

Festivals and Events

If you want a wild night out on the town, you're not going to get it in Pacific Grove. But there are a couple of family-friendly annual events in "America's Last Hometown." Recalling another era, Pacific Grove's **Good Old Days** (831/373-3304, www.pacificgrove. org, Apr.) is a weekend of good clean fun every April that includes a parade, a quilt show, pony rides, and live entertainment.

For more than 70 years, the kids of Pacific Grove have been getting dressed up like butterflies at the **Butterfly Parade and Bazaar** (831/373-3304, www.pacificgrove.org, first Sat. of Oct.), which welcomes the wintering monarch butterflies to the area every fall.

Pacific Grove's many bed-and-breakfasts get done up in Victorian-era holiday decor during the annual **Christmas at the Inns** (831/373-3304, www.pacificgrove.org, early Dec.).

SHOPPING

A canning factory no more, the **American Tin Cannery** (125 Oceanview Blvd., 831/372-1442, www.americantincannery.com, 10am-6pm daily) is an indoor mall with discount outlets for national brands including

Pendleton and Van Heusen. There's a hope to turn the complex into a luxury hotel sometime in the next few years.

Every great town needs a bookstore. Pacific Grove has that covered with **Bookworks** (667 Lighthouse Ave., 831/372-2242, www.bookworkspg.com, 9:30am-5:30pm daily), which sells new books and gifts and has a coffee shop (7am-5:30pm daily) on-site.

Bana Home Décor & Gifts (510 Lighthouse Ave., 831/324-4912, www.banahome.com, 10am-5pm Mon.-Sat., 10am-2pm Sun.) sells unique furniture at sometimes surprisingly fair prices right in downtown Pacific Grove.

Inside the purple-and-black storefront of **Vinyl Revolution** (309 Forest Ave., 831/646-9020, www.vinyl-rev.com, 10am-6pm Mon.-Sat., noon-5pm Sun.), you'll find a selection of fine new and used vinyl curated by the store's bearded owner and resident record expert, Bob Gamber.

FOOD
Seafood
One of the Monterey Peninsula's most lauded seafood restaurants is ★ **Passionfish** (701 Lighthouse Ave., 831/655-3311, www.passionfish.net, 5pm-9pm Sun.-Thurs., 5pm-10pm Fri.-Sat., $16-36), which is on a mission to spread the gospel about sustainable seafood; the top of the menu is adorned with a quote by Robert Redford about the importance of defending our natural resources, and every bill comes with a copy of the Monterey Bay Aquarium's Seafood Watch Guide. Dishes are creative and flavorful, and there are meat options in addition to seafood. The restaurant is also known for an extensive, moderately priced wine list. In addition to the very fine food and wine, the knowledgeable wait staff here could teach a course on seafood, and the atmosphere is just right.

Wild Fish (545 Lighthouse Ave., 831/373-8523, www.wild-fish.com, 11:30am-3pm and 5pm-8:30pm Sun.-Thurs., 11:30am-3pm and 5pm-9:15pm Sat.-Sun., $22-39)

sources seafood from all over the California coast. Menu items include whole fish and a bouillabaisse.

The Fishwife (1996 ½ Sunset Dr., 831/375-7107, www.fishwife.com, 11:30am-9pm Mon.-Fri., 11:30am-10pm Sat.-Sun., $12-22) occupies a fine spot out of downtown Pacific Grove near Asilomar Beach. Many of the seafood entrées have a Caribbean twist.

American
★ **Poppy Hall** (589 Lighthouse Ave., 831/204-9990, http://poppyhallpg.com, call for hours, $15-20) serves well-prepared, artfully presented food, from a signature salad (baby greens, sunflower seeds, globs of goat cheese all covered in a perfect lemon poppy seed dressing) to rotating entrées like skirt steak or prosciutto-wrapped trout. Flowers decorate the copper tables, and the long bar was carved from a Big Sur redwood tree. The beer and wine list is short but extremely well curated.

The **Beach House** (620 Ocean View Blvd., 831/375-2345, www.beachhousepg.com, 4pm-9pm daily, $18-38) is located right in Pacific Grove's Lovers Point Park, with views of the bay. Sit inside or on a heated and covered outdoor deck with an even better look down on the water. One way to experience both the views and the California cuisine is to come for the Beach House's popular Sunset Supper Menu (4pm-5:30pm daily), when a selection of entrées is $12-16. Make a reservation for a table during the Sunset Supper times so that you don't miss out on this superb promotion.

Mexican
A healthy, California-style take on Mexican food is done at the popular ★ **Michael's Grill & Taqueria** (1126 Forest Ave., 831/647-8654, www.michaelstaqueria.com, 10am-9pm Mon.-Sat., 10am-8pm Sun., $11-30), and there are shades of Cajun cooking in the blackened chicken and blackened shrimp used in the burritos and tostadas. Whether you order a burrito or a fajita salad or platter, you will get a tasty, stomach-stuffing meal.

A certain ingredient shows up everywhere at the very popular **Peppers Mexicali Café** (170 Forest Ave., 831/373-6892, www.pepperspg.com, 11:30am-9pm Mon. and Wed.-Thurs., 11:30am-9:30pm Fri.-Sat., 4pm-9pm Sun., $10-20). Posters of peppers adorn the walls of the narrow dining room and adjacent bar, while plastic peppers hang from the doorway between the two usually crowded rooms. The pepper also makes many appearances on the menu, whether it's as a citrus habanero marinade on the chicken or the roasted red pepper that tops the grilled snapper. This is not straight-up Mexican food, as evidenced by items like the winning Jamaican curry prawns with mango salsa. They also serve up glasses and pitchers of margaritas.

Italian

Il Vecchio (110 Central Ave., 831/324-4282, www.ilvecchiorestaurant.com, 11:30am-1:30pm and 4:30pm-8pm daily, $13-22) is a Pacific Grove favorite. The name Il Vecchio means "the old" and refers to traditional Italian fare like gnocchi with pesto. They make their pasta daily and offer traditional Italian takes on meats and seafood.

Mediterranean

The **Jeninni Kitchen & Wine Bar** (542 Lighthouse Ave., 831/920-2662, 4pm-close Thurs.-Tues., $18-30) has elevated Pacific Grove's dining scene. The menu changes frequently, but the Wagyu bullfighter's steak and the eggplant fries are favorites and the shawarma-style pork belly bursts with flavor. Sit in the dining area in the front of the building or walk up a few stairs to the bar area for small plates, wine, and craft beers. This is a great place for a glass of wine and a snack.

Latin American

Bringing a welcome dose of South American flair to Pacific Grove, **Café Guarani** (111 Central Ave., 831/747-1551, www.cafeguarani.com, 7am-5pm Thurs.-Tues., $4-15) serves coffee, yerba mate, and Paraguayan snacks like empanadas and baked goods stuffed with dulce de leche.

Vegetarian

Julia's Vegetarian Restaurant (1180 Forest Ave., Ste. F, 831/656-9533, www.juliasveg.com, 9am-10pm daily, $17-25) serves tasty, hearty fare; even carnivores will enjoy this vegetarian experience. This intimate restaurant located in a Pacific Grove strip mall has a unique menu for the area that includes entrées like a sweet yellow coconut curry dish starring a small rainbow of deliciously roasted vegetables. The owner is a real mycophile and incorporates locally foraged mushrooms in many menu items; look for them to show up in surprising places, including in the White Russian cocktail and in the caramel sauce that comes with the French toast.

Breakfast

The ★ **Red House Café** (662 Lighthouse Ave., 831/643-1060, www.redhousecafe.com, 8am-2:30pm Mon., 8am-9pm Tues.-Sun., $11-23) is easy to find. It is in a red Victorian building with a wraparound porch right on Pacific Grove's main drag. The breakfasts are legendary and include items like a smoked salmon Benedict and cinnamon brioche French toast.

Bakeries

Pavel's Backerei (219 Forest Ave., 831/643-2636, 7am-5pm Tues.-Fri., 7am-3pm Sat.) is one of the best bakeries on the Monterey Peninsula. They offer pastries, croissants, cinnamon rolls, and giant glazed donuts that you can eat in the small indoor seating area or out front.

Quick Bites

Part canning operation and part café, **Happy Girl Kitchen** (173 Central Ave., 831/373-4475, http://happygirlkitchen.com, café hours 8am-4pm) has an urban hipster feel that might make Portlanders or Bay Area folks feel at home. The café has a very basic menu of items, including toast with homemade jam and a

PB&J with milk. They also sell sandwiches, soups, and bowls of the day. Inside the shop are canned goodies like Meyer lemon marmalade and honeyed mandarin oranges. Take one of their classes on canning, pickling, or fermenting so that you can preserve your own foodstuffs.

Stop into **Goodies Deli** (518 Lighthouse Ave., 831/655-3663, www.goodiesdeli.com, 9:30am-4pm Mon.-Sat., $7-8) for a hearty sandwich. Thirty-two options include classics like Philly cheesesteaks and BLTs, as well as alternative choices like hot tofu and teriyaki chicken. The dining area is a bit sterile, so grab your sandwich to go for a picnic at nearby Lovers Point.

Markets
It took a while, but now Pacific Grove has its own farmers market. The **Pacific Grove Certified Farmers' Market** (Central Ave. and Grand Ave., http://everyonesharvest.org/farmers-markets/pacific-grove, 3pm-7pm Mon. summer, 3pm-6pm Mon. winter) sets up in front of Jewell Park on Mondays.

ACCOMMODATIONS
Pacific Grove is known for its bed-and-breakfasts, many located within old Victorian buildings. There are also a few hotels, motels, and the Asilomar Conference Grounds.

$150-250
Before becoming a bed-and-breakfast in 1983, ★ **The Old St. Angela Inn** (321 Central Ave., 831/372-3246, www.oldstangelainn.com, $165-290) was a rectory and then a convent. This B&B spoils its guests with cozy accommodations, a friendly staff, and terrific food. The nine homey rooms have pine antiques, live plants, and comfortable beds. The Whale Watch room has a nice balcony where you can try and catch a glimpse of the namesake marine mammal during migration season. Downstairs are common areas that are comfy but not stuffy. Out back is a brick patio with tables, chairs, a fire pit, and a waterfall fountain. Despite all these fine amenities, one

of the best features of The Old St. Angela Inn is its food. The afternoon teatime includes wine, a dessert, and an appetizer. (Hope for the indulgent pesto brie in a puff pastry!) The scrumptious breakfast includes yogurt, granola, muffins, and a hot sweet or savory item. All of it, including the yogurt, is made in-house.

The ★ **Gosby House Inn** (643 Lighthouse Ave., 800/527-8828, www.gosbyhouseinn.com, $150-360) has been taking care of visitors since the 1880s. Today the white-and-yellow Queen Anne-style Victorian, which sits right on downtown Pacific Grove's main street, is a welcome cross between a boutique hotel and B&B. Amenities include free Wi-Fi and flat screens in every room but one. Yet the inn's old photos, antiques, and complimentary breakfast are the kind of features that make B&Bs the favorite kind of accommodation for some travelers. The main house has 22 rooms, some with gas fireplaces. The two deluxe rooms available in the adjacent Carriage House each have a balcony, gas fireplace, roomy tile bathroom, and nice-sized soaking tub that allows even a tall individual to stretch out.

Staying overnight at the ★ **Asilomar Conference Grounds** (804 Crocker Ave., 831/372-8016, www.visitasilomar.com, $190-335) can feel a bit like going back to summer camp. There are lots of common areas on the 107 acres (43.3 ha), including the Phoebe Apperson Hearst Social Hall, where visitors can relax by a roaring fire or play pool at one of two billiards tables. There is a real range of accommodations here, from historic rooms to family cottages to modern rooms with a view of nearby Asilomar Beach. The rooms with an ocean view and a fireplace are definitely recommended for those who don't mind spending a little more money. Note that all the rooms here lack TVs and telephones. It's an incentive for you to head outdoors.

Over $250
Right across the street from the Asilomar Conference Grounds, the **Andril Fireplace**

Cottages (569 Asilomar Ave., 831/375-0994, www.andrilcottages.com, $200-900) are a cluster of cabins surrounded by pine forest. Most of the 1- to 5-bedroom structures have their own kitchens, private decks, and, as the name promises, fireplaces. There are also three basic motel-style units. Outdoor amenities include a whirlpool tub, Ping-Pong table, and some barbecue grills.

The most striking bed-and-breakfast on the coast of Pacific Grove, the Seven Gables Inn (555 Ocean View Blvd., 831/372-4341, www.sevengablesinn.com, $239-559) is perched just feet away from Lovers Point. Decorated with antique furniture and artwork, the Seven Gables Inn is for those who want to step back in time and experience ornate Victorian- and Edwardian-style lodging. Impressively, every single room has superb ocean views.

Pacific Grove's Ocean View Boulevard has a handful of stunning Queen Anne Victorian buildings perched over the ocean. One of the finest and most notable is the dark green-and-white Green Gables Inn (301 Ocean View Blvd., 831/375-2095 or 800/722-1774, www.greengablesinnpg.com, $260-410). For Victorian-era enthusiasts, the main building—which was built in 1888 and has a downstairs common area with multiple nooks offering full-window ocean views—is

the place to stay, with its impressive throwback feel and antique furnishings. The Gable Room has a ladder that allows you to climb into an attic-like gable. Behind the main inn is the Carriage House, which has five spacious rooms, each with a gas fireplace, jetted tub, and ocean views. Breakfast and afternoon snacks and wine are provided to guests of the inn.

TRANSPORTATION AND SERVICES

Most visitors drive into Pacific Grove via scenic Highway 1. From Highway 1, take the Route 68 West exit to downtown Pacific Grove.

To pick up pamphlets on Pacific Grove's sights and lodging options, stop in at the Pacific Grove Tourist Information Center (584 Central Ave., 831/373-3304, www.pacificgrove.org, 10am-5pm daily). Pacific Grove has its own banks, restaurants, and a post office (680 Lighthouse Ave., 831/373-2271, www.usps.com, 9am-4:30pm Mon.-Fri., 10am-1pm Sat.).

For medical needs, the Community Hospital of the Monterey Peninsula (CHOMP, 23625 Holman Hwy., 831/624-5311 or 888/452-4667, www.chomp.org) provides emergency services to the area. It is actually located closer to Pacific Grove than Monterey.

Northern Monterey County

North of Monterey are the coastal cities of Seaside, Marina, and Moss Landing. Seaside is a working-class community with some great inexpensive restaurants, while Marina has a couple of coastal state parks. Both cities were once home to the sprawling Fort Ord, a decommissioned base that now hosts students from California State University, Monterey Bay (CSUMB) instead of U.S. Army troops. Moss Landing is the northernmost town on

the Monterey County coast. It has a working fishing harbor and long, sandy beaches.

SEASIDE

Seaside is a working-class community directly north of Monterey on the Monterey Bay. It's also the most populated city on the Monterey Peninsula. The U.S. Army's Fort Ord, which was based in Seaside and Marina, closed in 1994 and the city dealt with the closure for decades. Now it's undergoing a resurgence, due in part to a handful of restaurants and

1: Gosby House Inn 2: Green Gables Inn

businesses that have popped up in recent years on Broadway Avenue.

Frog Pond Wetland Preserve

A seasonal pond is the main feature of the **Frog Pond Wetland Preserve** (Canyon Del Rey Rd. between General Jim Moore Blvd. and Highland St., 831/372-3196, www.mprpd. org, sunrise-sunset daily). The water draws frogs, ducks, and lizards to the area after winter rains. A 1-mile (1.6-km) path around the pond offers a very pleasant walk that includes a section with three redwood trees.

Golf

Initially constructed for Fort Ord's soldiers by a general, the golf courses at **Bayonet & Black Horse** (1 McClure Way, 831/899-7271, www.bayonetblackhorse.com, greens fees $60-165) are two Seaside courses that have been visited by golf pros like Arnold Palmer and Jack Nicklaus. Bayonet was designed by a left-hander and has narrow fairways. Black Horse is the course you want to play if you like long, rolling fairways and views of the bay.

Nightlife

Opened in 2019, **Other Brother Beer Co.** (877 Broadway Ave., 831/747-1106, http:// otherbrotherbeer.com, 11am-6pm Tues.-Thurs. and Sun., 11am-8pm Fri.-Sat.) quickly became a hotspot on the lower Broadway Avenue section of Seaside, which is essentially the city's downtown. Located inside an industrial building, the interior resembles a school cafeteria and has picnic tables, and friendly staff pour a variety of beers, including lagers, stouts, a rye IPA, and a wheat beer sweetened with honey. Some standout suds are the Roundabouter IPA and the Seasider pale ale. Also, on-site is the **Ad Astra Bread Company** (323/823-6772, www.adastrabread. com, 11am-6pm Tues.-Sun.), which makes snacks and flatbreads that you can enjoy with your beer and loaves of bread that you can take home.

Craft beer lovers from all over the Monterey Peninsula head to **Post No Bills** (600 Ortiz Ave., Sand City, 831/324-4667, www.postnobills.net, 3pm-close Mon.-Thurs., 1pm-close Fri.-Sun.), which is actually located in the tiny town of Sand City, which is surrounded by Seaside. This warehouse-like building with street art on the walls feels like something that would be in a hip part of the San Francisco Bay Area. It has 17 interesting craft beers on tap along with a few fridges stocked with cold beer that you can take off site. Post No Bills doesn't serve food, but they sometimes have a food truck out front, or you can bring in a meal from one of Seaside's eateries.

Lynn's Arcade (1760 Fremont Blvd., Ste. D1, 831/641-7173, http://lynnsarcade.square. site, 5pm-midnight Mon.-Fri., noon-midnight Sat., 10am-10pm Sun., $15 admission for unlimited games) bills itself as a "pinball parlor and can slangery"; what this means is that Lynn's has over 25 rotating vintage and modern pinball machines as well as a curated selection of over 60 types of craft beer. It also means that Lynn's is a great place for a casual night out.

Food
SEAFOOD
Seaside Seafood & Market (789 Trinity Ave., 831/394-2027, www. seasideseafoodmarket.com, 11am-7:30pm Tues.-Sat., 11am-3pm Sun., $14-26) offers seafood options—like a standout New Orleans-style cornmeal-crusted shrimp po' boy—as well as hosts **On the Bay BBQ** (www.bythebaybbq.com), which does classic Southern-style barbecue, including a pulled pork with an Alabama white sauce, spare ribs, and a smoked chicken. Save room for a bit of banana pudding for dessert!

SUSHI
Harumi (1760 Fremont Blvd., Ste. H4, 831/899-9988, http://harumiseaside.menu11. com, 11am-2:30pm and 5pm-9pm Mon.-Thurs., 11am-2:30pm and 5pm-10pm Fri., noon-2:30pm and 5pm-10pm Sat., noon-2:30pm and 5pm-9pm Sun., rolls $3-15) is

a large place with a large menu. The extensive sushi menu includes baked rolls and ingredients like deep-fried soft-shell crab and Japanese squash. With pitchers of beer on tap, the long bar can be a fun place to post up.

CLASSIC AMERICAN

Seaside has a plethora of worthy inexpensive restaurants that are worth seeking out if you don't mind leaving Monterey. **Googie Grill** (1520 Del Monte Blvd., 831/392-1520, 8am-9pm daily, $13-25) has a memorably silly name (googie is an ultramodern architectural style), but these guys take their comfort food seriously. The breakfast menu includes beignets, Benedicts, and biscuits drenched in gravy, but the best of the batch is arguably the corned beef hash topped with two eggs and hollandaise sauce. Lunch and dinner are eclectic, with everything from locally caught sand dabs and calamari to meatloaf and Danish meatballs.

Bayonet Grill (1 McClure Way, 831/899-5954, www.bayonetblackhorse.com, 7am-3pm Sat.-Thurs., 7am-7pm Fri., $12-15) is a bar and grill located at Bayonet & Black Horse golf courses, with sweeping views of the Monterey Peninsula. This locals' secret offers breakfast, lunch, and a legendary happy hour (3pm-7pm Fri.), with a superb vista as a backdrop.

MEXICAN

★ **Mi Tierra** (1000 Broadway Ave., 831/394-8113, 7am-9pm daily, $5-9) is a neighborhood Mexican supermarket with a superb taqueria in the back. Walk past slabs of *chicharrón* (pork rind) and whole fried tilapia under a glass case on your way to a small window and grill. The tacos are a tasty, inexpensive treat at $1.50 a pop. The best one is the al pastor, which comes with crunchy pork, chunks of pineapple, sprigs of cilantro, and a splash of salsa on a little tortilla bed.

There are many superb Mexican restaurants in Seaside, and one worth mentioning is **La Tortuga** (1257 Fremont Blvd., 831/394-8320, 6am-10pm daily, $6.50-15.50). The menu here is big and varied, but the tortas (Mexican sandwiches) are a definite highlight. The wide range of tortas includes breaded beef, chile relleno, and eggs-and-cactus versions.

With a welcoming staff and a brightly colored interior, **Jose's** (1612 Contra Costa St., 831/899-0345, 11am-10pm, $5-17) is a longtime Seaside fixture. More like a homey café than a taqueria, it's known for its hearty Mexican fare, including fajita platters and crab enchiladas. Jose's also serves up one of the best—and most potent—margaritas in town.

El Pollo Rey (1188 Broadway Ave., 831/717-4744, 10:30am-8pm Tues.-Sat., 10:30am-7pm Sun., $9-25) is all about grilled chicken and carne asada. Get the whole chicken with sides or a whole pound of grilled steak. The namesake burrito allows you to try both the chicken and steak together.

THAI

The most popular Thai restaurant on the peninsula is Seaside's **Baan Thai** (1760 Fremont Blvd., F1, 831/394-2996, http://baanthaiseaside.com, 11am-3pm and 4:30pm-8pm Mon.-Thurs., 11am-3pm and 4:30pm-8:30pm Fri., 3pm-8pm Sat., $12-18), which has been serving up delicious curries—try the chicken yellow curry—noodles, and rice dishes since 1997.

ITALIAN

★ **Gusto** (1901 Fremont Blvd., 831/899-5825, www.gusto1901.com, 11:30am-2:30pm and 4:30pm-8pm Wed.-Sun., $10-18) is one of Seaside's most popular restaurants. It puts reasonable prices on its pizzas and pastas, which include creative numbers like a rich short-rib ravioli dish and classics like a wholly satisfying lasagna and spaghetti with meatballs. The butternut squash ravioli has vegetarians covered. This lively restaurant also serves wine, beer, and cocktails.

DELI

A superb, high-end butcher shop, **The Meatery** (1534 Fremont Blvd., 831/656-8810, http://themeatery.us, 11am-6pm Tues.-Sun.,

$10-14) serves pre-made salads and sandwiches—like a banh mi, fried bologna sandwich, and cheesesteak—and has a hot-food bar with daily specials. It's also just a great place to pick up some steaks and other meats for the grill.

BREAKFAST

Run by two longtime locals, ★ **The Butter House** (1760 Fremont Blvd., B-1, 831/394-2887, http://thebutterhouse.com, 7:30am-2pm daily, $10-18) is a Seaside favorite with varied offerings. Traditional breakfast items like omelets, Benedicts, and chicken-and-waffles are on the menu, along with playful creations like lemon curd pancakes and "The Elvis"—featuring peanut butter, bananas, honey, and bacon on grilled sourdough—and Asian-influenced options like a breakfast fried rice. I'll let you in on a secret: The Butter House also does a delicious fried chicken biscuit sandwich with a honey sriracha sauce for just $5 a pop.

The Breakfast Club (1130 Fremont Blvd., 831/394-3238, http://bclubrestaurant.com, 7am-2pm daily, $10-16) is all about that first meal of the day. The extensive menu includes omelets, waffles, and eggs Benedicts, along with unique offerings like a Bananas Foster French toast and a chili verde breakfast burrito. This is a crowded locals' spot, but you can expect quick service from the fast-moving waitstaff.

COFFEE

The coffee served at ★ **Acme Coffee Roasting Co.** (485 Palm Ave., Ste. B, 831/393-9113, www.acmecoffeeroasting.com, 6:30am-3pm Mon.-Fri., 7am-3pm Sat.) is revered locally and served everywhere, from unassuming bakeries to Big Sur's fancy Sierra Mar restaurant. Head to an alley in Seaside to get a great cup of coffee at its source, whether it's the Americano made with the company's signature Motor City Espresso Blend or a creamy iced Vietnamese coffee. The coffee bar is just a counter in an open garage, but it's so popular that it hosts a pool of locals on weekend mornings.

Making Seaside's Broadway Avenue hipper, **Counterpoint Coffee** (565 Broadway Ave., 831/586-5888, 7am-7pm daily) always has staff-spun vinyl playing and serves up specialties like an espresso tonic. Its coffee drinks are made from beans roasted by Chromatic Coffee in San Jose, and the café also has beer on tap and lots of wines; the owner is a Georis, of Carmel Valley's Georis Winery.

Accommodations

The **Embassy Suites Monterey Bay** (1441 Canyon Del Rey, 831/393-1115, www.hilton.com/en/embassy, $189-389) has 225 bedrooms and living room suites located in a tower two blocks from the beach. The tall, yellowish building also has an indoor swimming pool, a fitness center, and a unique open-air atrium lobby.

Transportation

Seaside is adjacent to Monterey and very easy to reach by car. Take Del Monte Avenue northeast out of downtown Monterey until you arrive in Seaside, or jump on Highway 1 and take the Fremont Street or Canyon del Rey Boulevard exit into Seaside.

MARINA

The city of Marina is 8 miles (12.9 km) north of Monterey on Monterey Bay. A large part of Fort Ord was located in Marina. The former U.S. Army base is now the home of California State University, Monterey Bay; the Fort Ord Dunes State Park; and the Fort Ord National Monument. The community is also known for its sweeping sand dunes, long beach, and inexpensive restaurants and shops. With the land of the former fort still being developed, Marina has a lot of potential that it has not reached yet.

Marina State Beach

At **Marina State Beach** (end of Reservation Rd., 831/649-2836, www.parks.ca.gov, 8am-30 minutes after sunset, free), sand dunes give way to an expansive surf-slammed beach. The seemingly ever-present winds here make it a popular place for hang gliding and kite flying. There's a parking lot, bathrooms, and picnic tables for people who want to check out this beach known for its raw beauty.

Fort Ord Dunes State Park

The home to a U.S. Army post from 1917 to 1994, the dunes north of Monterey are a part of one of California's newest parks, **Fort Ord Dunes State Park** (831/649-2836, www. parks.ca.gov, 8am-30 minutes after sunset, free). Walk along a 4-mile (6.4-km) road past remnants of the military past, or head down to the remote beach for a stroll. The restored dunes, which had 700,000 pounds of contaminated materials removed before opening to the public, are home to threatened and endangered plant and animal species including Monterey spineflower, Menzies' wallflower, dune gilia, and the black legless lizard. The main section of the park has a parking lot, interpretive panels, and a coastal viewpoint along with a trail to the south heading to the beach. A campground is scheduled to be built in the park and open to the public in 2022.

To reach Fort Ord Dunes State Park from Monterey, head north on Highway 1 and take the Lightfighter Drive exit. Turn left onto 2nd Avenue and then take another left on Divarty Street. Take a right on 1st Avenue and follow the signs to the park entrance at the 8th Street Bridge over Highway 1.

Fort Ord National Monument

A large section of former Fort Ord land became the **Fort Ord National Monument** (831/582-2200, www.blm.gov, dawn-dusk daily) in 2012. This 7,200-acre swath of land east of Marina and Seaside has 86 miles (138 km) of rugged trails used by hikers, horseback riders, and wildflower enthusiasts, though it is primarily loved by mountain bikers.

Recreation
HIKING

Just north of Marina, the landscape gives way to open fields, rolling sand dunes, and vacant beaches. The **Salinas River National Wildlife Refuge** (Del Monte Ave., www.fws. gov, dawn-dusk daily) offers an entry point into this undeveloped area. The 367-acre (149-ha) refuge has two trails: the **River Trail** (1.2 mi/1.9 km round-trip, easy) and the **Beach Trail** (1.6 mi/2.6 km round-trip, easy). A worthwhile adventure is the **Shipwreck Hike,** which adds another 1.5 miles (2.4 km) round-trip to the Beach Trail. Take the Beach Trail out to the beach and then walk north for another 15-20 minutes, where you'll come upon a rusting barge beached in the sand and the surf. It hit the shore in 1983 and now serves as a perch for local anglers. If the waves are not too big, you can hop up onto its rusting deck and walk around. Just be careful. To reach the Salinas River National Wildlife Refuge, take the Del Monte Boulevard exit north of Reservation Road off Highway 1. Go left as it becomes a dirt road between fields. It can be muddy and rutted in winter, so don't attempt this during rugged conditions if you don't have four-wheel drive. There's an undeveloped parking lot at the end of the road.

Fort Ord Dunes State Park (831/649-2836, www.parks.ca.gov, 8am-30 minutes after sunset, free) has 4 miles (6.4 km) of carless roads that are nice for hiking, running, and biking.

HORSEBACK RIDING

Marina is home to the **Marina Equestrian Center** (California Ave. and 9th St., 831/521-6168, www.marinaequestrian.org, 9am-5pm daily, private one-hour lesson $60, private 45 min. lesson for children 8-12 $45), a public park operated by the Marina Equestrian Association. Lessons are available by calling 831/392-5267.

1: the burger at Salt Wood **2:** a delicious taco from Aki Fresh Mex **3:** shipwreck at the Salinas River National Wildlife Refuge

The **Monterey Bay Equestrian Center** (831/663-5712, www.montereybayequestrian. com, $115/1-hour ride, $135/1.5-hour ride) can help you achieve your romantic dream of riding a horse on the beach. The center takes riders out on the sands between Marina and Moss Landing.

ROLLER SKATING

Water City Skate (2800 2nd Ave., 831/384-0414, www.watercityskate.com, public skate times 2pm-5pm and 7pm-10pm Sat., 1pm-4pm Sun., admission $7, skate rental $3) is a big blue building on the former Fort Ord that houses a skating rink. Come on the weekends to get your skate on, or show up for a Monday-night lesson (5pm-5:30pm Mon., $10/one drop-in lesson, $50/10 weeks of lessons). It's also where the **Monterey Bay Derby Dames** (www.montereybayderbydames. org), a league of female roller derby competitors, have their bouts. Check their website for a schedule.

Food
SEAFOOD

The most upscale dining experience in Marina is at **Salt Wood** (3295 Dunes Dr., 831/883-5535, http://saltwoodkitchenandoysterette. com, 3pm-10pm Mon.-Fri., 10:30am-2:30pm and 3pm-10pm Sat.-Sun., $18-42). Gold fixtures and a marble bar give this restaurant an elegant feel. Classic entrées include burgers, steaks, chicken, and salmon. Alfresco dining just a few hundred yards from the ocean is available.

The **Poke Bar** (130 General Stillwell Dr., Ste. 106, 831/717-4570, www.pokebar monterey.com, 11am-8pm daily, $9-13) offers tasty poke at the right price, Signature bowls run $11.50 each. The spicy tuna has real kick! Vintage photos of the area adorn the walls in the otherwise generic setting.

MEXICAN

The mother-daughter duo behind ★ **Aki Fresh Mex** (265 Carmel Ave., 831/747-1074, http://aki-fresh-mex-restaurant.business.

site, 11:30am-7:30pm Mon.-Sat., $5-17) craft creative, high-end Mexican food. Almost everything in Aki Fresh is handmade, from the decor to the tortillas. The *chilaquiles* are hearty and tasty, while the tacos—especially *vampiro*-style (which includes fresh avocado wedges and grilled cheese)—are some of the best around. They also offer lesser-known Mexican dishes, like *guajolotes,* a massive sandwich with chorizo, cheese, and enchiladas piled between *telera* bread.

Papa Chevo's (3038 Del Monte Blvd., 831/884-9545, 6am-midnight Mon.-Thurs., 6am-2am Fri.-Sat., 6am-10pm Sun., $3.50-14) is a superb and unassuming taco shop. The tacos are fine, but a couple menu items make this spot worth checking out. One is the chile relleno burrito, where a whole battered chile relleno is stuffed into a tortilla with lettuce, rice, and enchilada sauce. The other is their glorious breakfast burrito (eggs, potatoes, cheese, and your choice of breakfast meat) that is served at all hours. There's also a shop in Seaside (1760 Fremont Blvd., 831/393-1610, 6am-midnight Mon.-Thurs., 6am-1am Fri.-Sat., 7am-10pm Sun.).

VIETNAMESE

Marina's **Noodle Bar** (215 Reservation Rd., Ste. E, 831/384-6225, http://noodlebar831. com, 11am-8pm Wed.-Mon., $6-9) serves large plates of fresh Vietnamese food at very reasonable prices. They have pho (soup), dry noodle bowls, sautéed noodle dishes, and fried rice plates. A large sweet-and-sour chicken with fried rice costs just $6.50 and is hearty enough for two meals. This little restaurant in a strip mall is very popular—expect to wait for a table on weekend evenings. They have an even smaller spot in Seaside (1944 Fremont Blvd., 831/392-0210, 11am-8pm Mon.-Sat.).

MEDITERRANEAN

A fast-casual version of the popular Dametra Café in Carmel, ★ **Dametra Fresh Mediterranean** (120 General Stilwell Dr., Ste. 110, 831/274-4444, http://

dametra.com, 11am-8:30pm Sun.-Thurs., 11am-9pm Fri.-Sat., $7-11) lets you choose a main ingredient (chicken kebab, lamb kebab, falafel) and enjoy it in a wrap it, on a plate, or in a salad. The buttery spanako-pita is a worthy appetizer. Although there's also a location inside Monterey's Del Monte Center, this outpost is the better option due to the presence of its adjacent sports bar, The General (11am-midnight daily). It has a historic bar top from the local for-mer military base and offers fine drinks. You can also bring Dametra food with you to the bar or order from a tweaked menu that includes fare like fries topped with gyro meat.

BREWPUBS

Marina has its own brewpub, the English Ales Brewery (223 A Reindollar Ave., 831/883-3000, http://englishalesbrewery. com, noon-midnight Fri.-Sat., noon-11pm Sun.-Tues. and Thurs., 12:30pm-11pm Wed., $6-12), which brews six flagship ales on-site, including the Fat Lip Amber Ale and the 1066 Pale Ale. Marina is a low-key town, and this brewpub feels like a neighborhood pub (in-cluding special member mugs hanging on the ceiling overhead). The food here includes burgers, sandwiches, and salads.

Accommodations

Just a few sandy steps from Marina State Beach is the Sanctuary Beach Resort (3295 Dunes Dr., 831/883-9478 or 855/693-6583, www.thesanctuarybeachresort.com, $426-1,150). All of the guest rooms and suites are as close to the beach as you'll get in a Monterey County accommodation. Enjoy your own pri-vate patio or balcony to watch the sunset and a gas fireplace for when the sun goes down. The staff can drive you around the property on a golf cart and there's an on-site heated pool and spa.

Transportation

Marina is a 10-minute drive north from Monterey on Highway 1. Just hop on the highway for 8 miles (12.9 km) and then exit at Del Monte Boulevard or Reservation Road.

MOSS LANDING

Located in the center of Monterey Bay, 25 miles (40 km) south of Santa Cruz and 15 miles (24 km) north of Monterey, Moss Landing is a picturesque, working fishing village; it helps if you can ignore the smokestacks of the towering Moss Landing Power Plant. Moss Landing Harbor is home to a fleet of fishing vessels. To the south of the harbor's mouth, Salinas River State Beach offers miles of wild, undeveloped shoreline. North of the inlet, Zmudowski State Beach is popular with local surfers during the winter months. Offshore, the Monterey Submarine Canyon is one of North America's largest submarine canyons. It's the reason that the Moss Landing Marine Laboratories and Monterey Bay Aquarium Research Institute have local addresses. The Moss Landing Chamber of Commerce web-site (www.mosslandingchamber.com) offers visitor information.

★ Elkhorn Slough

Elkhorn Slough is the second-largest sec-tion of tidal salt marsh in California after San Francisco Bay. The estuary hosts an amazing amount of wildlife that includes marine mam-mals and more than 340 bird species, which makes it one of the state's best birding spots. The best way to explore the slough is by kayak, where you can view rafts of lounging sea ot-ters and a barking rookery of California sea lions from water level.

Located in Moss Landing's North Harbor, which connects to the slough, Monterey Bay Kayaks (2390 Hwy. 1, 831/373-5357, www.montereybaykayaks.com, 9am-5pm daily, guided tours $60-85, kayak rental $35-50/day, SUP rental $45/four hours) has kayak rentals as well as a range of guided tours from a 2.5-hour paddle up the slough to monthly full-moon tours. While paddling a kayak is the recommended way to view the slough, the Elkhorn Slough Safari (Moss Landing Harbor, Dock A, 831/633-5555, www.

elkhornslough.com, adults $43, children $33, seniors $40) is a possibility for those who wish to take a 1.5- to 2-hour tour of the estuary by boat. Check the website for current tour times.

Recreation
BEACHES
Just north of Moss Landing's harbor, **Moss Landing State Beach** (Jetty Rd., 831/649-2836, www.parks.ca.gov, 8am-30 minutes after sunset daily) and **Zmudowski State Beach** (20 mi/32 km north of Monterey on Hwy. 1, 831/649-2836, www.parks.ca.gov, 8am-30 minutes after sunset daily) stretch for miles. They're mostly enjoyed by locals who fish, surf, or ride horses on the beach. To get there, take Struve Road and turn onto Giberson Road.

Just south of Moss Landing is the **Salinas River State Beach** (Potrero Rd., 831/649-2836, www.parks.ca.gov, 8am-30 minutes after sunset daily), which doesn't get as many visitors as other area beaches. Expect some serenity among a few horseback riders or anglers.

WHALE-WATCHING
For a glimpse of marine mammals in the wild, from gray whales to orcas, catch a ride with **Sanctuary Cruises** (7881 Sandholt Rd., 831/917-1042, www.sanctuarycruises.com, $45-55). Running on biodiesel, the 43-foot (13.1-m) ocean vessel *Sanctuary* takes passengers out daily for 2- to 3-hour and 3- to 4-hour cruises. **Blue Ocean Whale Watch** (7881 Sandholt Rd., 831/600-5103, www.blueoceanwhalewatch.com, adults $95, children $85, upper deck $115) also heads out into the bay for 4-hour whale-watching expeditions.

Entertainment
NIGHTLIFE
The **Moss Landing Inn** (7902 Hwy. 1, 831/633-9803, http://wenchilada.com, noon-close daily) is not a place to spend the night, but rather a dive bar where you can spend a few hours getting acquainted with the local

characters. It's connected to The Whole Enchilada restaurant and offers live music on weekends.

FESTIVALS AND EVENTS
The success of reality TV shows like *Antiques Roadshow* and *American Pickers* have people scouring yard sales and antiques shops for collectibles. On the last Sunday of July, Moss Landing is flooded with these enthusiasts for the annual **Moss Landing Antique Street Fair** (831/633-4501, www.mosslandingchamber.com). The giant outdoor antiques market has more than 200 booths selling collectibles, while other booths nearby serve local foods like fried fish and artichokes.

Food
SEAFOOD
As a harbor town, Moss Landing is probably best known for its seafood restaurants. The most popular is ★ **Phil's Fish Market** (7600 Sandholt Rd., 831/633-2152, www.philsfishmarket.com, 10am-8pm Sun.-Thurs., Fri.-Sat. 10am-9pm, $9-23), which is known for its cioppino—a hearty Italian American seafood stew that includes clams, mussels, fish, Dungeness crab, prawns, and scallops. A heaping bowl comes with salad and garlic bread. Another worthwhile order is the blackened sea scallops cooked with lemon butter and capers. This informal market/eatery has a bluegrass band playing on some nights.

AMERICAN
Housed in a distinct red-and-white building, the **Moss Landing Café** (421 Moss Landing Rd., 831/633-3355, 7am-2pm daily, $6-15) offers home-style breakfasts and lunches that utilize local ingredients, whether artichokes or seafood. The breakfast menu has some unique meetings of terrestrial and ocean items in dishes like the crab omelet, the fish and eggs, and an omelet with bacon, veggies, and your choice of oysters or squid. The Cajun fish sandwich with avocado salsa is a winner.

MEXICAN

The Whole Enchilada (7902 Hwy. 1, 831/633-3038, http://thewholeenchilada.party, 11:30am-9pm daily, $10-24) does seafood with a Mexican slant. Dine on Mexican-style cioppino or chile relleno stuffed with crab, shrimp, and cheese in the brightly colored dining room or outdoor patio.

LATIN AMERICAN

Part art gallery, part eatery, fanciful **Haute Enchilada Café & Gallery** (7902 Moss Landing Rd., 831/633-5843, www. hauteenchilada.com, 11am-9pm Mon.-Thurs., 9am-9pm Fri.-Sun., $14-30) is bursting with color. The menu includes items such as Peruvian empanadas and a grilled catch of the day.

THAI

Moss Landing even has a great place to get Thai food with the **Lemon Grass Restaurant** (413 Moss Landing Rd., 831/633-0700, www.lemongrassthaimosslanding.com, 11am-3pm and 4pm-9pm Tues.-Fri., 11am-9pm Sat.-Sun., $11-22). There are the typical pad Thais and curries, but there's also a roasted Cornish game hen and a seafood stir-fry with squid, scallops, shrimp, and mussels on the menu.

COFFEE SHOPS

The Power Plant Coffee + Store (7990 Hwy. 1, www.thepowerplant.store, 7am-4pm daily) nods to the nearby former plant and to the live plants that decorate the space. Sourcing from superb local purveyors including Acme Coffee, Ad Astra Bread, and Gizdich Ranch Pies, Power Plant boasts a pick-you-up menu that includes coffee drinks, smoothies, toasts, and a breakfast sandwich. There's also a small gift shop full of curated books, prepackaged snacks, and more.

Accommodations and Camping

With its nautical decor, the ★ **Captain's Inn** (8122 Moss Landing Rd., 831/633-5550, www.captainsinn.com, $199-300) is the perfect place to spend an evening in the fishing village. The inn offers rooms in two buildings: a historic structure that was once the site of the Pacific Coast Steamship Company and the Boathouse, where every room has a superb view of the nearby tidal marsh. The Boathouse rooms are recommended for animal lovers

The Power Plant Coffee + Store

and nautical enthusiasts. Wildlife watchers might be able to catch a glimpse of marine mammals or birds, while maritime fans can climb into bed sets crafted out of boats or boat parts. Wake up to a home-cooked breakfast that can be bagged if you are on the go.

Seeking solitude and miles of nearly empty coastline? The **Monterey Dunes Company** (407 Moss Landing Rd., 831/633-4883 or 800/553-8637, www.montereydunes.com, $345-690) rents 2- to 4-bedroom homes on the beach south of Moss Landing. Guests also have access to the development's tennis courts, swimming pool, saunas, and hot tub.

The **Moss Landing KOA Express** (7905 Sandholt Rd., 831/633-6800 or 800/562-3390, http://koa.com, $77-87) has almost 50 RV sites right in the Moss Landing Harbor area.

Transportation

Moss Landing is a 20-mile (32-km) drive from Monterey that under good traffic conditions should take about 20 minutes. Take Highway 1 north from Monterey. The highway switches from four lanes to two between Marina and Moss Landing, so expect some traffic congestion if you are traveling on a summer day or holiday weekend. Take a left on Moss Landing Road to travel to the heart of the fishing community.

Carmel

Carmel began as an artists' colony. The region's landscape seems to have been created by those artists: fanciful curlicue cypress trees, artfully arranged rocks, and a white-sand beach as blank as a canvas.

This most beautiful and glamorous of the Monterey Peninsula's communities has drawn admirers throughout time, from Father Junípero Serra, who preferred the Carmel Mission to all of his other California missions, to film icon Clint Eastwood, who was mayor of Carmel-by-the-Sea in the late 1980s.

More upscale than their neighbors, Carmel-by-the-Sea and Pebble Beach have long been vacation destinations for the well-heeled. Carmel-by-the-Sea is known as a quiet community with a predominately

Highlights

Look for ★ to find recommended sights, activities, dining, and lodging.

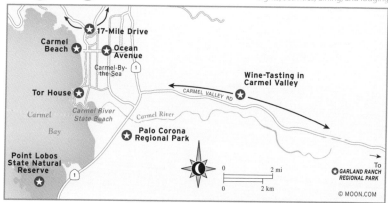

★ **Ocean Avenue:** The main thoroughfare of Carmel-by-the-Sea recalls a European town with its busy sidewalks, charming cafés, and cute boutiques (page 103).

★ **Tor House:** The stunning stone home of poet Robinson Jeffers and its adjacent Hawk Tower are monuments to the man's creative spirit. They still offer inspiration and fine views of Carmel's coastline (page 104).

★ **Point Lobos State Natural Reserve:** The crown jewel of California's impressive state park system has pocket coves, tidepools, forests of Monterey cypress, and diverse wildlife (page 104).

★ **Palo Corona Regional Park:** Only accessible with a permit, this stunning park has sweeping views of the Carmel coast from Inspiration Point (page 105).

★ **Carmel Beach:** One of the finest beaches on Monterey Bay, this is a great place for a stroll, a picnic, or catching a wave (page 107).

★ **17-Mile Drive:** This drive through Pebble Beach passes by mansions, beaches, golf courses, and the famed Lone Cypress (page 122).

★ **Wine-Tasting in Carmel Valley:** Carmel Valley's laid-back atmosphere makes for a fun day of tasting locally produced and bottled wines (page 126).

★ **Garland Ranch Regional Park:** This large county park offers some of the best hikes in Monterey County (page 130).

Carmel

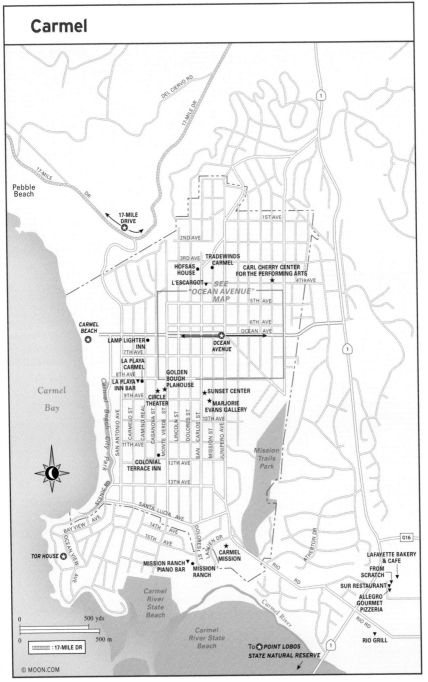

DEL CIERVO RD

17-MILE DR

17-MILE DR

Pebble
Beach

17-MILE
DRIVE

1ST AVE

2ND AVE

3RD AVE   TRADEWINDS
         CARMEL

HOFSAS
HOUSE   CARL CHERRY CENTER
                         FOR THE PERFORMING ARTS

L'ESCARGOT   SEE   4TH AVE
                "OCEAN AVENUE"
                    MAP

                                5TH AVE

                                6TH AVE

                            OCEAN AVE

CARMEL
BEACH

LAMP LIGHTER   OCEAN
INN   AVENUE
7TH AVE

LA PLAYA
CARMEL
8TH AVE   GOLDEN
LA PLAYA   BOUGH
INN BAR   PLAHOUSE
9TH AVE   CIRCLE
          THEATER   SUNSET CENTER
                         MARJORIE
Carmel   EVANS GALLERY
Bay   10TH AVE

11TH AVE

SAN ANTONIO AVE
CARMELO ST
CAMINO REAL
CASANOVA ST
MONTE VERDE ST
LINCOLN ST
DOLORES ST
SAN CARLOS ST
MISSION ST
JUNIPERO AVE

Mission
Trails
Park

COLONIAL
TERRACE INN
12TH AVE

13TH AVE

Carmel Beach City Park
SCENIC RD

SANTA LUCIA AVE

BAY VIEW AVE
                14TH AVE

OCEAN VIEW   15TH   AVE

DOLORES ST
LASUEN DR

TOR HOUSE   CARMEL
                       MISSION

MISSION RANCH
PIANO BAR   MISSION
               RANCH

RIO

Carmel
River
State
Beach

Carmel River

G16

LAFAYETTE BAKERY
& CAFE
FROM
SCRATCH

SUR RESTAURANT

ALLEGRO
GOURMET
PIZZERIA

RIO RD

ATHERTON DR
RIO RD

RIO GRILL

0   500 yds

0   500 m

: 17-MILE DR

© MOON.COM

Carmel
River
State
Beach

To POINT LOBOS
STATE NATURAL RESERVE

1

older crowd, but in recent years younger residents have opened bars and restaurants that have given the town a welcome jolt of energy. Indulge with a locally made fine wine or a round of golf on Pebble Beach's sacred greens. Even if you can't manage to overnight in the area, make sure to visit Carmel Beach and nearby Point Lobos State Natural Reserve, which has been called the "Crown Jewel of the California State Park System." Pebble Beach's 17-Mile Drive is a great drive that winds through a wealthy coastal enclave.

Adjacent Carmel Valley is more unassuming, but this sunny rural valley is home to some of the best wineries, a few high-end resorts, some great hiking, and something that the Carmel coast doesn't have in the summer: abundant sunshine.

PLANNING YOUR TIME

The primary sights of Carmel can be explored in a day, although a weekend is recommended to best experience the fruits of the local wineries.

The town of Carmel-by-the-Sea is a very charming and walkable coastal city, suitable for an overnight stay—although there are no hostels or inexpensive lodging options. The stunning white-sand beach and its European village-like downtown are worth your time.

Explore the windswept cypress trees, colorful tidepools, and easy trails of Point Lobos State Natural Reserve just 3 miles (4.8 km) south of town. Literature lovers should take a tour of the Tor House.

Pebble Beach is the place to stay if you are a golf fanatic or want to splurge on lodging. Here, it's all about catering to wealthy vacationers. The 17-Mile Drive is one of the region's most popular attractions, with exceptional natural scenery and stunning mansions to gawk at.

Carmel Valley is more rustic, relaxed, and spread out. It is also the epicenter of the area's growing wine industry and the region's most consistently sunny spot. Carmel Valley has the region's finest wineries and some laid-back tasting rooms. There's also some stellar hiking to be had at Garland Ranch Regional Park, and Carmel Valley Road (G-16) is one of the best scenic drives around.

CA-1 of Highway 1 connects Carmel-by-the-Sea to Monterey. Carmel Valley Road (G-16) winds east from Carmel-by-the-Sea into the more rustic Carmel Valley. Pebble Beach can be accessed from Carmel-by-the-Sea and Pacific Grove. Expect to pay the $10.50 entrance fee if you are not spending the evening at one of Pebble Beach's upscale lodges.

Carmel-by-the-Sea

There are no addresses in Carmel-by-the-Sea (frequently referred to as simply Carmel). There are lots of trees and no streetlights, and street signs are wooden posts with names written vertically, to be read while walking along the sidewalk, rather than driving down the street. There's little to do at night. These are a few clues as to how this village facing the Pacific Ocean maintains its lost-in-time charm.

Formerly a Bohemian enclave where local poets George Sterling and Robinson Jeffers hung out with literary heavyweights such as Jack London and Mary Austin, Carmel-by-the-Sea is now a popular vacation spot for the moneyed, the artistic, and the romantic. People come to enjoy the small coastal town's almost European charm: strolling its sidewalks and peering into the windows of upscale shops and art galleries, which showcase

Previous: Carmel Beach; coastal trail in Point Lobos State Natural Reserve; The Wine House in Carmel Valley.

Ocean Avenue

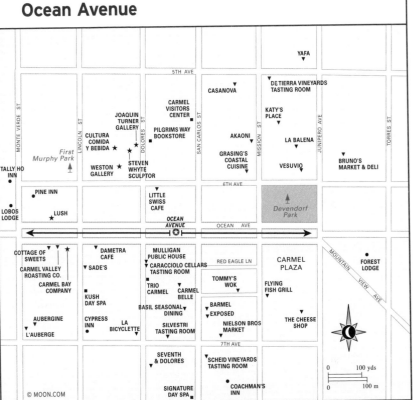

the work of sculptors, plein air painters, and photographers. Between the galleries are some of the region's most revered restaurants. The main thoroughfare, Ocean Avenue, slopes down to Carmel Beach, one of the finest on the Monterey Peninsula.

The old-world charms of Carmel can make it a little confusing for drivers. Because there are no addresses, locations are sometimes given via directions, for example: on 7th Avenue between San Carlos and Dolores Streets; or the northwest corner of Ocean Avenue. The town is compact, laid out on a plain grid system, so you're better off getting out of your car and walking anyway. Expect to share everything from Carmel's sidewalks to its restaurants with our canine friends. Carmel is very pro-pup.

SIGHTS
★ Ocean Avenue

With its wide, clean sidewalks, posh stores, bakeries, and restaurants, Ocean Avenue has a European feel. The main street of downtown Carmel-by-the-Sea can be crowded with humans and their dogs during summer and on holidays, but it is worth a stroll to get a taste of Carmel's unique personality. The road is four lanes wide with a tree-lined median separating the east- and west-traveling traffic. West of Lincoln Avenue, Ocean Avenue slopes toward the sea at a grade that recalls a ski run.

At the end of Ocean Avenue is one of the best places to access Carmel Beach.

Carmel Mission

Founded in 1771, **San Carlos Borromeo de Carmelo Mission** (3080 Rio Rd., 831/624-1271, www.carmelmission.org, 9:30am-5pm daily, $10 adults, $7 seniors, $5 children, children 6 and under free), more commonly known as the Carmel Mission, encompasses a collection of rambling buildings, living quarters, and courtyard gardens. Notable features of the complex are the restored church, with its gilded altar front and shrine to the Virgin Mary. There's a small memorial museum in a building off the second courtyard, but historical exhibits are on display throughout the buildings, showing a slice of the lives of friars. A working Catholic parish remains part of the complex, so be respectful when taking the self-guided tour.

The Carmel Mission is one of 21 California missions built by the Franciscan order—in the process displacing and enslaving the region's Indigenous peoples—in the 18th and 19th centuries. Father Junípero Serra personally founded 9 of them, and preferred the Carmel Mission to all of his other California missions. He lived, worked, and eventually died here. His grave and an ancillary chapel dedicated to his memory are located on-site. In 2015, when Serra was canonized by Pope Francis, this mission was the site of protests by Native Americans voicing dissent over Serra's treatment of Indigenous people.

Be sure to check out the mission's gardens, fountains, and small cemetery, which is home to the gravestone of Old Gabriel, a Native American who is believed to have lived to be 151 years old.

For more information about the area's Indigenous people and how they were affected by the arrival of the Spanish, pick up a copy of *The Ohlone Way: Indian Life in the San Francisco-Monterey Bay Area.*

★ Tor House

Local poet Robinson Jeffers penned nature poems to the uncompromising beauty of Carmel Point and nearby Big Sur. He built this rugged-looking castle on the Carmel coast in 1919. He named it **Tor House** (26304 Ocean View Ave., 831/624-1813, www.torhouse.org, tours 10am-3pm Fri.-Sat., adults $12, students $7) after its rocky setting, and he added the majestic Hawk Tower a year later.

Tor House Foundation volunteer docents lead 75-minute **tours** of the property that include a walk through the original home, which was hand built by Jeffers with giant stones. The poet once hosted luminaries like Ansel Adams, Charlie Chaplin, Edna St. Vincent Millay, and Dylan Thomas in the dining room, which offers fine views of Carmel Point and Point Lobos. The highlight of the tour is a visit to **Hawk Tower,** a four-story stone structure crowned with an open-air turret. Climb up a hidden staircase (not for the claustrophobic) or opt for the outside staircase to reach stunning views of Jeffers's property and the natural beauty that inspired his best work.

★ Point Lobos State Natural Reserve

Said to be the inspiration behind the setting of Robert Louis Stevenson's *Treasure Island,* **Point Lobos State Natural Reserve** (CA-1, 3 mi/4.8 km south of Carmel, 831/624-4909, www.parks.ca.gov and www.pointlobos. org, 8am-30 minutes after sunset daily winter, 8am-7pm daily spring-fall, $10/vehicle) is a wonderland of coves, hills, and jumbled rocks. The reserve's Cypress Grove Trail winds through a forest of antler-like Monterey cypress trees that are cloaked in striking red algae.

Half of the reserve is underwater, open for scuba divers who want to explore the 70-foot-high (21.3-m) kelp forests located just offshore.

Point Lobos also offers a lesson on the region's fishing history in the **Whaler's Cabin** (9am-5pm daily, staff permitting), a small wooden structure that was built by Chinese fishermen in the 1850s.

Dog-Friendly Carmel

a dog on Carmel Beach

Carmel-by-the-Sea has been called the most dog-friendly town in the nation, and with good reason. Dogs are allowed to run off-leash on the fine sands of **Carmel Beach.** Carmel Plaza has a drinking fountain for dogs, and even Carmel's most upscale boutiques put out dog bowls in front of their shops for passing dogs.

Many local hotels welcome dogs, though most add a nightly cleaning fee. **Cypress Inn, Coachman's Inn, Tradewinds Carmel, Lamp Lighter Inn,** and the **Hofsas House** can accommodate your pooch for nightly fees running $20-30 (see full listings in *Accommodations*).

Your dog can dine with you at a lot of local restaurants, but this might mean you have to eat outdoors on a patio. **Carmel Belle, Casanova, Grasing's Coastal Cuisine, Katy's Place, La Balena,** and **Tommy's Wok** are all dog-friendly options (see full listings in *Food*).

Terry's Lounge (inside the Cypress Inn, Lincoln and 7th Ave., 831/620-7454, www.carmelterrys.com, noon-11pm Sun.-Thurs., noon-midnight Fri.-Sat.) is a terrific dog-friendly bar with seating indoors and outside in a courtyard that resembles that of a Mediterranean villa.

The parking lots at popular Point Lobos tend to fill up frequently, so California State Parks is working on debuting a daytime reservation system in the near future.

★ Palo Corona Regional Park

Palo Corona Regional Park (200 yd/183 m south of Carmel River Bridge off Hwy. 1, 831/372-3196, www.mprpd.org, sunrise-sunset daily, free, reservation access permit required) is a stunning 4,350-acre (1,760-ha) park that offers sweeping views of the coastline from Pebble Beach to Point Lobos. It is also an important habitat for plant and animal species that include rare amphibians like the California red-legged frog and the tiger salamander. The 1.3-mile (2.1-km) hike to **Inspiration Point** is a must-do for its terrific vistas. The Monterey Peninsula Regional Park District runs the park and allows only 21 people to visit the property daily. **Access permits** are available online (www.mprpd.org) or by phone (831/372-3196).

BEACHES

★ Carmel Beach

Found at the end of Carmel-by-the-Sea's Ocean Avenue, **Carmel Beach** (Ocean Ave., 831/620-2000, http://ci.carmel.ca.us, 6am-10pm daily) is one of the Monterey Bay region's best beaches. Under a bluff dotted with twisted, skeletal cypress trees, it's a long, white, sandy beach that borders a usually clear blue-green Pacific. In the distance to the south, Point Lobos juts out from the land like a pointing finger, while just north of the beach, the green-as-billiard-table-felt golf courses cloak the grounds of nearby Pebble Beach. Like most of Carmel, Carmel Beach is very dog-friendly. On any given day, all sorts of canines fetch, sniff, and run on the white sand.

One of the best places to access the beach is at the west end of Ocean Avenue. There's a parking lot here, along with four beach volleyball courts, a wooden observation deck, and restrooms.

Carmel Beach allows beach **bonfires** (south of 10th Ave., 4pm-10pm daily) in designated smokeless fire pits, which are tall metal containers on small concrete slabs.

Carmel River State Beach

When Carmel Beach gets overrun, **Carmel River State Beach** (Carmelo Rd., 831/649-2836, www.parks.ca.gov, 8am-30 minutes after sunset daily) makes a great alternative. Actually, this mile-long beach is even better if you are a birder or scuba diver. The north end of the beach is the site of the Carmel River Lagoon and Wetlands Natural Preserve, where the Carmel River pools up before it reaches the ocean. Here, birders can see a range of birds from great blue herons to warblers. Monastery Beach is a very popular dive spot located at the southern end of the park. While it's great for advanced divers, the water offshore gets very deep very fast, making it a dangerous place for other ocean activities.

1: the view from Palo Corona Regional Park 2: a wooden bench overlooking scenic Carmel Beach

WINE-TASTING

The town of Carmel has over a dozen tasting rooms in its downtown area, despite the vineyards being in the nearby Carmel Valley or Santa Lucia Highlands. Visit the Carmel Chamber of Commerce website (www.carmelcalifornia.org) for a downloadable Carmel-by-the-Sea wine and spirits map that includes tasting rooms.

The family-owned **De Tierra Vineyards Tasting Room** (Mission St. and 5th Ave., 831/622-9704, www.detierra.com, 2pm-8pm Tues.-Thurs., noon-9pm Fri.-Sun. summer, 2pm-6pm Tues.-Thurs., noon-8pm Fri.-Sun. winter, tasting $20-25) has a range of wines, including a rosé, Syrah, merlot, chardonnay, red blend, Riesling, and a pinot noir. A chalkboard lists a cheese and chocolate plate menu. This is a place for great wine, good snacks, and occasional entertainment.

Dark and sleek **Caraccioli Cellars Tasting Room** (Dolores St. between Ocean Ave. and 7th Ave., 831/622-7722, www.caracciolicellars.com, noon-5pm daily, tasting $20) has a sophisticated atmosphere that reflects the upscale wines served; most start at $50 a bottle. Caraccioli's popular pours include a brut and a brut rosé that you can enjoy on the wooden slab bar. Its 2014 brut rosé won the Best U.S. Sparkling Wine 2020 trophy from the Champagne & Sparkling Wine World Championships. Th tasting room also offers a small selection of snacks, from locally spiced nuts to caviar.

Grammy-winning composer Alan Silvestri has scored everything from the TV series *CHiPs* and the movie *Forrest Gump* to the 2014 series *Cosmos*. He also makes wine in Carmel Valley, which can be sampled in the **Silvestri Tasting Room** (7th Ave. between Dolores St. and San Carlos St., 831/625-0111, www.silvestrivineyards.com, noon-7pm daily summer, noon-6pm Sun.-Thurs., noon-7pm Fri.-Sat. winter, tasting $10-15).

At Scheid Vineyards, Al Scheid and his employees take winemaking seriously, utilizing

10 vineyards in inland Monterey County from north of Soledad south to the county line. The estate vineyards produce 38 varietals of grapes but keep the best to themselves to make wines like their popular claret and 50/50, a cabernet sauvignon-Syrah mix that starts with a peppery kick before smoothing out. Sample their wares at the **Scheid Vineyards Carmel-by-the-Sea Tasting Room** (San Carlos St. and 7th Ave., 831/626-9463, www.scheidvineyards. com, noon-6pm daily, tasting $10-20), a clean, friendly space. There's a large map behind the counter that shows where all of the Scheid vineyards are located. A few large photographs on the wall show the vineyards and the winemaking process. They also have a location on the **River Road Wine Trail** (1972 Hobson Ave., Greenfield, 831/386-0316, 11am-5pm daily, tasting $5-10) that has an outdoor deck, a demo vineyard, and a bocce ball court.

Wrath Wines (Carmel Plaza, Ocean Ave. and Mission St., 831/620-1909, www. wrathwines.com, 11am-5pm daily, tasting $20) produces pinot noir, chardonnay, Syrah, and sauvignon blanc grapes in the nearby Carmel Highlands. Its Carmel-by-the-Sea tasting room is located in Carmel Plaza next door to The Cheese Shop.

RECREATION
Parks
Devendorf Park (Ocean Ave. and Junipero Ave., 831/624-3543, http://ci.carmel.ca.us) is downtown Carmel-by-the-Sea's best public place. This block-long park features a grassy lawn rimmed by live oaks, benches, and monuments honoring U.S. service people. It's the site of many Carmel-by-the-Sea events including the city's Fourth of July celebration, a Halloween parade, and an annual tree-lighting ceremony. It is also home to one of downtown's only public restrooms.

First Murphy Park (Lincoln St. and 6th Ave., 831/624-4447, www.carmelheritage.org) is owned by the city but maintained by the Carmel Heritage Society. The small park's primary feature is a 1902 home built by prominent Carmel architect Michael Murphy. The parcel also has a few benches, a native plant garden, some public art, and a public restroom topped by a wooden deck with views down to the ocean.

Surfing
Carmel Beach (Ocean Ave., 831/624-4909, 6am-10pm daily) has some of the area's most consistent beach breaks. Being a beach break, the sand bars shift, so the best spot on the beach frequently changes. The waves are usually at their finest from spring to late summer. The winds blow out a lot of area breaks in the spring, but Carmel Beach really comes alive during this time of year.

Contact **Carmel Surf Lessons** (831/915-4065, www.carmelsurflessons.com, group lessons $100/person, private lessons $200/person, $300/couple) if you want to learn to surf at Carmel Beach. To rent a board, head to **On the Beach** (693 Lighthouse Ave., Monterey, 831/646-9283, http://onthebeachsurfshop. com, 10am-6pm Sun.-Thurs., 10am-7pm Fri.-Sat., surfboard rental $30-35/day, wetsuit rental $20/day).

Scuba Diving
Just south of Carmel-by-the-Sea is a famed expert dive spot that one local has called the "Taj Mahal of local diving." The site is **Monastery Beach** (10-100 ft/3-30.5 m, expert), which is a beach dive off the southern end of Carmel River State Beach. It is best to enter on the north or south end of the beach, because the middle can have a strong current. (Do not attempt an entry during large swells!) The appeal of this dive is its dense sea life along with the fast-dropping, underwater Carmel Canyon offshore. You can dangle your fins above a wall that drops steeply more than 100 feet (30.5 m). The beach is right off Highway 1, 2.5 miles (4 km) south of the road's intersection with Carmel Valley Road.

Point Lobos State Natural Reserve (CA-1, 3 mi/4.8 km south of Carmel, 831/624-8413, www.parks.ca.gov, 8am-30 minutes after sunset daily winter, 8am-7pm daily spring-fall, diving permit $20-30) is known for its stunning terrestrial features, but there is a lot going on underwater as well. The reserve has the **Whaler's Cove** (20-45 ft/6.1-13.7 m, novice) and **Bluefish Cove** (40-100 ft/12.2-30.5 m, advanced) sites for divers. Whaler's is a beach dive easily accessible from the parking lot, while a boat or kayak is recommended to reach the deeper Bluefish Cove. Dive reservations can be made from two months to one day in advance. Two divers are required per reservation.

Hiking

Point Lobos State Natural Reserve (CA-1, 3 mi/4.8 km south of Carmel, 831/624-4909, www.parks.ca.gov and www.pointlobos.org, 8am-30 minutes after sunset daily winter, 8am-7pm daily spring-fall, $10/vehicle) has wonderful hikes. The hikes here involve little elevation gain but reward hikers with views of stunning coves, offshore marine life, and unique onshore vegetation. One of the best trails is the **Cypress Grove Trail** (Sea Lion Point parking lot, 0.8 mi/0.3 km round-trip, easy). This loop goes out on a finger of land with superb coast views, but the main attraction is the grove of wonderfully twisted Monterey cypress trees. That strange rust color on some of the tree branches? That is an algae that has carotene, the same pigment that causes carrots to have their orange coloring.

To view marine life, opt for the **Sea Lion Point Trail** (Sea Lion Point parking lot, 0.6 mi/1 km round-trip, easy). It offers vantage points to see a large sea lion colony on an offshore rock as well as the occasional sea otter backstroking through the kelp. The **South Shore Trail** (Bird Island parking lot, 1 mi/1.6 km one-way, easy) is a nice stroll along the reserve's south shore. There are views of the unique coastal geology that Edward Weston captured in his famous photos, as well as tidepools where you might be able to spot sea stars, anemones, and crabs.

A nice place for an easy hike in Carmel proper can be found at the **Mission Trail Park** (Rio Rd. and Ladera Dr., http://

ci.carmel.ca.us). This 35-acre (14.2-ha) parcel of canyon and woods has 5 miles (8 km) of hiking trails. A trail runs the whole length of the park, connecting eastern downtown to the Carmel Mission area.

Palo Corona Regional Park (200 yd/183 m south of Carmel River Bridge off Hwy. 1, 831/372-3196, www.mprpd.org, sunrise-sunset daily, free, reservation access permit required) has one of the best hikes in the Carmel area: the Palo Corona Trail's **Inspiration Point Hike** (1.3 mi/2.1 km round-trip, moderate). Access must be done in advance by securing a free **access permit** online (www.mprpd.org) or by phone (831/372-3196 ext. 2). The park allows just 21 visitors a day. The hike to Inspiration Point begins by passing through ranchland where cattle may be grazing. Then the dirt road winds up a hill that rises quickly from sea level like a wave. It offers views of the coastline framed by oak trees cloaked in lace lichen before arriving at a saddle with a redwood bench and picnic table. This is Inspiration Point, and it is worth spending some time here. To add a little more to your hike, continue on the Palo Corona Trail another 0.3 mile (0.5 km) one-way to **Animas Pond.** The endangered California red-legged frog calls this ecosystem home.

Spas

Carmel-by-the-Sea is as good a place as any to get a spa treatment. **Signature Day Spa** (San Carlos between 7th and 8th, 831/626-1998, http://signaturedayspa.com, 9am-9pm daily, $55-400) offers a variety of massages for your weary muscles, from classic Swedish style to a tasty sounding chocolate-oil massage.

ENTERTAINMENT

The events and entertainment in Carmel tend to center around either art or food. This town loves its haute culture, so you won't find too many sports bars or generic movie theaters here. Instead, enjoy classical music, a wealth of live theater, and a glass of wine in the mild evenings.

Bars and Clubs

Barmel (San Carlos St. between Ocean and 7th Aves., 831/626-2095, 2pm-midnight Sun.-Thurs., 2pm-1am Fri.-Sat.) has given Carmel's nightlife a youthful kick. It's the only bar in Carmel with live music (7pm-9pm Thurs.-Sat.). On weekends, a DJ party (from 9pm Fri.-Sat.) takes over after the live music ends.

One of downtown Carmel-by-the-Sea's more unassuming establishments, **Mulligan Public House** (Dolores and Ocean, 831/250-5910, http://mulliganspublichouse.com, 11am-midnight Mon.-Fri., 9am-midnight Sat.-Sun.) is decorated like an Irish golf bar; there's a narrow indoor dining and drinking area along with a heated, dog-friendly patio. Popular pub grub items include hot wings, Kobe beef sliders, and burgers. A true deal can be had here on Tuesdays, when beef and chicken tacos are sold for $1.25 each from 4pm-7pm.

Carmel's dive bar is **Sade's** (Lincoln St. and Ocean Ave., 831/624-0787, 4pm-1am daily, cash only). It's an intimate place with most seating placed around a U-shaped bar. In a place this small, you are bound to make some friends. Sade's accepts cash only.

For old-fashioned fun, head to the **Mission Ranch Piano Bar** (The Restaurant at Mission Ranch, 26270 Dolores St., 831/625-9040, www.missionranchcarmel.com, 4pm-11:30pm daily) for the nightly piano bar sing-along from 9pm to 11pm. It's possible you might spot owner Clint Eastwood joining the fun.

Bud's Bar (La Playa Carmel, Camino Real at 8th Ave., 831/293-6100, http://budscarmel.com, 2pm-10pm daily) is named for Bud Allen, who used to own La Playa, the hotel inside which the bar is located. Classic and classy, Bud's evokes earlier days with its signature cocktails, including a 1960s-style martini. One thing that sets Bud's apart from other high-end hotel bars is its "Dime Time"—a bartender rings a bell at their discretion once a day and all highballs and basic cocktails become available for just a dime (exact change needed) for just 10 minutes.

Live Music

Classical music aficionados will appreciate the dulcet tones of the musicians who perform for **Chamber Music Monterey Bay** (831/625-2212, www.chambermusicmontereybay.org). This society brings talented ensembles and soloists in from around the world to perform on the lovely Central Coast. One night you might find a local string quartet, and on another night, you'll get to see and hear a chamber ensemble. (String quartets definitely rule the small stage and intimate theater.) At its shows, all of which are performed at the **Sunset Cultural Center** (San Carlos St. at 9th Ave., 831/620-2048, www.sunsetcenter.org), Chamber Music Monterey Bay reserves up-front seats for children and their adult companions. The Sunset Cultural Center is a state-of-the-art performing center with more than 700 seats that hosts a true range of events and artistic endeavors, including rock shows, dance recitals, classical music concerts, and theater performances. Musical legends Willie Nelson, Jackson Browne, and Buddy Guy have all performed at this intimate venue.

Theater

Despite its small size, Carmel has a handful of live theater groups. In a town that defines itself by its love of art, theater arts don't get left out. Don't hesitate to ask the locals what's playing where when you're in town.

The **Pacific Repertory Theater** (831/622-0100, www.pacrep.org, prices vary) is the only professional theater company on the Monterey Peninsula. Its shows go up all over the region, most often in the **Golden Bough Playhouse** (Monte Verde St. and 8th Ave.), the company's home theater. Other regular venues include the **Forest Theater** (Mountain View St. and Santa Rita St.) and the **Circle Theater** (Casanova St. between 8th and 9th Aves.) within the Golden Bough complex. The company puts on dramas, comedies, and musicals both new and classic. You could see a work of Shakespeare or a family favorite like Disney's *The Little Mermaid*. Check the website for upcoming shows, and buy tickets online or over the phone to guarantee you'll get seats while you're in town.

Located in a quiet residential area, the Carl Cherry Center for the Arts (4th Ave. and Guadalupe St., 831/624-7491, http://carlcherrycenter.org, 11am-4pm Wed.-Fri.) was the former home of a Carmel artist and her inventor husband. When they passed away, they left the building to the city with the provision that it would be a place that carries on Carmel's artistic tradition. The one-room gallery hosts rotating exhibits, while the 50-seat theater has infrequent plays and events.

Festivals and Events

Relais & Chateaux is an international collection of gourmet restaurants and luxury hotels. In 2014, they debuted the Relais & Chateaux GourmetFest (831/622-5909, www.gourmetfestcarmel.com, Mar.) in Carmel. The event brings chefs from Relais & Chateaux together with winemakers for 20 unique events including dinners, demos, mushroom hunts, and bike rides.

In a town famed for art galleries, one of the biggest events of the year is the Carmel Art Festival (Mission St. between Ocean Ave. and 6th and Devendorf Park at Mission St., 831/626-4000, www.carmelartfestival.org, May). This three-day event celebrates visual arts in all media with shows by internationally acclaimed artists at galleries, parks, and other venues all across town. This wonderful festival also sponsors here-and-now contests, including the prestigious plein air (outdoor painting) competition. Visitors get a rare opportunity to witness the artists outdoors, engaging in their creative process as they use the Carmel scenery for inspiration. Round out your festival experience by bidding on paintings at the end-of-event auction. You can get a genuine bargain on original artwork while supporting both the artists and the festival. Perhaps best of all, the Carmel Art Festival is a great place to bring your family—a wealth of children's activities help even the youngest festivalgoers become budding artists.

For a more classical experience, one of the most prestigious festivals in Northern California is the Carmel Bach Festival (831/624-1521, www.bachfestival.org, July). For 15 days, Carmel-by-the-Sea and its surrounding towns host dozens of classical concerts. Naturally the works of J. S. Bach are featured, but you can also hear renditions of Mozart, Vivaldi, Handel, and other heavyweights of Bach's era. Choose between big concerts in major venues or intimate performances in modest spaces with only a small audience between you and the beautiful music. Concerts and recitals take place literally every day of the week—budget-conscious music lovers can just as easily enjoy the festival in the middle of the week as on the weekends.

During the summer, the Forest Theater (Mountain View St. and Santa Rita St., 831/626-1681, www.foresttheaterguild.org, $7) puts on its popular Films in the Forest series. Under the stars and trees, movie lovers can take in classics like *The Princess Bride* or cult favorites like *The Big Lebowski*. It's okay to bring in a bottle of wine or some snacks to sample during the flicks. Be sure to also pack a blanket to soften the blow of the theater's wooden bench seats. Visit the Forest Theater website for the summer film schedule.

An entry into Carmel's annual food and wine events, A Taste of Carmel (831/624-3877 or 800/550-4333, http://tasteofcarmel.org, Nov.) showcases the region's wines and cuisine. Expect appearances by popular Carmel-by-the-Sea restaurants, local wineries, and a couple of area breweries.

SHOPPING
Downtown

Shopping is a sport in Carmel, and Carmel-by-the-Sea offers a lot of upscale shopping opportunities on Ocean Avenue, from high-end national retailers like Tiffany & Co. to locally owned shops.

The Joaquin Turner Gallery (Dolores between 5th and 6th, 831/869-5564, www.joaquinturner.com, 11am-5pm Thurs.-Mon., by appointment Tues.-Wed.) has paintings that nod to the works of early 20th-century Monterey Peninsula artists. Turner also co-authored *Preserving Nature: A Field Guide to the Art and Artists of the Monterey Bay,* which indicates where famous local art pieces were painted.

One of the best galleries in town is the **Weston Gallery** (6th Ave. between Dolores and Lincoln, 831/624-4453, www.westongallery.com, 11am-5pm Tues.-Sun.), which highlights the photographic work of 20th-century masters, including Ansel Adams, Robert Mapplethorpe, Edward Weston, and more. A tiny art gallery owned by a local photographer, **Exposed** (Carmel Square, San Carlos St. and 7th Ave., 831/238-0127, www.galleryexposed.com, 1pm-3pm Sat., 5pm-8pm first Fri. of the month) is worth a peek.

Local artists display their fine art within the Sunset Cultural Center's **Marjorie Evans Gallery** (Sunset Cultural Center, San Carlos St. at 9th Ave., 831/620-2040, www.sunsetcenter.org, 10am-2pm Thurs.-Fri., by appointment Mon.-Wed.). The exhibits change every month.

When your head starts spinning from all the art, head to **Carmel Plaza** (Ocean Ave. and Mission St., 831/624-0138, www.carmelplaza.com, 10am-6pm Mon.-Sat., 11am-5pm Sun.), which offers lots of ways to part with your money. This outdoor mall has luxury fashion shops like Tiffany & Co. as well as the hip clothing chain Anthropologie. But don't miss locally owned establishment **The Cheese Shop** (800/828-9463, www.thecheeseshopinc.com, 11:30am-5pm daily), which sells delicacies like cave-aged Gruyere cheese that you can pair with a local wine. As for the vino, the shop has one of the finest ranges on the peninsula.

Worth a browse is the eclectic **Carmel Bay Company** (Ocean Ave. and Lincoln St., 831/624-3868, www.carmelbaycompany.com, 10am-5pm daily), which features copper armoires and a fascinating collection of vintage photographic prints.

Pilgrim's Way Books (Dolores between 5th and 6th, 831/624-4955, www.pilgrimsway.com, 11:30am-5pm daily) is an independent bookstore with new releases, classics, and a nice selection of local authors. They also sell New Age-y items including white-sage wands and incense. In an alleyway alongside the bookstore is The Secret Garden, a garden decor shop and calm space with bamboo, succulents, wind chimes, and water features.

For the environment lover in your life, pick

Carmel Plaza

up natural milk-based paint or books like *The Gorgeously Green Diet* at **Eco Carmel** (San Carlos St. and 7th Ave., 831/624-1222, www. ecocarmel.com, 10am-6pm Mon.-Tues. and Thurs.-Sat., 10:30am-6pm Wed., 11am-5pm Sun.).

Inside handmade cosmetic store **Lush** (Ocean Ave. and Lincoln St., 831/708-6914, www.lush.com, 11am-6pm daily) blocks of rough-cut soaps resemble cheeses (but with a different smell). Part of an international chain, Lush does colorful bath, shower, body, and hair supplies.

The **Cottage of Sweets** (Ocean Ave. between Monte Verde and Lincoln Sts., 831/624-5170, www.cottageofsweets.com, 10am-8pm Mon.-Thurs., 10am-9pm Fri.-Sat.) is a stunning little Carmel structure with moss on the roof and ivy running up its exterior. Inside, it's a sweet tooth's dream with homemade fudge, imported candies, and more than 50 kinds of licorice.

The Barnyard Shopping Village

Just east of Highway 1 is **The Barnyard Shopping Village** (24600 Carmel Rancho Ln., 831/624-8886, www.thebarnyard.com, 10am-6pm Mon.-Sat., 11am-5pm Sun.). Its multistory buildings are home to more than 45 mostly local merchants, with everything from art and home furnishings to beauty products, as well as eight locally owned restaurants. Particularly notable is the **Steven Whyte Sculpture Gallery** (831/620-1917, www.stevenwhytesculptor.com, 9am-4:30pm Wed., 9am-5pm Thurs. and Mon., 9am-6pm Fri., 10am-6pm Sat., 10am-4pm Sun.), where you can watch the artist create amazing life-sized sculptures in his open studio.

The Crossroads Shopping Center

The Crossroads Shopping Center (243 Crossroads Blvd., 831/625-4106, www. thecrossroadscarmel.com, 10am-6pm Mon.-Sat., noon-5pm Sun.) is the southernmost place to shop in Carmel before Highway 1 heads into the wilds of Big Sur. Local businesses like **Lula's Chocolates** (244 Crossroads Blvd., 831/626-3327, www.lulas. com, 10am-5pm Mon.-Sat., 11am-5pm Sun.) and **River House Books** (208 Crossroads Blvd., 831/626-2665, 10am-6pm Mon.-Sat., 10am-5pm Sun.) populate the shopping center, along with a few restaurants like longtime favorite **Rio Grill** (101 Crossroads Rd., 831/625-5436, www.riogrill.com, 11:30am-9:30pm daily). It's also a good place to stock up on supplies before continuing to Big Sur, with a 24-hour Safeway grocery store.

FOOD
Seafood

The **Flying Fish Grill** (Mission St. between Ocean Ave. and 7th Ave., 831/625-1962, http://flyingfishgrill.com, 5pm-10pm daily, $24-39) serves Japanese-style seafood with a California twist in the Carmel Plaza open-air shopping mall. Entrées include rare peppered-ahi, black-bean halibut, and clay pot dinners for two. You might even score a market-price meal of Monterey abalone. Enjoy it all in the dimly lit, wood-walled establishment.

Sushi

★ **Akaoni** (Mission St. and 6th Ave., 831/620-1516, 5:30pm-8:30pm Mon.-Tues., 11:30am-1pm and 5:30pm-8:30pm Wed.-Sat., $7-40) is a superb hole-in-the-wall sushi restaurant. Sit at the bar or one of the few tables, if you can get in. The menu includes tempura-fried oysters, soft-shell crab rolls, and *unagi donburi* (eel bowl). Check the daily specials on the whiteboard for the freshest seafood, including items flown in from Japan or caught right out in the bay. For adventurous diners, the live Monterey spot prawn is the freshest seafood you'll ever eat.

A one-room sushi and sake bar in downtown Carmel, **Toro Sushi** (Dolores St. between 5th Ave. and 6th Ave., 831/574-3255, http://torosushicarmel.com, noon-8pm daily, $12-20) has a small menu focused on traditional, well-sourced seafood. It includes classic rolls (Philadelphia, spicy tuna, rainbow) along with some seared rolls and creative offerings like a tempura-fried jalapeño pepper stuffed with spicy tuna and cream cheese. Not feeling fishy? Toro does a superb chicken *katsu* entrée—perfectly crispy fried chicken cut into strips. Sake flights featuring five tastings cost $25.

American

★ **Sur Restaurant** (3601 The Barnyard Shopping Village, 831/250-7188, www. surcarmel.com, 11:30am-9pm Tues.-Sun., $19-35) is the latest creation by well-known restauranteur Billy Quon. The menu accommodates most appetites with meal-sized appetizers, salads, seafood, and meat, including a popular fried chicken and waffle entrée. The food and ambience, complemented by fine cocktails, craft beers, and wines by the bottle and glass, make this a worthwhile destination.

Tucked into San Carlos Square, ★ **Stationaery** (San Carlos Square, San Carlos St. between 5th Ave. and 6th Ave, 831/250-7183, www.thestationaery.com, 8am-2pm and 4pm-8pm Wed.-Mon., $12-34) is run by a husband-and-wife team who source their ingredients from local farms and ranches. The small restaurant delivers high-quality meals for brunch, lunch, and dinner. On the rotating menu you might find chilaquiles, a potato pancake with salmon, or a decadent burger. There's also a lobster roll with a caviar topping for those that want to spoil themselves.

Grasing's Coastal Cuisine (6th Ave. and Mission St., 831/624-6562, http://grasings. com, 11am-9pm Mon.-Fri., 10:30am-9pm Sat.-Sun., $28-64) serves the creations of chef Kurt Grasing in a cute cottage atmosphere that is quintessential Carmel. Begin by flipping through the impressive 42-page wine list in which cabernets, pinots, and Burgundies are well represented. The dinner menu has a chophouse section, featuring fine steaks from Nebraska. Another notable entrée is the tasty paella studded with prawns, clams, mussels, and spicy sausage in a tomato broth over orzo and vegetables. In the high-ceilinged dining room, waiters in vests and ties serve guests, while the outdoor patio is dog-friendly.

The **Rio Grill** (101 Crossroads Blvd., 831/625-5436, www.riogrill.com, 11:30am-9:30pm daily, $15-42) has been luring diners to the Crossroads Shopping Center for decades. The grill's menu includes Southwest/Tex-Mex fare like a quesadilla of the day and stuffed poblano peppers. The popular happy hour (4pm-6:30pm Mon.-Fri., 4pm-10pm Sun.) offers a taste of the restaurant's cuisine in the bar, which is decorated with murals of local luminaries.

Mexican

Cultura Comida y Bebida (Dolores between 5th and 6th, 831/250-7005, www. culturacarmel.com, 2pm-8pm Tues.-Fri., noon-8pm Sat.-Sun., $18-28) will satisfy adventurous diners with superb upscale Mexican cuisine. Try the *chapulines* (toasted grasshoppers) appetizer or skip ahead to the smoked pork cheeks with mole or a plantain burrito. There's also a large mescal menu.

Asian Fusion

Pangaea Grill (Ocean Ave. near Lincoln St., 831/624-2569, www.pangaeagrillcarmel. com, 8am-9pm, $18-40) really stands out in Carmel's sea of Mediterranean and European restaurants. The friendly owners and staff have a wide-ranging menu that includes pastas, seafood, and steaks, but it's their "East Meets West" items that stand out. This includes the Korean short ribs and the kimchee fried rice. Along with the food, they have tasty cocktails and coveted wines from Pisoni Family Vineyards on their drink menu. It's all served in a stylish interior with glass lights hanging from the ceiling and abstract ocean scenes decorating the walls.

Chinese

For an authentic hole-in-the-wall locals' dining experience, seek out **Tommy's Wok**

1: Stationaery **2:** Toro Sushi **3:** Rise & Roam
4: Pangaea Grill

(San Carlos St. between Ocean Ave. and 7th Ave., 831/624-8518, www.tommyswokcarmel. com, 11:30am-2:30pm and 4:30pm-8:30pm Tues.-Sun., $10-16). You can dine in or take out items like the moo shu pork. It's often crowded.

French

If the international feel of Carmel-by-the-Sea has put you in the mood for European food, have dinner at the quaint French eatery **La Bicyclette** (Dolores St. at 7th Ave., 831/622-9899, www.labicycletterestaurant.com, 8am-10:45am, 11:45am-3:30pm, and 5pm-10pm daily, $19-38). The dinner menu changes nightly but always includes wood-fired pizzas. Owned by the same family, **Casanova** (5th Ave. between Mission St. and San Carlos St., 831/216-3811, www.casanovacarmel.com, 5pm-9:30pm Mon.-Thurs., 5pm-10pm Fri., 11am-3pm and 5pm-10pm Sat., 11am-3pm and 5pm-9:30pm Sun., $23-49) oozes romance. This charming Carmel fixture does a dinner menu that focuses on rustic French and Italian cuisine with a touch of Belgian influence as well. Expect pastas along with a small range of meat and seafood entrées. The restaurant built a special room to house a table that artist Vincent Van Gogh once dined on.

L'Escargot (Mission St. and 4th Ave., 831/620-1942, www.escargot-carmel.com, 5:30pm-11:30pm daily, $27-42) is a fine French restaurant. The menu often includes indulgent favorites like rack of lamb, roasted duck breast, and steak frites. The wine list skews French and Californian.

Italian and Pizza

Vesuvio (6th Ave. and Junipero St., 831/625-1766, http://chefpepe.com/restaurants/vesuvio, 4pm-11pm daily, $17-38) is an Italian restaurant serving dishes like tri-colored cannelloni, gnocchi, and wood-oven pizzas. There's also a great burger topped with bunches of caramelized onions, oozing cambozola cheese, and a chipotle aioli on a housemade roll. The restaurant also has a popular rooftop bar—which achieved tabloid notoriety

in 2016 when actor Bill Murray tossed some fans' cellphones off of it—with fire pits, heat lamps, and love seats.

It's difficult to secure a reservation at popular **La Balena** (Junipero St. between 5th and 6th Aves., 831/250-6295, http://labalenacarmel.com, noon-10pm Tues.-Sun., $21-35), a farm-to-kitchen Italian restaurant. Menu items change, but may include freshly made pastas or a slow-braised lamb shank. The fried half-chicken entrée is a local favorite.

Basil (Ocean and 7th, 831/626-8226, www.basilcarmel.com, 11:30am-9pm Tues.-Thurs. and Sun., 11:30am-10pm Fri.-Sat., $24-45) is tucked back along a corner of the Paseo San Carlos Courtyard. The intimate interior has just nine tables with some seating on a covered outdoor patio. Menu items may include locally sourced goat or a black-squid ink linguine with Monterey Bay squid and Mendocino sea urchin sauce. The five-hour braised barbecue short ribs are tender, tasty, and worthwhile. Basil was Carmel's first certified green restaurant.

Allegro Gourmet Pizzeria (3770 The Barnyard Shopping Village, 831/626-5454, http://allegropizzeria.com, 11am-9pm daily, $7-30) doesn't just serve up your standard slice of pie. There are some inspired creations here, including a chicken Thai peanut pie and a gorgonzola cheese pizza with roasted red peppers and pistachios. The pizzeria also serve salads, pastas, and paninis.

Light-filled and modern, **Rise & Roam** (Mission St. and 7th Ave., 831/574-2900, 7am-7pm daily, $10-28) is an upscale pizza joint/bakery located on a street corner in downtown Carmel. The Roman-style pizzas are hearty, rustic, and flavorful, with a crust that resembles an airy focaccia. The bakery side serves up house-made loaves of bread, cookies, coffees, and teas.

Mediterranean

While **Dametra Café** (Ocean Ave. at Lincoln St., 831/622-7766, www.dametracafe.com, 11am-11pm daily, $14-34) has a wide-ranging international menu that includes an all-American cheeseburger and Italian dishes like spaghetti alla Bolognese, it's best to go with the lively restaurant's signature Mediterranean food. The Greek chicken kebab entrée is a revelation, with two chicken and vegetable kebabs drizzled with a distinct aioli sauce, all served over yellow rice and with a Greek salad. The owner and his staff have been known to serenade evening diners.

Come into **Yafa** (5th Ave. and Junipero St., 831/624-9232, www.yafarestaurant.com, 5pm-10pm daily, $14-30), and you'll feel like you have suddenly become a member of a giant Mediterranean family. Owner and manager Ben Khader and his father will make you feel utterly welcome as you enter this popular one-room restaurant. The restaurant makes dining fun, with occasional eruptions of singing, dancing, and clapping. The menu includes pastas (lamb ravioli, lobster ravioli) along with Mediterranean classics (Moroccan chicken, lamb kebabs). Try the Aleppo Kefta platter, starring a tasty ground beef-and-lamb kebab mixture.

Steakhouse

Carmel's dining scene was missing a steakhouse until **Seventh & Dolores** (7th Ave. and Dolores, 831/293-7600, www.7dsteakhouse.com, 11:30am-10pm Mon.-Fri., 10am-10pm Sat.-Sun., $22-88). Inside the architecturally stunning building is a restaurant helmed by meat-loving local chef Todd Fisher, who is dedicated to celebrating being a carnivore. High-end steaks from Niman Ranch are dry-aged for 3-4 weeks (which explains their price tag of $34-88). Or opt for the $22 burger, a wildly rich and flavorful blend of dry-aged beef, filet mignon, and brisket whipped with bone marrow. Since the dinner entrées can be pricey, visit at lunch or during Social Hour (4pm-6pm Sun.-Thurs.). Marble counter-top seats are available at the raw bar.

Breakfast

Katy's Place (Mission St. between 5th and 6th, 831/624-0199, www.katysplacecarmel.

com, 7am-1pm daily, $10-30) serves gigantic, classic breakfasts such as Denver omelets and biscuits and gravy, inside or outside on a redwood-shaded deck. This longtime local favorite serves 20 different combinations of eggs Benedict, including the Benedict Romanoff with smoked salmon and caviar, and a Hawaiian version with bacon and pineapple.

Carmel Belle (Doud Craft Studios, Ocean Ave. and San Carlos St., 831/624-1600, www.carmelbelle.com, 8am-6pm Thurs.-Tues., 8am-8pm Wed., $6-25) is a little eatery with a big attention to detail. In the open section of an indoor mall, Carmel Belle serves up creative fare for breakfast and lunch, including an open-faced breakfast sandwich featuring a slab of toast topped with a poached egg, thick strips of bacon, a bed of arugula, and wedges of fresh avocado. Its slow-cooked Berkshire pork sandwich with red onion-currant chutney is a perfect example of what can happen when savory meets sweet.

The **Little Swiss Café** (6th Ave. and Dolores St., 831/624-5007, 7:30am-3pm Mon.-Sat., 8am-2pm Sun., $10-13) is a perennial local go-to for breakfast. Grab a booth and gaze at the murals covering the walls. You might notice something is off when you spot a penguin or the Eiffel Tower hidden in the European countryside. The café favorites include blintzes and egg Benedicts.

From Scratch Restaurant (3626 The Barnyard Shopping Village, 831/625-2448, http://fromscratchrestaurant.com, 8am-2pm Thurs.-Tues., $7-16) has been featured on the Food Network's *Diners, Drive-ins and Dives*. Start your day with pancakes, a skillet platter, an omelet, or the wildly popular nacho-style huevos rancheros. Lunch options include wraps, soups, salads, and a crustless quiche of the day.

Bakeries and Coffee Shops

Run by a French master baker and a French pastry chef, **Lafayette Bakery** (3672 The Barnyard Shopping Village, Ste. E22, 831/915-6286, www.lafayettebakery.com, 7am-6pm Mon.-Sat., 7am-4pm Sun.) can tempt as much

as any Paris bakery. The delectable goods, including artisan breads, pastries, and baguette sandwiches, are showcased at the counter.

The **Carmel Valley Coffee Roasting Co.** (Ocean Ave. between Lincoln St. and Monte Verde St., 831/626-2913, www.carmelcoffeeroasters.com, 6am-5pm Sun.-Thurs., 6am-6pm Fri.-Sat.) is a great place to get caffeinated during a walk around Carmel-by-the-Sea. The brick-floored café has a few seats and tables on an upper level at which to drink or eat a pastry or premade sandwich. There are two other locations in Carmel, at the Crossroads Shopping Center (246 Crossroads Shopping Center, 831/626-8784, 7:30am-5pm daily) and at The Barnyard Shopping Village (3720 The Barnyard Shopping Village, 831/620-0844, 7am-3:30pm daily).

Markets

★ **Bruno's Market & Deli** (6th Ave. and Junipero St., 831/624-3821, www.brunosmarket.com, 7am-8pm daily) is the place to pick up supplies for a Carmel Beach picnic. It has great made-to-order sandwiches, and if there is a long line at the counter, they have a batch of premade sandwiches, including meatloaf, turkey, and sausage, in a fridge across from the deli case. Bruno's also has a good selection of sodas and juices to wash it all down.

Nielsen Bros. Market (7th Ave. and San Carlos St., 831/624-6441, http://nielsenbros.com, 7am-8:30pm daily) is the market to stop at if you are looking to buy fine wines or rare liquors. The wine room has local labels and sometimes hosts a wine consultant. The market makes sandwiches and has basic goods.

ACCOMMODATIONS
$150-250

Just two blocks from the beach, the ★ **Lamp Lighter Inn** (Ocean Ave. and Camino Real, 831/624-7372, www.carmellamplighter.com, $225-425) has 11 rooms located in five blue-and-white cottages. The units have a comfortable, beachy decor befitting their location. The cottages encircle a nice courtyard area that has two fire pits, which are perfect for hanging out with old friends or making new ones. Guests are treated to an afternoon wine-and-cheese reception and a morning continental breakfast that they can enjoy in the courtyard. This is a pet-friendly property, and two of the units even have fenced-in backyards.

Lobos Lodge (Monte Verde St. and Ocean Ave., 831/624-3874, www.loboslodge.com, $205-465) sits right in the midst of downtown Carmel-by-the-Sea, making it a perfect spot from which to dine, shop, and admire the endless array of art in this upscale town. Each of the 30 rooms and suites offers a gas fireplace, a sofa and table, a bed in an alcove, and enough space to stroll about and enjoy the quiet romantic setting. All but two of the rooms have a patio or balcony where you can enjoy the product of a local vineyard outside. In the morning, guests are treated to a continental breakfast and a newspaper.

The Bavarian-inspired, locally owned **Hofsas House** (San Carlos St. between 3rd and 4th Aves., 831/624-2745, www.hofsashouse.com, $158-335) offers surprisingly spacious rooms in a quiet neighborhood within easy walking distance of downtown Carmel. If you have a crew, Hofsas House has family suites for rent with two bedrooms and two bathrooms. If you can, get an ocean-view room with a patio or balcony and spend some time sitting outside looking over the town of Carmel out toward the serene (from a distance) Pacific waters. The property also has a heated swimming pool, a sauna, and continental breakfast for guests.

Located in a neighborhood just a block from Carmel Beach, **Colonial Terrace Inn by the Sea** (San Antonio Ave. between 12th and 13th Aves., 831/624-2741, www.thecolonialterrace.com, $235-535) is the best place in the small town to fall asleep to the white noise of breaking waves. In addition to superb ocean views from the property,

1: abalone appetizer at Basil **2:** Allegro Gourmet Pizzeria **3:** Carmel Belle **4:** Nielsen Bros. Market

Colonial Terrace has a nice brick courtyard surrounded by blooming flowers that guests can enjoy on the area's warmer days.

Tally Ho Inn (Monte Verde St. and 6th Ave., 800/652-2632, www.tallyho-inn.com, $229-379) seeks to conjure a feeling of the English countryside with its flowers, gardens, and fireplaces. The units all have private decks and marble bathrooms. Spend a little more for a room with a fireplace or hot tub.

You'll figure out that the **Pine Inn** (Ocean Ave. and Lincoln St., 831/624-3851 or 800/228-3851, www.pineinn.com, $189-389) was built in a different time when you enter the hotel lobby, which has wood paneling and is decorated with antiques. Constructed in 1889, the inn has unique rooms, including some with marble bathrooms and hot tubs. A breakfast buffet is served to guests on weekday mornings. The complex is home to a handful of shops and **Il Fornaio,** an Italian restaurant.

Outside of downtown Carmel, **Mission Ranch** (26270 Dolores St., 831/624-6436, 800/538-8221, www.missionranchcarmel.com, $125-345) is a sprawling old ranch complex with views of sheep-filled pastures and Point Lobos in the distance. If you get a glimpse of Mission Ranch's owner, it might just make your day: It's none other than Hollywood icon and former Carmel-by-the-Sea mayor Clint Eastwood. Overnight options range from a rustic bunkhouse to modern rooms with jetted tubs and private decks. On the grounds is a restaurant with a nightly sing-along piano bar that is popular with Carmel's silver-haired crowd.

The **Carmel River Inn** (26600 Oliver Rd., 831/624-1575 or 800/882-8142, http://carmelriverinn.com, $169-299) has two sets of accommodations on its 10 acres (4 ha) near the Carmel River: inn rooms and cottages. The inn rooms have basic amenities including mini-fridges and coffeemakers. Some of the one- or two-bedroom cottages have gas fireplaces.

Over $250

Touted by *Architectural Digest,* ★ **Tradewinds Carmel** (Mission St. and 3rd Ave., 831/624-2776, www.tradewinds.com, $250-550) brings a touch of the Far East to California. Inspired by the initial proprietor's time spent in Japan, the 28 serene hotel rooms are decorated with Asian antiquities and live orchids. Outside, the grounds feature a water fountain that passes through bamboo shoots and horsetails, along with a meditation garden, where an oversized Buddha head overlooks a trio of cascading pools. A stay comes with continental breakfast that includes French pastries and fruit.

Landmark Carmel-by-the-Sea hotel ★ **Cypress Inn** (Lincoln St. and 7th Ave., 831/624-3871 or 800/443-7443, www.cypress-inn.com, $249-650) welcomes both human and dog guests in a white, ornate Mediterranean-inspired building. The property was co-owned by actress, singer, and animal rights activist Doris Day, who passed away in 2019. Her influence is notable throughout the hotel, from her movie posters adorning the walls downstairs to the fact that every one of the inn's rooms is dog-friendly. This is one of the most pro-pup hotels in the whole state: There are dog cookies at the front desk, water bowls are situated around the hotel, and dog beds and towels are provided by request. The rooms all come with complimentary cream sherry, fruit, and snacks for guests, while some also have fireplaces and/or jetted tubs. Human visitors are also treated to a breakfast in the morning that includes several hot items. In the standout Tower Suite, a multilevel unit, the bedroom is located in a tower with views of the sea.

The ★ **Forest Lodge** (Ocean Ave. at Torres St. and Mountain View Ave., 831/624-7372, www.carmelforestlodge.com, $255-375), with its trees and several terraces, feels like it's in the middle of a park. It's in a tranquil location, yet Ocean Avenue is just a few feet down the hill. The six units are in three different buildings that have seen extraordinary figures pass through, including Albert Einstein and photographer Edward Weston. The uniquely decorated units all have fridges, microwaves, and complimentary items like cream sherry.

The Forest Lodge is ideal for larger parties and families: Even the smallest unit, the Garden House, has two bedrooms.

The initial structure at ★ **La Playa Carmel** (El Camino Real at 8th Ave., 831/293-6100 or 800/582-8900, www.laplayahotel.com, $379-1,044) was a mansion built for a member of the Ghirardelli family by a renowned landscape painter in 1905. Though La Playa underwent an extensive remodel in 2012, it still has many features from an earlier era, including its wood-walled bar, a stained-glass window, and a tiled staircase. Beginning with check-in, you'll feel at home when you are handed a welcoming glass of champagne or sangria and take in the cozy lobby with its gas fireplace. Half of the 75 classic and cozy rooms look out on nearby Carmel Beach, Pebble Beach, and Point Lobos, and the beach is only two blocks away. La Playa's grounds are worthy of exploration, from the collection of newspapers in the library to the heated outdoor pool and the oversized chessboard and pieces in the courtyard. The staff will treat you to an afternoon wine reception, an evening dessert of fresh-baked cookies, and a breakfast that includes a hot item like a quiche. La Playa Carmel is easily one of the best places in town for spoiling yourself.

Coachman's Inn (San Carlos St. and 8th Ave., 831/624-6421, www.coachmansinn.com, $250-400) is a small downtown motel with 30 clean, well-appointed rooms that include large flat-screens, mini-fridges, microwaves, and Keurig coffeemakers. Some also have gas fireplaces and jetted spa tubs. A stay includes access to a gated patio that has a hot tub, sauna, and exercise bike. Breakfast and afternoon snacks and wine are provided.

L'Auberge Carmel (Monte Verde St. and 7th Ave., 831/624-8578, www.laubergecarmel.com, $325-800) is a luxurious hotel located in a former apartment building dating to the 1920s. Every one of its 20 rooms is unique, and all have radiant floor heating in the bathrooms and in-room espresso machines. The rooms are decorated in a French country style and include striking black-and-white photos of the coast by Carmel photographer Helmet Horn. A stay includes a fully prepared breakfast and valet services. This is the kind of place where the staff tries to accommodate your every request.

South of downtown Carmel-by-the-Sea, the **Tickle Pink Inn** (155 Highland Dr., 800/635-4774, www.ticklepinkinn.com, $349-729) is located in the Carmel Highlands, which is otherwise known as the gateway to Big Sur.

La Playa Carmel

The inn's cutesy name comes from the couple that used to reside in the inn: California state senator Edward Tickle and his wife Bess Tickle. All of the 35 rooms and suites have balconies (except for one, which has a bay window). Seventeen units also warm guests with in-room fireplaces. Other amenities include an outdoor hot tub, an evening wine-and-cheese reception, and an expanded continental breakfast with homemade pastries.

TRANSPORTATION AND SERVICES

As you try to read the addresses in Carmel-by-the-Sea and begin to explore the neighborhoods, you'll realize something interesting. There are no street addresses. (Some years ago, Carmel residents voted not to enact door-to-door mail delivery, thus there is no need for numeric addresses on buildings.) So, you'll need to pay close attention to the street names and the block you're on. Just to make things even more fun, street signs can be difficult to see amid the mature foliage, and a dearth of streetlights can make them nearly impossible to find at night. If you can, show up during the day to get the lay of the land before trying to navigate after dark.

Car

If you've made it to Monterey by car, getting to Carmel is a piece of cake. The quick and free way to get to Carmel from the north or the south is via Highway 1. From Highway 1, take Ocean Avenue into the middle of downtown Carmel. A more expensive but more beautiful route is via Pebble Beach's 17-Mile Drive.

Services

You'll find the Carmel Visitors Center (Carmel Plaza, second floor, Ocean Ave. between Junipero and Mission, 831/624-2522 or 800/550-4333, www.carmelchamber.org, 10am-5pm Mon.-Sat., 11am-4pm Sun.) right in the middle of downtown Carmel-by-the-Sea.

For more information about the town and current events, pick up a copy of the weekly *Carmel Pine Cone* (www.pineconearchive.com), the local newspaper. It also has a (possibly unintentionally) funny police log.

The nearest major medical center to Carmel-by-the-Sea and the Carmel Valley is in nearby Monterey: the Community Hospital of the Monterey Peninsula (23625 Holman Hwy., Monterey, 831/624-5311, 888/452-4667, www.chomp.org).

Pebble Beach

Located between Pacific Grove and Carmel, the gated community of Pebble Beach lays claim to some of the Monterey Peninsula's best and highest-priced real estate. Pebble Beach is famous for the scenic 17-Mile Drive and its collection of high-end resorts, restaurants, spas, and golf courses owned by the Pebble Beach Company, a partnership that includes golf legend Arnold Palmer and film legend Clint Eastwood. In February, Pebble Beach hosts the annual AT&T Pebble Beach National Pro-Am, a charity golf tournament that pairs professional golfers with celebrities.

SIGHTS
★ 17-Mile Drive

The best way to take in the stunning scenery of Pebble Beach is 17-Mile Drive. But don't get too excited yet—long ago, the all-powerful Pebble Beach Corporation realized that the local scenery is also a precious commodity, and began charging a toll ($10.50/vehicle); entrances are at Pacific Grove and Carmel. The good news is that when you pay the fee at the gatehouse, you receive a map of the drive that describes the parks and sights that you will pass along the winding coastal road: the much-photographed Lone Cypress, the beaches of Spanish Bay, and Pebble Beach's golf course, resort, and housing complex. If you're in a hurry, you can get from one end of the 17-Mile Drive to the other in 20 minutes. But go slowly and stop often to enjoy the natural beauty of the area (and get your money's worth). There are plenty of turnouts where you can stop to take photos of the iconic cypress trees and stunning coastline. You can picnic at many of the beaches, most of which have basic restroom facilities and ample parking lots. It's worth noting that your gate fee will be reimbursed if you spend over $35 or more in one of Pebble Beach's restaurants, which is easy to do.

RECREATION
Biking

Traveling the 17-Mile Drive by bike means you don't have to pay the $10.50 vehicle admission fee. It's also a great bike route. Cyclists can enjoy the smells and sounds of the spectacular coastline in a way that car passengers just can't. Expect fairly flat terrain with lots of twists and turns, and a ride that runs . . . about 17 miles (27 km). Foggy conditions can make this ride a bit slick in the summer, but spring and fall weather are perfect for pedaling.

Monterey's Adventures by the Sea (299 Cannery Row, 831/372-1807, www.adventuresbythesea.com, 9am-8pm daily summer, 9am-5pm daily winter, standard bike rentals $35/day, electric bike rentals $75/day) offers bike rentals for cruising 17-Mile Drive. Take it easy and rent an electric bike.

On the Carmel end, Mad Dogs & Englishmen (Corner of Ocean Ave. and Mission St., 831/250-7687, http://maddogsenglishmen.com, 9:30am-5pm Tues.-Sun., bike rentals $75-95/day) has a selection of quality bikes, including electric bicycles, for rent. Some options have infant seats or sidecars if you have a child or dog coming along for the ride.

Golf

There's no place for golfing quite like Pebble Beach. Golf has been a major pastime here since the late 19th century; today avid golfers come from around the world to tee off inside the gated community. You can play courses trodden by the likes of Tiger Woods and Jack Nicholson, pause a moment before you putt to take in the sight of the stunning Pacific Ocean, and pay $200 or more for a single round of golf.

One of the Pebble Beach Resort courses, the 18-hole, par-72 Spyglass Hill (1700 17-Mile Dr., 800/877-0597, www.pebblebeach.com, $415) gets its name from the Robert Louis Stevenson novel *Treasure Island*. Don't be fooled—the holes on this beautiful course may be named for characters in an adventure novel, but that doesn't mean they're easy. Spyglass Hill boasts some of the most challenging play in this golf course-laden region. Expect a few bogeys, and tee off from the championship level at your own (ego's) risk.

Another favorite with the Pebble Beach crowd is the famed 18-hole, par-72 Poppy Hills Golf Course (3200 Lopez Rd., 831/622-8239, www.poppyhillsgolf.com, $250). Though it's not managed by the same company, Poppy Hills shares amenities with Pebble Beach golf courses. Expect the same level of care and devotion to the maintenance of the course and your experience as a player.

The Pebble Beach Golf Links (1700 17-Mile Dr., 800/877-0597, www.pebblebeach.com, $575) has been called nothing short of the nation's best golf course by *Golf Digest*. The high ranking might have something to do with the fact that some of the fairways are perched above the Pacific Ocean. The course has hosted six men's championships and is one of three courses utilized during the popular AT&T Pro-Am.

Less pricey to play than the Pebble Beach Golf Links course, The Links at Spanish Bay (2700 17-Mile Dr., 800/877-0597, $295) course is located on some of Pebble Beach's native sand dune habitat and has the most ocean views of any Pebble Beach course. Due to the environmental sensitivity of the grounds, the course caps the number of players and spectators on the greens.

Spas

Of course, there's a spa in Pebble Beach, named **The Spa at Pebble Beach** (1518 Cypress Dr., 800/877-0597, www.pebblebeach.com, 8:30am-7:30pm daily, massages $95-425), and it's a Forbes Five-Star recipient. The spa has specialty massages for golfers before or after a day on the greens.

Kayaking and Stand-Up Paddleboarding

Pebble Beach's **Stillwater Cove** (adjacent to The Beach & Tennis Club) on the south end of 17-Mile Drive is a terrific place to kayak or stand-up paddleboard. There is a public boat launch here to get your craft in the water. Offshore is an island that blocks swells, and there is a kelp forest behind it. To the north is Pescadero Point, while Arrowhead Point is to the south. **Adventures by the Sea** (831/372-1807, www.adventuresbythesea.com, $85 pp) does guided tours of Stillwater Cove. To bring in your own kayak or SUP, you'll have to pay the Pebble Beach admission fee and then head to the coastal access ramp.

ENTERTAINMENT AND EVENTS

One of Pebble Beach's iconic experiences is watching and listening as a bagpiper performs in front of The Inn at Spanish Bay as the sun sets into the nearby Pacific Ocean. **The Bagpiper at Spanish Bay** (The Inn at Spanish Bay, 2700 17-Mile Dr., 5:45pm-6:30pm mid-Mar.-mid-Nov., 4:30pm-5:15pm mid-Nov.-mid-Mar.) begins playing on the first tee at The Links at Spanish Bay. The Lobby Lounge's outdoor terrace is a terrific vantage point. He finishes up 45 minutes later at the Spanish Bay fire pits near the second green. Watching the bagpiper is open to all guests visiting Pebble Beach and a great way to end the day.

If you dream of watching Bill Murray or Kevin Costner play golf—and who doesn't?—plan a trip to Pebble Beach in February for the **AT&T Pebble Beach National Pro-Am** (831/649-1533, www.attpbgolf.com, Feb., event prices vary). This almost week-long tournament pairing pro golfers with Hollywood celebrities is the biggest annual event in Pebble Beach and arguably the whole Monterey Peninsula.

The biggest epicurean event on the peninsula is the annual **Pebble Beach Food & Wine** (866/907-3663, www.pbfw.com, Apr., event prices vary). Hobnob with celebrity chefs from your favorite cooking shows and restaurants during four days of wine-tastings, cooking demos, and indulgent dinners.

The **Concours d'Elegance** (831/622-1700, www.pebblebeachconcours.net, Aug., event prices vary) is a showcase of upscale and rare automobiles, held on the 18th hole of the Pebble Beach Golf Links. Former *Tonight Show* host and car enthusiast Jay Leno almost always attends this annual event.

FOOD

To experience the luxury of Pebble Beach without dropping your savings on a night's stay, consider having lunch, dinner, or a drink in the exclusive community before heading back to less expensive lodging in nearby Pacific Grove or Monterey.

The Hawaiian fusion cuisine of celebrity chef Roy Yamaguchi takes center stage at **Roy's at Pebble Beach** (The Inn at Spanish Bay, 2700 17-Mile Dr., 800/877-0597, www.pebblebeach.com, 6:30am-10pm daily, $26-78). Island-inspired dishes include seafood and sushi, all with an Asian flair. Standouts include the Japanese-style butterfish, blackened rare ahi, and honey mustard beef short ribs.

Another option at The Inn at Spanish Bay is **Peppoli** (The Inn at Spanish Bay, 2700 17-Mile Dr., 800/877-0597, www.pebblebeach.com, 6pm-10pm daily, $20-100), which is intimate and upscale. Its modernized Tuscan cuisine includes a decadent lasagna stuffed with filet mignon, while the wine list is wide-ranging.

If you want to experience Pebble Beach in a low-key way, **The Tap Room** (The Lodge at Pebble Beach, 1700 17-Mile Dr., 800/877-0597, www.pebblebeach.com, 11am-midnight daily, $17-52) is your place. This wood-walled bar serves burgers, brisket, and a Kobe beef filet mignon. The prime rib chili is also worth your time. The Tap Room has 14 beers on tap at an inflated price ($10.75), yet it will all be money well spent if you end up spending the afternoon drinking with Bill Murray, an occasional customer.

Golfers may not need to know much more than that **The Bench Restaurant** (The Lodge at Pebble Beach, 1700 17-Mile Dr., 800/877-0597, www.pebblebeach.com, 11am-10pm daily, $18-31) overlooks the famed 18th hole of the Pebble Beach Golf Links. The chef employs wood-roasting and open-flame cooking techniques to create wood-fired Brussels sprouts, grilled steaks, flatbreads, and small plates. This is the Lodge at Pebble Beach's most casual restaurant, and a great place to experience Pebble Beach luxury without draining your bank account.

ACCOMMODATIONS

You need to drop some serious money to stay in Pebble Beach. Expect luxury amenities at **The Lodge at Pebble Beach** (1700 17-Mile Dr., 831/647-7500 or 800/654-9300, www.pebblebeach.com, $990-7,550), located by the 18th hole of the Pebble Beach Golf Links. A stay includes an opportunity to play the coveted course. Most rooms and suites have wood-burning fireplaces as well as private patios or balconies. Some of the high-end rooms have their own spas, while the Fairway One Cottages have a view of the first hole of the Pebble Beach Golf Links. A stay also includes access to The Beach & Tennis Club, which has a heated outdoor pool, a whirlpool spa, and a tennis pavilion.

Like The Lodge at Pebble Beach, **The Inn at Spanish Bay** (2700 17-Mile Dr., 831/647-7500 or 800/654-9300, www.pebblebeach.com, $870-4,980) has rooms with fireplaces and decks or patios. Sixty-four of the inn's rooms have sweeping views of the nearby ocean. There's also a retail arcade, fitness center, heated outdoor pool, and tennis pavilion on-site.

A favorite of the luxury crowd, **Casa Palmero** (1518 Cypress Dr., 831/647-7500 or 800/877-0597, www.pebblebeach.com, $1,150-4,000) has just 24 rooms on its Mediterranean-style estate. The units all have large soaking tubs and wood-burning fireplaces for a romantic mood. Amenities include a billiards table, a library, and an outdoor heated pool.

view from The Lodge at Pebble Beach

TRANSPORTATION

There are several gates to get into Pebble Beach, including three in Pacific Grove and one in Carmel. Admission to Pebble Beach is $10.50 if you aren't staying here. You can get the fee waived if you are going in to dine at a Pebble Beach restaurant. Just make a reservation and tell the guard at the entry gate that you have one.

Carmel Valley

When the Carmel coastline gets socked in with summer fog, locals flock inland to the reliably sunny Carmel Valley. But locals aren't the only people making their way to this corridor through the Santa Lucia Mountains. Carmel Valley is becoming known as a burgeoning but still unassuming wine region due to its tasty cabernet sauvignons, merlots, and other reds.

The landscape changes quickly as you leave the coast: You'll see the mountains rising above you, and the land is dotted with farms, ranches, and orchards. Thirteen miles (20.9 km) east of Highway 1 is the unincorporated Carmel Valley Village. This small strip of businesses hugging Carmel Valley Road includes a collection of wineries, tasting rooms, restaurants, and even an Old West saloon.

SIGHTS

Earthbound Farms

One of the largest purveyors of organic produce in the United States, Earthbound Farms began at the Earthbound Farms Farm Stand (7250 Carmel Valley Rd., 831/625-6219, www.earthboundfarm.com, 8am-5pm Mon.-Sat., 9am-5pm Sun.). This 2.5-acre (1-ha) farm and roadside stand offers visitors easy access to its smallish facility in the Carmel Valley. Drive up to the farm stand and browse a variety of organic fruits, veggies, flowers, and premade meals. The stand also features a coffee and fruit smoothie bar. Outdoors, you can ramble into the fields, checking out the river rock labyrinth and the kids' garden (yes, kids can look *and* touch).

Carmel Valley Village

The social and business center of Carmel Valley is the Carmel Valley Village, an unincorporated business district 13 miles (20.9 km) inland from the junction of Carmel Valley Road and Highway 1. This is the easiest place to go wine-tasting without doing a lot of driving, as there are six tasting rooms on the southeast side of the village just feet away from one another. There are also several fine restaurants and a classic Western tavern called the Running Iron Restaurant and Saloon.

TOP EXPERIENCE

★ Wine-Tasting

The Carmel Valley's tiny size necessarily limits the number of vineyards and wineries that can set up shop there. But this small, charming wine region makes for a perfect wine-tasting day trip from Carmel, Monterey, or even Big Sur. Small crowds, light traffic, and meaningful tasting experiences characterize this area, which still has many family-owned wineries. Some of the best wineries are clustered together. You'll get personal attention and delicious wines, all in a gorgeous green setting.

CHESEBRO WINES

Chesebro Wines (19 E. Carmel Valley Rd., Ste. D, 831/659-2125, www.chesebrowines.com, 1pm-6pm Thurs.-Fri., noon-6pm Sat.-Sun. and holidays, tasting $10) offers smart, affordable wines from Mark Chesebro, a former Bernardus Winery employee. Offerings include chardonnays, pinot noirs, Grenache rosés, and a vermentino—its signature white wine.

Carmel Valley

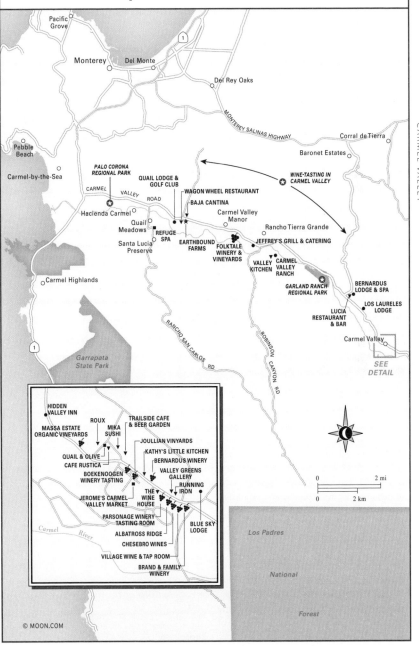

Pacific Grove
Monterey
Del Monte
Del Rey Oaks
MONTEREY SALINAS HIGHWAY
Corral de Tierra
Pebble Beach
Baronet Estates
Carmel-by-the-Sea
PALO CORONA REGIONAL PARK
QUAIL LODGE & GOLF CLUB
WAGON WHEEL RESTAURANT
BAJA CANTINA
WINE-TASTING IN CARMEL VALLEY
CARMEL VALLEY ROAD
Hacienda Carmel
Carmel Valley Manor
Quail Meadows
Rancho Tierra Grande
REFUGE SPA
Santa Lucia Preserve
EARTHBOUND FARMS
FOLKTALE WINERY & VINEYARDS
JEFFREY'S GRILL & CATERING
VALLEY KITCHEN
CARMEL VALLEY RANCH
Carmel Highlands
GARLAND RANCH REGIONAL PARK
BERNARDUS LODGE & SPA
LOS LAURELES LODGE
LUCIA RESTAURANT & BAR
RANCHO SAN CARLOS RD
ROBINSON CANYON RD
Carmel Valley
SEE DETAIL
Garrapata State Park

HIDDEN VALLEY INN
ROUX
TRAILSIDE CAFE & BEER GARDEN
MASSA ESTATE ORGANIC VINEYARDS
MIKA SUSHI
JOULLIAN VINYARDS
QUAIL & OLIVE
KATHY'S LITTLE KITCHEN
CAFE RUSTICA
BERNARDUS WINERY
BOEKENOOGEN WINERY TASTING
VALLEY GREENS GALLERY
JEROME'S CARMEL VALLEY MARKET
THE WINE HOUSE
RUNNING IRON
PARSONAGE WINERY TASTING ROOM
ALBATROSS RIDGE
BLUE SKY LODGE
CHESEBRO WINES
VILLAGE WINE & TAP ROOM
BRAND & FAMILY WINERY
Carmel River

Los Padres

National

Forest

0   2 mi
0   2 km

© MOON.COM

I. BRAND & FAMILY WINERY

I. Brand & Family Winery (19 E. Carmel Valley Rd., 831/298-7227, www.ibrandwinery. com, noon-6pm Wed.-Sun., tasting $18) is a small family operation with three labels (Le P'Tit Paysan, La Marea, I. Brand) that appeal to three different price points. Winemaker Ian Brand gravitates toward uncommon varietals with grapes sourced from small growers. He also was named 2018's Winemaker of the Year by the *San Francisco Chronicle,* quite an accomplishment due to the strong competition in the region. Enjoy his wine in the cozy, casual tasting room as vintage vinyl plays on the in-house record player.

PARSONAGE VILLAGE VINEYARD

At **Parsonage Village Vineyard** (19 E. Carmel Valley Rd., 831/659-7322, www. parsonagewine.com, 11am-5pm daily, tasting $10-20), you'll taste wonderful Syrahs, hearty cabernet sauvignons, and surprisingly deep and complex blends—the Snosrap (that's Parsons spelled backwards) table wine is inexpensive for the region and incredibly tasty. If you find a vintage you love at Parsonage, buy it then and there since it sells out of many of its wines every year. The tiny tasting room displays quilts.

ALBATROSS RIDGE

Albatross Ridge (19 E. Carmel Valley Rd., 831/293-8896, http://albatrossridge.com, noon-7pm Sun.-Mon. and Thurs., noon-8pm Fri.-Sat., tasting $18-25) grows 25 acres (10.1 ha) of chardonnay and pinot noir grapes on a steep ridge near town. Taste the fruits of the winemakers' labors in their neat, white building in Carmel Valley Village.

BERNARDUS WINERY

The **Bernardus Winery** (5 W. Carmel Valley Rd., 831/298-8021 or 800/223-2533, www. bernardus.com/winery, 11am-5pm daily, tasting $12-20) offers varietals like chardonnay, pinot noir, and sauvignon blanc that come from cool coastal vineyards, but the pride of the winery is the Bordeaux-style blended red

Marinus Vineyard wine, made from grapes grown on its vineyard estate just a couple of miles away from this tasting room. If you're interested and lucky, you might also get to sip some small-batch vintages of single-vineyard wines that are only available here.

BOEKENOOGEN VINEYARD & WINERY

Boekenoogen Vineyard & Winery (24 W. Carmel Valley Rd., 831/659-4215, www. boekenoogenwines.com, 11am-5pm daily, tasting $15-20) offers pinot noirs, chardonnays, and Syrahs at its tasting room, as well as a garden patio for those sunny Carmel Valley afternoons.

JOULLIAN VINEYARDS

Joullian Vineyards (2 Village Dr., 831/659-8100, http://joullian.com, noon-4pm Tues.-Sun. by appointment, tasting $45-100) was the first winery to make a zinfandel in Carmel Valley. Now its well-regarded wines include cabernet sauvignons, Syrahs, and chardonnays as well. It pours its wines in a unique stone building and offers an hour-long artisan tasting as well as a more in-depth executive tasting that can last up to three hours.

FOLKTALE WINERY AND VINEYARDS

Folktale Winery and Vineyards (8940 Carmel Valley Rd., 831/293-7500, www. folktalewinery.com, 11am-8pm daily, tasting $20) promises to liven up the local wine scene as "an extension of your backyard," with bocce, horseshoes, and corn hole. The winery has teamed up with local radio station KRML to put on concerts in their barrel room, with acts like Lukas Nelson, G. Love, and Fantastic Negrito.

THE WINE HOUSE

After the wineries close, **The Wine House** (1 E. Carmel Valley Rd., 831/298-7438, www.

1: Earthbound Farms **2:** I. Brand & Family Winery's tasting room

thewinehousecv.com, 2pm-9pm Thurs., 2pm-10pm Fri.-Sat., 2pm-8pm Sun.) becomes the hangout for the area's tasting room servers and any visitors who want to keep on going. Choose from a list of 50 local and European wines or from six rotating taps of craft beer. Inside is an old farmhouse feel, while the large outdoor area has fire pits, a bocce ball court, and corn hole. There's a real youthful energy here.

WINE TOURS

The **Wine Trolley** (209 Figueroa St., Monterey, 831/624-1700, www.toursmonterey.com, $119-169) picks up in downtown Monterey to take riders on five-hour tours of Carmel Valley. You'll visit 3-5 wineries with a stop for lunch at Mika Sushi or Plaza Linda. **Dream Tours By-the-Sea** (200 Clock Tower Pl., Ste. D206, 831/888-7555) does customized wine-tasting and vineyard tours of the Carmel Valley area.

RECREATION
★ Garland Ranch Regional Park

The 4,462-acre (1,806-ha) **Garland Ranch Regional Park** (700 W. Carmel Valley Rd., 831/372-3196, www.mprpd.org, sunrise-sunset daily, free) allows hikers to take in all sorts of natural ecosystems, from oak woodlands to redwood forests. With the park's elevation ranging 200-2,000 feet (61-610 m) above sea level, it is also a great place to get a workout, and boasts the best **hiking trails** in Carmel Valley. The **Lupine Loop** (1.4 mi/2.3 km round-trip, easy) is a level, dog-friendly trail that circles around a flat part of the park. On the other end of the spectrum, the **Snively's Ridge Trail-Sky Loop** (6 mi/9.7 km round-trip, difficult) involves a very steep hike up to a ridge that offers views of the ocean and mountains. The **Mesa Trail** (1.6 mi/2.6 km one-way, moderately strenuous) climbs to a saddle with valley views and a small pond.

To experience a less visited section of the park, secure a free permit to explore **Kahn Ranch,** a 1,100-acre (445-ha) addition east of the main park. A highlight here is the **Hitchcock Loop Trail** (3.6 mi/5.8 km round-trip, moderate), which travels up to mountain views and back down along a well-maintained trail. The seasonal **Fern Falls,** tucked away in a lush canyon, can be accessed via a short spur just off the Hitchcock Loop Trail. Kahn Ranch allows just 10 cars to visit a day; free passes are available on the park's website, but must be

trail in Garland Ranch Regional Park's Kahn Ranch

obtained at least two weekdays in advance of your visit.

Golf

If you want to play golf in the sun, head out to Carmel Valley. The **Quail Lodge & Golf Club** (8505 Valley Greens Dr., 831/620-8808, www.quaillodge.com, $125-185) has an 18-hole course with 10 lakes, as well as an academy to improve your game.

Spas

After an exhausting day of wine-tasting in Carmel Valley, unwind at **Refuge Spa** (27300 Rancho Carlos Rd., 831/620-7360, www.refuge.com, 10am-7pm daily, admission $52, treatments $155-292). Sprawled over 2 acres (0.8 ha) in the shadow of the Santa Lucia Mountains, this adult water park includes warm waterfalls tumbling into soaking pools and two kinds of cold plunge pools: one that is comparable to the body-shocking temperature of a mountain stream in the Sierra, and the other close to the chilling temp of the nearby Pacific Ocean. Don't miss the eucalyptus steam room, where a potent minty cloud of steam will purge all of your body's impurities.

Swimming

When summer fog takes over the Monterey Peninsula, locals head inland to the almost-always sunny Carmel Valley. For river swimming, head to **The Bucket,** a fabled swimming hole in the Carmel River. (It's nick-named the Bloody Bucket, either because visitors have cut their feet on the jagged rocks or as a reference to a tavern that once existed nearby—regardless, it's a good idea to wear footwear.)

Find the swimming hole by driving 13 miles (20.9 km) east on Carmel Valley Road from the junction of Carmel Valley Road and Highway 1. Look for a place to park after passing the Camp Stephanie road sign on Carmel Valley Road. Walk down Carmel Valley Road and look for a hole in the fence just before the Stone Pine sign. Duck through the fence and descend on the path to the Carmel River.

Off-Roading

Learn how to drive over piles of rocks and navigate steep trail ascents in a four-wheel drive vehicle at the **Land Rover Experience Driving School** (Quail Lodge & Golf Club, 8000 Valley Greens Dr., 831/620-8854, www.quaillodge.com, 9am-5pm daily, two hours $425/vehicle) at the Quail Lodge & Golf Club. The driving instructor can also teach you about winching, vehicle recovery, and expedition travel.

ENTERTAINMENT

Bars

While many of Carmel Valley's ranches are being transformed into vineyards, the **Running Iron Restaurant and Saloon** (24 E. Carmel Valley Rd., 831/659-4633, www.runningironrestaurantandsaloon.com, 11am-2am Mon.-Fri., 10am-2am Sat., 9am-2am Sun.) keeps the region's cowboy past alive. This watering hole's Old West style includes branding irons and other cowboy paraphernalia hanging from the ceiling and the walls. In addition to serving beer, wine, and liquor, the Running Iron offers an extensive food menu with seafood, burgers, steaks, and ribs.

The **Village Wine & Tap Room** (19 E. Carmel Valley Rd., 760/224-5675, 1pm-8pm daily) is where wine industry workers go to unwind. It offers wine, of course, along with 10 draft beers and four TVs playing whatever sports game is happening at the time.

Festivals and Events

Carmel Valley Village shows off its local wines and locally produced art at the daylong **Carmel Valley Art & Wine Celebration** (831/659-4000, www.carmelvalleychamber.com, June, free).

SHOPPING

Taste something besides wine at **The Quail & Olive** (14 Del Fino Pl., 831/659-4288, http://quailandolive.com, noon-5pm daily). This specialty food store allows you taste their balsamic vinegars and olive oils. Olive oils come in rosemary, basil, truffle, and bacon versions.

FOOD

Sushi

The opening of Mika Sushi (9 Del Fino Pl., www.mikasushicv.com, 11am-2:30pm and 4pm-8pm daily, $6-25) made the Carmel Valley dining scene a bit more cosmopolitan and diverse. A local favorite, the restaurant showcases high-end raw seafood and sake, with artfully presented nigiri and superb sushi rolls like a rich and tasty creation featuring snow crab, cream cheese, and avocado with baked salmon on top. Mika wins extra points for its outdoor patio, where you can dine with your dog.

American

★ Café Rustica (10 Del Fino Pl., 831/659-4444, www.caferusticacarmel.com, 11am-2:30pm and 5pm-9pm Tues.-Sun., $15-35) offers some of Carmel Valley's best food for the best value. Specialties include the nightly fish (the petrale sole is superb), Hungarian goulash, sausages, and creative pizzas. The interior has a rustic, faux-alpine vibe with stone walls, and there's an outdoor patio for the valley's frequent sunny afternoons. Note that wine is served by the bottle and quarter-liter (about one-third of a bottle) instead of by the glass.

The Lucia Restaurant & Bar (Bernardus Lodge & Spa, 415 W. Carmel Valley Rd., 831/658-3400, www.bernarduslodge.com, 7am-2:30pm and 5pm-9pm daily, $22-58, chef's tasting menu $125) is led by revered local chef Cal Stamenov. Lucia utilizes the nearby land, using herbs from the garden out front and serving wines created from the adjacent vineyard. The menu includes high-end seafood and meat options. Oenophiles should consider wine pairings, including the superb Bernardus Pisoni pinot noir and the Bernardus Ingrid's chardonnay; the knowledgeable and friendly staff can properly guide you. The dining room puts the focus on the vineyard out front, with a counter looking toward the vines and an outdoor terrace. This is a great place to get a feel for what makes Carmel Valley special.

Waking up late? The Trailside Café (3 Del Fino Pl., 831/298-7453, http://trailsidecafecv.com, 10am-8pm daily, $9-18) serves breakfast omelets, Benedicts, and beignets until 4pm. It's worth returning later in the afternoon or evening for dinner and a taste of their rotating craft beers. The seasonal beer garden hosts live music on weekends in summer.

Oozing atmosphere with its mahogany-paneled walls and stone fireplace, the Los Laureles Restaurant & Saloon (313 W. Carmel Valley Rd., 831/659-2233, http://loslaureles.com, 4pm-9pm daily, $9-22) offers classics including burgers and buffalo wings.

Mexican

Sip a wide range of tasty, intoxicating margaritas on the large wooden deck at Baja Cantina (7166 Carmel Valley Rd., 831/625-2252, www.carmelcantina.com, 11:30am-11pm Mon.-Fri., 11am-midnight Sat.-Sun., $13-20). Catch a sports game on one of the big-screen TVs and enjoy the car memorabilia covering the walls. The menu includes hearty Americanized Mexican cuisine, like rosemary chicken burritos and wild mushroom and spinach enchiladas. Even the nachos are worthwhile—they have so much baked cheese that they resemble a casserole.

For inexpensive Mexican food, visit Kathy's Little Kitchen (13 W. Carmel Valley Rd., 831/659-4601, 7am-8pm Tues.-Sat., 8:30am-3pm Sun., $5-8) for a range of dishes from asada fries to tacos. The breakfast burrito is a standout.

French

A native of France, chef Fabrice Roux brings French and Spanish cuisine to Roux (6 Pilot Rd., 831/659-5020, www.rouxcarmel.com, 11:30am-3pm and 5pm-8pm Mon. and Thurs.-Fri., 10am-3pm and 5pm-8pm Sun., $20-34). The restaurant's specialty is their paella, which is made for two.

1: Mika Sushi 2: Jerome's Carmel Valley Market

Breakfast

Carmel Valley has two fine breakfast places that are worth a drive from the coast. ★ **Jeffrey's Grill & Catering** (112 Mid Valley Center, 831/624-2029, www.jeffreysgrillandcatering.com, 8:30am-2:30pm Tues.-Sun., $7-15) serves creative breakfast plates from an inconspicuous space in a Carmel Valley strip mall. The menu includes sausages served with apple fritters and an omelet with sweet pasilla peppers countered by salty ham. The weekend specials go more outside the box, with smoked turkey hash and grilled lamb served with eggs.

A famed Carmel Valley breakfast spot is the **Wagon Wheel Restaurant** (7156 Carmel Valley Rd., 831/624-8878, 6:30am-2pm daily, $7-15). This down-home place is decorated with horseshoes, ropes, and other Western knickknacks. The menu includes hearty three-egg dishes, oatmeal pancakes, and biscuits drenched in sausage gravy.

Markets

Jerome Viel, the former chef at Carmel Valley's Will's Fargo, owns **Jerome's Carmel Valley Market** (2 Chambers Ln., 831/659-2472, http://jeromescarmelvalleymarket.com, 7am-7pm Mon.-Sat., 7am-6pm Sun.), which showcases a range of culinary delights. The spotlight here is on local items, whether it's wine, coffee, custom cuts of meat, or produce. The deli makes made-to-order sandwiches that are less than $10 and perfect for taking on a hike or picnic. On Fridays, Jerome's serves up a traditional paella to go, a local favorite.

ACCOMMODATIONS

Under $150

There's plenty of space to absorb Carmel Valley's sunshine at the ★ **Blue Sky Lodge** (10 Flight Rd., 831/659-2256, www.blueskylodge.com, $119-413), whether on your unit's private patio or sundeck or in the lodge's courtyard, which has a pool, a lawn, a multiperson hot tub, table tennis, and lots of lounge chairs. The units have thick carpeting and are a bit dated, but in a charming, retro-chic way.

Six of the rooms also have kitchens. Behind the pool is a comfy common room with a fireplace, an extensive library, a piano, a lot of houseplants, and a computer for guest use. The Blue Sky Lodge's location can't be beat—it is just a few hundred feet up from Carmel Valley Village and its many tasting rooms.

$150-250

For folks who come to Carmel Valley to taste wine, hike in the woods, and enjoy the less-expensive golf courses, **Hidden Valley Inn** (102 W. Carmel Valley Rd., 831/659-5361, www.visithiddenvalleyinn.com, $159-249) offers a perfect spot to rest and relax. The inn is ideally situated at the start of the village. Amenities include an outdoor, heated saltwater pool and an extended continental breakfast.

Hosting guests on and off since 1915, the former ranch at **Los Laureles Lodge** (313 W. Carmel Valley Rd., 831/659-2233, www.loslaureles.com, $150-300) can put you up in a guest room, a honeymoon cottage, or a three-bedroom house ($660). Enjoy the property's restaurant, saloon, and, most of all, its swimming pool and adjacent pool bar.

Golfers may opt to stay at the **Quail Lodge & Golf Club** (8205 Valley Greens Dr., 831/624-2888, $195-870), which is known for its 18-hole championship golf course. The renovated guest rooms and suites all have an outdoor patio or balcony. There's also an on-site pool and restaurant.

Over $250

To truly spread out and relax, book a stay at the 500-acre (202-ha) ★ **Carmel Valley Ranch** (1 Old Ranch Rd., 855/687-7262, www.carmelvalleyranch.com, $570-1,600). The units here are all spacious suites ranging 650-1,200 square feet (60.4-111.5 sq m) with fireplaces and decks to take in the valley views and wild turkeys trotting through the grounds. With rooms this nice you may be tempted to stay inside, but Carmel Valley Ranch has so many outdoor activities that it feels like an upscale summer camp. An activity calendar comes with your stay and includes everything from a beekeeping class to horseback riding and nightly s'mores roasting over an open fire. At **Spa Aiyana** (831/626-2586, 8:30am-7pm daily, massages $145-280), masseurs use lavender grown on-site in their treatments. The **Carmel Valley Ranch Golf Course** (831/620-6406, resort guests $165, non-guests $180) is an 18-hole course that winds into the hills. Don't miss the amazing saltwater swimming pool long enough for laps and the infinity hot tub overlooking some beautiful oak trees and the resort's vineyard.

Having first opened in the 1960s, the **Carmel Valley Lodge** (8 Ford Rd., 831/659-2261, www.valleylodge.com, $239-363) is just a one-block walk from the village, which is ideal if you are going to do some wine-tasting. The property has 12 remodeled rooms along with 19 renovated ones. For groups, the lodge rents a three-bedroom/two-bathroom cottage with a full kitchen for $610 a night. The locally owned boutique lodge's grounds include a garden, an Olympic-sized pool, a yoga pavilion, and an outdoor patio where complimentary breakfasts are served.

The **Bernardus Lodge & Spa** (415 W. Carmel Valley Rd., 831/658-3400, www.bernarduslodge.com, $325-875) has luxury guest rooms with high-end features like two-person soaking tubs, oversized patios, and limestone fireplaces. The property has other notable features, including an outdoor heated pool, two tennis courts, a croquet lawn, and a fitness room that is open 24 hours daily.

TRANSPORTATION AND SERVICES

To get to Carmel Valley, take Highway 1 to Carmel Valley Road, which is a major intersection with a stoplight. Take Carmel Valley Road east for 13 miles (20.9 km) to the Carmel Valley Village, where most of the area's restaurants and wineries are located.

Call or visit the website of the **Carmel Valley Chamber of Commerce** (831/659-4000, www.carmelvalleychamber.com) for basic information before arriving. Most services are available in nearby Carmel-by-the-Sea, but the unincorporated community of Carmel Valley has a **post office** (11 Via Contenta, 831/659-8839, www.usps.com, 9am-4:30pm Mon.-Fri.) and a **Safeway** (104 Mid Valley Center, 831/624-4600, 6am-10pm daily).

The nearest major medical center to Carmel Valley is in nearby Monterey: The **Community Hospital of Monterey** (23625 Holman Hwy, Monterey, 831/624-5311, 888/452-4667, www.chomp.org).

Salinas

Salinas Valley is one of the country's most pro-ductive agricultural regions. Its hub, Salinas, is a small city dominated by agriculture. To literature lovers, it's known as the hometown of Pulitzer Prize-winning author John Steinbeck.

Salinas is more unassuming than the nearby cities of the Monterey Peninsula and has a significant population of farmers, cowboys, field laborers, and blue-collar workers. The best way to get a feel for Salinas's small-town ambience is to spend a little time in Oldtown, where Main Street is lined with local businesses. Steinbeck fans should spend some time at the illuminating National Steinbeck Center and the Steinbeck House, where the author lived during the early part of his life.

Outside of Salinas, inland Monterey County offers many worthy

Highlights

Look for ★ to find recommended sights, activities, dining, and lodging.

★ **National Steinbeck Center:** Learn about Nobel Prize-winning author John Steinbeck and his relationship to Salinas at this multimedia museum (page 139).

★ **The Steinbeck House:** A meal here gives Steinbeck fans an intimate experience in the place where the author spent his formative years (page 140).

★ **River Road Wine Trail:** Take in stunning views of Salinas Valley as you sip fine pinot noirs and chardonnays along this unassuming wine route (page 141).

★ **Tassajara Zen Mountain Center:** Naturally occurring hot springs and a unique Zen Buddhist retreat make this remote mountain spot worth seeking out (page 147).

★ **Hiking at Pinnacles National Park:** One of the nation's youngest national parks, Pinnacles has crags, caves, and other unique features, many of which can only be reached by trails like the Juniper Canyon Loop and Moses Spring-Rim Trail Loop (page 148).

★ **San Juan Bautista:** Less than an hour northeast of Monterey, San Juan Bautista is a scenic small town that you may recognize—it's where key scenes in Alfred Hitchcock's *Vertigo* were filmed (page 152).

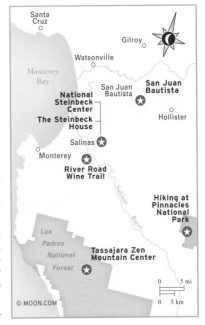

Salinas and Vicinity

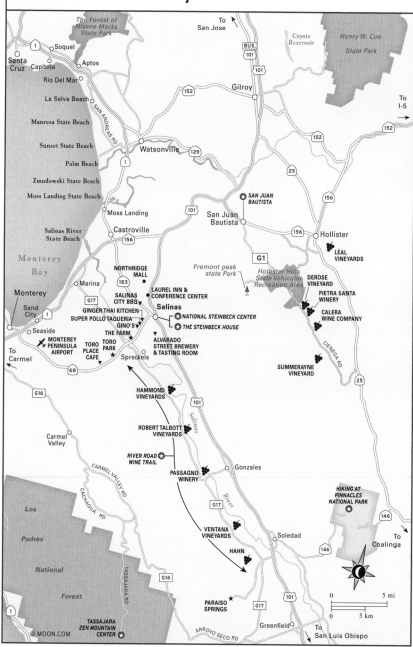

To San Jose

Coyote Reservoir

Henry W. Coe State Park

The Forest of Nisene Marks State Park

Soquel

Santa Cruz

Capitola

Aptos

Rio Del Mar

La Selva Beach

Manresa State Beach

Sunset State Beach

Palm Beach

Zmudowski State Beach

Moss Landing State Beach

Salinas River State Beach

Monterey Bay

Monterey

Sand City

Seaside

To Carmel

Gilroy

Watsonville

Moss Landing

Castroville

NORTHRIDGE MALL

Marina

SALINAS CITY BBQ

GINGER THAI KITCHEN
SUPER POLLO TAQUERIA
GINO'S
THE FARM

MONTEREY PENINSULA AIRPORT

TORO PLACE CAFE

TORO PARK

Spreckels

SAN JUAN BAUTISTA

San Juan Bautista

Hollister

LÉAL VINEYARDS

Fremont peak state Park

Hollister Hills State Vehicular Recreation Area

DEROSE VINEYARD

PIETRA SANTA WINERY

CALERA WINE COMPANY

LAUREL INN & CONFERENCE CENTER

Salinas

NATIONAL STEINBECK CENTER
THE STEINBECK HOUSE

ALVARADO STREET BREWERY & TASTING ROOM

SUMMERAYNE VINEYARD

HAMMOND VINEYARDS

Carmel Valley

ROBERT TALBOTT VINEYARDS

RIVER ROAD WINE TRAIL

PASSAGNO WINERY

Gonzales

HIKING AT PINNACLES NATIONAL PARK

To Coalinga

VENTANA VINEYARDS

HAHN

Soledad

Los Padres National Forest

PARAISO SPRINGS

TASSAJARA ZEN MOUNTAIN CENTER

Greenfield

To San Luis Obispo

To I-5

To Carmel

Salinas River

Carmel Valley Rd

Cachagua Rd

Tassajara Rd

Arroyo Seco Rd

© MOON.COM

0   5 mi

0   5 km

attractions and unique experiences that are spread throughout the region's hotter, drier interior. On the eastern side of Salinas Valley is Pinnacles National Park, which has caves and jagged rock formations perfect for hikers and climbers alike. The western side of the valley is lined with some of the county's best vineyards and tasting rooms, especially along the River Road Wine Trail. You can also climb the 5,856-foot (1,785-m) Junípero Serra Peak, or reflect in an Eastern-inspired setting at the Tassajara Zen Mountain Center.

Just north of the county line, the historic town of San Juan Bautista may look familiar to film fans: The historic downtown and mission were the setting of many pivotal scenes in Alfred Hitchcock's masterpiece *Vertigo*. Nearby, 3,169-foot (966-m) Fremont Peak in Fremont Peak State Park offers one of the area's best views of the Monterey Bay as well as some of the Central Coast's finest stargazing.

Be aware that Salinas and inland Monterey are almost always hotter than the Pacific Ocean-cooled peninsula. Bring lots of water and plenty of sunscreen.

PLANNING YOUR TIME

Salinas is Monterey County's largest city and a popular attraction for fans of writer John Steinbeck. The best place to visit in Salinas is its Oldtown area, where the National Steinbeck Center is located. There are chain hotels in Salinas, but you can find better (albeit more expensive) lodging on the Monterey Peninsula.

Inland Monterey is pretty spread out, so it doesn't make sense to try and get to everything in a couple of days. Instead, focus on which area sounds the most interesting. The Eastern Los Padres is a great place for outdoor enthusiasts. Fort Hunter Liggett is for those that treasure out-of-the-way places. A superb day can be made by hiking in Pinnacles National Park and then visiting the tasting rooms of the River Road Wine Trail while heading back to Monterey or Salinas. San Juan Bautista is in neighboring San Benito County, and is worth an afternoon of exploration for people interested in early California history. Gilroy makes a fine stopping point on trips between Monterey and the Bay Area.

SALINAS
SALINAS

Salinas

Salinas is the major city of the Salinas River Valley, a fertile agricultural region dubbed the "Salad Bowl of the World." The Monterey County seat's other claim to fame is as the hometown of Nobel Prize-winning author John Steinbeck, which explains why the local library, an elementary school, and a produce company are named after him. The Oldtown Salinas area situated around Main Street has the city's best restaurants, shops, and the National Steinbeck Center.

It's best to confine your visit to Oldtown Salinas due to crime in other parts of the city. Avoid East Salinas, where a lot of the city's gang violence occurs.

SIGHTS

Main Street is the main thoroughfare of **Oldtown Salinas** and the best section of town to visit. Lined with local shops, restaurants, and historic buildings, Main Street feels like it has been the same for decades (probably why the 2001 film *Bandits*, starring Bruce Willis, Billy Bob Thornton, and Cate Blanchett, filmed scenes here). The National Steinbeck Center is located at the north end of the one-way street.

★ National Steinbeck Center

The **National Steinbeck Center** (1 Main St., 831/796-3833, www.steinbeck.org,

---

Previous: Main Street in Oldtown Salinas; The Steinbeck House; Pinnacles National Monument.

Oldtown Salinas

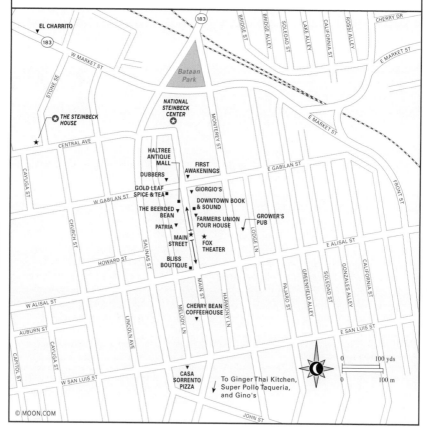

10am-5pm daily, adults $15, seniors and students $12, children 6-17 $7, children 5 and under free) utilizes multimedia displays that employ sight, sound, and even touch to tell the story of Salinas's most popular son, famed writer John Steinbeck. The permanent exhibit includes lengthy book passages, photos, footage from film adaptations, and sets mocked up to resemble scenes from the author's novels, lending insight into the life of the author of the classics *The Grapes of Wrath*, *East of Eden*, *Cannery Row*, and *Of Mice and Men*. Much of the museum showcases Steinbeck's relationship with Salinas and the surrounding region. A highlight is

the camper that Steinbeck used to journey across America and write the 1962 travelogue *Travels with Charley*.

★ The Steinbeck House

A yellow Victorian in downtown Salinas, **The Steinbeck House** (132 Central Ave., 831/424-2735, http://steinbeckhouse.com, 11:30am-2pm Tues.-Sat., $12-14) is where John Steinbeck was born and spent his early years. There is no museum here, but rather a restaurant that serves lunch in the parlor, living room, middle bedroom, and guest bedroom of Steinbeck's former home. The Victorian-style interior is still decorated with Steinbeck family photos. The entrées change weekly, but the sandwiches stay the same—including the decadently gooey brie, apple, and chicken. In the cellar-level gift shop, *The Steinbeck House Cookbook* is sold alongside early edition novels by the famed author and unexpected items like Steinbeck whiskey glasses. Tours ($10 pp) of the house are given during summer on Sundays between 11am and 1pm. There are no set times for the tours, and they last 30-45 minutes.

★ River Road Wine Trail

Just 10 miles (16.1 km) south of Salinas, the River Road Wine Trail (http://riverroadwinetrail.com) runs about 40 miles (64 km) down to Soledad, comprising a collection of seven wineries in the Santa Lucia Highlands, a region known for its chardonnays and pinot noirs. The drive along River Road and Foothill Road makes for a scenic back-road excursion, and the tasting rooms rarely get too crowded, meaning the employees will have more time to interact and answer your questions. Allot about half a day to explore the wine trail—it's a perfect afternoon adventure.

Pessagno Winery (1645 River Rd., 831/675-9463, http://pessagnowines.com, noon-5pm Mon.-Fri., 11am-5pm Sat.-Sun., tasting $15) touts itself as the source for "exclusive luxury wines." Its 5,900-acre (2,388-ha) vineyard in the nearby Santa Lucia Highlands is known for its pinot noir and chardonnay grapes. The team behind Pessagno also runs the Puma Road Winery (32720 River Rd., 831/675-3548, http://pumaroad.com, noon-5pm Thurs.-Mon., tasting $15) on the River Road Wine Trail. It also has an outpost in downtown Monterey, Puma Road on the Plaza.

At the southern end of the trail outside Soledad, the spacious Hahn Winery Tasting Room (37700 Foothill Dr., 831/678-4555, www.hahnwinery.com, 11am-5pm daily, tasting $20) is known for its superb outdoor deck and emphasis on wines not readily available in the marketplace. As at other River Road wineries, the chardonnays and pinot noir are the focus. Sip your wine at the long bar or on the deck for stellar views of the Salinas Valley and the Gabilan Mountains, or opt for an ATV Adventure Tour (1.5 hours, $45), which includes a trip to the vineyard's highest point, a stop at the wine cellar, and a tasting in the winery's VIP room.

The Steinbeck House

RECREATION
Parks

Toro Park (501 Monterey-Salinas Hwy. 68, 831/755-4895, www.co.monterey.ca.us, 8am-dusk daily, $8-10/vehicle, $2/pedestrian) is a great place to recreate just 6 miles (9.7 km) from downtown Salinas. The 4,756-acre (1,925-ha) park has hiking, biking, and horseback-riding trails, softball fields, volleyball courts, and horseshoe pits. Take a steep, challenging hike on the **Ollason Peak Loop** (9 mi/14.5 km round-trip, strenuous, 1,650-ft/503-m elevation gain), which climbs to the 1,800-foot (549-m) summit of Ollason Peak. This is a great place to visit in the spring, when the hills are covered in wildflowers. The 2020 River Fire burned a great deal of the park, so check on conditions before arrival.

ENTERTAINMENT
Nightlife

Oldtown Salinas has a sports bar in **Dubber's** (172 Main St., 831/676-0256, www.dubbersbarandgrill.com, 11am-midnight daily). The walls are decorated with sports gear and flat-screen TVs for taking in your favorite team's game. Watch all the action while sipping one of the eight beers on tap. The bar also serves pub grub like fish-and-chips, burgers, and hot dogs.

Farmers Union Pour House (217 Main St., 831/975-4890, 3pm-9pm Tues.-Thurs., 3pm-11pm Fri.-Sat.) has a rotating menu of craft beer and wine on tap. The comfortable, brick-walled establishment has unique features, including historical clocks and a green wall of hanging beer bottles.

An indication of Alvarado Street Brewery's tasty takeover of Monterey County is its Salinas-based **Alvarado Street Brewery & Tasting Room** (1315 Dayton St., Ste. E, 831/800-3332, http://asb.beer, 3pm-8pm Tues.-Fri., 1pm-8pm Sat.-Sun.). At this informal facility, beer fans can drink while surrounded by brewing equipment, as well as buy growlers, cans, and bottles to go. Alvarado Street Brewery also plans to open a restaurant and bar in Oldtown Salinas at 301 Main Street in 2022.

Cinema

One of Oldtown Salinas's draws is **Maya Cinemas** (153 Main St., 831/757-6292, www.mayacinemas.com), the first of a small, mostly California-based movie theater chain that caters to Latinx communities. Its screens first-run movies along with movies in Spanish.

Dubber's in Oldtown Salinas

Festivals and Events

The **California Rodeo Salinas** (Salinas Sports Complex, 1034 N. Main St., 831/775-3100 or 800/549-4989, www.carodeo.com, July) is one of the city's biggest events and the largest professional rodeo in California. For four days, more than 700 cowboys and cowgirls come to Salinas to compete in bull-riding events. There's also live music, parties, and mutton busting, where children (ages 4-7, under 60 lb/27.2 kg, $25) take part in a sheep-riding competition.

Salinas honors its most famous export every even year with the **Steinbeck Festival** (National Steinbeck Center, 1 Main St., 831/775-4721, www.steinbeck.org, Aug.). The weekend-long celebration of the author's life includes talks, tours, parties, and panel discussions.

Every fall, the sky above Salinas fills with aerobatic planes and skydivers for the annual **California International Airshow** (Salinas Municipal Airport, 30 Mortensen Ave., 844/647-7469, www.salinasairshow.com, Sept.). Come see legendary flight demonstration teams like the U.S. Navy Blue Angels and the U.S. Air Force Thunderbirds soar through the air. All proceeds from this two-day event benefit local charities.

SHOPPING
Oldtown Salinas

Oldtown Salinas (831/205-0795, http://oldtownsalinas.com), based around Main Street, is a pleasant place to shop, with easy parking and restaurants scattered throughout. The **Halltree Antique Mall** (202 Main St., 831/757-6918, www.halltreeantiquemall.com, 10am-5:30pm Mon.-Fri., 10:30am-5pm Sat.-Sun.), in a large building that was a gentleman's club and then a bank, has 22 antiques vendors. There's a little of everything sold here, from coins and jewelry to furniture and kitchenware.

Thankfully, Steinbeck's hometown has a great bookstore in **Downtown Book & Sound** (222 Main St., 831/477-6700, www.downtownbookandsound.com, 10am-9pm daily). The 2,500-square-foot (232-sq-m) space has row upon row of books, including a nice local interest section and many books by local authors. The store holds numerous book events.

Head to **Gold Leaf Spice & Teas** (8 1/2 Gabilan St., 831/753-7700, www.goldleafspiceandteas.com, 10am-5pm Tues.-Fri., 9am-3pm Sat.) to taste teas, olive oils, and balsamic vinegars. This one-room shop/tea lounge has a multitude of canisters of tea and "sniffer jars" to take in the many spices for sale. Their most popular item is matcha, a powdered green tea.

For women's contemporary clothing, try **Bliss Boutique** (266 Main St., 831/757-4055, http://bebeautifulinbliss.com, 11am-5:30pm Mon.-Fri., 10am-5pm Sat.).

FOOD
Barbeque

You can smell the smoked, mouthwatering scents at ★ **Salinas City Barbeque** (700 W. Market St., 831/758-2227, www.salinascitybbq.com, 11am-9pm Mon.-Sat., 11am-8pm Sun., $9-30) from a block away. Inside the homey restaurant, you'll find different regional takes on barbeque, including St. Louis-style pork ribs, North Carolina-inspired pulled pork with vinegar molasses, and Central Coast tri-tip (the tri-tip is the way to go, especially when paired with homemade barbeque sauce). They also serve a rotating menu of eight craft beers on tap and glasses of sweat tea, which officially validates them as a real-deal barbeque joint.

Mexican

The family behind ★ **El Charrito** (122 W. Market St., 831/424-9446, www.elcharrito.com, 6am-5:30pm Mon.-Sat., 7am-5pm Sun., $3-8) ran a small market for 35 years before realizing that their greatest asset was the Mexican food made from their family recipes and their truly superb homemade flour tortillas. Following this epiphany, they pulled out their shelves and replaced them with a long counter, where staff dish out delicious

burritos, tortas, and bowls. Their burritos may be smaller than others, but what they lack in size, they make up for in taste. They wrap everything from carne asada to chile relleno to *chicharrón* (pork rind) in the stellar tortillas. Wash it all down with a refreshing agua fresca.

Super Pollo Taqueria (1237 S. Main St., 831/424-4930, 8am-7pm Mon.-Fri., 8am-4pm Sat., $5-17) is an unassuming eatery short on ambience, but its food is widely loved. It's known for its burritos, including breakfast, carne asada, carnitas, and chicken versions.

Thai

At **Ginger Thai Kitchen** (1104 S. Main St., 831/422-8424, http://gingerthaikitchen.com, 11am-2:30pm and 4:30pm-8:30pm Tues.-Fri., noon-8pm Sat.-Sun., $9-17), expect tasty Thai classics, including curries, noodle dishes, and rice plates. There are options for vegetarians like soy vegetarian duck. Cool off from the spicy dishes with beer or a California wine.

Italian

Founded in 1975 by an Italian immigrant, ★ **Gino's** (1410 S. Main St., 831/422-1814, www.ginosfamilyrestaurantgroup.com, 4:30pm-10pm Mon., 11am-3pm and 4:30pm-9pm Tues.-Thurs., 11am-3pm and 4:30pm-10pm Fri., 4:30pm-10pm Sat., $12-40) is a Salinas institution, set in a multi-room building with a patio. This family-friendly restaurant is where locals come for special occasions. The food here is hearty home-style Italian, like pasta, pizza, chicken Parmesan, and abalone-style calamari piccata. The appetizer meatballs braised in a spicy tomato garlic sauce are a good place to start.

European

Patria (228 Main St., 831/424-5555, 11:30am-2pm and 3pm-close daily, $10-38) is not the kind of restaurant you might expect in unassuming Salinas. The interior has a rustic

European feel due to its artwork, exposed wooden beams, and antler chandelier hanging in the foyer. The kitchen is run by a German chef, who offers items like spaetzle and jaeger schnitzel on the dinner menu. Patria also has a serious Italian influence exemplified by its house-made pastas and pizzas. Try the caramelized onion and thyme pizza with loads of smoked bacon, goat cheese, and a bacon béchamel sauce.

Steakhouse

Grower's Pub (227 Monterey St., 831/754-1488, www.growerspub.com, 11am-3pm and 4pm-8pm daily, $19-42) is on the fancier side of Salinas's dining options, and one of the priciest restaurants in town. This white-tablecloth place is a throwback to another era, from its 1940s bar to its popular slow-roasted prime rib. Check out the historic photos of Salinas decorating the walls.

Breakfast and Brunch

There is no better place to start a day in Salinas than at ★ **First Awakenings** (171 Main St., 831/784-1125, www.firstawakenings.net, 7am-2pm daily, $9-12). Menu options include a carnitas scramble, frittatas, eggs Benedict, and huevos rancheros. It also has a Pacific Grove location (125 Oceanview Blvd., 831/372-1125, 7am-2pm Mon.-Fri., 7am-2:30pm Sat.-Sun.).

On Highway 68, you'll find an old-school breakfast and lunch spot at the **Toro Place Café** (Monterey-Salinas Hwy. 68, 831/484-1333, 6:30am-2:30pm Mon.-Sat., 7:30am-1:30pm Sun., $6-15). This back-roads joint serves breakfast (egg scrambles, rib eye and eggs, etc.) and a burger-heavy lunch menu. The diner is featured in the Netflix series *Ratched*. It's 7 miles (11.3 km) southwest of Salinas.

Coffee Shops

Oldtown Salinas has a couple of coffee shops. **The Beerded Bean** (210 Main St., 831/202-0966, www.thebeerdedbean.com, 6am-9pm Mon.-Wed., 6am-11pm Thurs.-Sat., 6am-3pm Sun.) serves both coffee drinks and

1: Downtown Book & Sound **2:** Salinas City Barbeque **3:** burrito at El Charrito **4:** the throwback sign at Grower's Pub

craft beer. Popular coffee drinks include a Mexican mocha and a dulce latte. The six beers on tap feature local and regional breweries. The Beerded Bean also hosts live music. **Cherry Bean Coffeehouse** (332 Main St., 831/424-1989, www.cherrybeancoffeehouse. com, 5:30am-7pm Mon.-Fri., 6:30am-6pm Sat.-Sun.) roasts its own beans and attracts a more alternative crowd. Its walls are decorated with the works of local artists.

Farmers Markets

Salinas is known for its agriculture, so it comes as no surprise that the city hosts five farmers markets each week in peak season. The single year-round market is the **Downtown Salinas Saturday Farmers Market** (Gabilan St. between Main St. and Salinas St., www.wcfma. org, 9am-2pm Sat.). The seasonal markets are the **Alisal Farmers Market** (632 E. Alisal St., www.everyonesharvest.org, 11am-4pm Tues. June-Sept.), the **Natividad Farmers Market** (1441 Constitution Blvd., 831/384-6961, www.everyonesharvest.org, 11am-3:30pm Wed. May-Oct.), and the **Salinas Valley Memorial Market** (Salinas Valley Memorial Hospital, 450 E. Romie Lane, 2pm-5:30pm Fri. May-Oct., 12:30pm-4:30pm Nov.).

ACCOMMODATIONS

Salinas has a range of moderately priced lodging options. Locally owned **Laurel Inn & Conference Center** (801 W. Laurel Dr., 831/449-2474, www.laurelinnsalinas.com,

$129-149) is near US 101 and is a five-minute drive to Oldtown Salinas. Amenities include a complimentary hot breakfast, a heated pool, and the adjacent Black Bear Diner.

TRANSPORTATION AND SERVICES

Salinas is 20 miles (32 km) from Monterey; the drive takes about 30 minutes if CA-68 is not backed up. It is not a good idea to drive from Monterey to Salinas around 5pm, when two-lane CA-68 gets crowded with commuters. From Monterey, take CA-1 north, then merge right onto CA-68 and head east. The highway becomes South Main Street as it enters Salinas.

For information on Salinas, stop into Oldtown's **Salinas 411** (222 Main St., 831/435-4636, www.salinas411.org, 11am-8pm daily). Their website has information about restaurants, lodging, and attractions, along with a Salinas-centric smartphone app. Salinas has three **post offices:** at 100 West Alisal Street (831/758-1204, www.usps.com, 8:30am-5pm Mon.-Fri.), 303 North Sanborn Road (831/757-7704, 9am-4:30pm Mon.-Fri.), and 1011 Post Drive (831/770-7124, 8:30am-5pm Mon.-Fri., 10am-4pm Sat.).

Salinas has two hospitals: **Salinas Valley Memorial Hospital** (450 E. Romie Lane, 831/757-4333, www.svmh.com) and **Natividad Medical Center** (1141 Constitution Blvd., 831/755-4111, www. natividad.com).

Inland Monterey County

At 1.5 times the size of the state of Delaware, Monterey County is a big place. While the Monterey Peninsula and the Big Sur coast get most of the area's visitors, the inland portion of the county and its neighboring region boast a burgeoning wine country, an uncrowded national park, and a few out-of-the-way gems worth seeing.

EASTERN LOS PADRES NATIONAL FOREST

The western side of Los Padres National Forest is in Big Sur, and thus receives many visitors. The eastern portion of Los Padres has worthwhile destinations with fewer people. Compared to the coast, it's hotter and drier here during summer, so bring ample water.

Los Padres Reservoir

The Los Padres Dam on the Carmel River is responsible for the **Los Padres Reservoir.** The area is worthwhile for hikers and backpackers who want to experience the Carmel River Valley. A good day hike is the **Carmel River Trail to Danish Creek** (5.6 mi/9 km round-trip, moderate, 300-ft/91.4-m elevation gain), which meanders along the western edge of the Los Padres Reservoir before reaching Danish Creek.

GETTING THERE

Los Padres Reservoir is about an hour drive from Monterey. Head south out of Monterey on CA-1 and turn left on Carmel Valley Road. Turn right on Tassajara Road, and then take another right on Cachagua Road. Finally, take a left on Nason Road and follow it almost 2 miles (3.2 km) to the reservoir.

The drive from Salinas is also about an hour. Head south on South Main Street and stay on it as it becomes CA-68. Continue east, then turn left on Laureles Canyon Road, which takes you over the mountain. Turn left on Carmel Valley Road, then turn right on Tassajara Road. Take another right on Cachagua Road. Finally, take a left on Nason Road and follow it to the reservoir.

★ Tassajara Zen Mountain Center

Tucked on the eastern edge of Los Padres National Forest, **Tassajara Zen Mountain Center** (39171 Tassajara Rd., 888/743-9362, www.sfzc.org, 9am-9pm daily late Apr.-mid-Sept., day use adults $35, children $12) is known for its naturally occurring hot springs and is where Buddhist scholars study in a monastic setting. Run by the San Francisco Zen Center, Tassajara is closed to the public from late September to early April so that students can study, meditate, and work in peace. During the summer, the grounds are open for daily and overnight visits.

The primary attractions here are the Japanese-style **bathhouses** that offer access to the hot springs. (During daytime hours,

men and women must use separate bathhouse facilities.) Day guests are also welcome to hike the grounds and dip into the outdoor pool. There are also shared **dorm rooms** and **private cabins** ($125-446) available for those who want to spend the night in this tranquil setting. A stay includes three vegetarian meals a day.

GETTING THERE

The Tassajara Zen Mountain Center is more than an hour's drive from Monterey. Head south out of Monterey on CA-1 and turn left on Carmel Valley Road, which you continue on for about 20 miles (32 km). Then turn right on Tassajara Road and stay on it for just over a mile before taking a slight left. The last 4 miles (6.4 km) are unpaved and steep.

From Salinas, head south on South Main Street and stay on it as it becomes CA-68. From CA-68, turn left on Laureles Canyon Road. On the other side of the mountain, turn left on Carmel Valley Road. Turn right on Tassajara Road and stay on it for about a mile before taking a slight left.

The center is reached by driving a windy, mountainous, unpaved road for 14 miles (22.5 km). The road is not navigable to vehicles with automatic transmissions and low clearance. First-time overnight guests are advised to secure a seat in the seven-person **passenger van** (10:30am and 1:15pm daily, based on demand, $63/round-trip pp) that leaves from Jamesburg, which is about 15 miles (24 km) south of Carmel Valley.

Arroyo Seco Recreation Area and Campground

When it gets hot out, people come in droves to the **Arroyo Seco Recreation Area** (47600 Arroyo Seco Rd., 831/385-5434, www.fs.usda.gov, day use 8am-7pm summer, 9am-4pm winter, $10/vehicle) for the deep, cold pools of the Arroyo Seco River. There are swimming holes right upon entering the area, but a better option is to hike 1 mile (1.6 km) up Indian Mary Road (closed to vehicular traffic) to reach the **Arroyo Seco Gorge.** The deep pool of this stunning gorge is surrounded by rocky cliffs.

Spend the night at one of the 50 RV or tent sites at **Arroyo Seco Campground** (877/444-6777, www.recreation.gov, $25-125) if you want multiple swimming days. Some sites can be reserved in advance, while others are first-come, first-served. The campground can accommodate RVs, but there are no hook-ups. Developed sites have access to showers and flush toilets, while the primitive sites have just vault toilets.

This is a popular spot for day trips. On summer weekends the day-use parking areas are known to quickly fill.

GETTING THERE

The trip to Arroyo Seco takes a good 1.5 hours to reach from Monterey. Take CA-1 out of the coastal city before heading east on CA-68. Exit at Speckels Boulevard and follow the roadway until it turns into Harris Street. Turn right on Abbott Street and continue to US-101 South. After about 20 miles (32 km), exit at Arroyo Seco Road. Take Arroyo Seco Road for another 20 miles (32 km).

Arroyo Seco is just an hour from Salinas. Drive south on US-101 for almost 30 miles (48 km) and exit at Arroyo Seco Road. Take Arroyo Seco Road for about 20 miles (32 km).

TOP EXPERIENCE

PINNACLES NATIONAL PARK

Pinnacles National Park (5000 Hwy. 146, 831/389-4427 ext. 4487, www.nps.gov/pinn, west entrance 7:30am-8pm daily, east entrance 24 hours daily, $30/vehicle, $25/motorcycle, $15/person on foot or bicycle) is made up of naturally occurring castles of rock spires, towers, walls, canyons, and caves that rise up above the Gabilan Mountains on the east side of Salinas Valley. A natural wonder created by volcanic activity, Pinnacles had been a national monument since 1908, until it was elevated to national park status in 2013. This stunning 26,000-acre (10,522-ha) park

has more than 30 miles (48 km) of hiking trails along with rock faces that are popular with climbers and some of the world's largest talus caves, which are created when boulders become lodged in narrow canyons. Pinnacles is home to wildlife like California condors, Townsend's big-eared bats, California red-legged frogs, 100 species of wildflowers, and 400 bee species.

Pinnacles National Park can be accessed on both its western and eastern sides via Highway 146, though the highway does not traverse the park. The eastern side receives much more visitation. The parks sees the most visitors during spring; in March and April, there may be lines of cars on the east side on weekends and holidays. Most people arrive 10am-2pm, so avoid this time of day if possible.

For visitors coming from Monterey or Salinas, the west side of the park is about 15 minutes closer. The western side has the shortest trails to the Balconies Caves and the High Peaks area, while the eastern side is the best place to access Bear Gulch Cave and the Bear Gulch Reservoir. For information on the west side of the park, visit the **West Pinnacles Visitor Contact Station** (831/389-4427 ext. 4487, 9am-4:30pm Thurs.-Mon.). The eastern side of the park has even more infrastructure, including the **Bear Gulch Nature Center** (10am-4pm daily), **Campground Store** (831/200-1722, 9:30am-5pm daily), and **Pinnacles Park Store** (831/389-4485, 9am-4pm Thurs.-Mon.), where books, souvenirs, water, and flashlights are sold. The eastern side of the park also offers ranger-led programs on weekends; check the park's website and social media sites for upcoming events.

★ Hiking

Pinnacles has more than 30 miles (48 km) of hiking trails that traverse the park. They are the only way to reach unique features like the High Peaks, the Balconies Caves, and Bear Gulch Reservoir.

1: fantastic rock formations at Pinnacles National Park **2:** a hiker climbing a rock staircase in Pinnacles National Park

One of the best ways to experience the geology of Pinnacles is to do the west side's **Juniper Canyon Loop** (Chaparral Trailhead, 4.3 mi/6.9 km round-trip, strenuous, 1,215-ft/370-m elevation gain). Begin on the Juniper Canyon Trail and climb 2,605-foot (794-m) Scout Peak, where you may spot a condor soaring overhead. Then the hike gets exciting as you traverse a steep and narrow section of the High Peaks Trail. This 0.7-mile (1.1-km) portion climbs across the rock-strewn ridgeline via steps carved into the rock, with handrails for support. It's almost like a beginner's version of Yosemite's famed Half Dome hike. Another worthwhile hike from the west side is the **Balconies Cliffs-Balconies Cave Loop** (Chaparral Trailhead, 2.4 mi/3.9 km round-trip, easy to moderate, 100-ft/30.5-m elevation gain). The highlight here is an 0.4-mile (0.6-km) section that passes through the talus caves. Bring a flashlight!

From the east side, hikers are closer to two standout features of the park: **Bear Gulch Cave** and **Bear Gulch Reservoir.** The **Moses Spring-Rim Trail Loop** (Bear Gulch Day Use Area, 2.2 mi/3.5 km round-trip, moderate, 500-ft/152-m elevation gain) takes in both Bear Gulch Cave—a cavern with a lush feel thanks to a stream running through it—and Bear Gulch Reservoir, which was built by the Civilian Conservation Corps. The hike includes a short tunnel, a large rock overhang, and a few sets of steep stairs cut into the rock. Hikers on the east side can reach the Balconies Caves via the **Old Pinnacles Trail** (Old Pinnacles Trailhead, 5.3 mi/8.5 km round-trip, moderate, no elevation gain). A more intense hike from this end of the park is the **Condor Gulch-High Peaks Loop** (Bear Gulch Day Use Area, 5.3 mi/8.5 km round-trip, strenuous, 1,300-ft/396-m elevation gain).

Camping

Visitors to Pinnacles can pitch a tent at the **Pinnacles Campground** (2400 CA-146, Pacines, information 831/200-1722, reservations 877/444-6777, www.recreation.gov, $35 tent site, $45 RV site), accessible only from the park's east side. The sites have picnic tables and fire rings, and some RV sites have electrical hookups. Tent cabins ($129) are also available, but you'll still need to bring your own bedding.

Getting There

The drive from Monterey to Pinnacles National Park's west side takes just over an hour. Take CA-68 east out of the Monterey Peninsula and exit at Spreckels Boulevard. Spreckels Boulevard turns into Harris Road. Take a right onto Abbott Street and then go south on US-101. Exit in Soledad and take CA-146 east for 10 windy miles (16.1 km) until you reach the park.

The park's west side is 45 minutes from downtown Salinas. Simply take US-101 south to Soledad. Then head east on CA-146 until you reach the park.

The drive from Monterey to the park's eastern side is longer and more involved. Expect it to take an hour and a half. Take CA-1 north before hopping east onto CA-156, then go north on US-101. Take Highway 156 east until Hollister. Then turn right on San Juan Road, which becomes 4th Street. Turn right onto San Benito Street and then left on Nash Road, which becomes Tres Pinos Road. From there, take a right on CA-25 until it reaches CA-146, then head into the park.

The park's east side is just over an hour drive from Salinas. Take US-101 north from Salinas and get off at the San Juan Bautista/Hollister exit (Highway 156 East). Follow CA-156 east until you reach Hollister. Then turn right on San Juan Road, which becomes 4th Street. Turn right onto San Benito Street and then left on Nash Road, which becomes Tres Pinos Road. From there, take a right on CA-25 until reaching CA-146, then head into the park.

FORT HUNTER LIGGETT AREA

Fort Hunter Liggett is a 165,000-acre (66,773-ha) U.S. Army Reserve training facility located in a scenic oak-dotted valley. Although much of the region is closed to the public, there are a few worthy, off-the-beaten-track sites, including a former William Randolph Hearst ranch house-turned-hotel and Monterey County's tallest peak. All visitors to Fort Hunter Liggett must have a valid driver's license, vehicle registration, and proof of insurance to pass through the base.

Hearst Hacienda Lodge

The **Hearst Hacienda Lodge** (10 Infantry Rd., 831/386-2900, http://hunterliggett. armymwr.com/programs/historic-hacienda, $50-200) is a historic gem of southern Monterey County. The Mission Revival-style complex with its unique dome tower was designed by Hearst Castle architect Julia Morgan for William Randolph Hearst. The newspaper magnate used the lodge as a ranch headquarters for his employees and a place to entertain guests, including Spencer Tracy, Clark Gable, and Errol Flynn. The lodge is now in the National Register of Historic Places. Overnight options range from Cowboy Rooms with shared bathrooms to suites with two bedrooms and a fully equipped kitchen. Each room comes with breakfast foods stored in the fridge so that you won't have to leave the base for your first meal. The **Hearst Hacienda Lounge** (call 831/386-2171 or 831/386-3068 for hours) is the place to grab a beer or cocktail in the complex.

Mission San Antonio de Padua

The third mission founded by Junípero Serra in 1771, **Mission San Antonio de Padua** (end of Mission Rd., 831/385-4478, www. missionsanantonio.net, 10am-4pm daily, adults $5, children under 12 $3) is a quiet place that hasn't changed much since California's early days; it's quite stunning in how far away it feels from the rest of the world. It's the primary attraction in the Fort Hunter Liggett

area, along with the Hearst Hacienda Lodge, which was designed to reflect the mission's architecture. The mission once had a water-powered gristmill, a tannery, and a lumber storage facility. The site retains its chapel and adjacent courtyard, along with a Salinan Indian cemetery and a museum showcasing artifacts from the mission era and early California times.

Junípero Serra Peak

At 5,857 feet (1,785 m), **Junípero Serra Peak** is the tallest peak in Monterey County and the Santa Lucia Mountain Range. The **Santa Lucia Trail** (12 mi/19.3 km round-trip, difficult) offers a way to reach the top with a steep, switchbacked 3,724-foot (1,135-m) climb. The summit is home to a dilapidated tower and several places where you can get fine views of the region. Snow frequently blankets the mountain in winter. To reach the trailhead from Fort Hunter Liggett, take a left on Del Venturi Road, which becomes Milpitas Road. Follow it until you enter Los Padres National Forest. Continue until you see the trailhead and small parking area.

Santa Lucia Memorial Park and The Indians

Located within the nearby Los Padres National Forest, **The Indians** are sandstone rock formations prime for exploring and climbing. Past the noticeable terrain is **Santa Lucia Memorial Park** (877/444-6777, www. recration.gov, $20), with eight campsites in the oak and pine trees. One of the eight sites is a first-come, first-served option while the rest can be reserved in advance. To reach the area, from Mission Road turn onto Del Venturi Road and travel 18 miles (29 km) to the campground.

Getting There

It is an hour and 40-minute drive from Monterey to the Fort Hunter Liggett area. Take CA-1 out of the coastal city for 0.5 mile (0.8 km) before hopping on CA-68 East for 7.5 miles (12.1 km). Exit at Spreckels Boulevard and follow that road 1.6 miles (2.6 km) until it turns into Harris Street. Continue on Harris 2 miles (3.2 km), then turn right on Abbott Street and go 2 miles (3.2 km) to US-101 South. Keep on the highway for 39 miles (63 km) and then exit at Jolon Road/County Highway G14. Continue down Jolon Road for 18 miles (29 km) before taking a right on Mission Road, which goes into the base. Remember you must have a valid driver's license, vehicle registration, and proof of insurance to drive into Fort Hunter Liggett.

From Salinas, the drive to Fort Hunter Liggett is an hour and 15 minutes. Take US-101 south out of Salinas and exit at Jolon Road/County Highway G14. Continue down Jolon Road for 18 miles (29 km) before taking a right on Mission Road, which goes into the base.

★ SAN JUAN BAUTISTA

Located in the San Juan Valley between Salinas and Gilroy, San Juan Bautista is a small, scenic city dotted with historic landmarks. There is much to recommend here for California history enthusiasts, including San Juan Bautista State Historic Park and one of the few Spanish plazas left in the state, as well as Mission San Juan Bautista. A block away from the historic park, the town's 3rd Street is lined with historic structures that house antiques stores, restaurants, and gift shops. If San Juan Bautista looks familiar, it's because the town and mission played a prominent role in Alfred Hitchcock's masterpiece *Vertigo*.

The hillside adjacent to the mission is the former site of the Camino Real, a 600-mile (970-km) trail connecting the California missions. Below the rise, look for visible evidence of the San Andreas Fault, which has caused many of the state's earthquakes. Just south of town, Fremont Peak State Park's 3,169-foot (966-m) summit draws people for its superb views of the Monterey Bay and the night sky.

San Juan Bautista State Historic Park
San Juan Bautista State Historic Park

(2nd St. at Mariposa St. and Washington St., 831/623-4881, www.parks.ca.gov, 10am-4:30pm daily, adults $3, children under 16 free) is composed of the buildings that rim the town's plaza, which give a feel for what life was like here back in the late 1800s. It's possible to experience the park in just one or two hours. Start your tour of the park in the Plaza Hotel, a former 18-room lodging establishment with fully furnished re-creations of the hotel's dining room, private card room, parlor, saloon, and a guest room.

The Castro-Breen Adobe, adjacent to the hotel, uses old photos and interpretive displays to detail two of the town's prominent early families that resided in the building. Across 2nd Street and overlooking the plaza is the Plaza Stable, which shelters a fleet of stagecoaches, wagons, and carriages. Other buildings of interest include the blacksmith shop, the Zanetta House, the jail, and the settler's cabin.

The park puts on several events a year, including an antique firearm display, Dutch cooking demonstrations, living-history days, and a special *Vertigo* event with tours, dinner, and a screening of the film on the Plaza Lawn. Check the website for dates. A tour lasting 1-1.5 hours can be reserved for up to 10 people (831/623-4881, $70). Be on the lookout for strange occurrences while wandering through the park's old buildings; it is said that many ghosts reside on the premises.

Mission San Juan Bautista

Dedicated in 1812, **Mission San Juan Bautista** (406 2nd St., 831/623-4528, 9:30am-4:30pm daily, adults $4, seniors $3, students $2, children 5 and under free) has the state's largest mission chapel, which is three aisles wide. After the 1906 San Francisco earthquake, sections of the mission, including the side walls of the chapel, had to be replaced. Upon entering the chapel, look for the impressive and ornate main altar, which holds six

1: Plaza Hotel in San Juan Bautista State Historic Park **2:** the settler's cabin in San Juan Bautista State Historic Park

statues. Also keep an eye out for the cat door that's carved into the Guadalupe Chapel's blue door. Cats were kept on the mission grounds and allowed to enter the chapel to control the mouse population.

The padre's former living quarters now serve as the complex's museum, with a model of the grounds along with a collection of vestments. There's a collection of Native American artifacts that tell the story of the area's original inhabitants before and after the construction of the mission. Adjacent to the church is a cemetery that is thought to be the final resting place of more than 4,000 Native American, Spanish, Mexican, and American people. The mission was the setting of the climax in Hitchcock's *Vertigo*, although the bell tower depicted in the film was a painting, as the mission's original bell tower had been torn down.

Fremont Peak State Park

Eleven miles (17.7 km) south of San Juan Bautista, **Fremont Peak State Park** (San Juan Canyon Rd. off Hwy. 156, 831/623-4255, www.parks.ca.gov, 8am-30 minutes after sunset daily, $6/vehicle) has one of the best views of the Monterey Bay area from its 3,169-foot (966-m) mountaintop, letting visitors take in both the Salinas and San Benito Valleys. Drive close to the summit and then hike 0.5 mile (0.8 km, one-way, moderate) for the best views.

Fremont Peak offers more than a look down below. The state park is one of the best places in the region for stargazing. It has an **observatory** (831/623-2465, http://fpoa.net, programs 8pm or 8:30pm Sat. Apr.-Oct.) with a 30-inch (76-cm) diameter telescope that hosts summer astronomy programs on Saturday nights. In addition, there is a **campground** (800/444-7275, www.reservecalifornia.com, $25) with 25 primitive sites.

Recreation

If off-roading is your thing, head for the hills. Specifically, the **Hollister Hills State Vehicular Recreation Area** (7800 Cienega Rd., 831/637-3874, http://ohv.parks.ca.gov, dawn-dusk daily, $5/vehicle), which has more than 150 miles (242 km) of trails created for four-wheel-drive vehicles, ATVs, and motorcycles. The Upper Ranch area caters to four-wheel drives and motorcycles, while the Lower Ranch is just for motorbikes and ATVs. Hollister Hills also has seven **campgrounds** (first-come, first-served, $10).

Performing Arts

Theater company **El Teatro Campesino** (705 4th St., 831/623-2444, www.elteatrocampesino.com) began with members performing skits on flatbed trucks and union halls to highlight the plight of farmworkers during the 1965 Delano Grape Strike. In 1971 the theater company, led by Luis Valdez (the playwright who wrote *Zoot Suit* and directed the 1987 film *La Bamba*), moved to San Juan Bautista. Today the company does original productions like the annual *La Virgen del Tepeyac,* performed during the holiday season, which is about Our Lady of Guadalupe.

Food

Chef Jarad Gallagher worked in kitchens in London and Paris as well as Michelin-starred Bay Area restaurants like Michael Mina's Chez TJ before opening ★ **The Smoke Point BBQ & Provisions** (206 4th St., 831/593-5009, http://thesmokepoint.com, noon-7pm daily, $12-18). Not to knock those impressive accomplishments, but this inspired but casual barbecue joint and market may be his crowning achievement. The smoked pulled pork sandwich is full of tender, flavorful meat enlivened by the crunch of potato chips and spice of jalapeño peppers. Another recommended sandwich is the Dr. Pepperoncini, a braised beef short rib with au jus. House-made sauces range from a classic Kansas City version to an Alabama white sauce made of horseradish and lemon. The stellar food along

1: pulled pork sandwich at The Smoke Point BBQ & Provisions **2:** Vertigo Coffee

with the friendly staff, full bar, and outdoor dining areas mean this spot transcends your standard barbecue joint.

JJ's Homemade Burgers (100 The Alameda, 831/623-1748, 11am-8pm Mon.-Thurs., 11am-7pm daily, $11-15) is a throwback burger joint with modern prices. All of the burgers here are made with beef from the Central Valley's Harris Ranch. Options include bacon cheeseburgers, Hawaiian burgers, and the El Jefe Burger, topped with bacon, avocado, jack cheese, grilled onions, and jalapeños. Dine inside under biker decor or out front on the patio. Get your photo on the wall if you can complete the JJ's Burger Challenge: Consume a four-patty burger, fries, and a milkshake in 20 minutes or less.

Vertigo Coffee (81 4th Ave., 831/623-9533, www.vertigocoffee.com, 8am-8pm Wed.-Sun.) is a great place for a pick-me-up while exploring San Juan Bautista. Vertigo roasts its beans in-house and makes drip coffee, espresso, and Americanos. The impressive café also bakes its pastries on the premises and makes pizzas in a rustic wood-fired oven. It has a stellar selection of curated local canned craft beers and bottles of wine.

On a sunny afternoon, it's hard to beat dining in the outdoor courtyard and garden at **Jardines de San Juan** (115 3rd St., 831/623-4466, 11:30am-9pm Sun.-Thurs., 11:30am-10pm Fri.-Sat., $7-20). The menu includes Mexican staples like tacos, tostadas, and burritos, while regional specialties are served on Friday, Saturday, and Sunday nights. They also offer some interesting margaritas, including a spicy mango version and an avocado one.

Accommodations

There are just two lodging options in San Juan Bautista. The **Hacienda de Leal** (410 The Alameda, 831/623-4380, www.liveloveleal.com, $145-225) is a boutique hotel with 42 rooms and suites. All rooms have hardwood floors and custom-made wood furniture along with iPhone docking stations and flat-screen TVs. There is also a nice courtyard area with a fountain and a pet playground. All guests are treated to a continental breakfast in the morning.

The other option in town is the **Posada de San Juan** (310 4th St., 831/623-4030, www.posadadesanjuanbautista.com, $155-175), which is centrally located in the town near bars and restaurants. A stay in one of the 34 rooms includes a light breakfast in the morning. This Spanish-style hotel has hosted the likes of Clint Eastwood, Linda Ronstadt, and Cheech Marin. Some of the rooms have fireplaces and soaking tubs.

Transportation

San Juan Bautista is just outside of Monterey County, a 35-minute drive from downtown Monterey. Head north on CA-1 and then east on CA-156. The two-lane highway dead-ends into US-101. Head north on US-101 and then turn off on the CA-156 exit toward San Juan Bautista and Hollister. Take CA-156 east for 2 miles (3.2 km) before taking a left toward San Juan Bautista's downtown area.

The town is a 25-minute drive from nearby Salinas. Take US-101 north and take the CA-156 exit toward San Juan Bautista and Hollister. Take CA-156 east for 2 miles (3.2 km) before taking a left toward San Juan Bautista's downtown area.

GILROY

Gilroy is located in Santa Clara County, 16 miles (26 km) south of San Jose. It is known as the "Garlic Capital of the World" due to the pungent crop that you can sometimes smell while passing through the city on US 101. The city is the home of the Gilroy Gardens Family Theme Park and the Gilroy Premium Outlets, and it hosts the annual Gilroy Garlic Festival. Gilroy makes for a nice place to stop while traveling between Monterey and the Bay Area, as it's about the halfway point between the two destinations.

Gilroy Gardens Family Theme Park

The **Gilroy Gardens Family Theme Park**

(3050 Hecker Pass Hwy., 408/840-7100, www.gilroygardens.org, 11am-5pm Mon.-Fri., 10am-6pm Sat.-Sun., adults $58, children $48) is a family-friendly amusement park featuring the Quiksilver Express Mine Coaster. The other rides include a carousel, a raft that floats through gardens, and a swing around a giant mushroom. The theme park is also known for its Circus Trees, which have been shaped and grafted to resemble hearts and chain-link fences. Ticket discounts are available online.

Festivals and Events

Gilroy is known as "The Garlic Capital of the World," and the annual **Gilroy Garlic Festival** (Christmas Hill Park, 7050 Miller Ave., 408/842-1625, http://gilroygarlicfestival.com, July, adults $20, children and seniors $10) celebrates the flavorful plant over a summer weekend. Be adventurous and try garlic ice cream or other gourmet foods. Events include cook-offs, craft-making, live music, and the crowning of Miss Gilroy Garlic. Be aware that if you are traveling through Gilroy during this weekend, there will be major traffic jams on US 101.

Shopping

Beyond garlic, Gilroy is known for its sprawling outlet mall, which draws shoppers from all over Central California. **Gilroy Premium Outlets** (681 Leavesley Rd., Ste. 175, 408/842-3729, www.premiumoutlets.com, 10am-9pm Mon.-Sat., 10am-7pm Sun.) has 145 outlet stores, ranging from preppy clothes retailer Abercrombie & Fitch to surfwear company Volcom. You can also pick up shoes from Timberland, necklaces from Kay Jewelers, and cookware from Le Creuset.

Food

Gilroy is home to an In-N-Out Burger. Another fast option is **Barbecue 152** (8295 Monterey Rd., 408/842-4499, http://bbq152.com, 11:30am-9pm daily, $7-25). It has a classic barbecue joint menu of meat (pulled pork, ribs, tri-tip, chicken, and spicy hot links) and sides (potato salad, coleslaw, and beans).

The **Garlic City Café** (7461 Monterey St., 408/847-7744, 8am-9pm Tues.-Sun., $15-20) utilizes the city's favorite edible plant in its calamari steak sandwich and its pasta. The signature soup is none other than cream of garlic.

Getting There

It takes 45 minutes to travel from Monterey to Gilroy, and closer to 1.5 hours on a summer or holiday weekend. Take CA-1 north out of Monterey and hop on CA-156 going east. Take the two-lane road to US-101, and then head north for about 20 miles (32 km) until you hit Gilroy.

Driving from Salinas to Gilroy can take just 30 minutes. Get on US-101 heading north and travel 25 miles (40 km) until you reach the city limits.

Santa Cruz

There's no place like Santa Cruz. Even in the left-leaning Bay Area, you won't find another town that has embraced cultural experimentation, radical philosophies, and progressive politics quite like this little beach city.

Santa Cruz has made out-there ideas into a kind of municipal cultural statement. Everyone does their own thing: Surfers ride the waves, nudists laze on the beaches, tree-huggers wander the redwood forests, tattooed and pierced punks wander the main drag, and families walk their dogs along West Cliff Drive.

Most visitors come to Santa Cruz to hit the Boardwalk and the beaches. Locals and UC Santa Cruz students tend to hang downtown on Pacific Avenue and stroll on West Cliff. Local food qualifies as a hidden

Highlights

Look for ★ to find recommended sights, activities, dining, and lodging.

★ **Santa Cruz Beach Boardwalk:** One of the state's last beach boardwalks, this amusement park is a blast of throwback fun with its iconic wooden roller coaster and arcade (page 162).

★ **Pacific Avenue:** Santa Cruz's liveliest street is packed with the city's best restaurants, shops, and bars. It also serves as a runway for the city's eclectic characters to strut their stuff (page 162).

★ **Santa Cruz Surfing Museum:** Perched above Santa Cruz's most well-known break, Steamer Lane, this one-room museum honors the seaside city's most popular pastime (page 167).

★ **Surfing in Santa Cruz:** The shape and direction of Santa Cruz's coastline means that there is a near-constant parade of waves suitable for surfers of all abilities (page 168).

★ **Wilder Ranch State Park:** Just west of Santa Cruz, this park provides a great way to experience the region's coastal beauty, whether you're a hiker or mountain biker (page 192).

★ **Davenport:** This small coastal community is surrounded by terrific beaches with sea stacks offshore (page 193).

★ **Año Nuevo State Park:** See nature in action at this park, where one of the world's

largest groups of elephant seals congregates (page 196).

★ **Roaring Camp Railroads:** Experience the redwood forests of the Santa Cruz Mountains via train at this popular attraction (page 197).

treasure, with a myriad of international cuisines represented and enjoyed.

The West Side is the section of town northwest of the San Lorenzo River that includes the Boardwalk, Steamer Lane, West Cliff Drive, and the university, and it tends toward families with children. The East Side has fewer attractions, but offers a vibrant surf scene situated around Pleasure Point.

Outside Santa Cruz proper, several tiny towns blend into appealing beachside suburbia. Aptos and Capitola lie to the east along the coast. They've each got their own shopping districts, restaurants, and lodgings, as well as charming beaches.

Heading west and north up the coast, Santa Cruz's buildings quickly give way to scenic bluffs dotted with attractions like Wilder Ranch State Park, the tiny town of Davenport, and Año Nuevo State Park, with its gigantic elephant seals.

The redwood-forested Santa Cruz Mountains are home to the quirky communities of Felton, Ben Lomond, and Boulder Creek. It's also a great place to take a walk in the forest, at Big Basin Redwoods State Park or Henry Cowell Redwoods State Park.

PLANNING YOUR TIME

Santa Cruz is ideal for a two- to three-day trip. In that amount of time, you can enjoy the rides of the Santa Cruz Beach Boardwalk, go surfing, explore downtown's Pacific Avenue,

and head into the Santa Cruz Mountains to experience redwood forests, or travel west and north up the coast for secluded beaches and elephant seals.

Summers can be particularly crowded in Santa Cruz due to masses of people from San Jose and the Bay Area traveling to the city for the Boardwalk and beaches. During this time, parking can be a real nightmare, especially since many residential areas near the beach have resident-only parking. On summer days when Monterey is socked in with fog, the sun is often shining in Santa Cruz.

Consider visiting Santa Cruz in the off-season, when hotel room prices are a lot more affordable. Note that the Boardwalk rides are closed on weekdays in the off-season, and many restaurants and other businesses in the area have reduced hours.

Highway 1 connects Santa Cruz to Monterey and Carmel. During the morning and evening rush hours, this part of Highway 1 can be jammed, especially the southbound section from the Highway 17/Highway 1 junction down to the 41st Avenue exit.

Highway 9 connects Santa Cruz to the mountain towns of Felton, Ben Lomond, and Boulder Creek, and it can be closed in the winter for long periods due to mudslides. Highway 17, traversing the mountains en route to San Jose and Silicon Valley, is a steep, windy road that sees lots of accidents.

Previous: wave breaking off a beach in Santa Cruz; wild and beautiful Davenport Beach; surfing in Santa Cruz.

Santa Cruz and Vicinity

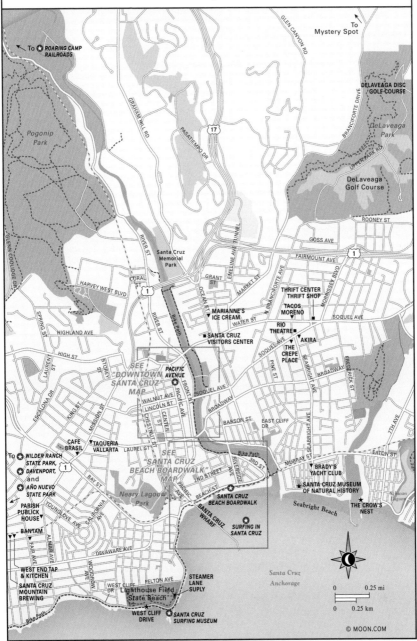

To Mystery Spot

GLEN CANYON RD

DELAVEAGA DISC GOLF COURSE

BRANCIFORTE DRIVE

DeLaveaga Park

UPPER PARK RD

DeLaveaga Golf Course

ROONEY ST

GOSS AVE

FAIRMOUNT AVE

To ★ ROARING CAMP RAILROADS

GRAHAM HILL RD

PASATIEMPO DR

17

Pogonip Park

GLEN-COOLIDGE DR

RIVER RD

Santa Cruz Memorial Park

CORAL ST

HARVEY WEST BLVD

1

EMELINE AVE TUNNEL

GRANT ST

OCEAN ST

MARKET ST

BRANCIFORTE AVE

MORRISSEY BLVD

THRIFT CENTER THRIFT SHOP

TACOS MORENO

SOQUEL AVE

SPRING ST

HIGHLAND AVE

RIVER ST

WATER ST

MARIANNE'S ICE CREAM

■ SANTA CRUZ VISITORS CENTER

RIO THEATRE ■

■ AKIRA

HIGH ST

LAUREL ST

STOREY ST

SEE DOWNTOWN SANTA CRUZ MAP

PACIFIC AVENUE

FRONT ST

SOQUEL AVE

PINE ST

SOQUEL AVE

THE CREPE PLACE

SEABRIGHT AVE

BROADWAY

FREDERICK ST

7TH AVE

ESCALONA DR

KING ST

MISSION ST

WALNUT AVE

LINCOLN ST

CHESTNUT ST

CENTER ST

PACIFIC AVE

BROADWAY

BARSON ST

EAST CLIFF DR

CAFE BRASIL

TAQUERIA VALLARTA

LAUREL ST

SEE "SANTA CRUZ BEACH BOARDWALK" MAP

Bike Path

3RD ST

MURRAY ST

EATON ST

EATON ST

To ★ WILDER RANCH STATE PARK, ★ DAVENPORT, and ★ AÑO NUEVO STATE PARK

1

BAY ST

2ND STREET

BEACH ST

RIVERSIDE AVE

BRADY'S YACHT CLUB

★ SANTA CRUZ MUSEUM OF NATURAL HISTORY

Swan Lagoon

PARISH PUBLICK HOUSE

BANTAM

YOUNGLOVE AVE

CALIFORNIA ST

ALMAR AVE

Neary Lagoon Park

PACIFIC AVE

SANTA CRUZ BEACH BOARDWALK

SANTA CRUZ WHARF

★ SURFING IN SANTA CRUZ

Seabright Beach

★ THE CROW'S NEST

WEST END TAP & KITCHEN

SANTA CRUZ MOUNTAIN BREWING

FAIR AVE

DELAWARE AVE

WOODROW AVE

WEST CLIFF DR

PELTON AVE

STEAMER LANE SUPLY

Santa Cruz Anchorage

0   0.25 mi

0   0.25 km

WEST CLIFF DRIVE

Lighthouse Field State Beach

★ SANTA CRUZ SURFING MUSEUM

Blue Path

© MOON.COM

Sights

★ SANTA CRUZ BEACH BOARDWALK

The Santa Cruz Beach Boardwalk (400 Beach St., 831/423-5590, www.beachboardwalk.com, hours vary daily late May-late Aug., Sat.-Sun. and holidays the rest of the year weather permitting, parking $15-30/day, holiday weekends $20-40) has a rare appeal that beckons to young children, too-cool teenagers, and adults of all ages. It's been immortalized in popular culture in 1980s-era teenybopper vampire classic *The Lost Boys* and Jordan Peele's mind-bending 2019 horror film *Us*.

The amusement park rambles along each side of the east end of the Boardwalk. The Giant Dipper is an old-school wooden roller coaster that opened in 1924 and still gives riders a thrill. The Double Shot shoots riders up a 125-foot (38.1-m) tower for great views before free-falling straight down. For chills, there's the Fright Walk, a high-tech version of a haunted house. The Boardwalk also offers several kids' rides. Entry is free, but you must either buy per-ride tickets ($4-7 per ride) or an all-day rides wristband ($28-36).

At the other end of the Boardwalk, avid gamesters choose between traditional midway games, laser tag and a laser maze, mini-golf, and the Casino Arcade, which has a large collection of video games, along with the classics: air hockey, pinball, and Skee-Ball. The arcade is sometimes open even when the boardwalk rides are closed.

After you've worn yourself out playing games and riding rides, you can take the stairs down to the broad, sandy beach below the Boardwalk. It's a great place to flop down and sun yourself, or brave a dip in the cool Pacific surf. Granted, it gets a bit crowded in the summertime. But you've got all the services you could ever want right here on the Boardwalk, plus the sand and the water (and the occasional strand of kelp). What could be more perfect?

SANTA CRUZ WHARF

The 0.5-mile-long (0.8-km) Santa Cruz Wharf (21 Municipal Wharf, 831/420-5725, www.cityofsantacruz.com, 5am-2am daily, parking $1 per 20 min.) claims to be the longest wooden wharf in the coastal United States. Built in 1914, it was originally used for commercial purposes. Today it's used for recreational purposes, including fishing, strolling, and sightseeing, with both pedestrian and vehicle lanes. It's also home to several restaurants (mostly serving seafood) and shops. At the western end there are places to observe the sea lions hanging out on the pilings below.

★ PACIFIC AVENUE

The center of downtown Santa Cruz is Pacific Avenue, stretching nine blocks from Water Street to Laurel Street. The vibrant, two-lane road is lined with many of the city's finest restaurants, shops, bars, and entertainment options, including the three-screen, art deco Del Mar Theatre. At the northern end is a handsome clock tower. The sidewalks are often jammed with shoppers, street performers, panhandlers, and sightseers.

For information on Santa Cruz, stop by the Downtown Information Kiosk (1130 Pacific Ave., K2, 831/332-7422, www.downtownsantacruz.com, 11am-6pm Sun.-Thurs., 11am-8pm Fri.-Sat. May-Oct., 11am-6pm Tues.-Thurs. and Sun., 11am-7pm Fri.-Sat., Nov.-Apr.).

NATURAL BRIDGES STATE PARK

At the tip of the West Side, Natural Bridges State Park (2531 West Cliff Dr., 831/423-4609, www.parks.ca.gov, 8am-sunset daily, $10) used to have three coastal arches right

Santa Cruz Beach Boardwalk

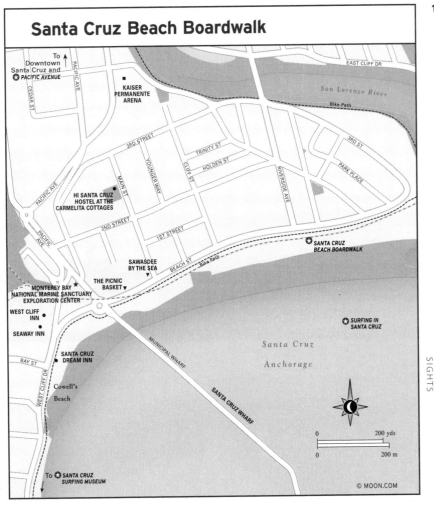

To Downtown Santa Cruz and ✪ PACIFIC AVENUE

PACIFIC AVE

CEDAR ST

KAISER PERMANENTE ARENA

EAST CLIFF DR

San Lorenzo River

Bike Path

3RD STREET

TRINITY ST

HOLDEN ST

CLIFF ST

3RD ST

PARK PLACE

MAIN ST

YOUNGER WAY

RIVERSIDE AVE

PACIFIC AVE

HI SANTA CRUZ HOSTEL AT THE CARMELITA COTTAGES

2ND STREET

1ST STREET

BEACH ST

Bike Path

✪ SANTA CRUZ BEACH BOARDWALK

SAWASDEE BY THE SEA ▼

THE PICNIC BASKET ▼

PACIFIC AVE

★ MONTEREY BAY NATIONAL MARINE SANCTUARY EXPLORATION CENTER

WEST CLIFF INN

SEAWAY INN

BAY ST

SANTA CRUZ DREAM INN

WEST CLIFF DR

Cowell's Beach

MUNICIPAL WHARF

SANTA CRUZ WHARF

✪ SURFING IN SANTA CRUZ

Santa Cruz Anchorage

To ✪ SANTA CRUZ SURFING MUSEUM

0   200 yds
0   200 m

© MOON.COM

offshore; today only one arch remains. This picturesque state park has a beach that falls back deeply, crossed by a creek that feeds into the sea. An inconsistent break makes surfing at Natural Bridges fun on occasion, while the near-constant winds bring out windsurfers nearly every weekend. Hardy sun-worshippers brave the breezes, bringing out their beach blankets, umbrellas, and sunscreen on rare sunny days (usually in late spring and fall). Back from the beach, a wooded picnic area has tables and grills. Beyond the picnic tables, the park has a monarch butterfly preserve, where the migrating insects take over the eucalyptus grove during the fall and winter.

Tidepools range out to the west side of the beach. You can access them by a somewhat scrambling short hike (0.25-0.5 mi/0.4-0.8 km) on the rocky cliffs. These odd little holes filled with sea life aren't like most tidepools—many are nearly perfectly round depressions in the sandstone cliffs worn away by harder stones as the tides move tirelessly back and forth. To avoid causing harm, don't touch the

delicate residents of these pools. Rangers offer guided tours (year-round at low tide) of the tidepools. Visit the visitors center for the current tour schedule.

MONTEREY BAY NATIONAL MARINE SANCTUARY EXPLORATION CENTER

The Monterey Bay National Marine Sanctuary Exploration Center (35 Pacific Ave., 831/421-9993, http://montereybay.noaa.gov, 10am-5pm Wed.-Sun., free) teaches visitors about the protected waters off Santa Cruz and Monterey. Just across the street from Cowell's Beach and the Santa Cruz Wharf, this two-story facility built and operated by the National Oceanic and Atmospheric Administration (NOAA) has exhibits on the water quality, geology, and marine life of the continental United States' largest marine sanctuary. Highlights include a 15-minute film screened upstairs and an interactive exhibit where visitors get to control a remote operational vehicle (ROV) with an attached camera in a large aquarium. The downstairs has a gift shop with books, T-shirts, and postcards. The center also practices environmental sensitivity: The building is built from mostly recycled or reused construction waste and runs on solar power.

SANTA CRUZ MISSION STATE HISTORIC PARK

Believe it or not, weird and funky Santa Cruz started out as a mission town. Santa Cruz Mission State Historic Park (144 School St., off Mission St. and Emmett St., 831/425-5849, www.parks.ca.gov, 10am-4pm Mon. and Thurs.-Sat., noon-4pm Sun., free) was one of the later California missions, dedicated in 1791. Today, the attractive white building with its classic red-tiled roof welcomes visitors to its active Holy Cross church and historical museum. The park's accessible buildings are

not the original complex built by the Spanish fathers in the 18th century. Instead, they're a replica that was built in the 1930s. The park acknowledges the trauma that the mission system inflicted on California's Native Americans, and one of the better museum exhibits relates the story of the local Ohlone and Yokuts peoples. After touring the complex and grounds, be sure to stop in at the Galeria, which houses the mission gift shop and a stunning collection of religious vestments—something you won't see in many other California missions.

SANTA CRUZ MUSEUM OF ART & HISTORY

A block off Pacific Avenue, the Santa Cruz Museum of Art & History (705 Front St., 831/429-1964, www.santacruzmah.org, 10am-8pm daily, adults $10, seniors and students $8) showcases contemporary art alongside Santa Cruz County's history. Rotating exhibition topics have included Santa Cruz's LGBTQ community and local skateboard artist Jim Phillips. There's an outdoor sculpture garden on the museum's rooftop.

LONG MARINE LABORATORY

While the Monterey Bay Aquarium down the road in Monterey provides the best look into the nearby bay, the Long Marine Laboratory (100 Shaffer Rd., 831/459-3800, http://seymourcenter.ucsc.edu, 10am-5pm Tues.-Sun. Sept.-June, 10am-5pm daily July-Aug., adults $8, seniors, students, and children $6) is a worthwhile stop for people interested in sea creatures and marine issues. The large, attractive complex at the end of Delaware Avenue sits right on the edge of the cliff overlooking the ocean—convenient for the research done primarily by students and faculty of UCSC.

Your visit will be to the Seymour Marine Discovery Center, the part of the lab that's open to the public. You'll be greeted outside the door by a full blue whale skeleton that's lit up at night. Inside, instead of a standard

---

1: Santa Cruz Beach Boardwalk 2: Monterey Bay National Marine Sanctuary Exploration Center

Downtown Santa Cruz

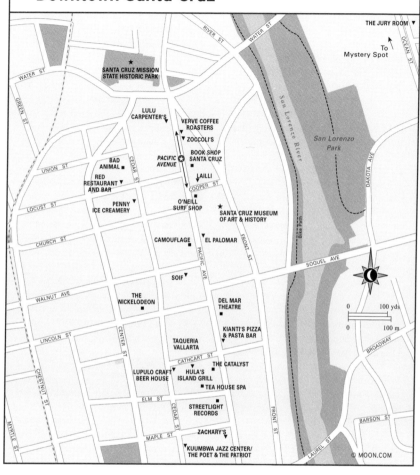

aquarium setup, you'll find a marine laboratory similar to those used by scientists elsewhere in the complex. The aquariums showcase fascinating creatures, including monkey face eels and speckled sand dabs, while displays highlight environmental issues like shark finning. Kids particularly love the touch tanks, while curious adults enjoy checking out the seasonal tank that contains the wildlife that's swimming around outside in the bay *right now*.

If you've never been to Long/Seymour

before, the best way to introduce yourself to the lab is to take a tour. **Tours** run at 1pm, 2pm, and 3pm Tuesday-Sunday. An abbreviated 11am family tour is available for those with small children. Sign up an hour in advance to be sure of getting a slot.

UNIVERSITY OF CALIFORNIA, SANTA CRUZ

The **University of California, Santa Cruz** (1156 High St., 831/459-0111, www.ucsc.edu)

might be the single most beautiful college campus in the country. Set in the hills above downtown Santa Cruz, the classrooms and dorms sit underneath groves of coast redwood trees, among tangles of ferns and vines that are home to woodland creatures. The Office of Admissions (Cook House, 10am-4pm Mon.-Fri.) and the UCSC website provides self-guided tour maps. Or just find a parking lot and wander out into the woods like the students do, looking for a perfect circle of trees to sit and meditate within.

Porter Cave

The UCSC campus has some other natural wonders: caves, which are located in a gulch behind Porter and Kresge Colleges. Porter Cave is the easiest to find and the best for beginning spelunkers. Enter the subterranean chamber by descending down a 20-foot (6.1-m) steel ladder. The cave can get quite muddy, so wear clothes you don't mind getting dirty. To find the cave, go behind Porter College and follow the trail across the meadow and into the trees. Then head right alongside Empire Grade Road. Look for a concrete block that marks the cave opening. Bring a flashlight.

UC Santa Cruz Arboretum

Budding botanists should visit the UC Santa Cruz Arboretum (1156 High St., 831/502-2998, http://arboretum.ucsc.edu, 8am-5pm daily, adults $5, children $2). The 135-acre (54.6-ha) outdoor garden showcases the diverse plants of Australia, New Zealand, South Africa, and California. The "World Tour" is a self-guided path through highlights of the arboretum with different species identified along the way. With plants from both the northern and southern hemispheres, there's always something blooming. Free tours are available the first Saturday of every month at 11am and begin in front of Norrie's Gift & Garden Shop.

McHenry Library

Deadheads and fans of 1960s counterculture have another reason to visit UCSC:

the Grateful Dead Archive (second floor of McHenry Library, Steinhart Rd., http://guides.library.ucsc.edu/gratefuldeadarchive). Artifacts from the popular rock band are displayed in the library's Dead Central Gallery, while visitors can peruse items in the reading room.

★ SANTA CRUZ SURFING MUSEUM

Just feet away from Santa Cruz's best-known surf spot, Steamer Lane, the tiny Santa Cruz Surfing Museum (1701 West Cliff Dr., 831/420-6289, www.cityofsantacruz.com, 10am-5pm Thurs.-Tues. July 4-Labor Day, noon-4pm Thurs.-Mon. Labor Day-July 3, donation requested) is housed within a still-operating lighthouse. Opened in 1986, it is the world's first museum dedicated to the water sport. Run by the Santa Cruz Surfing Club Preservation Society, the one-room museum has pictures of Santa Cruz's surfing culture from the 1930s to the present. One haunting display on shark attacks includes a local surfboard with bite marks from a great white shark.

THE MYSTERY SPOT

Santa Cruz has its own kitschy tourist trap: The Mystery Spot (465 Mystery Spot Rd., 831/423-8897, www.mysteryspot.com, 10am-6pm Mon.-Fri., 10am-8pm Sat.-Sun. summer, 10am-4pm daily winter, $8, children under 3 free, $5 parking) is a tiny piece of land just outside of Santa Cruz where gravity fails. Balls roll uphill and people can stand off the side of a wall. It may be an area of spatial distortion where the laws of physics don't apply . . . or it may be a collection of optical illusions.

SANTA CRUZ MUSEUM OF NATURAL HISTORY

Housed in a former library within the city's Seabright neighborhood, the Santa Cruz Museum of Natural History (1305 East Cliff Dr., 831/420-6115, www.santacruzmuseum.org, 11am-4pm Tues.-Fri., 10am-5pm Sat.-Sun., adults $4, seniors and

Surf City

There's a plaque outside the **Santa Cruz Surfing Museum** that explains how three Hawaiian princes introduced surfing to California in 1885. Apparently, they rode redwood planks from a nearby lumber mill on waves at the mouth of the San Lorenzo River in Santa Cruz.

While Santa Cruz's claim as the birthplace of surfing on the mainland is not disputed, the popular surfing town calling itself "Surf City" has raised the hackles of Southern California's Huntington Beach, which also likes to have its tourist T-shirts adorned with "Surf City." In 2006, Huntington Beach was awarded exclusive use of the title "Surf City" by the U.S. Patent and Trademark Office and went after Santa Cruz beachwear stores that sold T-shirts with the words "Santa Cruz" and "Surf City."

Despite Huntington Beach's aggressive legal action, the residents of Santa Cruz might have the last laugh. In 2009, *Surfer Magazine* proclaimed Santa Cruz as "The Real Surf City, USA" in a piece about the best surf towns. To Huntington Beach's chagrin, it didn't even make the magazine's top 10 list.

students $2, under 18 free) has exhibits covering the Indigenous people of the Monterey Bay region and the area's plant and animal diversity, with a live honeybee display and a live snake. Outdoors, there is a garden that imparts sustainable gardening techniques and information about native plants.

Recreation

BEACHES

Natural Bridges State Park (2531 West Cliff Dr., 831/423-4609, www.parks.ca.gov, 8am-sunset daily, $10) is one of Santa Cruz's best beaches, but the city also boasts two other excellent beaches. Lots of beginning surfers rode their first waves at **Cowell's Beach** (350 West Cliff Dr.). This West Side beach sits right at a crook in the coastline and features a reliable small break that lures new surfers by the dozens.

At the east end of Santa Cruz, down by the harbor, beachgoers flock to **Seabright Beach** (East Cliff Dr. at Seabright Ave., 831/427-4868, 6am-10pm daily, free) all summer long. This miles-long stretch of sand, protected from the worst of the winds by the surrounding cliffs, is a favorite retreat for sunbathers and loungers. While there's little in the way of snack bars, permanent volleyball courts, or facilities, you can still have a great time at Seabright. There is a lot of soft sand to lie in, plenty of room to play football or set up your own volleyball net, and, of course, easy access to the chilly Pacific Ocean. There's no surfing here—Seabright has a shore break that delights skim-boarders but makes wave riding impossible.

TOP EXPERIENCE

★ SURFING

The coastline of Santa Cruz has more than its share of great surf breaks. The water is cold, demanding full wetsuits year-round, and the shoreline is rough and rocky. But that doesn't deter the hordes of locals who ply the waves every day they can.

The best place for beginners is **Cowell's** (stairs at West Cliff Dr. and Cowell's Beach). The waves rarely get huge here, so they provide long, mellow rides, perfect for surfers just getting their balance. Because the Cowell's break is acknowledged as the newbie spot,

1: Santa Cruz Surfing Museum **2:** Natural Bridges State Park

the often-sizeable crowd tends to be polite to newcomers and visitors.

Visitors who know their surfing lore will want to surf the more famous spots along the Santa Cruz shore. Pleasure Point (between 32nd Ave. and 41st Ave.) encompasses a number of different breaks. You may have heard of The Hook (steps at 41st Ave.), a well-known experienced longboarder's paradise. But don't mistake The Hook for a beginner's break; the locals are protective of the waves here and aren't always friendly toward inexperienced newcomers. The break at 36th and East Cliff (steps at 36th Ave.) can be a better place to go on weekdays—on the weekends, the intense crowding makes catching your own wave a challenge. Up at 30th and East Cliff (steps at 36th Ave.), you'll find shortboarders catching larger, long peeling sets if there is a swell in the water. When the point breaks are crowded, consider 26th Avenue, a rare beach break in town. Parking is easiest at nearby Moran Lake Park off East Cliff Drive.

The most famous break in all of Santa Cruz can also be the most hostile to newcomers. Steamer Lane (West Cliff Dr. between Cowell's and the Santa Cruz Surfing Museum) has a fiercely protective crew of locals. But if you're experienced and there's a swell coming in, Steamer Lane offers some of the best waves on the California coast.

Yes, you can learn to surf in Santa Cruz despite the distinct local flavor at some of the breaks. Check out either Club Ed Surf School and Camps (831/464-0177, www. club-ed.com, beginner group lesson $100 pp, private lessons $130/hour) or the Richard Schmidt School (849 Almar Ave., 831/423-0928, www.richardschmidt.com, 2-hour class $120 pp, private lessons $200/hour) to sign up for lessons. Who knows, maybe one day the locals will mistake you for one of their own.

STAND-UP PADDLEBOARDING

The latest water-sports craze has definitely hit Santa Cruz. Stand-up paddleboarders vie for waves with surfers at Pleasure Point and can also be found in the Santa Cruz waters with less wave action. Covewater Paddle Surf (726 Water St., 831/600-7230, http://covewater.com, 2-hour private lesson $200) conducts beginner stand-up paddleboarding (SUP) classes in the relatively calm waters of the Santa Cruz Harbor. They also rent SUPs ($35-60/day).

HIKING AND BIKING

To walk or bike where the locals do, just head out to West Cliff Drive. This winding street with a full-fledged sidewalk trail running its length on the ocean side is the town's favorite walking, dog walking, jogging, skating, scootering, and biking route. Start at Santa Cruz Municipal Wharf and go 2.75 miles (4.4 km) to Natural Bridges State Park (the west end of West Cliff). You'll pass the *To Honor Surfing* statue along with flowering ice plant and views of the ocean studded with sea stacks. Bring your camera if you're strolling West Cliff on a clear day—you won't be able to resist taking photos of the sea, cliffs, and sunset. Watch for fellow path-users, as it can get crowded.

To rent a bike for cruising West Cliff Drive, head over to Pacific Ave Cycles (318 Pacific Ave., 831/471-2453, 10am-6pm daily, hourly bike rental $8-15, daily bike rental $25-55). The small shop with single- and multiple-speed bikes for rent is just a few blocks east of the start of West Cliff Drive.

DISC GOLF

For disc golfers, the DeLaveaga Disc Golf Course (DeLaveaga Park, 850 Branciforte Dr., $2 parking) is like the Pebble Beach of disc golf courses, a famed place known by most who play the sport. Created in 1984 as a host site for the World Disc Championship, this 27-hole course still draws more than 100 players a day. Its most famous hole is 26, which is a long 600 feet (183 m) from tee box to basket. Many a disc has been lost here. There's an active DeLaveaga Disc Golf Facebook page if you have any questions.

SAILING

You don't have to ride a surfboard to get into the waters off Santa Cruz. *Chardonnay II* (790 Mariner Park Way, 831/423-1213, www.chardonnay.com, adults $50-68, children $23-32) is a 70-foot sailboat with a large deck and seating area that does weekend sunset sails, champagne brunches, afternoon pizza parties, Hawaiian food parties, and more.

Another way to get onto the bay is through **Lighthall Yacht Charters** (Santa Cruz Harbor, 831/429-1970, www.lighthallcharters.com, two-hour sail $320-370). They do two-hour outings and private charter sails on their fleet of three yachts, ranging 32-42 feet (9.8-12.8 m) long. Passengers are free to bring their own food and drink on board. The skipper is highly knowledgeable about the area.

SPAS

It's hard to beat a hot-water soak after a day of surfing Santa Cruz's breaks or walking the city's vibrant downtown area. The **Tea House Spa** (112 Elm St., 831/426-9700, www.teahousespa.com, 11am-11pm Mon.-Thurs., 11am-midnight Fri.-Sun., spa rooms $16-42/hour, massages $60-180) is a half-block off Pacific Avenue and offers private hot tubs with views of a bamboo garden. It's not a fancy facility, but the tubs will warm you up and mellow you out.

The **Well Within Spa** (417 Cedar St., 831/458-9355, http://wellwithinspa.com, 10am-midnight daily, spa rooms and outdoor spas $18-30 pp/hour, massages $55-130) has indoor spa rooms and outdoor spas and offers massages.

SPECTATOR SPORTS

In 2012, Santa Cruz became home to the Santa Cruz Warriors, an NBA Development League team associated with the Golden State Warriors. The team plays in the **Kaiser Permanente Arena** (140 Front St., 831/713-4400, http://santacruz.gleague.nba.com, tickets $17-160), an indoor arena just west of downtown. The sporting facility can accommodate more than 2,500 spectators.

a view along West Cliff Drive

Entertainment

BARS AND CLUBS

Lovers of libations should grab a drink at **Red Restaurant and Bar** (200 Locust St., 831/425-1913, www.redrestaurantandbarsc. com, 5pm-1:30am Mon.-Sat., 5pm-1am Sun.), located upstairs in downtown Santa Cruz's oldest building; it dates to 1877. With its dark wood paneling and burgundy barstools, Red feels like an old speakeasy. Creative cocktails include signature creations like the Jean Grey, a mix of house-infused Earl Grey organic gin, lemon, and simple syrup. The bar also has a nice selection of 30 craft and Belgian beers on tap, as well as serves a comprehensive late-night menu until 1am for those who need some food to soak up the alcohol.

A drinking establishment on the West Side, the **Parish Publick House** (841 Almar Ave., 831/421-0507, www.theparishpublick.com, 11am-2am daily) serves 16 beers on draft and pub grub from its space in a strip mall. The food menu includes wings, burgers, and sandwiches.

The Jury Room (712 Ocean St., 831/426-7120, 6am-2am daily), a dive bar just east of downtown, is a local favorite for its cheap drinks, free pool, and jukebox filled with punk rock songs. Their motto is "cement floors, heavy pours." It's also got creepy cred: It was once the hangout of 1970s serial killer Edmund Emil Kemper and was featured in the Netflix series *Mindhunter*.

The Crêpe Place (1134 Soquel Ave., 831/429-6994, www.thecrepeplace.com, 11am-midnight Mon.-Thurs., 11am-1am Fri., 9am-midnight Sat.-Sun.) has been around in different locations around town since 1973. This Soquel Avenue Victorian has been its base of operations since 1990. It's now a hangout for the hipster crowd, which is drawn in by the high-profile indie rock acts and popular Bay Area bands that perform in its intimate front room. They also have outdoor seating and a comprehensive menu of creative crêpes.

There aren't any boats at **Brady's Yacht Club** (413 Seabright Ave., 831/425-9854, 10am-2am daily), a welcoming dive bar in the Seabright neighborhood where friendly locals may be playing a game of pool or dice. The bar is cluttered with knickknacks, and branches and Christmas lights hang in the rafters. They have some beer on tap and a deal on Moscow mules (vodka, ginger beer, and lime juice), served in a copper mug for just $6. Cash only.

LIVE MUSIC

The Catalyst (1011 Pacific Ave., tickets available at www.etix.com), right downtown on Pacific Avenue, hosts a variety of reggae, rap, and punk acts from Snoop Dogg to Agent Orange. Neil Young and Crazy Horse's 2021 live album *Way Down in the Rust Bucket,* is a recording of their legendary 1990 performance at the venue. Be sure to check the calendar when you buy tickets—some shows are 21 and over. The 800-person main concert hall is a standing-room-only space, while the balconies offer seating. The bar is located downstairs adjacent to the concert space. The vibe tends to be low-key, but it depends on the night and the event. The Catalyst Atrium, a smaller room in the same building, snags some superb national touring bands. You can buy tickets online or by phone; purchasing in advance is recommended, especially for national acts.

Named one of the greatest jazz venues in the world by *DownBeat* magazine, the **Kuumbwa Jazz Center** (320 Cedar St., 831/427-2227, www.kuumbwajazz.org) is a 200-seat treasure. It puts on over 130 intimate concerts a year, aided by a superb sound and lighting setup. Past performers have included Bobby Hutcherson, Pharaoh Sanders, Christian McBride, Wynton Marsalis, and Charles Lloyd.

The Crow's Nest (2218 East Cliff Dr., 831/476-4560, www.crowsnest-santacruz.

Santa Cruz Craft Brews

Santa Cruz's craft brewing scene has exploded. The best way to sample the city's suds is with Brew Cruz (831/222-0120, www.scbrewcruz.com, $45/person), an army green tour bus with a refrigerated cooler on board. The tour begins (and ends) at the Dream Inn (175 West Cliff Dr.), stopping at three local breweries over a four-hour period. For beer fans who want to do their own tour, there's plenty of places to visit.

On the West Side, the Santa Cruz Mountain Brewery (402 Ingalls St., 831/425-4900, www.scmbrew.com, 11:30am-10pm daily) serves organic brews in a taproom and outdoor beer garden. Expect to find seven of the flagship beers on tap, including an IPA and seasonal brews. Just around the corner, Humble Sea Brewing (820 Swift St., 831/621-2890, http://humblesea. com, noon-9:30pm Mon.-Thurs., Fri. noon-10pm, 11am-10pm Sat., 11am-9pm Sun.) is known for its cloudy, flavorful IPAs. Sample its "experiments in beer" in the small but charming outdoor beer garden or the modest indoor area.

Beer connoisseurs flock to Capitola's Sante Adairius (103 Kennedy Dr., Capitola, 831/462-1227, http://rusticales.com, 3pm-8pm Tues.-Thurs., 1pm-8pm Fri.-Sun.) for beers with bold flavor, including some barrel-aged farmhouse ales. A tasting room is also in Santa Cruz (1315 Water St., 831/201-4141, 2pm-9pm Mon.-Thurs., noon-10pm Fri.-Sat., noon-9pm Sun.).

At Soquel's Discretion Brewing (2703 41st Ave., Ste. A, Soquel, 831/316-0662, www. discretionbrewing.com, 11:30am-9pm daily), fine beer shares the tasting room with fine food, courtesy of chef Brad Briske of acclaimed restaurant HOME. The tasting menu includes the brewery's popular and award-winning Uncle Dave's Rye IPA and Oh Black Lager. Briske's culinary creations include fish sandwiches and beef tongue tacos, but the shoestring potatoes with a sesame aioli dipping sauce may be the best snack to accompany a Discretion beer. The brewery has both indoor and outdoor spaces.

A couple of fine beer bars are also in the area. In downtown Santa Cruz, Lúpulo Craft Beer House (233 Cathcart St., 831/454-8306, www.lupulosc.com, 11:30am-10pm Sun.-Thurs., 11:30am-11:30pm Fri.-Sat.) has 16 rotating craft beers on tap and more than 100 types of bottled beer (which can also be taken to-go). This husband-and-wife-owned business also conducts brewing demos, tastings, and other events. A small-bites menu features tacos, salads, and sandwiches. Soquel's Beer Thirty Bottle Shop & Pour House (2504 S. Main St., Soquel, 831/477-9967, www.beerthirtysantacruz.com, 11am-10pm daily) has a large outdoor beer garden, 30 taps, and a fine selection of bottles to bring home.

com) is as a venue for all kinds of live music acts. Rock, soul, reggae, and funk bands typically play Tuesday-Saturday. Sundays are live comedy evenings, and Tuesdays are reggae jam nights.

A former 1940s movie house, the Rio Theatre (1205 Soquel Ave., 831/423-8209, www.riotheatre.com) hosts everything from film festivals to performances by international touring acts like Ladysmith Black Mambazo and Built to Spill. Check the theater's website for a full list of upcoming events.

A short drive east of downtown, Moe's Alley (1535 Commercial Way, 831/479-1854, www.moesalley.com) draws nationally touring rock, reggae, blues, funk, and jam bands to its venue every night of the week except Mondays. Moe's accommodates audiences of around 300 people. Previous performers have included Fantastic Negrito, Antibalas, The Blasters, and King Gizzard & the Lizard Wizard.

CINEMA

Santa Cruz has two great downtown movie theaters: The Nickelodeon (210 Lincoln St., 831/359-4523, www.landmarktheatres.com), a classic art house movie theater, and the art deco Del Mar Theatre (1124 Pacific Ave., 831/359-4447, www.landmarktheatres.com), which dates to 1936. Both screen independent features, foreign films, and the occasional

Hitchcock's Santa Cruz

Famed film director Alfred Hitchcock had a deep connection to the Santa Cruz area. It began in earnest in 1940, when Hitchcock bought a 200-acre (80.9-ha) estate in the Santa Cruz Mountains near Scotts Valley as a second home. From then on, the Santa Cruz area was part of his work. In the 1941 film *Suspicion*, the Santa Cruz coastline stands in for the English countryside. It's rumored that the mansion in his 1960 masterpiece *Psycho* was based on the former Hotel Mc-Cray, which is now the Sunshine Villa senior living facility on Beach Hill. The town of Santa Cruz is even mentioned in *The Birds* as the place that the strange phenomena in the film first occurred. Today, the former Hitchcock estate is the Heart O' the Mountain Winery. Unfortunately, it is not open to the public.

big-budget flick. The Del Mar also frequently shows a slate of midnight movies; Del Mar's Theater 1 is known for roomier seats. Check the website for details.

COMEDY

For a good laugh in Santa Cruz, **The Crow's Nest** (2218 East Cliff Dr., 831/476-4560, www.crowsnest-santacruz.com, 9pm Sun., $7) hosts a weekly stand-up comedy show. Because the show runs on Sunday nights, The Crow's Nest takes advantage of the opportunity to hire big-name comics who have been in San Francisco or San Jose for weekend engagements. This lets folks see headliners in a more casual setting for a fraction of the cost of the big-city clubs. The Crow's Nest, with its great views out over the Pacific, also has a full bar and restaurant. You can enjoy drinks and dinner while you get your giggle on.

THEATER

When the long-running Shakespeare Santa Cruz went belly-up in 2013, the nonprofit **Santa Cruz Shakespeare** (831/460-6396, box office 831/460-6399, www.santacruzshakespeare.org, July-Aug., prices vary) formed, in 2014, so Bard lovers could still get their fix. Recent productions, presented in **The Grove at DeLaveaga Park** (501 Upper Park Rd.), have included *The Comedy of Errors* and Jane Austen's *Pride and Prejudice*.

The **Jewel Theatre Company** (administration 408/482-1057, box office 831/425-7506,

www.jeweltheatre.net) is the only Santa Cruz County troupe that produces plays throughout the year. You may be able to catch something like Eugene O'Neill's *A Moon for the Misbegotten* or the 1930s-musical comedy *Me and My Girl*. Plays are mounted at the **Colligan Theater at the Tannery Arts Center** (1010 River St.), a 182-seat venue with a rise between rows so that all ticketholders can view the stage.

FESTIVALS AND EVENTS

Every winter when the rains start and the mushrooms emerge, Santa Cruz celebrates with three days of fun(gi) at the **Fungus Fair** (Louden Nelson Community Center, 301 Center St., 831/222-0000, http://ffsc.us, Jan., $5-10). The festivities include talks, cooking demonstrations, a dinner, and displays of different types of mushrooms.

Watch surf kayakers and stand-up paddleboarders compete on the giant winter swells at **Santa Cruz Paddlefest** (Steamer Lane, 831/724-5692, http://santacruzpaddlefest.com, Mar., free), which unfolds over three days. The event includes a stand-up paddleboard race from Cowell's Beach to the Santa Cruz Harbor and back, along with a popular SUP and surf kayaking competition at Steamer Lane. Crowds gather on West Cliff Drive to catch the action. Food trucks and merchandise booths set up along the cliffside.

Woodies were pre-1950s cars with partial wood bodies that are associated with early surf culture. Woodies on the Wharf (Santa Cruz Wharf, 21 Municipal Wharf, 831/420-5273, www.santacruzwoodies.com, late June, free) finds more than 200 of these cool cars and trucks displayed on the wharf.

Sure, Santa Cruz can be an out-there place, but it still does traditional events like the Santa Cruz County Fair (Santa Cruz County Fairgrounds, 2601 East Lake Ave., Watsonville, 831/724-5671, www.santacruzcountyfair.com, Sept.). With five fun days full of carnival rides, livestock, and entertainment, the big annual event happens in nearby Watsonville.

Shopping

PACIFIC AVENUE

For a small city, Santa Cruz has a bustling downtown, centered on Pacific Avenue, which extends from Water Street to Laurel Street for about nine blocks. At the northern end, shoppers peruse antiques, clothing, and kitchenware. In the middle, you can grab a cappuccino, a cocktail, or a bite to eat in one of the many independent eateries. At the south end, visitors can purchase body jewelry or tattoos. The sidewalks are often jammed with shoppers, street performers, panhandlers, and sightseers. It's a good idea to park in one of the structures a block or two off Pacific Avenue and walk from there.

Bookshop Santa Cruz (1520 Pacific Ave., 831/423-0900, www.bookshopsantacruz.com, 9am-10pm Sun.-Thurs., 9am-11pm Fri.-Sat.) is a superb independent bookstore with new and used books. It's been in business since 1966 and occupies a 20,000-square-foot (1,858-sq-m) space right on Pacific Avenue. Check the staff recommendations if you are looking for a new favorite author. Bookshop Santa Cruz also hosts regular readings by literary heavy hitters like Michael Chabon and Jennifer Egan. Another wholly original bookseller is Bad Animal (1011 Cedar St., 831/900-5031, www.badanimalbooks.com, 10am-9pm Wed.-Thurs. and Sun., 10am-10pm Fri.-Sat.), a bookstore, wine bar, and café. The books here lean toward vintage as well as transgressive, revolutionary, and psychedelic works. The wines are organic and biodynamic. Bad

O'Neill Surf Shop in downtown Santa Cruz

Animal also hosts an eclectic array of events, from poetry readings to wine school.

Santa Cruz's Jack O'Neill is credited with making cold-water surfing possible with the invention of the wetsuit. His **O'Neill Surf Shop** (110 Cooper St., 831/469-4377, www.oneill.com, 10am-8pm Sun.-Thurs., 10am-9pm Fri.-Sat.) specializes in surfboards, brand-name clothing, and, of course, wetsuits. If your trip to California has gotten you hooked on riding the waves, and you just have to invest in your own equipment, O'Neill can be a good place to start. You can also buy a T-shirt or some sweats here—handy if you didn't pack quite right for Central Coast summer fog. There's also another location in Capitola (1115 41st Ave., 831/475-4151, 9am-8pm Mon.-Fri., 8am-8pm Sat.-Sun.).

If you want to buy clothes in Santa Cruz, chances are you're looking for a secondhand store—and this town has plenty of them. One of the largest of these sits only a block off Pacific Avenue—the aptly, if redundantly, named **Thrift Center Thrift Store** (1305 Water St., 831/429-6975, 9am-8pm Mon.-Sat., 10am-6pm Sun.). This big, somewhat dirty retail space offers a wide array of cheap secondhand clothes. You'll need to hunt a bit to find that one perfect vintage item, but isn't that the fun of thrift shopping?

Camouflage (1329 Pacific Ave., 831/423-7613, www.shopcamouflauge.com, 10am-10pm Mon.-Thurs., 10am-11pm Fri.-Sat., 10am-8pm Sun.) is an independent, family-owned, and women-friendly adult store. The first room contains mostly lingerie and less-shocking items. Dare to walk through the narrow black-curtained passage and you'll find the *other* room, which is filled with grown-up toys designed to please women of every taste and proclivity.

Stop by **Streetlight Records** (939 Pacific Ave., 831/421-9200, www.streetlightrecords.com, noon-8pm Sun.-Mon., 11am-9pm Tues.-Thurs., 11am-9pm Fri.-Sat.) to pick up the latest music for your drive down the coast. With records and turntables making a serious comeback, Streetlight is also the place in Santa Cruz to find new and used vinyl.

Food

SEAFOOD

Hula's Island Grill (221 Cathcart St., 831/426-4852, www.hulastiki.com, 11:30am-10pm Sun.-Thurs., 11:30am-11pm Fri.-Sat., 4:30pm-10pm Mon., $12-23) has a fun surf theme that fits perfectly with Santa Cruz's culture. Surfing movies play on loop and paraphernalia covers the walls while diners enjoy a diverse menu featuring seafood as well as burgers, bowls, tacos, and curries. They also have a Monterey location.

A Santa Cruz fixture for over 50 years, **The Crow's Nest** (2218 E. Cliff Dr., 831/476-4650, http://crowsnest-santacruz.com, 9am-9pm daily, $16-38) is a fun place for casual dining—with a menu leaning heavily on seafood—an extensive cocktail menu, and fine views of the Santa Cruz Harbor meeting the ocean. It's a nice spot to watch the sunset over the Pacific.

SUSHI

East of downtown, ★ **Akira** (1222 Soquel Ave., 831/600-7093, http://akirasantacruz.com, 11am-11pm daily, rolls $10-17) is a modern sushi bar with interesting creations. Some of the rolls here employ unconventional ingredients like skirt steak, sriracha sauce, and spicy truffled shoestring yams. It also serves more typical items including Philly rolls, spider rolls, and spicy tuna rolls. This being Santa Cruz, skateboard art decorates some of the walls. At happy hour (2pm-4pm daily), diners can snack on appetizers and enjoy sake, beer, or wine.

NEW AMERICAN

Right downtown, the **Soif Restaurant & Wine Bar** (105 Walnut Ave., 831/423-2020, www.soifwine.com, 5pm-9pm Mon.-Thurs., 5pm-10pm Fri.-Sat., entrées $16-30) has locally sourced sustainable and organic fare to go with your glass of red or white wine. Snack from the small-plate menu or sample some exotic cheeses. The entrées have an Italian tinge.

With its contemporary and warm interior, **Suda** (3910 Portola Dr., 831/600-7068, www.eatsuda.com, 4pm-9pm Mon.-Thurs., 4pm-10pm Fri., 10am-10pm Sat., 10am-9pm Sun., $10-30) brings a downtown feel to the East Side. The menu splits the difference between comfort food (burgers, shoestring fries) and healthier California fare (a kale Caesar salad, a vegetable bowl). It has a nice long bar along with a few high-top tables for sampling some of their classic and creative cocktails or one of the 22 beers on draft.

MEXICAN

Santa Cruz has some great taquerias, but **Tacos Moreno** (1053 Water St., 831/429-6095, 11am-8pm daily, $6-11, cash only) may be the best, as evidenced by the locals lined up outside the nondescript eatery during lunch. Tacos Moreno serves just the basics: burritos, tacos, quesadillas, and beverages to wash them down. The standout item is the al pastor burrito supreme with crispy barbecued pork, cheese, sour cream, and guacamole, among other savory ingredients. It also has two Capitola locations: beachfront (201 Esplanade, 831/515-7507, 10am-8pm daily) and at King's Plaza Shopping Center (1601 41st Ave., 831/464-8810, 10am-8pm daily).

El Palomar (1336 Pacific Ave., 831/425-7575, http://elpalomarsantacruz.com, 11am-3pm and 5pm-9pm Mon.-Wed., 11am-10:30pm Fri., 10am-10:30pm Sat., 10am-9pm Sun., $13-27) is located in the dining room of an old luxury hotel. Enjoy shrimp enchiladas or chicken mole while mariachi bands rove around and play to diners. Jose's Special Appetizer ($17) can be a light meal for two, though don't forget to try El Palomar's tasty guacamole. Their informal taco bar is great for a quick bite and drink. Stop in for happy hour (3pm-6pm Mon.-Fri.), when superb deals include $5 margaritas and $2 street tacos.

Taqueria Vallarta (608 Soquel Ave., 831/457-8226, http://taqueriavallartaonline.com, 9am-10pm Sun.-Thurs., 9am-11pm Fri.-Sat., $4.50-11) has a Mexican food empire in Santa Cruz County, with three locations in Santa Cruz alone. Vallarta's dominance is due to their inexpensive but tasty menu. Their super quesadilla alone will fill you up, while the jumbo burrito with your choice of meat can easily stuff you silly for two meals. The other Santa Cruz locations include 893 41st Avenue (831/464-7022, 9am-11pm daily) and 1221 Mission Street (831/426-7240, 9am-10pm Sun.-Wed., 9am-11pm Thurs.-Sat.).

SOUTH AMERICAN

Painted jungle green with bright yellow and blue trim, you can't miss this totally Santa Cruz breakfast and lunch joint. **Cafe Brasil** (1410 Mission St., 831/429-1855, www.cafebrasil.us, 8am-3pm daily, $6-11) serves up the Brazilian fare its name promises. In the morning, the fare runs to omelets and Brazilian specialties, including a dish with two eggs topping a steak. Lunch includes pressed sandwiches, meat and tofu dishes, and Brazilian house specials. They also have a smoothie and juice bar to counteract your meat intake.

THAI

Just feet from the Boardwalk, **Sawasdee by the Sea** (101 Main St., 831/466-9009, www.sawasdeesoquel.com, 11am-9:30pm Sun.-Thurs., 11am-10pm Fri.-Sat., $7-18) does great Thai food in a restaurant with large windows that have views of the beach and wharf. The menu is long and daunting, but there are curries, noodle dishes, fried rice plates, salads, and soups. Downstairs is a bar with beers on tap and unique cocktails like a potent vodka-spiked Thai iced tea. The bar area also has a small (just three tables) outside deck that is perfect for a sunny afternoon. Sawasdee is at

the top of the hill at the corner of 1st Street and Main Street.

AFGHAN

★ **Laili** (101 B Cooper St., 831/423-4545, http://lailirestaurant.com, 11:30am-2:30pm and 5pm-close Tues.-Sun., $12-29) is in a sleek, modern building with an open kitchen and marbled bar that oozes style. This cuisine complements the space—which includes a back patio surrounded by vine-covered walls and string lights—with artfully prepared dishes ranging from a cilantro Caesar salad to *bolani*, a vegan flatbread. Meals begin with a hefty serving of naan and dipping sauce. The filet mignon kebab, three tender pieces of meat with dipping sauces, is exceptional.

PIZZA

An untold number of surfers have stopped by ★ **Pleasure Pizza** (4000 Portola Dr., 831/475-4002, http://pleasurepizzasc.com, 11am-9pm daily, $3-6) for a slice after a morning of surfing nearby Pleasure Point or The Hook. This unassuming shack is just a couple of blocks from the waves. The large, tasty slices are served on paper plates in a somewhat dingy building decorated with old surfboards and local surfing photos. Surfing legend Jay Moriarity once worked here (as immortalized in the 2012 film about his life, *Chasing Mavericks*). On Tuesdays, slices of cheese pizza go for just $2. There is also a downtown location (1415 Pacific Ave., 831/600-7859, 11am-9pm Mon.-Thurs., 11am-10pm Fri.-Sun.).

Right on bustling Pacific Avenue, **Kianti's Pizza & Pasta Bar** (1100 Pacific Ave., 831/469-4400, www.kiantis.com, 11am-9pm Sun.-Thurs., 11am-10pm Fri.-Sat., $13-21) draws in crowds with individual and family-size servings of pastas, pizzas, and salads. Pizza toppings range from traditional Italian ingredients to more creative options; one pie is covered with seasoned beef, lettuce, tomatoes, avocado, and tortilla chips. People are also drawn in by Kianti's full bar and outdoor seating area right on Pacific Avenue.

Bantam (1010 Fair Ave., Ste. J, 831/420-0101, www.bantam1010.com, 4:30pm-8pm Tues.-Sat., $13-24) has a small menu dominated by thin-crust wood-fired pizza. Unique ingredients, including spicy honey and Brussels sprouts, abound at this hipsterish space decorated with subway tiles and reclaimed wood.

GASTROPUB

The **West End Tap & Kitchen** (334 Ingalls St., 831/471-8115, http://westendtap.com, 11:30am-9:30pm Sun.-Thurs., 11:30am-10pm Fri.-Sat., $10-24) creates food to pair with their fine craft beers and wines. Their 18 beers and four wines on tap can be enjoyed with salads, sandwiches, flatbreads, or a house-ground burger. West End is a hip, airplane hangar-like space where wooden barrels serve as both furniture and decor.

GOURMET CONCESSION STAND

Overlooking one of Santa Cruz's most popular surf spots, **Steamer Lane Supply** (698 West Cliff Dr., 831/316-5240, http://steamerlanesc.com, 9am-6:30pm daily, $4-11) is a concession stand in Lighthouse Field State Beach that's perfect for a snack while walking along West Cliff Drive. There are sandwiches, bowls, and breakfast tacos, though the focus is on quesadillas in all sorts of varieties: kale, kimchi, tuna, pulled pork, and more. It also sells surf wax, leashes, and other essential surf gear if you're planning to hit the nearby waves.

SANDWICHES

Just feet from the corndog-slinging Boardwalk is ★ **The Picnic Basket** (125 Beach St., 831/427-9946, www.thepicnicbasketsc.com, 7am-9pm Sat.-Sun. summer, 7am-4pm Mon.-Fri., 7am-4pm daily winter, $3-9), a casual eatery with a simple menu of tasty, locally sourced goodness. The attention to detail here shines through even on a deceptively simple

1: ahi sandwich at The Crow's Nest **2:** the brightly colored Cafe Brasil

turkey, cheese, and avocado sandwich. Other options include breakfast dishes, salads, mac-and-cheese, and even local beer and wine. Dine inside or out front, where you can take in the sounds of the bustling Boardwalk.

Zoccoli's (1534 Pacific Ave., 831/423-1711, www.zoccolis.com, 8am-6pm Mon.-Sat., 10am-6pm Sun., $6-8) is an old-fashioned Italian deli that serves warm sandwiches, soups, green salads, and pasta salad from behind a long case. The breaded-chicken pesto sandwich with roasted red peppers and Swiss cheese is hard to beat. A pulled pork sandwich is available on Fridays and Saturdays.

BREAKFAST

There is almost always a line spilling out of ★ Cliff Café (815 41st Ave., 831/476-1214, 8am-1pm Thurs.-Tues., $8-12). That's partly because this intimate café has just six tables. The other reason is because of the great service and superb omelets, tofu dishes, and pancakes. The pesto and Swiss cheese omelet with an addition of bacon (done extra crispy) is highly impressive.

A downtown breakfast favorite since 1985, Zachary's (819 Pacific Ave., 831/427-0646, www.zacharyssantacruz.com, 7am-2:30pm Tues.-Sun., $5-12) makes everything in-house including their breads and rolls. Choose between favorites like the sourdough pancakes, the pesto scramble, and the corned beef hash and eggs. Zachary's is housed in a building that dates back to 1912. The restaurant has high ceilings and is decorated with a variety of plants.

COFFEE AND BAKERIES

★ Verve Coffee Roasters (1540 Pacific Ave., 831/471-7726, www.vervecoffee.com, 6:30am-9pm daily) offers a hip, open space with lots of windows at the northern edge of Pacific Avenue. It roasts its own beans in the nearby Seabright neighborhood. After ordering your drink at the counter, look for a seat in this frequently crowded coffee shop. There are also have locations on the East Side at 846 41st Avenue (831/706-2369, 7am-6pm daily) and

104 Bronson Street, Suite 19 (831/216-4448, 7am-5pm daily).

Lulu Carpenter's (1545 Pacific Ave., 831/439-9200, www.lulucarpenters.com, 6am-midnight daily) serves great coffee downtown. It has the distinction of being the first business to reopen on Pacific Avenue after the 1989 Loma Prieta earthquake. Lulu's hosts live music on Fridays and Saturdays. Other locations are at 925 Soquel Avenue (6am-6pm daily) and 930 Almar Avenue (5am-2pm daily).

DESSERTS

Santa Cruz has two favorite local ice cream shops. Marianne's (1020 Ocean St., 831/458-1447, http://mariannesicecream.com, 10am-11pm Sun.-Thurs., 10am-midnight Fri.-Sat.) has served scoops of butter brickle and other flavors since 1947. It has 105 flavors, including the recommended creations "Heaven" and "1020." Marianne's is in a bright red building with a retro sign; you can't miss it. The Penny Ice Creamery (913 Cedar St., 831/204-2523, www.thepennyicecreamery. com, noon-11pm daily) is the relative new-comer—being in business since 2010—and serves hipster-approved flavors like whiskey custard and orange star anise sorbet. Penny also has an East Side location at 820 41st Avenue (noon-9pm Sun.-Thurs., noon-10pm Fri.-Sat.).

MARKETS

Any self-respecting hippie community should have a market that sells organic and natural foods. Santa Cruz's superb mini-chain, New Leaf Community Market (1101 Fair Ave., 831/426-1306, http://newleaf.com, 7am-9pm daily), offers a local alternative to Whole Foods. Stock up on groceries or grab a meal of sandwiches, smoothies, or the terrific chicken pesto quesadilla at the flagship Fair Avenue location on the West Side or at their locations downtown (1134 Pacific Ave., 831/425-1793, 8am-9pm daily) and in Capitola (1210 41st Ave., 831/479-7987, 8am-9pm daily).

The nonprofit Santa Cruz Community

Farmers' Markets (831/454-0566, www.santacruzfarmersmarket.org) runs three community markets in Santa Cruz with goods and food from more than 100 farms and vendors. The **Downtown Farmers Market** (Cedar St. and Lincoln St., 1pm-6pm Wed. spring-summer, 1pm-5pm Wed. winter) operates a block north of Pacific Avenue, while the **Live Oak Farmers Market** (15th St. and East Cliff Dr., 9am-1pm Sun.) is staged in a strip mall parking lot on the East Side. Finally, the **Westside Market** (Western Dr. and Mission St., 9am-1pm Sat.) takes place on the western boundary of town.

Tucked into a space by the Santa Cruz Museum of Art and History, the **Abbott Square Market** (725 Front St., http://abbottsquaremarket.com, 7am-10pm Sun.-Thurs., 7am-midnight Fri.-Sat.) is a hipster take on a food court. It houses vendors like Cat & Cloud Coffee, Veg On the Edge, and Belly Goat Burger and also has entertainment, including yoga, dance, and outdoor movie screenings.

Accommodations

Though there are no campgrounds in Santa Cruz proper, there are several near the beach in the Capitola and Aptos areas. The Santa Cruz Mountains also have camping opportunities. Most of these are so close to Santa Cruz that they make fine places to stay while exploring the city if you don't mind a bit of a drive.

UNDER $150

Staying at a hostel in Santa Cruz just feels right. And the **Santa Cruz Hostel** (321 Main St., 831/423-8304, www.hi-santacruz.org, dorm beds $40-50, private rooms $80-130) offers the area's only real budget lodging. These historic renovated cottages are just two blocks from the Santa Cruz Beach Boardwalk. They're clean, cheap, and close to Cowell's Beach. The big, homelike kitchen is open for guest use and may even be hiding some extra free food in its cupboards. Expect all the usual hostel-style amenities: a nice garden out back, an outdoor deck, free linens, laundry facilities, and a free guest computer. The private rooms are a deal due to their size and cleanliness.

Located among a strip of motels on Ocean Street, the **Continental Inn** (414 Ocean St., 831/429-1221, www.continentalinnsantacruz.com, $89-379) doesn't look like much from the outside. But inside, most of the rooms have hardwood floors, and all include a fridge and microwave. A stay includes continental breakfast and access to a pool and spa. It is also a short walk to Santa Cruz's downtown.

$150-250

The ★ **Seaway Inn** (176 West Cliff Dr., 831/471-9004, www.seawayinn.com, $229-469) offers a night's stay in a great location across from Cowell's Beach for a moderate price, as beach accommodations go. The rooms are clean but not fancy, and the bathrooms are small. All have a shared patio or deck out front with chairs. The 18 units in the main building have TVs with DVD players, along with microwaves and mini-fridges. In addition, there are family suites that can accommodate up to six adults.

OVER $250

The ★ **Santa Cruz Dream Inn** (175 West Cliff Dr., 831/426-4330, www.dreaminnsantacruz.com, $400-629) is in a location that cannot be beat. Perched over Cowell's Beach and the Santa Cruz Wharf, the Dream Inn has 165 rooms, all with striking ocean views and either a private balcony or a shared common patio. The rooms have a retro-chic feel that matches perfectly with the vibrant colors of the nearby Santa Cruz Boardwalk. On a sunny day, it would be difficult to ever leave the Dream Inn's sundeck,

which is located right on Cowell's Beach. You can take in the action of surfers, stand-up paddleboarders, and volleyball players from the comforts of the deck's heated swimming pool or large multi-person hot tub. Or you could just relax on a couch or reclining chair while sipping a cocktail from the poolside bar.

The ★ West Cliff Inn (174 West Cliff Dr., 831/457-2200, www.westcliffinn.com, $260-450) is a gleaming white mansion topping the hill above Cowell's Beach and the Boardwalk. This three-story historic landmark was constructed in 1877 and was the first of the bluff's "Millionaires' Row" residences; it was transformed into an elegant inn in 2007. The nine rooms in the main house have stunning white marble bathrooms, and some have oversized soaking tubs. If your room is on a higher floor, use the inn's dumbwaiter to transport your luggage. The more moderately priced and pet-friendly "Little Beach Bungalow" is behind the main house. All guests can fill up on breakfast in the morning and wine and appetizers in the afternoon. The inn's veranda and second-floor balcony provide wonderful views.

Escape the busy Boardwalk and downtown areas for the Ocean Echo Inn & Beach Cottages (401 Johans Beach Dr., 831/462-4192, www.oceanecho.com, $229-649), a secluded gem on the East Side. The inn is just 53 footsteps (the innkeepers' count) down to a locals' pocket beach known to some as Sunny Cove and to others as Johan's Beach. The inn's property is thought to have been a farm once, and its water tower, chicken coop, and carriage house have all been converted into cozy cottages. There are 15 units at Ocean Echo, including cottages and inn rooms. Each is different, and 11 of the 15 units have full kitchens. There are multiple outdoor decks on-site, along with a ping-pong table and some grills for cooking out.

The large pool deck at the Hotel Paradox (611 Ocean St., 831/425-7100, www. hotelparadox.com, $289-629) is the boutique hotel's best asset. Take advantage of Santa Cruz's sunshine at the tempting pool and large hot tub that can accommodate a dozen or more. The rooms are clean and modern with flat-screen TVs and Keurig coffeemakers. Opt for a unit on the ground floor with a small outdoor deck area, or choose a room higher up with a view of the pool action.

High up on a hilltop, the Chaminade Resort & Spa (1 Chaminade Ln., 831/475-5600, www.chaminade.com, $330-430) occupies an impressive 300 acres (121 ha). Occupy your time at the fitness center, heated outdoor pool, tennis courts, hiking trails, or The Spa at Chaminade (831/465-3465, 10am-8pm Mon.-Fri., 9am-8pm Sat.-Sun., massages $120-190).

Transportation and Services

Visitors planning to drive or bike around Santa Cruz should get themselves a good map, either before they arrive or at the visitors center in town. Navigating the winding, occasionally broken-up streets of this oddly shaped town isn't for the faint of heart. CA-1, which becomes Mission Street on the West Side, acts as the main artery through Santa Cruz and down to Capitola, Soquel, Aptos, and coastal points farther south. You'll find that CA-1 at the interchange to CA-17, and sometimes several miles to the east, is often a parking lot. No, you probably haven't come upon a major accident or a special event; it's just like that a lot of the time.

CAR

If you're driving to Santa Cruz from Silicon Valley, you have two choices of roads. Most drivers take fast, dangerous Highway 17. This narrow road doesn't have any switchbacks and

1: Seaway Inn 2: Santa Cruz Dream Inn 3: West Cliff Inn 4: Ocean Echo Inn & Beach Cottages

is the main truck route "over the hill." Most locals take this 50-mile-per-hour (81 kph) corridor fast—probably faster than they should. Each year, several people die in accidents on Highway 17. So, if you're new to the road, keep to the right and take it slow, no matter what the traffic to the left of you is doing. Check traffic reports before you head out; Highway 17 is known to be one of the worst commuting roads in all of the Bay Area, and the weekend beach traffic in the summer jams up fast in both directions, too.

For a more leisurely drive, you can opt for two-lane Highway 9. The tight curves and endless switchbacks will keep you at a reasonable speed, and you can use the turnouts to let the locals pass. On Highway 9, your biggest obstacles tend to be groups of bicyclists and motorcyclists, both of whom adore the slopes and curves of this technical driving road. The good news is that you'll get an up-close-and-personal view of the gorgeously forested Santa Cruz Mountains, complete with views of the valley to the north and ocean vistas to the south.

Parking

Parking in Santa Cruz can be its own special sort of horror. Downtown, head straight for the parking structures one block from Pacific Avenue on either side. They're much easier to deal with than trying to find street parking. The same goes for the beach and Boardwalk areas. At the Boardwalk, just pay the fee to park in the big parking lot adjacent to the attractions. You'll save an hour and a possible car break-in or theft.

BUS

In town, the buses are run by the **Santa Cruz Metro** (831/425-8600, www.scmtd.com, adults $2 per ride, passes available), with routes running all around Santa Cruz County.

You can probably find a way to get nearly anywhere you'd want to go on the Metro.

SERVICES

While it can be fun to explore Santa Cruz just by using your innate sense of direction and eye for the bizarre, those who want a bit more structure to their travels can hit the **Santa Cruz County Visitors Center** (303 Water St., Ste. 100, 800/833-3494 or 831/425-1234, www.santacruz.org, 9am-noon and 1pm-4pm Mon.-Fri., 11am-3pm Sat.-Sun.) for maps, advice, and information. Or stop by the **Downtown Information Kiosk** (1130 Pacific Ave., K2, 831/332-7422, www.downtownsantacruz.com, 11am-6pm Sun.-Thurs., 11am-8pm Fri.-Sat. May-Oct., 11am-6pm Tues.-Thurs. and Sun., 11am-7pm Fri.-Sat., Nov.-Apr.) on Pacific Avenue.

The daily *Santa Cruz Sentinel* (www. santacruzsentinel.com) offers local news plus up-to-date entertainment information. The free weekly newspaper *Good Times* (www. gtweekly.com) is also filled with upcoming events.

The **post office** (850 Front St., 831/426-0144, www.usps.com, 9am-5pm Mon.-Fri.) is a block off Pacific Avenue.

Medical treatment is available at **Dominican Hospital** (1555 Soquel Ave., 855/404-5720, www.dignityhealth.org).

Santa Cruz is wired. You'll be able to access the Internet in a variety of cafés and hotels. There are Starbucks locations here, and many indie cafés compete with their own (sometimes free) Wi-Fi.

Santa Cruz has plenty of banks and ATMs (including some ATMs on the arcade at the Boardwalk). Bank branches congregate downtown near Pacific Avenue. The West Side is mostly residential, so you'll find a few ATMs in supermarkets and gas stations, but little else.

Capitola and Aptos

Just east of Santa Cruz, Capitola was founded as the vacation resort Camp Capitola in the late 1800s before becoming the seaside hamlet of Capitola-by-the-Sea around 1900. Said to be the Pacific Coast's oldest seaside resort town, Capitola Village has all the features you'd want in a small oceanside city, including an esplanade, a wharf, and a sandy beach split by Soquel Creek. The few blocks that comprise downtown are scenic, with shops and restaurants worth visiting.

Aptos is east of Capitola. This unincorporated area is home to the Forest of Nisene Marks State Park and Seacliff State Beach. At the state park is the epicenter of the 1989 Loma Prieta Earthquake. Seacliff is popular for its pier, which leads out to a sunken concrete ship.

SIGHTS

Capitola Village

With its colorful buildings, narrow staircases, and long sandy beach, **Capitola Village** is a great place to wander around for a couple hours. Pick up a self-guided walking tour map from the **Capitola Historical Museum** (410 Capitola Ave.) to learn about 38 scenic locations and historic sites. Strolling along the footpath by Soquel Creek feels a bit like wandering the Venice Beach canals in Southern California, and offers views of an old train bridge spanning the creek and buildings like the Windmill House. Just downstream, the Capitola Wharf begins at the pastel-colored buildings of the Venetian Court—the first condominium project in California—and stretches 855 feet (261 m) into the bay. A bird's-eye view of the village can be attained by climbing the **Depot Hill Stairs** (El Camino Medio and Monterey Ave.), 86 steep steps to the Depot Hill subdivision, which dates to 1884.

New Brighton State Beach

One of the region's most popular sandy spots is **New Brighton State Beach** (1500 Park Ave., Capitola, 831/464-6329, www.parks. ca.gov, 8am-sunset daily, $10/vehicle). This forest-backed beach has everything: a strip of sand that's perfect for lounging and swimming, a forest-shaded campground for both tent and RV campers, hiking trails, and ranger-led nature programs. The **Pacific Migrations Visitor Center** (Memorial Day-Labor Day 10am-4pm Wed.-Sun., March 28-Memorial Day 10am-4pm Tues.-Sat.) focuses on interpreting the movements of humans and other animals. New Brighton can get crowded on sunny summer days, but it's nothing like the wall-to-wall people of the popular Southern California beaches. Call in advance to make camping reservations at this popular state park.

Seacliff State Beach

Seacliff State Beach (201 State Park Dr., Aptos, 831/685-6500, www.parks.ca.gov, 8am-sunset daily, $10/vehicle) is otherwise known as "the beach with the shipwreck." The concrete vessel SS *Palo Alto*, connected to the shore by a fishing pier, was once a floating attraction with a ballroom and restaurant before its hull cracked. The wreck is closed to the public, but you can get close to it on the pier. The bluff-sheltered beach is a mile long, and has a **visitors center** (831/685-6444, 10am-4pm Wed.-Sun.) with a model of the *Palo Alto* and a viewing tank filled with tidepool organisms.

The Forest of Nisene Marks State Park

Take a walk at **The Forest of Nisene Marks State Park** (4 mi/6.5 km north of Aptos on Aptos Creek Rd., 831/763-7063, www.parks. ca.gov, sunrise-sunset daily, $8/vehicle), once

Land of Medicine Buddha

For a unique experience, visit the **Land of Medicine Buddha** (5800 Prescott Rd., Soquel, 831/462-8383, http://landofmedicinebuddha.org, day-use gate 7am-5:30pm daily, $5/donation), north of Capitola in the shade of the Santa Cruz Mountains. The 108-acre (43.7-ha) facility is home to an active Buddhist community. Spin one of the giant, intricately decorated prayer wheels or take a thought-provoking walk on the **Eight Verses Pilgrimage Loop** (0.75 mi/1.2 km round-trip, easy), a stroll that passes eight Buddhist quotes. It is also possible to book a room or yurt for an overnight stay ($125 pp).

the site of serious logging operations but now shaded by second-growth redwoods. Mountain bikers can ride up the fire road through the center of the park, while hikers can head out on more than 30 miles (48 km) of hiking trails that take off from the roadway. You can also hike with your dog on parts of the park below the Portner Family Picnic Area, which is unusual in a state park. One popular hike is the **Loma Prieta Grade Trail** (4.6 mi/7.4 km round-trip, moderate, 350-ft/107-m elevation gain), which follows an old railway bed up to the remnants of a lumber camp. Another point of interest within the park is the epicenter of the 1989 Loma Prieta Earthquake, which interrupted the World Series and caused the collapse of a section of San Francisco's Bay Bridge.

Manresa State Beach

One of the nicest stretches of beach in Santa Cruz County, **Manresa State Beach** (1445 San Andreas Rd., 831/724-3750, www.parks.ca.gov, $10/vehicle, 8am-sunset daily) draws beachgoers and surfers to its sandy shores. Advanced surfers are fond of the nice, less-crowded break at Manresa, especially in the summer. The large parking lot has restrooms and an outdoor shower. There's free parking in the residential area just south of the beach's entrance.

Sunset State Beach

Surrounded by agricultural fields, **Sunset State Beach** (201 Sunset Beach Rd., Watsonville, 831/763-7063, 8am-sunset daily, $10/vehicle) in southern Santa Cruz County

feels like it is in the middle of nowhere despite being just 16 miles (26 km) south of Santa Cruz. Pine trees shade the campground on the bluffs above a truly wild beach. The oceanside picnic spots are pleasant if the wind isn't too bad.

FOOD
Seafood

Longtime Capitola fixture **Paradise Beach Grille** (215 Esplanade, Capitola, 831/476-4900, www.paradisebeachgrille.com, 11:30am-9:30pm, $12-40) closed during the 2020 pandemic but was rescued by a purchase from the owners of The Crow's Nest in Santa Cruz. There are no plans to change the seafood-heavy menu—like mahi mahi fish tacos, coconut prawns, sugar-and-spice salmon. The food's good, but the prime location on Capitola's Esplanade and the fun atmosphere makes it even better. At night, the outdoor deck hanging over Soquel Creek offers a romantic view of city lights reflecting on the water.

American

Just inland from Capitola, ★ **Café Cruz** (2621 41st Ave., Soquel, 831/476-3801, www.cafecruz.com, 11:30am-9pm Mon.-Thurs., 10:30am-10:30pm Fri., 11:30am-10pm Sat., 5pm-9pm Sun., $16-36) is a local favorite known for its rotisserie chicken. Watch the meat twirling away on the spit as the cooks craft other entrées in the open kitchen. There's also a heated patio for those who want to head outdoors. This place is very popular, even on weeknights.

The **Shadowbrook Restaurant** (1750 Wharf Rd., Capitola, 831/475-1511, www.

1: seaside Capitola **2:** footpath in Capitola Village

shadowbrook-capitola.com, 4pm-8:30pm Mon.-Fri., 2pm-9pm Sat., 2pm-8:30pm Sat., $22-36) is where to celebrate a special occasion. The adventure begins with a cable car ride down to the restaurant, which is perched on a steep slope above Soquel Creek. Entrées include blackened lamb, filet mignon, and a salmon dish that has been touted in *Bon Appétit Magazine*. Be sure to get your photo taken if it's a special occasion. If you're staying within a 3-mile (4.8-km) radius of the restaurant, Shadowbrook will pick you up and shuttle you via a 1950 Dodge (free, but tips are appreciated); reserve a ride when you make your dinner reservations.

Barbecue

One of the best barbecue joints in the region, ★ **Aptos St. BBQ** (8059 Aptos St., Aptos, 831/662-1721, www.aptosstbbq.com, 7am-9pm daily, $12-32) is a down-home spot that does a combination of Kansas City and Texas barbecue styles. All of the meats—tri-tip, chicken, pulled pork, ribs—are smoked over seasoned oak wood. The popular brisket takes 14 hours to cook. To round it out, the eatery offers 37 curated craft beers on tap, has outdoor seating, and hosts live blues nightly.

Southern

Roux Dat (35555 Clares St., Suite G, 831/295-6372, http://rouxdatcajuncreole.com, 11am-7pm daily, $8-13) dishes out New Orleans-style fare in a casual space in a Capitola strip mall. The classic stews—jambalaya, gumbo, étouffée—are warming on a cold day. Other items include po'boys and tasty hush puppies with mustard dipping sauce. This being the Santa Cruz area, there are gluten-free, vegan, and vegetarian options. The eatery also has another location in downtown Santa Cruz's Abbott Square (118 Cooper St., Unit B, 831/888-6500, 11am-7pm daily).

French

Café Sparrow (8042 Soquel Dr., Aptos, 831/688-6238, www.cafesparrow.com, 11:30am-2pm and 5:30pm-9pm Mon.-Fri., 11am-2pm and 5:30pm-9pm Sat., 9am-2pm

and 5:30pm-9pm Sun., $20-40) serves country French cuisine that's consistently tasty. Whatever you order, it will be fantastic. The seafood is noteworthy, as are the steaks. Café Sparrow's kitchen prepares all the dishes with fresh ingredients, and the chef (who can sometimes be seen out in the dining room checking on customer satisfaction with the food) thinks up innovative preparations and creates tasty sauces. He's also willing to accommodate special requests and dietary restrictions with good cheer. For dessert, treat yourself to the profiteroles, which can be created with either ice cream or pastry cream.

Deli

Gayle's Bakery (Upper Village Shopping Center, 504 Bay Ave., Capitola, 831/462-1200, www.gaylesbakery.com, 6:30am-8:30pm daily, $4-17) is a lot more than a place to pick up baked goods. This 10,000-square-foot (929-sq-m) facility has a rotisserie and deli that serves salads, sandwiches, hot entrées, and nightly blue-plate specials. This place can get quite crowded so be ready for a line.

The Palm Deli (3000 Valencia Ave., Aptos, 831/688-3354, www.thepalmdeli.com, 7am-5pm daily, $5-12) has such a wide selection of sandwiches that it could keep lunch interesting for weeks. Part market, part coffee bar, and part deli, this unassuming locals' joint serves cold takeout sandwiches, hot paninis, salads, and daily specials like a slow-roasted pulled pork and barbecued tri-tip. Some creative selections include a ham-and-cheese sandwich enlivened with a pineapple chutney and a spicy buffalo chicken breast panini.

ACCOMMODATIONS

The ★ **Monarch Cove Inn** (620 El Salto Dr., Capitola, 831/464-1295, www.monarchcoveinn.com, $250-440) is on a property with manicured gardens, gurgling fountains, towering palm trees, a monarch butterfly sanctuary, and a marvelous view of

1: Capitola restaurants overlooking Soquel Creek
2: classic New Orleans stew from Roux Dat

Monterey Bay curving from Moss Landing to Monterey. The grounds were once a private retreat for two English families, and then a resort that hosted noted guests such as Mary Pickford and Al Capone. The inn's Victorian mansion is divided into nine units along with two suites, all of which have private entrances. The Carriage House Cottage, with a full kitchen, private outdoor deck, private gazebo, and private hot tub, is one of two cottages available. A continental breakfast is delivered to guests each morning. Capitola is just a 10-minute walk away.

A boutique hotel right on the Esplanade, the **Capitola Hotel** (210 Esplanade, 831/476-1278, www.capitolahotel.com, $300-479) has 10 small and simple but nicely decorated rooms. At any rate, you'll probably want to spend your stay at the nearby beach or eating and drinking at the row of restaurants located just feet away. There's one dog-friendly room (Martinique) and a room ideal for close-knit groups or families (Grand Cayman); it has a small kitchenette, private patio, and two beds. The friendly staff serve a continental breakfast and offer weekend wine and cheese service.

It's difficult to miss the **Capitola Venetian Hotel** (1500 Wharf Rd., Capitola, 831/476-6471, www.capitolavenetian.com, $289-650), the cluster of brightly colored Mediterranean-style buildings on Soquel Creek. This longtime Capitola fixture has one-, two-, and three-bedroom units, all with kitchens. Some also have fireplaces.

For a vacation full of sun and sand, book one of the 283 suites at the **Seascape Beach Resort** (1 Seascape Beach Resort Dr., Aptos, 831/688-6800, $400-800), all of which have a kitchen and fireplace. The grounds include a pool, spa, fitness center, beach access, and two restaurants: **Sanderlings** and **Palapas.**

Camping

Whether you want an inexpensive place to stay while exploring nearby Santa Cruz or just want to camp near a beach, the Santa Cruz state beach campgrounds in Capitola and Aptos fit the bill. The biggest and possibly best camping option is at **New Brighton State Beach** (1500 Park Ave., Capitola, 800/444-7275, www.reservecalifornia.com, $35). There are more than 100 campsites in a 93-acre (37.6-ha) area situated on a bluff above the beach. Santa Cruz is just 6.5 miles (10.5 km) away.

RV campers have 26 sites with full hookups and 37 non-hookup sites to choose from at **Seacliff State Beach** (201 State Park Rd., Aptos, 800/444-7275, www.reservecalifornia.com, $55). Those without much to carry can opt for the 60 walk-in campsites at the **Manresa Uplands Campground** (205 Manresa Beach Rd., La Selva Beach, 800/444-7275, www.reservecalifornia.com, $35) in Manresa State Beach.

Less than 4 miles (6.4 km) from Manresa State Beach, **Sunset State Beach** (201 Sunset Beach Rd., Watsonville, 800/444-7275, www.reserveamerica.com, $35) is an underrated and worthy place to pitch a tent. It feels far from Santa Cruz, but the city is only a 20-minute drive north.

TRANSPORTATION AND SERVICES

The village of Capitola is just 6 miles (9.7 km) east of Santa Cruz. Hop onto CA-1 South and for almost 5 miles (8 km) before exiting at Bay Avenue/Porter Street. Take a slight right onto Bay Avenue and continue for almost 0.5 mile (0.8 km). Then take a right on Capitola Avenue and follow almost another 0.5 mile (0.8 km) to the village.

Aptos is 8 miles (12.9 km) east of Santa Cruz. Take CA-1 South about 7 miles (11.3 km) and exit on State Park Drive.

For information about the Capitola area, you can call the **Capitola Soquel Chamber of Commerce** (831/475-6522, www.capitolachamber.com) or visit their website. The Capitola **post office** (826 Bay Ave., Capitola, 831/475-5948, www.usps.com, 9am-4:30pm Mon.-Fri., 10am-1pm Sat.) is available if you need to send a package or a postcard.

1: Monarch Cove Inn **2:** Capitola Venetian Hotel

Excursion to Corralitos

Corralitos Brewing Company

Twenty miles (32 km) east of Santa Cruz, tucked below the Santa Cruz Mountains, Corralitos is a community of vineyards and farmlands. Since 1957, Corralitos has been a mecca for meat eaters thanks to the **Corralitos Market & Sausage Company** (569 Corralitos Rd., 831/722-2633, http://corralitosmarketsausagecompany.com, 8am-6pm Mon.-Sat., 9am-5pm Sun.) and its smoked sausages and marinated tri-tips, ribs, and chicken. The house-made sausages are their claim to fame, with flavors including the very popular "Cheezy Bavarian," a beef and pork sausage with chunks of sharp cheddar cheese. You can purchase hot sandwiches like the tasty tri-tip from the back counter.

The **Corralitos Brewing Company** (2536 Freedom Blvd., 831/728-2311, www.

Northern Santa Cruz Coast

The northern coastal section of Santa Cruz is made up of agricultural lands, parks, open spaces, and secluded beaches dotted with sea stacks. Residents of this region have started calling this stretch of coastline the Slowcoast, due to its rural, unrushed attitude. Recently, there has been an effort to transform 5,800 acres (2,347 ha) of this coastline into the Santa Cruz Redwoods National Monument.

★ WILDER RANCH STATE PARK

West of Santa Cruz's city limits, the land on both sides of Highway 1 suddenly gives way to farmland perched atop coastal terraces. The best place to get a feel for this mostly undeveloped stretch of coastline is to visit **Wilder Ranch State Park** (1401 Coast Rd., 831/423-9703, www.parks.ca.gov, 8am-sunset daily, $10/vehicle). The park allows visitors to step back in time and discover what it was like to live on a ranch more than 100 years ago at its many living-history demonstrations. Other annual events include gardening demonstrations and the Old-Fashioned Independence Day Celebration. Get your bearings at the **Visitor Center & Store** (10am-4pm Thurs.-Sun.).

corralitosbrewingco.com, 4pm-8pm Tues.-Fri., noon-8pm Sat.-Sun.) provides the perfect place to get suds to go with your Corralitos Market sausages. This beautiful tasting room is attached to the owner's family's lumber store, which explains the interior filled with stunning woodwork—from redwood beams and madrone hardtops to Monterey pine floors and ceilings. The beer here is superb. The taproom has 10 draft beers brewed on-site, including a terrific red ale and their flagship IPA. On the front porch are barrel tables and wood-slab seats for those who would rather sip their suds outdoors.

If you prefer a pinot noir or chardonnay with your smoked sausage sandwich, head down the Corralitos Wine Trail (www.corralitoswinetrail.com). Here you can visit a number of family-owned wineries: Windy Oaks Winery (550 Hazel Dell Rd., 831/786-9463, www.windyoaksestate.com, noon-5pm Sat., tasting $20-25), Alfaro Family Vineyards (420 Hames Rd., 831/728-5172, www.alfarowine.com, noon-5pm Sat., tasting $15), Nicholson Vineyards (2800 Pleasant Valley Rd., 831/724-7071, www.nicholsonvineyards.com, noon-5pm Sat., tasting $15), El Vaquero Vineyards (2901 Freedom Blvd., 831/607-8118, www.elvaquerowinery.com, 3pm-6pm Fri., noon-6pm Sat.-Sun., tasting $12), Lester Estate Wines (1950 Pleasant Valley Rd., 831/728-3793, http://deerparkranch.com, noon-4pm Sat., tasting $15), and Storrs Winery & Vineyards (1560 Pleasant Valley Rd., 831/724-5030, www.storrswine.com, Sat.-Sun. by appointment, tasting $22-30).

Technically, Slice Project (300 Main St., Watsonville, 831/319-4851, www.sliceprojectpizza.com, 2pm-8pm Wed.-Sat., 2pm-7pm Sun., $4-40) isn't in Corralitos, but it is just south via Freedom Boulevard in the adjacent city of Watsonville. The terrific family-owned pizza joint does NYC-inspired slices and, even better, Detroit-style square pizzas. Add in an impressive craft beer selection, and Slice Project makes a very worthy detour.

Corralitos is just a 20-minute drive from Santa Cruz. Head out of town on CA-1 South toward Watsonville. After about 8 miles (12.9 km), exit onto Freedom Boulevard. Turn left on Freedom Boulevard and follow it for almost 3 miles (4.8 km). Then go straight on Hames Road for 0.5 mile (0.8 km) before turning right on Pleasant Valley Road, which you continue on for another 0.5 mile (0.8 km). Take the first left to get back on Hames Road and take it 1.5 miles (2.4 km). Then turn right on Corralitos Road to get into the heart of Corralitos.

For those who would rather check out the park's natural beauty in the present, there are more than 35 miles (56 km) of trails at Wilder Ranch. The Old Cove Landing Trail (2.5-mi/4-km, easy) is a flat hike out to the coastline, which is pocketed with sea caves and usually decorated with wildlife, from elegant cormorants to harbor seals lazing on the coastal shelves.

The east side of the park is very popular with mountain bikers for its beginner to intermediate climbs with coastal views. The Wilder Ridge Loop (6.3 mi/10.1 km) provides a good introduction to the park's trails along with its coastal views. The Enchanted Loop (2 mi/3.2 km) traverses more technical terrain.

Getting There

Wilder Ranch State Park is less than a 10-minute drive west from downtown Santa Cruz. Head out on Mission Street, which doubles as CA-1, for about 3 miles (4.8 km).

★ DAVENPORT

Nine miles (14.5 km) north of Santa Cruz's West Side, the small community of Davenport (pop. 400) sits on the coastline's scenic bluffs. Right off Highway 1, Davenport has a tiny town center with some charming eateries and a wine bar, as well as the two-cell Davenport Jail, a Mission Revival-style building that now houses a small museum. Across the street from town is a dirt pullout that offers access to Davenport Beach and some coastal headlands that are a great spot for whale-watching during winter. The region around Davenport is worth exploring for its stunning beaches, coastal cliffs, and unique sea stacks offshore.

Shark Fin Cove

Less than 1 mile (1.6 km) south of Davenport on the west side of Highway 1 sits the aptly named **Shark Fin Cove**. This popular pull-off for photographers looks out over a small, vertical island that rises out of the sea like a shark fin. The formation is a remnant of the mudstone cliff that surrounds the adjacent beach.

Davenport Landing Beach

Santa Cruz County has a lot of fine beaches, and **Davenport Landing Beach** (Davenport Landing Rd.) is one of its best. Located almost 2 miles (3.2 km) north of town on Davenport Landing Road, it is a scenic stretch of sand bookended by rocky terraces and looming headlands. It also has a beachside swing set with a fine ocean view. Rumored to have once been a whaling port, this beach is popular with surfers, who like the right- and left-breaking waves on either side of the beach, and windsurfers, who turn up for the afternoon winds. A sea cave with a large opening can be found on the north end of the beach and accessed during low tide. Facilities include pit toilets and a wheelchair-accessible ramp to the beach.

The beach is also the location of **American Abalone Farms** (245 Davenport Rd., http://americanabalone.com, 10am-4pm Sat.-Sun.), an aquaculture business that raises California red abalone. It operates a **seafood market** (Sat.-Sun.) that sells live abalone, pounded abalone steaks, oysters, sea urchins, and Dungeness crab.

Wine-Tasting

Beauregard Wine Bar (450 Hwy. 1, 831/425-7777, www.beauregardvineyards.com, 10am-5pm daily, tasting $25) has fine coastal views at its Davenport location. Beauregard's wines—pinot noir, Syrah, chardonnay—are made from grapes grown in the mountains behind the tasting room.

Food

In a small community, some businesses have to be more than one thing. The **Whale City Bakery Bar & Grill** (490 Hwy. 1, 831/423-9009, www.whalecitybakery.com, 6:30am-8pm Fri.-Wed., 6:30am-9pm Thurs., $7-13) certainly fits this bill. It's a bakery, restaurant, bar, coffee shop, live music venue, and community gathering place. The menu items include burgers, sandwiches, and a few seafood options. On Thursday nights, they stay open later for live music performances.

Davenport Roadhouse (1 Davenport Ave., 831/426-8801, http://davenportroadhouse.com, 8:30am-3pm Mon., 8:30am-9pm Tues.-Fri., 8am-9pm Sat., 8am-8:30pm Sun., $12-21) is a gourmet option in little Davenport. The menu ranges from wood-fired pizzas to a ribeye steak with fries. The restaurant also has a taco night on Tuesday and a Wednesday night fixed-price menu for two.

You can pick your own fruit at the **Swanton Berry Farm** (25 Swanton Rd., 831/469-8804, www.swantonberryfarm.com, 8am-5pm daily). April and May are the months for pick-your-own strawberries. Or stop by the stand and purchase a berry pie, jar of jam, or strawberry drink.

Getting There

Davenport is a simple 9-mile (14.5-km) drive north of Santa Cruz on CA-1. You'll see the buildings on your right and a large dirt pull-out on the left.

RANCHO DEL OSO AND WADDELL BEACH

A section of Big Basin Redwoods State Park reaches the coastline at **Rancho Del Oso and Waddell Beach** (17 mi/27 km north of Santa

1: spring in Davenport **2:** Davenport Landing Beach

Cruz on Hwy. 1, 831/338-8860, www.parks. ca.gov). The primary attraction of this inland section of the park is the **Rancho del Oso Nature and History Center** (3600 CA-1, 831/427-2288, http://ranchodeloso.org, noon-4pm Sat.-Sun.). The museum is housed within an old ranch house where one of President Herbert Hoover's relatives resided and has exhibits on the region's natural and cultural history. To reach the center, take a right on the dirt road before the Waddell Creek Bridge and follow it inland to the structure.

There are also a couple of short walks that leave from the nature center. Popular with birders, the **Marsh Trail** (0.4 mi/0.6 km one-way, easy) goes alongside the marsh and Waddell Creek.

On the west side of the highway is **Waddell Beach.** This is one of the area's best places for windsurfing and kitesurfing. It can be quite entertaining to watch the boarders carve across the sea and launch themselves into the sky.

★ AÑO NUEVO STATE PARK

Año Nuevo State Park (1 New Year's Creek Rd., Pescadero, 650/879-2025, www.parks. ca.gov, 8:30am-sunset daily, $10/vehicle) is one of the California coast's truly wild places. The beach is one of the largest mainland breeding spots of the elephant seal—up to 10,000 seals can pile up in the sand here. Offshore, the giant marine mammals have overrun the abandoned buildings of Año Nuevo Island. Great white sharks circle the small island, waiting for an opportunity to snack on one of the seals.

The only way to experience this stunning display of nature up close is by taking a 2.5-hour **guided tour** (www. reservecalifornia.com, $7 plus a $3.99 reservation fee) between December 15 and March 31. Other reasons to visit include a secluded cove and the Marine Education Center (8:30am-4:30pm daily), with its exhibits, bookstore, and theater.

Getting There

Año Nuevo State Park is located in San Mateo County right above the Santa Cruz County/San Mateo County line. From Santa Cruz, Año Nuevo is a half-hour drive north on CA-1.

PIGEON POINT LIGHTHOUSE

On a secluded section of coast, the **Pigeon Point Lighthouse** rises 115 feet (35.1 m) above its headlands perch and the crashing Pacific Ocean. Built in 1871, the structure is tied with Point Arena Lighthouse in Mendocino County for the title of tallest lighthouse on the West Coast. Even cooler: You can spend an evening on the grounds at the ★ **Pigeon Point Lighthouse Hostel** (210 Pigeon Point Rd. at Hwy. 1, 650/879-0633, www.norcalhostels.org/pigeon, dorm beds $25-32, private rooms $82-186). It has simple but comfortable accommodations, both private and dorm style. Amenities include three kitchens, free Wi-Fi, a fire pit, and beach access. But the best amenity of all is the cliff-top hot tub ($8/half hour).

Getting There

The Pigeon Point Lighthouse is located in San Mateo County and can be reached via a simple half-hour drive north up CA-1 out of Santa Cruz.

Santa Cruz Mountains

Less than 10 miles (16.1 km) outside the city, the Santa Cruz Mountains feel a world away from Santa Cruz's bustling Pacific Avenue and Boardwalk. The mountains are cloaked in forests of coast redwoods and dotted with parks. Along Highway 9 and the San Lorenzo River is a string of scenic mountain towns, starting with **Felton, Ben Lomond,** and **Boulder Creek,** the latter of which is just 13 miles (20.9 km) from Santa Cruz. Boulder Creek is also the best of the bunch, with colorful storefronts and a few eateries lining Highway 9 amid a backdrop of forested mountain ridges.

SIGHTS
★ Roaring Camp Railroads

One of the best ways to experience the redwoods is to hop on a train at **Roaring Camp Railroads** (5401 Graham Hill Rd., Felton, 831/335-4484 or 831/335-4400, www. roaringcamp.com). There are two train trips to choose from: The **Redwood Forest Steam Train** (year-round, adults $33, children $24, 1.25 hours round-trip) and the **Santa Cruz Beach Train** (Apr.-Sept., adults $35, children $27, 3 hours round-trip). Both of these trains chug through the towering redwood forests that cloak the Santa Cruz Mountains. Pulled by a diesel electric engine, the Beach Train passes through Henry Cowell Redwoods State Park and travels along the San Lorenzo River as it makes its way down to the Boardwalk. There's a one-hour layover at the Boardwalk before it climbs back up into the mountains. The Redwood Forest Steam Train is a narrow-gauge steam locomotive that billows impressive clouds of steam as it climbs Bear Mountain. Along the way, it offers close views of coast redwoods that are up to 1,800 years old. Both trains have a guide who narrates your journey over the clanking machinery of the locomotives. Passengers ride outdoors on open-air cars, so bring a sweater and sunblock.

Bigfoot Discovery Museum

Most people believe if Bigfoot lived anywhere, it would be in the dense forests of Northern California. The folks at the **Bigfoot Discovery Museum** (5497 Hwy. 9, Felton, 831/335-4478, www. bigfootdiscoverymuseum.com, 11am-6pm Wed.-Mon., donations appreciated) maintain that the hairy biped has also been seen in the Santa Cruz Mountains. This little red building with wooden Bigfoot carvings out front is an essential stop for conspiracy theorists and lovers of quirky attractions. Inside, there is information on local Bigfoot sightings, plaster footprints of what is said to be Bigfoot, and the iconic 1967 film footage of the beast striding across the screen, which plays on continuous loop. A fun section of the small museum is devoted to Bigfoot in popular culture, from its appearance on the label of Sierra Nevada Brewing Co.'s Bigfoot Ale to toys associated with the 1987 film *Harry and the Hendersons.*

Mount Hermon Redwood Canopy Tours

Experience the coast redwoods from way up high at the **Mount Hermon Redwood Canopy Tours** (Mount Hermon Conference Center, 17 Conference Dr., 831/430-4357, http://mounthermonadventures.com, $99). Taking their lead from Costa Rica's popular rainforest canopy tours, these two-hour guided adventures involve traversing six zip lines and two sky bridges to gain a unique perspective on California's sky-scraping trees.

PARKS
Henry Cowell Redwoods State Park

Henry Cowell Redwoods State Park (101 N. Big Trees Park Rd., Felton, 831/335-4598, www.parks.ca.gov, sunrise-sunset daily, $10/vehicle) is the closest of the Santa Cruz Mountain parks to downtown Santa Cruz.

Just over 6 miles (9.7 km) away from the coastal city, the 4,650-acre (1,882-ha) park's highlight is a stand of virgin coast redwoods that can be experienced via the **Redwood Grove Loop Trail** (trailhead by the nature center, 0.8 mi/1.3 km round-trip, easy). Some unique natural features along the loop are the Fremont Tree, in whose burnt-out trunk Gen. John C. Fremont is said to have spent a night, and the albino redwood trees, which have white needles due to a lack of chlorophyll.

There's a section of the park worth visiting during warm days for the so-called **Garden of Eden** (6am-sunset daily), a spot featuring deep pools of the San Lorenzo River and a nice beach. It's also known as a frequent nude sunbathing spot. To reach it, drive out of Santa Cruz 3 miles (4.8 km) toward Felton on Highway 9. Look for the sign for the north entrance of the park, and then drive into the dirt pullout on the right with the green metal gates. Park your vehicle and pass through the southern gate. Follow the trail downhill and take a right at the next fork. When you hit the train tracks, take a right and walk until you see the "No Campfire" and "No Alcoholic Beverages" signs. Follow the steep trail down to the river and the Garden of Eden.

Another adventure can be had hiking to some **lime kiln ruins** (3 mi/4.8 km round-trip, moderate) in the park's **Fall Creek Unit** (Felton Empire Rd. off Hwy. 9). The abandoned stone structures manufactured lime in the late 1800s and early 1900s. To reach this site, start at the south end of the Fall Creek Unit on the Bennett Creek Trail. Then continue onto the Fall Creek Trail and the South Fork Trail.

Big Basin Redwoods State Park

The ancient trees at **Big Basin Redwoods State Park** (21600 Big Basin Way, Boulder Creek, 831/338-8860, www.parks.ca.gov, 6am-sunset daily, $10/vehicle), some of them as tall as 375 feet (114 m), inspired the creation of California's first state park in 1902. Decorating this 18,000-acre state park are

multiple waterfalls, rock formations pocked with Native American mortar holes, and wildlife ranging from bright yellow banana slugs to stealthy coyotes. Sadly, Big Basin suffered extensive wildfire damage in 2020, although, thankfully, many of the coastal redwoods survived. The best way to experience them is hiking Big Basin's miles of trails, still in the process of recovery. Check the park's website for an update on conditions before making plans.

Castle Rock State Park

Crowning the top of the Santa Cruz Mountains, **Castle Rock State Park** (15000 Skyline Blvd., 408/868-9540, 8am-sunset daily, $10/vehicle) is best known for its weathered sandstone rock formations that resemble giant slabs of Swiss cheese. Goat Rock is one of several destinations for the region's rock climbers. The 5,150-acre (2,084-ha) park also has 34 miles (55 km) of hiking trails. The **Saratoga Gap and Ridge Trail Loop** (trailhead at main parking lot, 5.6 mi/9 km round-trip, moderate) hits most of the park's best sites, including Goat Rock, Castle Rock Falls, and the Russell Point Overlook.

FOOD

The **Cowboy Bar & Grill** (5447 Hwy. 9, Felton, 831/335-2330, www.feltoncowboy.com, 11am-9pm Wed.-Mon., $11-26) gives comfort food a ride in the saddle. Tablecloths resemble spotted cowhides. This longtime Felton favorite serves meat in sauces and creations like a yam cake dish topped with chicken and cheese in a pool of sweet jalapeno glaze. There's a nice outdoor patio, or dine inside amid a museum's worth of cowboy memorabilia.

Casa Nostra (9217 Hwy. 9, Ben Lomond, 831/609-6132, http://ristorantecasanostra. com, 11am-9pm Mon.-Thurs., 11am-10pm Fri., 8:30am-10pm Sat., 8:30am-9pm Sun., $20-27) is a quirky Italian restaurant perfectly at home in the Santa Cruz Mountains.

1: Roaring Camp Railroads **2:** one of the cabins at Felton's Fern River Resort

1

2

Tasty dishes include *rigatoni alla Bolognese* and eggplant parmesan. The indoor dining room has tables built from locally produced redwood. There's also outdoor seating under live redwood trees and a taproom serving a dozen local beers.

ACCOMMODATIONS

The 15 red wooden cabins at the **Fern River Resort** (5250 Hwy. 9, Felton, 831/335-4412, www.fernriver.com, $200-700) are in a park-like setting amongst redwood trees on the shore of the San Lorenzo River. The largest cabins accommodate eight people; the smallest is a studio the size of a hotel room. A handful of wooden decks overlook the river, perfect for a sunny afternoon. The summer-camp-like grounds have a community fire pit, a badminton court, a ping-pong table, and a gazebo garden.

Jaye's Timberlane Resort (8705 Hwy. 9, Ben Lomond, 831/336-5479, www.jayestimberlane.com, $105-195) has 10 cabins spread across a 7-acre (2.8-ha) plot of land. All of the one- or two-bedroom units have full kitchens and some have fireplaces. Each one has its own private deck for taking in the forest. The grounds have a solar-heated pool, a horseshoe pit, and a ping-pong table.

Camping

The Santa Cruz Mountains are an ideal place to pitch a tent. **Henry Cowell Redwoods State Park** (2591 Graham Hill Rd., Scotts Valley, 800/444-7275, www.reservecalifornia.com, Apr.-Oct., $35) has 113 campsites in a section of the park that is a five-minute drive or 45-minute hike from Cowell's popular redwood grove. The campground closes during the winter.

TRANSPORTATION AND SERVICES

When Highway 9 is open, it's only a 7-mile (11.3-km) drive from Santa Cruz to Felton on the mountainous road. It usually takes half an hour to get to Boulder Creek from Santa Cruz along a 15-mile (24-km) stretch of the road. To avoid the windy bottom section of Highway 9, take CA-17 toward San Jose for just more than 3 miles (4.8 km) before exiting on Mt. Hermon Road. Then continue on that road for almost 4 miles (6.4 km) before turning right on Graham Hill Road. After 0.25 mile (0.4 km), Graham Hill Road hits Highway 9 in Felton.

Felton has its own **post office** (6101 Gushee St., 831/335-8015, www.usps.com, 9am-4pm Mon.-Fri., 11:30am-2pm Sat.). Boulder Creek has one, too, at 200 Lorenzo Street (831/338-4865, www.usps.com, 9:30am-4pm Mon.-Fri.).

Big Sur

Big Sur is not a town, a rock, or a beach, but rather the stunning 90-mile (145-km) stretch of coastline between Carmel and San Simeon. Highway 1, which runs through Big Sur, is one of the world's iconic coastal drives.

There is a lot to see off the precipitous roadway, including skyscraping coast redwoods, waterfalls decorating cliff faces, steep mountains and their accompanying valleys, and rugged beaches that are as scenic as any along the California coast.

Big Sur is a collision of land and sea as well as a juxtaposition of vibrant colors: green hills, orange cliffs, and blue seas. It is a place for contemplation, recreation, relaxation, and rejuvenation. Even with Big Sur's rising popularity, it's still possible to find a peaceful parcel to take

Highlights

Look for ★ to find recommended sights, activities, dining, and lodging.

★ **Big Sur Coast Highway:** This stretch of Highway 1 is known as one of the most beautiful drives in the world (page 205).

★ **Point Sur Light Station:** One of California's most stunning lighthouses is perched atop a looming 360-foot-tall (110-m) rock surrounded on three sides by ocean. Take a worthwhile three-hour tour to learn about its history (page 206).

★ **Andrew Molera State Park:** This sprawling, lightly developed park offers access to a stunning stretch of coast. It offers great hiking options, like the Ridge Trail and Panorama Trail Loop (page 208).

★ **Pfeiffer Beach:** With rock formations offshore and purple sand, this is one of Big Sur's most picturesque spots (page 209).

★ **Henry Miller Memorial Library:** Dedicated to preserving the idiosyncratic artistic spirit of former resident and acclaimed author Henry Miller, this quirky arts outpost is both bookstore and cultural center (page 211).

★ **Julia Pfeiffer Burns State Park:** This park's claim to fame is McWay Falls, which pours right into the Pacific (page 211).

★ **Sand Dollar Beach:** This is one of the largest stretches of sand on Big Sur's rugged coastline (page 213).

in the majesty of the natural world, whether it's whales moving and spouting off the coast like locomotives or California condors swirling above your head like campfire embers.

The range of restaurant and lodging options in Big Sur mirrors the gap between the area's towering peaks and deep canyon floors. Visitors can pitch a tent by the Big Sur River or opt to spend a night in one of the region's famed luxury hotels: the Post Ranch Inn and the Ventana Big Sur. Or make a picnic with takeout food from the Big Sur Deli or watch the sunset drop from Nepenthe's stunning outdoor deck.

The region has inspired all sorts of artists, including risqué writer Henry Miller, beat icon Jack Kerouac, nature poet Robinson Jeffers, and indie rock frontman Ben Gibbard of Death Cab for Cutie; most likely, it will inspire you, too.

PLANNING YOUR TIME

Summer is the busy season for Big Sur, though its booming popularity makes it an increasingly year-round destination. Summer is when there can be frequent coastal fog. Away from the coast, the Big Sur Valley can offer some relief from the fog. Reservations are essential for hotels and campsites during the summer, when options are pricey and scarce. Fall is the ideal time for a trip to the area, with warmer temperatures and fewer crowds.

Big Sur is almost always recovering from some natural disaster. The 2020 Dolan Fire burned sections of Julia Pfeiffer Burns State Park, Limekiln State Park, and the Ventana Wilderness. And the twisting two-lane Highway 1—the only road in and out of Big Sur—frequently undergoes construction and closures; the "burn scar" from the Dolan Fire caused a mudslide in 2021, sweeping parts of the highway into the ocean. Always check the **California Department of Transportation's website** (www.dot.ca.gov) for information about highway closures and possible delays. The locals' place for information is the **BigSurKate blog** (http://bigsurkate.blog).

A lot of people drive through Big Sur in a day, taking Highway 1 from Carmel to San Simeon and pulling off at the road's many turnouts to take in the views. If you are driving slower than most traffic on Highway 1, pull over into a pullout and allow the traffic to pass. To stop for photos, turn into the nearest pullout. Give the drivers behind you enough notice that you will be slowing down and turning. Outdoors enthusiasts who want to get off the highway and *really* experience Big Sur will need at least a couple days. The Big Sur Valley (26 mi/42 km south of Carmel) is a good place to stay if you want both a great outdoors experience and amenities such as restaurants and lodging. The valley is also home to Pfeiffer Big Sur State Park, which has nearly 200 campsites. The south coast of Big Sur—the stretch from Lucia to San Simeon—has significantly fewer amenities; there are a few campgrounds and the Treebones Resort.

A trip to Big Sur involves planning. It's a good idea to secure supplies and gas before entering the region (at Carmel in the north or Cambria in the south). While the area does have a few markets, you will pay higher prices for a smaller selection of goods. Definitely fill up your tank before heading into Big Sur. While there are a few gas stations on the 90-mile (145-km) stretch of coastline, you will pay a premium; gas stations here have made headlines for having the most expensive gas in the nation.

Consider visiting famous and very popular attractions like Pfeiffer Beach, Nepenthe, and McWay Falls at off-peak hours to better enjoy them.

Big Sur

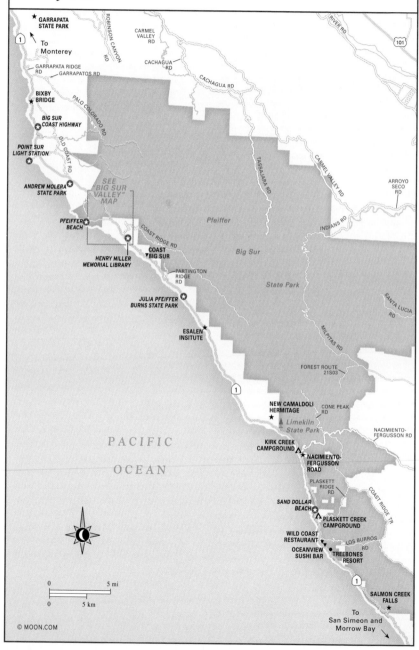

GARRAPATA STATE PARK

To Monterey

ROBINSON CANYON RD

CARMEL VALLEY RD

CACHAGUA RD

CACHAGUA RD

RIVER RD

101

GARRAPATA RIDGE RD
GARRAPATOS RD

BIXBY BRIDGE

PALO COLORADO RD

BIG SUR COAST HIGHWAY

OLD COAST RD

POINT SUR LIGHT STATION

ANDREW MOLERA STATE PARK

SEE "BIG SUR VALLEY" MAP

PFEIFFER BEACH

COAST RIDGE RD

COAST BIG SUR

HENRY MILLER MEMORIAL LIBRARY

PARTINGTON RIDGE RD

JULIA PFEIFFER BURNS STATE PARK

ESALEN INSITUTE

Pfeiffer

Big Sur

State Park

TASSAJARA RD

CARMEL VALLEY RD

INDIANS RD

ARROYO SECO RD

SANTA LUCIA RD

MILPITAS RD

FOREST ROUTE 21S03

1

NEW CAMALDOLI HERMITAGE

CONE PEAK RD

Limekiln State Park

NACIMIENTO-FERGUSSON RD

KIRK CREEK CAMPGROUND

NACIMIENTO-FERGUSSON ROAD

PACIFIC

OCEAN

PLASKETT RIDGE RD

SAND DOLLAR BEACH

COAST RIDGE TR

PLASKETT CREEK CAMPGROUND

WILD COAST RESTAURANT

LOS BURROS RD

OCEANVIEW SUSHI BAR

TREEBONES RESORT

0   5 mi

0   5 km

1

SALMON CREEK FALLS

To San Simeon and Morrow Bay

© MOON.COM

Respecting the Sur

Over the past few years Big Sur's popularity has exploded, due in part to gushing travel articles, social media posts starring the region's photogenic attractions, some very successful PR campaigns by Monterey County's hospitality organizations, and being featured in popular films and TV shows, including HBO's *Big Little Lies*. Many of Big Sur's businesses and residents depend on tourism dollars for their survival, but the surge in visitors has led to issues that endanger the residents and the environment. Do your part to help protect this unique region; here are a few tips to be a safe and responsible traveler in Big Sur:

- **Share the roads:** Many drivers stop right in the middle of the highway to snap photos, but this endangers other vehiclists. Pull over to take your picture, and if the pullout area is already full, continue on to find another spot along the road or make plans to return later.

- **Visit popular attractions at off-hours:** If possible, visit famous sites like Bixby Bridge, McWay Falls, and Pfeiffer Beach on weekdays or before 10am on weekends and holidays to prevent over-crowding.

- **Respect park closures:** Due to the many natural disasters that occur in Big Sur—wildfires, floods, landslides—there are sometimes closures at the region's state parks and national forests. Please respect these closures so that sensitive habitats have time to fully recover.

- **Stay on public lands:** There are over 1,000 Big Sur residents, including many who work in the region's restaurants, bars, and hotels. Please respect their privacy.

- **Don't camp illegally or build illegal campfires:** Only camp in designated campsites to preserve the area's natural resources. Only make fires in designated fire pits and follow all current campfire regulations; an illegal campfire in 2016 resulted in a massive wildfire.

- **Leave no trace:** Big Sur does not have enough facilities—restrooms, trash cans—to deal with the increasing number of visitors, so be prepared to pack out what you bring in.

Sights

TOP EXPERIENCE

★ BIG SUR COAST HIGHWAY

Even if you're not up to tackling the endless hiking trails and deep wilderness backcountry of Big Sur, you can still get a good sense of the glory of this region just by driving through it. The **Big Sur Coast Highway,** a 90-mile (145-km) stretch of Highway 1, is quite simply one of the most picturesque roads in the country. A two-lane road, Highway 1 twists and turns with Big Sur's jagged coastline, running along precipitous cliffs and rocky beaches, through dense redwood forests, over historic bridges, and past innumerable parks. In the winter,

you could spot migrating whales offshore spouting fountains of air and water, while spring finds yucca plants feathering the hillsides and wildflowers coloring the landscape. Construction on this stretch of road was completed in the 1930s, connecting Cambria to Carmel. You can start out at either of these towns and spend a whole day making your way to the other end of the road.

The road has plenty of wide turnouts set into picturesque cliffs to make it easy to stop to admire the glittering ocean and stunning wooded cliffs running right out to the water. There can be frequent highway delays due to road construction. For photos, please pull off the road at turnouts along the highway.

GARRAPATA STATE PARK

The 3,000-acre (1,214-ha) **Garrapata State Park** (CA-1, 6.7 mi/10.8 km south of Carmel, 831/624-4909, www.parks.ca.gov, 8am-30 minutes after sunset daily, free) is Big Sur's northernmost park. Just 3 miles (4.8 km) south of Point Lobos, the park includes the popular Soberanes Point and namesake Garrapata Beach.

At Soberanes Point, trails circle out onto headlands. Make the short climb to the top of Whalers Peak, a knob on the west side of the highway. More substantial hikes depart from the east side of the highway, including the strenuous Rocky Ridge Trail and the Soberanes Canyon Trail, which begins in a cacti-studded landscape and travels into a redwood canyon.

One of Big Sur's best and most easily accessed beaches, Garrapata Beach is just more than 2 miles (3.2 km) south of Soberanes Point. Pass through Gate 18 or Gate 19 to get down to the sand. The beach's southern side has some rocky coves and caves. Be careful of dangerous sleeper waves here.

BIXBY BRIDGE

You'll probably recognize **Bixby Bridge** (CA-1, 13.5 mi/21.7 km south of Carmel, 5.5 mi/8.9 km south of Garrapata State Park) when you come upon it on Highway 1 in Big Sur. The picturesque, cement, open-spandrel arched bridge is one of the most photographed bridges in the nation, and over the years it has been featured in car commercials as well as the opening credits of HBO series *Big Little Lies*. The bridge was built in the early 1930s as part of the massive government works project that completed CA-1 through the Big Sur area, finally connecting the north end of California to the south.

Today, you can pull out north of the bridge to take photos or just look out at the attractive span and Bixby Creek flowing into the Pacific far below. Get another great view of the bridge by driving a few hundred feet down the dirt Old Coast Road, which is located on the bridge's northeast side. Be careful pulling off the road here as there is lots of traffic and only a small area to park.

OLD COAST ROAD

Before the Bixby Bridge spanned the impressive Bixby Canyon, the **Old Coast Road** was the route that Big Sur locals used to get to Carmel. This 10-mile (16.1-km) dirt road provides a scenic drive through ranchland and redwood forests with views of the coastline at either end. The road is best traversed with a four-wheel drive vehicle, although a confident driver with a two-wheel drive and some clearance can pull off this road during the dry summer months.

Begin just north of Bixby Bridge where the Old Coast Road starts its trek inland. Stop after 100 yards (91.4 m) or so for one of the best vantage points of Bixby Bridge, spread across the deep canyon like a giant spider web, with the blue Pacific as a backdrop. Continue on, eventually descending into a redwood forest along the Little Sur River. The road rises once again, offering great views of the Big Sur River Valley to the south, Andrew Molera State Park down below, and Point Sur to the north. The road returns to CA-1 across from Andrew Molera State Park. Be aware of local traffic and expect to share the road with hikers and bikers.

★ POINT SUR LIGHT STATION

Sitting lonely and isolated out on its cliff, the **Point Sur Light Station** (CA-1, 20 mi/32 km south Carmel, 6.7 mi/10.8 km south of Bixby Bridge, 831/625-4419, www.pointsur.org) crowns the 361-foot-high (110-m) volcanic rock Point Sur. It keeps watch over ships navigating near the rocky waters of Big Sur. It's the only complete 19th-century light station in California that you can visit, and even here access is severely limited. First lit in 1889, this now fully automated light station

1: the iconic Bixby Bridge **2:** Point Sur Light Station **3:** coastal view along Highway 1 in Big Sur **4:** Pfeiffer Beach

still provides navigational aid to ships off the coast.

If you're interested in going inside the light station, park your car off CA-1 on the west side by the farm gate. A guide meets visitors there at designated times for **Point Sur tours** (10am and 2pm Wed. and Sat., 10am Sun. Apr.-Sept., 1pm Wed., 10am Sat. Oct.-Mar., adults $15, children $5) and leads them up the paved road 0.5 mile (0.8 km) to the light station. Once there, you'll climb the stairs up to the light, explore the restored keepers' homes and service buildings, and walk out to the cliff edge. Expect to see a great variety of wildlife, from brilliant wildflowers in the spring to gray whales in the winter to flocks of pelicans flying in formation at any time of year. Dress in layers; it can be sunny and hot or foggy and cold, winter or summertime, and sometimes both on the same tour! Tours last three hours and require more than a mile of walking, with a bit of slope, and more than 100 stairs. If you need special assistance for your tour or have questions about accessibility, call 831/667-0528 as far in advance as possible of your visit to make arrangements.

Families stopped living and working in the tiny stone compound in 1974. But is the lighthouse truly uninhabited? Take one of the **moonlight tours** (adults $25, children $10, check website for upcoming tours) to learn about the haunted history of the light station buildings.

The docents at Point Sur Light Station also offer tours of the **Point Sur Naval Facility** (2:30pm Sat., adults $10, ages 6-17 $5, children 5 and under free), the cluster of buildings just south of Point Sur. The abandoned buildings and grounds are a relic from the Cold War when the U.S. Navy created a secret base in Big Sur, where they attempted to listen in on Soviet submarines offshore. Learn about this little-known history and tour buildings in varying states of decay.

★ ANDREW MOLERA STATE PARK

At 4,800 acres (1,942 ha), **Andrew Molera State Park** (CA-1, 22 mi/35 km south of Carmel, 3.1 mi/5 km south of Point Sur Light Station, 831/667-1112, www.parks.ca.gov, 8am-sunset, $10/vehicle) is a great place to immerse yourself in Big Sur's coastal beauty and rugged history. Among its many assets is the Big Sur River, one of the area's best hikes (the Ridge Trail and Panorama Trail Loop), and a long, sweeping beach decorated with driftwood huts.

Today, the **Cooper Cabin** is a remnant from the park's past. The redwood structure built in 1861 is the oldest building standing on the Big Sur coast. The **Molera Ranch House Museum** (831/667-2956, http://bigsurhistory. org, 11am-3pm Sat.-Sun. summer) displays stories of the life and times of Big Sur's human pioneers and artists as well as the wildlife and plants of the region. Take the road signed for horse tours (no longer offered) to get to the ranch house. Next to the ranch house is the **Ventana Wildlife Society's Discovery Center** (831/620-0702, www.ventanaws.org, 10am-4pm Sat.-Sun. Memorial Day-Labor Day). This is the place to learn about the successful reintroduction of the California condor to the region.

The park has numerous hiking trails (page 216), such as the **Ridge Trail and Panorama Trail Loop,** also known as Eight-Mile Loop, which runs down to the beach and up into the forest along the river. Many trails are open to cycling as well. Most of the park trails lie to the west of the highway.

PFEIFFER BIG SUR STATE PARK

The most developed park in Big Sur is **Pfeiffer Big Sur State Park** (CA-1, 26 mi/42 km south of Carmel, 2.7 mi/4.3 km south of Andrew Molera State Park, 831/667-1112, www.parks.ca.gov, 8am-sunset, $10/vehicle). It's got the Big Sur Lodge, a restaurant and café, a shop, an amphitheater, a somewhat incongruous softball field, plenty of hiking-only trails, and lovely redwood-shaded campsites. This park isn't situated by the beach; it's up in the coastal redwoods forest, with a network of roads that can be driven or biked up into the

Big Sur as Writer's Muse

With so much beauty, it's no wonder that Big Sur has stirred the souls of many of the country's finest writers. Poet Robinson Jeffers was one of the first famous writers to pen praises to Big Sur's beauty. His poems, including "Bixby's Landing" and "The Place for No Story," aptly impart a feeling of the region's rugged character.

Big Sur-based novelist Lillian Bos Ross wrote firsthand about the challenges of living in the area with her Big Sur Trilogy, beginning with 1942's *The Stranger,* a National Book Award winner that was later made into the 1974 film *Zandy's Bride,* starring Gene Hackman and Liv Ullmann.

Henry Miller is the best known of the writers that spent significant time in Big Sur. He resided in the area from 1944 to 1962. His 1957 novel *Big Sur and the Oranges of Hieronymus Bosch* is a portrait of the region during the time he lived there. The **Henry Miller Memorial Library** (48603 CA-1, 30 mi/48 km south of Carmel, 0.25 mi/0.4 km south of Nepenthe, 831/667-2574, www. henrymiller.org, 11am-6pm Wed.-Mon., free) is a nonprofit arts center that celebrates the late author. It has framed photos of Miller along with a bookstore that sells some of the works that influenced the controversial writer.

Another heavyweight literary figure that spent time in the area and wrote about his experiences is Beat writer Jack Kerouac. His dark 1962 novel *Big Sur* goes into unflinching detail about a depressing, alcohol-soaked time that he spent in fellow writer Lawrence Ferlinghetti's Bixby Canyon cabin. The novel was adapted into a 2013 film of the same name starring Jean-Marc Barr and Kate Bosworth.

Other well-known writers have had Big Sur inform their careers to lesser extents. In 1961, Gonzo journalist Hunter S. Thompson worked as a security guard at the hot springs now known as the **Esalen Institute.** His time there helped form the basis of his first feature article in a national magazine, titled "Big Sur: The Tropic of Henry Miller."

Richard Brautigan, who is best known for his 1967 novella *Trout Fishing in America,* was also inspired to write about Big Sur. His 1964 cult favorite novel *A Confederate General from Big Sur* sprang out of some time he spent visiting a friend on Big Sur's south coast.

Thomas Steinbeck's 2002 *Down to a Soundless Sea* has seven stories, most of which are about Big Sur's early settlers. The author was the son of Nobel Prize-winning author John Steinbeck.

trees and along the Big Sur River. It is one of the best parks in the area to see Big Sur's redwoods and a great place to dip into the cool Big Sur River.

Pfeiffer Big Sur has the tiny **Ernst Ewoldsen Memorial Nature Center** (Warden's Path, south side of Big Sur River, open seasonally 10am-2pm Fri.-Sun.; call park to confirm hours), where a condor flight simulator is located. The historic **Homestead Cabin,** located off the Big Sur Gorge Trail, was once the home of part of the Pfeiffer family, who were the first European immigrants to settle in Big Sur. They ushered in Big Sur's reputation as a vacation destination by forming Pfeiffer's Ranch Resort on what is now the site of the Big Sur Lodge.

The **Nature Trail** (0.7 mi/1.1 km roundtrip, easy) leaves from the Big Sur Lodge and provides an introduction to the park's natural assets. Pick up a guide to do this self-guided tour from the end of the trail across from Day Use Lot No. 2. Learn about the park's plant life, including bay laurels, oaks, redwoods, and poison oak, along with information about forest fire damage and decomposition.

No bikes or horses are allowed on trails in this park, which makes it quite peaceful for hikers.

★ PFEIFFER BEACH

Big Sur has plenty of striking meetings of land and sea, but **Pfeiffer Beach** (end of Sycamore Canyon Rd., 805/434-1996, www. campone.com, 9am-8pm daily, $10/vehicle) is definitely one of the coastline's most picturesque spots. This frequently windswept beach has two looming rock formations right where

Big Sur Valley

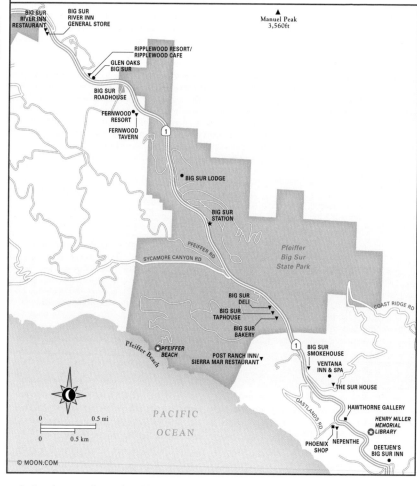

the beach meets the surf, and both of these rocks have holes that look like doorways, allowing waves and sunlight to pass through. Occasionally, purple sand colors the beach; it is eroded manganese garnet from the bluffs above. Note it can be incredibly windy here some days.

Getting There

For newcomers, getting to Pfeiffer Beach is a bit tricky. The turn-off for Sycamore Canyon Road is 27 miles (43 km) south of Rio Road in Carmel. The beach is at the end of the second paved road on the right, south of the Big Sur Station. Motorists (no motor homes) must then travel down a narrow, windy, 2-mile (3.2-km) road before reaching the entrance booth and the beach's parking lot. It's part of the adventure. This road gets extremely busy, and the staff at the top of the road will not allow vehicles down Sycamore Canyon Road if the parking lot is full. Try

to avoid visiting around the peak hours of noon and 2:30pm.

★ HENRY MILLER MEMORIAL LIBRARY

A number of authors have spent time in Big Sur, soaking in the remote wilderness and sea air to gather inspiration for their work. Henry Miller lived and wrote in Big Sur for 18 years, and his 1957 novel *Big Sur and the Oranges of Hieronymus Bosch* describes his time here. Today, the **Henry Miller Memorial Library** (48603 CA-1, 30 mi/48 km south of Carmel, 0.25 mi/0.4 km south of Nepenthe, 831/667-2574, http://henrymiller.org, 11am-6pm Wed.-Mon., free) celebrates the life and work of Miller and his brethren in this quirky community center, museum, coffee shop, and gathering place. What you won't find is a typical lending library or slicked-up museum. Instead, inside is a well-curated bookstore featuring the works of Miller as well as other authors, like Jack Kerouac and Richard Brautigan, along with a crew of employees who are always ready to strike up a conversation. There is also a bookshelf devoted to literary works that influenced Miller; it includes novels by Joseph Conrad, Fyodor Dostoevsky, and others. The controversial writer was also a rabid table tennis player, so a table is available outside for those who'd like to play a game or work on their serve.

Over the years, the library has become an important arts and music center for the Central Coast. Its small redwood-shaded lawn hosts concerts, literary events, and film screenings. Live music performances have included shows by big names including The Flaming Lips, the Red Hot Chili Peppers, and the Yeah, Yeah, Yeahs.

★ JULIA PFEIFFER BURNS STATE PARK

One of Big Sur's best postcard-perfect views can be attained at **Julia Pfeiffer Burns State Park** (CA-1, 37 mi/60 km south of Carmel, 7.7 mi/12.4 km south of Henry Miller Memorial Library, 831/667-1112, www.parks.ca.gov,

8am-sunset, $10/vehicle). Julia Pfeiffer Burns State Park also has some of the best day hiking in the area. At an unmarked section of the park to the north, visitors can access a number of noteworthy trails (page 219). Although many of these were damaged in the 2020 Dolan Fire, they're expected to reopen; check the park's website for trail conditions and closures.

McWay Falls

Take the **Overlook Trail** (0.6 mi/1 km round-trip, easy) along a level, wheelchair-friendly boardwalk. Stroll under CA-1 and past the Pelton wheelhouse to take in the stunning view of **McWay Falls.** The 80-foot-high (24.4-m) waterfall cascades year-round off a cliff and onto the beach of a remote cove, where the water wets the sand and trickles out into the sea. The water of the cove gleams bright cerulean blue against the slightly off-white sand of the beach; it looks more like the South Pacific than California. Anyone with an ounce of love for the ocean will want to build a hut right there beside the waterfall. But you can't. In fact, the reason you'll look down on a pristine and empty stretch of sand is that there's no way down to the cove that is even remotely safe.

The waterfall once spilled right into the ocean, but that all changed after a giant landslide just north of the cove occurred in 1983. This massive slide of dirt and rock closed Highway 1 for almost a year. To reopen the road, eight million cubic yards (six million cubic m) of dirt and debris had to be pushed into the sea. Eventually, this sediment washed into McWay Cove and created the beach below McWay Falls.

You can also catch views of McWay Falls from a highway pullout just north of the park entrance, near mile marker 36.2.

NEW CAMALDOLI HERMITAGE

Removed from society and its flood of sounds, the **New Camaldoli Hermitage** (62475 CA-1, 52 mi/84 km south of Carmel, 0.5 mi/0.8

km south of Lucia, 831/667-2456 or 831/667-5126, www.contemplation.com) is located 2 miles (3.2 km) above Highway 1 on a stunning Big Sur ridgeline. The 900-acre (364-ha) facility at 1,300 feet (396 m) is home to a community of Roman Catholic monks who reside at the serene site for contemplation and prayer. New Camaldoli is named for a Tuscan hermitage founded by Saint Romauld in 1012.

Day-use visitors are welcome to explore the public portions of the grounds, including the **New Camaldoli Hermitage Bookstore** (1:30pm-4:30pm daily), and attend the daily **Eucharist** (5pm Mon.-Thurs., 11:30am Fri., 6:30am Sat., 11am Sun.) in the chapel, where robed monks sing, speak, and meditate. Strategically placed benches around the property allow visitors to take in the soothing sea and the enveloping silence.

LIMEKILN STATE PARK

The 716-acre (290-ha) **Limekiln State Park** (63025 CA-1, 52 mi/84 km south of Carmel, 2 mi/3.2 km south of Lucia, 805/434-1996, www.parks.ca.gov, 8am-sunset daily, $10/vehicle) is a small park with redwoods, an impressive waterfall, ruins from the region's rugged past, a nice beach on the stunning coastline, and a campground. The park is named for four limekilns located 0.5 mile (0.8 km) from the coast in a redwood forest. These large rusted kilns can be accessed via the park's Limekiln Trail. For just three years beginning in 1887, the Rockland Lime and Lumber Company extracted and processed limestone rock deposits in these kilns using wood fires to purify the stones.

Also worth hiking to is **Limekiln Falls,** a 100-foot-high (30.5-m) waterfall that splashes down a rock face in two distinct prongs. The beach is a sandy stretch littered with boulders that has the Limekiln Creek Bridge as a backdrop. A single picnic table plopped in the sand provides a terrific place for a picnic lunch. The park also has a campground with 32 sites.

NACIMIENTO-FERGUSSON ROAD

The only road that traverses Big Sur's Santa Lucia Mountains, the **Nacimiento-Fergusson Road** (54 mi/87 km south of Carmel, 4 mi/6.4 km south of Lucia) offers spectacular coastal views to those who are willing to wind up this twisty, paved, 1.5-lane road. Simply drive a few miles up to see an eyeful of the expansive Pacific Ocean or to get above Big Sur's summer fog. It also heads in and out of infrequent redwood forests on the way up. The road connects Highway 1 to US-101, passing through Fort Hunter Liggett army base on its journey. The road is frequently closed during the winter months and is not recommended for those who get carsick. To check if it's open, call the Monterey Ranger District (831/385-5434).

MILL CREEK

Mill Creek (CA-1, 55 mi/89 km south of Carmel, 5 mi/8km south of Limekiln State Park, www.campone.com, 10am-6pm daily, $10) is a Forest Service day-use area right off Highway 1. This is one of several places along Big Sur's south coast that provide easy access to the rocky coastline. Take a walk on the boulder-strewn beach or enjoy the small picnic area, which has tables, grills, and two pit toilets for a worthwhile driving break.

★ SAND DOLLAR BEACH

Sand Dollar Beach (59 mi/95 km south of Carmel, 9 mi/14.5 km south of Lucia, www.campone.com, 10am-6pm daily, $10/vehicle) is one of Big Sur's biggest and best beaches. On Big Sur's south coast, this half-moon-shaped beach is tucked under cliffs that keep the wind down. Although frequently strewn with rocks, the beach is a great place to plop down for a picnic or an afternoon in the sun. From the beach, enjoy a striking view of Big Sur's south coast mountains, including Cone Peak, rising like a jagged fang from a long ridgeline. A series of uncrowded beach breaks offers waves for surfers even during the flatter summer months.

1: Limekiln Falls 2: Sand Dollar Beach 3: Julia Pfeiffer Burns State Park

The area around the parking lot has picnic tables with raised grills, pit toilets, and a pay phone. If the parking lot is full, you can park on the dirt pullout to the south of the entrance.

JADE COVE

Jade Cove (CA-1, 60 mi/97 km south of Carmel, 0.7 mi/1.1 km south of Sand Dollar Beach) is a rock-jumbled coastal indentation that is said to have a jade-veined underwater cave offshore. This is the place where jade diver Don Wobber found the giant boulder of jade that now resides at the Pacific Grove Museum of Natural History. It's possible to find jade at low tide on this rocky stretch of shore.

Getting to the cove involves walking about 100 yards (91.4 m) through an open field before descending a steep rocky path, the bottom section of which is so steep that ropes have been set up to help people into and out of the cove.

WILLOW CREEK

Willow Creek (CA-1, 62 mi/100 km south of Carmel, 2.4 mi/3.8 km south of Jade Cove, www.campone.com, 10am-6pm daily, $10), with its rugged, boulder-strewn beach, is one of the best places to find jade on Big Sur's south coast. This Forest Service day-use area is right off the highway and has a nice coastal overlook. If you have time, take the steep, short road under the highway bridge and down to sea level. Here, you can wander among the rocks searching for naturally occurring chunks of jade at low tide. Or just stand in Willow Creek, which has water that is strained through a series of rocks on its way to the sea. Straight offshore is Gorda Rock, a sea stack said to resemble a large woman. Willow Creek has two pit toilets.

SALMON CREEK FALLS

One of the southern portions of Big Sur's best natural attractions is **Salmon Creek Falls** (CA-1, 70 mi/113 km south of Carmel, 8.8 mi/14.2 km south of Willow Creek). Flowing year-round, a pair of waterfalls pours down rocks more than 100 feet (30.5 m) high, their streams joining halfway down. To get a great perspective of the falls, take an easy 10-minute walk over a primitive trail littered with rocks from the highway.

The unmarked parking area is a pullout in the middle of a hairpin turn on Highway 1.

TOURS

One way to visit Big Sur is to let someone else do all of the work. **Big Sur Tours & More** (831/241-2526, www.bigsurtoursandmore. com, $430) offers a four-hour guided tour of the area in a Volvo or Rolls Royce. Tours can accommodate 2-4 people. Possible stops include Bixby Bridge, Nepenthe, and McWay Falls.

Big Sur Guides (831/594-1742, www. bigsurguides.com, $125-200) is run by Stephen Copeland, who does all sorts of tours, ranging from helicopter and whale-watching tours to art gallery tours to a Jack Kerouac tour along the Big Sur coast. He also does a daily guided hike from the Carmel Highlands Inn (120 Highlands Dr., Carmel, $30/person) that lasts 1-1.5 hours.

1: Willow Creek **2:** Garrapata State Park

Hiking

Only a small portion of Big Sur is accessible by car. Many of the region's best sights—waterfalls tucked into redwood canyons, remote beaches, expansive vistas from steep mountain peaks—can only be experienced on foot. Big Sur's hiking trails also provide an opportunity to see the little details that make the area special, from wildflowers splashed across hillsides to bright yellow banana slugs inching under dark redwood trees.

It should be noted that Big Sur hikes can be more of a challenge than expected due to the region's steep V-shaped mountains and accompanying sheer-walled canyons. In addition, summer and fall can see high temperatures on Big Sur's ridgelines. Be prepared with lots of water and a snack when heading out on a substantial day hike.

Big Sur is located in a particularly volatile region, prone to forest fires, mudslides, and floods, which can affect highway and trail access. Before lacing up your hiking boots and heading out, check conditions on the **California State Parks website** (www.parks.ca.gov), which maintains updated information on trail openings and closures for Garrapata State Park, Andrew Molera State Park, Pfeiffer Big Sur State Park, Julia Pfeiffer Burns State Park, and Limekiln State Park.

GARRAPATA STATE PARK

Garrapata State Park (CA-1, 6.7 mi/10.8 km south of Carmel, 831/624-4909, www.parks.ca.gov, 8am-30 minutes after sunset daily) has most of the features that make Big Sur such a famed destination for outdoor enthusiasts: redwood trees, rocky headlands, pocket beaches, and ocean vistas from steep hills and mountains. Garrapata, which means "tick" in Spanish, includes Garrapata Beach, northern Big Sur's finest beach, and miles of coastline. To experience the grandeur of the coastline, wander about the **Soberanes Point Trail** (2 mi/3.2 km round-trip, easy), which loops around Soberanes Point and includes a quick climb up to Whale Peak, a hill with nice views. Stroll along the beach, scramble up the cliffs for a better view of the ocean, or check out the seals, sea otters, and sea lions near Soberanes Point. In the wintertime, grab a pair of binoculars to look for migrating gray whales passing quite close to shore here.

The **Soberanes Canyon Trail** (1.4 mi/2.3 km one-way, moderate) to the east of the highway showcases two of the region's ecosystems. This hike begins in a wide, exposed canyon covered in chaparral and cacti. As the trail continues, the canyon narrows while following Soberanes Creek and is shaded by redwood trees.

Expect little in the way of facilities here. You'll park in a wide spot on Highway 1, and if you're lucky you might find a pit toilet for use.

ANDREW MOLERA STATE PARK

Andrew Molera State Park (CA-1, 22 mi/35 km south of Carmel, 3.1 mi/5 km south of Point Sur Light Station, 831/667-1112, www.parks.ca.gov, 8am-sunset, $10/vehicle) has several hiking trails that run down to the beach and up into the forest along the river. The beach is a mile walk down the easy, multiuse **Creamery Meadow Trail** (2 mi/3.2 km round-trip, easy) that leaves from the parking lot, crosses a seasonal footbridge (open June 15-Oct.), passes through a meadow, and ends at a long beach where the Big Sur River empties into the ocean.

If you prefer to get a better look at the river, take the flat, moderate **Bobcat Trail** (5.5 mi/8.9 km round-trip, easy) and perhaps a few of its ancillary loops. You'll walk right along the riverbank, enjoying the local microhabitats.

For a longer and more difficult trek up

the mountains and down to the beach, take the **Ridge Trail and Panorama Trail Loop** (8 mi/12.9 km round-trip, moderate, 1,000-ft/305-m elevation gain), also known as the **Eight-Mile Loop.** This is one of the best coastal hikes in Big Sur. You'll start at the parking lot on the **Creamery Meadow Trail,** then make a left onto the long and fairly steep **Ridge Trail** to get a sense of the local ecosystem. Then turn right onto the **Panorama Trail,** which has sweeping views of the coast, including Molera Point and Point Sur, as it runs down to the coastal scrublands. Be sure to take the small **Spring Trail** (0.2 mi/0.3 km round-trip, easy) down a driftwood-littered gully to a scenic stretch of beach. Hike back out and take a left connecting to the **Bluffs Trail,** which takes you back to Creamery Meadow along the top of a marine terrace. A shorter version of this hike be done at low tide by taking the Creamery Meadow Trail to the Bluffs Trail to the Spring Trail. Then just hike north back up the beach, where you can connect back to the Bluffs and Creamery Meadow Trails to the parking lot. There's much to see along the way, including purple-sand beaches, unique rock formations, and a few sea caves. The whole loop is about 5.5 miles (8.9 km).

The **Headlands Trail** (2 mi/3.2 km round-trip, easy) takes hikers to headlands overlooking where the Big Sur River spills into the ocean. It begins at the Surfer's Pullout, a pullout 0.25 mile (0.4 km) north of the park entrance, and takes you past the historic Cooper Cabin and alongside the Big Sur River before reaching a short, steep section with stairs. There's no beach access on this hike unless you ford the river.

A fairly short but steep hike that is never crowded is the **East Molera Trail** (3 mi/4.8 km round-trip, strenuous, 1,300-ft/396-m elevation gain), which is located on the east side of Highway 1. From the main parking lot, walk to the white barn and take the tunnel under the road that leads to the trail. The trail is a steep series of switchbacks that climb up to a saddle with coast views to the west and a glimpse of the imposing, pyramid-shaped Pico Blanco to the east.

At the park entrance, you'll find bathrooms but no drinkable water and no food concessions.

PFEIFFER BIG SUR STATE PARK

For a starter walk at **Pfeiffer Big Sur State Park** (CA-1, 27 mi/43 km south of Carmel, 2.7 mi/4.3 km south of Andrew Molera State Park, 831/667-1112, www.parks.ca.gov, 30 minutes before sunrise-30 minutes after sunset, $10/ vehicle), hop on the **Nature Trail** (0.7 mi/1.1 km round-trip, easy), which leaves from the Big Sur Lodge. You can pick up a guide to the area's native plants to take a self-guided tour. Another short stroll is the out-and-back **Valley View Trail** (2 mi/3.2 km round-trip, moderate, 500-ft/152-m elevation gain) to the **Valley View Overlook,** where you can peer down the Big Sur Valley to Point Sur in the distance.

The **Buzzard's Roost Trail** (3 mi/4.8 km round-trip, moderate, 750-ft/229-m elevation gain) explores the portion of the park on the west side of Highway 1. Climb from the river's edge through redwoods and oak trees on the way up to the summit of Pfeiffer Ridge, where you'll have a view of the coastline. Other coastal hikes, such as Molera's Eight-Mile Loop, have better vistas.

For a longer, more difficult, and more interesting hike that leaves the park and goes into the adjoining Ventana Wilderness, start at the Homestead Cabin and head to the **Mount Manuel Trail** (8 mi/12.9 km round-trip, strenuous, 3,150-ft/960-m elevation gain). From the Y-intersection with the Oak Grove Trail, it's 4 miles (6.5 km) of sturdy hiking up a steep grade to Mount Manuel, a 3,379-foot (1,030-m) peak that looms high over the Big Sur Valley. On summer days, during the trail's initial climb, it's possible to hear swimmers in the Big Sur Gorge below. The tallest point has some rocks and a view of the ocean behind Pfeiffer Ridge. Bring lots of water for this hike.

The best option for a hot, sunny day is the

short hike and rock scramble to the **Big Sur River Gorge** (0.5 mi/0.8 km round-trip), a scenic spot where you can wade in the chilly river between some steep canyon walls. The trail begins at the back of the campground, or can be reached from Day Use Lot No. 3. This adventure will get you wet. Stay mindful of the many slippery rocks along the way. Diving and jumping off the rocks is prohibited and very hazardous.

This is one of the few Big Sur parks to offer a full array of services. Before you head out into the woods, stop at the **Big Sur Lodge** restaurant and store complex to get a meal and some water, and to load up on snacks and sweatshirts. Between the towering trees and the summer fogs, it can get quite chilly and somewhat damp on the trails.

COAST RIDGE ROAD

If you hike it far enough, **Coast Ridge Road** (2 mi/3.2 km south of Big Sur Station, off CA-1, open June-Oct.) rewards with sweeping, unobstructed views of the Big Sur Valley and the Big Sur backcountry. Originating by the Ventana Big Sur, this gated dirt road is usually closed from November to May. Coast Ridge Road climbs fast, so within a few miles hikers can attain stunning views of the Big Sur River Valley, Point Sur, the massive monolith of Mount Manuel, and the rocky line of peaks known as the Ventana Double Cones. It is possible to do a satisfying out-and-back hike on the road.

JULIA PFEIFFER BURNS STATE PARK

Julia Pfeiffer Burns State Park (CA-1, 37 mi/60 km south of Carmel, 7.7 mi/12.4 km south of Henry Miller Memorial Library, 831/667-1112, www.parks.ca.gov, day use 30 minutes before sunrise-30 minutes after sunset, $10/vehicle) is a great place for a hike.

Located in Julia Pfeiffer Burns State Park,

Partington Cove (35 mi/56 km south of Carmel, 6 mi (9.7 km) south of Henry Miller Memorial Library) is 2 miles (3.2 km) north of the park's main entrance at a noticeable bend in Highway 1. The west side of the road is where you pick up the **Partington Cove Trail** (1 mi/1.6 km round-trip, easy, 200-ft/61-m elevation gain), an underrated walk that goes to a striking, narrow coastal inlet. It begins as a steep dirt road. It soon reaches a bridge over Partington Creek and continues through a 60-foot-long (18.3-m) tunnel blasted into the rock. The trail arrives at a cove where John Partington used to ship out the tanbark trees that he had harvested in the canyon above. There is a bench at the end of the trail offering views of the cove and the coastline to the south. To reach the trailhead from the north, drive 9 miles (14.5 km) south of Pfeiffer Big Sur State Park on Highway 1. Look for a big bend in the road to the east with dirt pullouts on either side. Park here and then begin your hike where the gated road departs from the west side.

On the east side of Highway 1 across from the Partington Cove Trail pullout, you can access the **Tan Bark Trail and Tin House Loop** (5.6 mi/9 km round-trip, strenuous, 1,600-ft/488-m elevation gain). The hike begins in a redwood forest along Partington Creek and climbs to an oak forest. At the top is the Tin House, an abandoned building known for its tin exterior. To make the hike a loop, descend down the steep fire road and then cross the highway at the bottom to the scenic overlook. It's about a 1-mile (1.6-km) walk north along Highway 1 back to your car.

Some of the park's best trails include the **Ewoldsen Trail** (4.5 mi/7.2 km round-trip, moderate, 1,500-ft/457-m elevation gain) and the **Waters Trail** (1.2 mi/1.9 km one-way, easy). These trails were damaged in the 2020 Dolan Fire but are expected to reopen; check the park's website for updates on conditions.

LIMEKILN STATE PARK

Limekiln State Park (63025 CA-1, 52 mi/84 km south of Carmel, 14.4 mi/23.2 km south

---

1: Mount Manuel in Pfeiffer Big Sur State Park
2: hikers on Waters Trail in Julia Pfeiffer Burns State Park

of Pfeiffer Burns State Park, 805/434-1996, www.parks.ca.gov, 8am-sunset daily, $10/vehicle) has only one major trail, but it's worth your time. The **Limekiln Trail** (1 mi/1.6 km round-trip, easy, 170-ft/51.8-m elevation gain) begins by heading up the canyon on the dirt road that passes the campground. After crossing Hare Canyon Creek on a footbridge, the trail travels up beside the scenic Limekiln Creek through a redwood forest standing in bright green puddles of ferns and sorrel. Up past a third bridge, the trail comes to the large, rusty kilns topped with tufts of vegetation.

On the way up or back, be sure to take the **Limekiln Waterfall Spur Trail** (0.5 mi/0.8 km round-trip, easy), located about 100 feet (30.5 m) past the second bridge. The trail traverses the creek multiple times over logs and bridges made of planks of lumber. This short detour leads to its namesake 100-foot (30.5-m) waterfall, which splashes down a vegetation-cloaked rock face. On a warm day, duck your head under the left falls for an invigorating experience.

The **Hare Creek Trail** (1 mi/1.6 km round-trip, easy, 150-ft/45.7-m elevation gain) includes a walk on the campground road before crossing the footbridge over Hare Creek. When the trail forks, the left fork becomes the Limekiln Trail and the right fork heads up a canyon where Hare Creek spills over rocks. The walk ends at a small waterfall.

NACIMIENTO-FERGUSSON ROAD AREA

Nacimiento-Fergusson Road (54 mi/87 km south of Carmel, 4 mi/6.4 km south of Lucia) offers access to one of Big Sur's most stunning hikes, the Cone Peak Trail, as well as the rarely crowded **Mill Creek Trail** (3 mi/4.8 km round-trip, moderate, 500-ft/152-m elevation change). The latter trail can be reached by driving up to a noticeable bend in Nacimiento-Fergusson Road about 0.8 mile (1.3 km) from its junction with Highway 1. This trail goes up the namesake creek bed in

a redwood forest and is best ended at the unofficial camp 1.5 miles (2.4 km) up.

Cone Peak dominates the skyline of Big Sur's south coast. This impressive mountain rises from sea level to 5,150 feet (1,570 m) in just 3 miles (4.8 km). It is also the second-tallest peak in the Santa Lucia Mountains, about 700 feet (213 m) shorter than nearby Junípero Serra Peak. Although it takes some mountain driving to get to its trailhead, the **Cone Peak Trail** (5 mi/8 km round-trip, moderate, 1,150-ft/351-m elevation change) offers a moderate hike that pays big dividends. The trailhead can be reached by driving Nacimiento-Fergusson Road 7 miles (11.3 km) from Highway 1 up to the dirt Coast Ridge Road. Take a left on Coast Ridge Road (also called Cone Peak Road), then drive 6 miles (9.7 km) to a small parking area by the trailhead. The trail itself is exposed and climbs steadily. The last 0.25-mile (0.4-km) is challenging. The astounding 360-degree views from the top include Ventana Double Cone to the north and the broad-shouldered Junípero Serra Peak to the east. Most impressive is the view to the west, where mountains drop precipitously toward the sea. A defunct fire lookout crowns the peak and can be climbed for an even better view.

Coast Ridge Road is usually **closed November-May.** Call the U.S. Forest Service Office in King City (831/385-5434) to make sure the road is open before departing. When Coast Ridge Road is closed, you can hike in on the dirt road, but it adds an extra 12 miles (19.3 km) to your round-trip journey.

PACIFIC VALLEY AREA

Pacific Valley (59 mi/95 km south of Carmel, is a distinct, broad coastal terrace designated with a green-and-white sign just south of Mill Creek. The coastal terrace boasts headlands that poke into the sea like spread-out fingers. It's also home to the lightly used **Prewitt Loop Trail** (12 mi/19.3 km round-trip, strenuous, 1,500-ft/457-m elevation gain). The trail does a long loop inland from the Pacific Valley coast. Past Stag Camp, 4 miles (6.4 km) in, trail conditions deteriorate. Hardy hikers can continue up and then down to Pacific Valley Station, a Forest Service facility. It will be almost a mile's walk north back to the initial trailhead off Highway 1. This trail is most rewarding during wildflower season in spring. There is trailhead parking at a pullout off Highway 1. It is located 57 miles (92 km) south of Carmel and 0.8 mile (1.3 km) north of the Pacific Valley Ranger Station.

To explore the western edge of Pacific Valley, opt for the **Pacific Valley Bluffs Trail** (0.7 mi/1.1 km round-trip, easy). Start across from the Pacific Valley Ranger Station and take the wooden steps over the fence line. The trail passes through an open meadow where cattle sometimes graze. It makes its way out to bluffs over the ocean and continues southwest before ending at a small sand dune.

RAGGED POINT

The **Ragged Point Cliffside Trail** (85 mi/137 km south of Carmel, 1 mi/1.6 km round-trip, moderate, 300-ft/91.4-m elevation gain) originates on the edge of the Ragged Point Inn's property and descends down to a black-sand beach. The bottom is also the base of the 300-foot (91.4-m) **Black Swift Falls.** Those who aren't up for the steep climb can take in the region from a viewing platform on top of the cliff. Ragged Point Inn (19019 CA-1, Ragged Point) is 85 miles (137 km) south of Carmel and 20 miles (32 km) north of San Simeon.

BACKPACKING

If you long for the solitude of backcountry camping, the **Ventana Wilderness** (www.fs.usda.gov) is ideal. This area comprises the peaks of the Santa Lucia Mountains and the dense growth of the northern reaches of Los Padres National Forest. It has 167,323 acres (67,713 ha) of steep V-shaped canyons and mountains that rise to more than 5,000 feet (1,524 m). You'll find many trails beyond the popular day hikes of the state parks, especially as Big Sur stretches down to the south. Farther south in Big Sur, there's also the less visited **Silver Peak Wilderness** (www.fs.usda.gov),

a 31,555-acre (12,770-ha) parcel on the southwest Big Sur coast. There are many points from which to access the wilderness in Big Sur. Call the **Monterey Ranger District** (831/385-5434) or check the **Ventana Wilderness Alliance** (www.ventanawild.org) to find reports on trail conditions, and stop in at Big Sur Station to get the latest news on the backcountry areas.

The Pine Ridge Trail originates from **Big Sur Station** (47555 CA-1, 28 mi/45 km south of Carmel, 0.6 mi/1 km south of Pfeiffer Big Sur State Park) and is the most popular backcountry trail in Big Sur. It reopened in 2021 after being closed for five years due to extensive fire and flood damage.

Big Sur Station

By far the most popular backpacking trail in Big Sur, the **Pine Ridge Trail** cuts across the center of the Ventana Wilderness, connecting Big Sur Station on the west side to China Camp on the east. The backcountry camp that most people hike to is **Sykes Camp** (11 mi/17.7 km one-way from Big Sur Station, strenuous). Once known for its riverside hot spring pools, the U.S. Forest Service has decided not to allow new construction to harness the hot pools due to extreme overuse and environmental degradation previously. Not too worry as there are many other stunning camps to visit including, the riverside **Ventana Camp** (4.3 mi/6.9 km one-way, strenuous), the closest backcountry campground to Big Sur Station and beautiful **Redwood Creek Camp** (12 mi/19.3 km one-way, strenuous). To hike the Pine Ridge Trail from the west side, pay the $10 day parking fee, pick up a campfire permit at Big Sur Station, and self-register at the trailhead.

Kirk Creek Area

Less crowded than the Pine Ridge Trail, the **Vicente Flat Trail to Vicente Flat Camp** (10.6 mi/17.1 km round-trip, moderate-strenuous) heads up toward Cone Peak, the jagged mountain rising in the distance, while gaining sweeping views of the coast. It is on the South Coast of Big Sur across from the Kirk Creek Campground, which is 4 miles (6.4 km) south of Lucia and 38 miles (61 km) south of Pfeiffer Big Sur State Park on CA-1. The trail starts with switchbacks and climbs almost 2,000 feet (610 m) along hillsides that are painted with wildflowers during the spring months. After 1.4 miles (2.3 km), the trail reaches a ridge with coast views. Continue on to Vicente Flat Camp with its large redwoods near Hare Creek. You can also do this as a grueling up-and-back day hike.

The **Cone Peak Loop** (15 mi/24 km round-trip, strenuous) offers a multiday backpacking trip that ascends the 5,150-foot (1,570-m) Cone Peak from sea level. The loop leaves from the Kirk Creek area and travels up the Vicente Flat Trail to Vicente Flat Camp. It then utilizes the Stone Ridge Trail, the Gamboa Trail, the Coast Ridge Trail, the Cone Peak Trail, Cone Peak Road, and the Vicente Flat Trail to make a circular route to and from the high peak. Overnight opportunities include the backpacking camps at Vicente Flat Camp, Goat Camp, Ojito Camp, and Trail Springs Camp.

Silver Peak Wilderness

The **Silver Peak Wilderness** is located on the south end of the Big Sur coast near the Monterey County-San Luis Obispo County border. It has waterfalls, redwoods, and fine coast views like the Ventana Wilderness, but it receives less foot traffic than its northern neighbor. One relatively easy way to experience the Silver Peak Wilderness is to embark on the **Salmon Creek Trail to Spruce Creek Camp** (4 mi/6.4 km round-trip, moderate). The Salmon Creek Trailhead is off a noticeable turn on CA-1, 8 miles (12.9 km) south of Gorda and 27 miles (43 km) south of Big Sur Station. After about 10 minutes on the trail, a spur trail heads to the left to get closer to the impressive Salmon Creek Falls. The main trail is to the right and continues upward, winding in and out of the creek canyon along the way. Spruce Creek Camp is situated at the intersection of Spruce Creek and Salmon Creek. If you still have energy, continue on to **Estrella Camp** (6.5 mi/10.5 km round-trip, strenuous). The trail passes by some waterfalls on Salmon Creek on the way to the backcountry camp.

Recreation

MOUNTAIN BIKING

It's possible to mountain bike in Big Sur, although you'll have to bring your own bike or rent one in Carmel. **Andrew Molera State Park** (CA-1, 3.1 mi/5 km south of Point Sur Light Station, 831/667-1112, www.parks. ca.gov, 30 minutes before sunrise-30 minutes after sunset, $10/vehicle) has a few trails open to bikes. One of the easiest is the **Creamery Meadow Trail** (2 mi/3.2 km round-trip, easy) that goes along the side of its namesake meadow to the beach. Another more rigorous option is the **Ridge Trail** (6.4 mi/10.3 km round-trip, strenuous) that climbs 1,000 feet (305 m) to views of the coast stretching north to Point Sur. Be aware that you may encounter hikers and horseback riders while riding.

Across the highway from Molera, the **Old Coast Road** offers lots of hill climbs for riders who want to break a sweat. The 10-mile (16.1-km) road heads inland before reaching the coast again to the north of Bixby Bridge. Do a section or attempt the whole road.

FISHING

No harbors offer deep-sea charters around Big Sur, but if your idea of the perfect outdoor vacation includes a rod and reel, you can choose between shore and river fishing. Steelhead run up the Big Sur River to spawn each year, and a limited fishing season follows them up the river into **Pfeiffer Big Sur State Park** and other accessible areas. Check with Fernwood Resort (831/667-2422, www.fernwoodbigsur.

Stargazing

Far away from the bright lights of San Francisco and Los Angeles, Big Sur offers some of the finest views of the starry skies on the California coast. Constellations are even more compelling when viewed through the tops of redwood trees and glittering above the Pacific Ocean. Here are a few tips for stargazing in the region:

- **Visit in autumn or winter:** Many people visit Big Sur in the summer, when chances of seeing stars are slimmest due to frequent fog. In fall, the skies are usually clear, while the crisp winter nights also tend to be good for skygazing (save for evenings that bring some cloud cover or rain).

- **Head inland:** The marine layer near the coast can blot out the night sky. Try heading up the Old Coast Road or Nacimiento-Fergusson Road. The backpacking camps in the Ventana Wilderness are also a good bet.

- **Download an astronomy app:** Before heading to Big Sur (where connectivity is rare), download an app to your phone. A couple of options include Star Tracker, which is free, and SkySafari ($3), which lets you point your phone toward the sky to identify particular stars and constellations.

- **Join a stargazing program: Pfeiffer Big Sur State Park** offers few astronomy programs every summer; check its website for upcoming events. On the other end of the spectrum, both of Big Sur's luxury hotels—**Ventana Big Sur** and **Post Ranch Inn**—offer stargazing activities to their guests. Ventana Big Sur has a Star Bathing program (two hours, $150 pp) that includes stargazing while sitting in a plot of old-growth redwoods. Post Ranch Inn offers a free group activity of stargazing to its guests in the late summer and early fall.

com) and the other lodges around Highway 1 for the best spots during the season of your visit.

The numerous creeks that feed into and out of the Big Sur River are home to their fair share of fish. The regional office of the California Department of Fish and Game (call 831/649-2870 or email askmarine@wildlife. ca.gov, http://wildlife.ca.gov) can give you specific locations for legal fishing, season information, and rules and regulations.

If you prefer the fish from the ocean, you can cast off several of the beaches for the rockfish that scurry about in the near-shore reefs. Garrapata State Beach has a good fishing area, as do the beaches at Sand Dollar.

SCUBA DIVING

There's not much for beginner divers in Big Sur. Expect cold water and an exposure to the ocean's swells and surges. Temperatures are in the mid-50s in the shallows, dipping into the 40s as you dive deeper down. Visibility is 20-30 feet (6.1-9.1 m), although rough conditions can diminish this significantly; the best season for clear water is September-November.

The biggest and most interesting dive locale here is Julia Pfeiffer Burns State Park (CA-1, 12 mi/19.3 km south of Pfeiffer Big Sur State Park, 831/667-1112, www.parks. ca.gov, 8am-sunset daily). You'll need to acquire a dive permit through Ranger Kraft at 831/667-0193. The park, along with the rest of the coast of Big Sur, is part of the Monterey Bay National Marine Sanctuary. You enter the water from the shore, which gives you the chance to check out all the ecosystems, beginning with the busy life of the beach sands before heading out to the rocky reefs and then into the lush green kelp forests.

Divers at access-hostile Jade Cove (CA-1, 0.7 mi/1.1 km south of Sand Dollar Beach) aren't usually interested in cute, colorful nudibranchs or even majestic gray whales. Jade Cove divers come to stalk the wily jade pebbles and rocks that cluster in this special spot. The semiprecious stone striates the coastline

California Condors

With wings spanning 10 feet (3 m) from tip to tip, the California condors soaring over the Big Sur coastline are some of the area's most impressive natural treasures. But, in 1987, there was only one bird left in the wild, and it was taken into captivity as part of a captive breeding program. The condors' population had plummeted due to its susceptibility to lead poisoning, along with deaths caused by electric power lines, habitat loss, and being shot by indiscriminate humans.

Now the reintroduction of the high-soaring California condor, the largest flying bird in North America, to Big Sur and the Central Coast is truly one of conservation's greatest success stories. In 1997, the Monterey County-based nonprofit **Ventana Wildlife Society** (VWS) began releasing the giant birds back into the wild. In 2006, a pair of condors were found nesting in the hollowed-out section of a redwood tree and, as of 2021, more than 90 wild condors soar above Big Sur and the surrounding area.

a California condor in Big Sur

The species recovery in the Big Sur area means that you may be able to spot a California condor flying overhead while visiting the rugged coastal region. Look for a tracking tag on the condor's wing to determine that you are actually looking at a California condor and not just a big turkey vulture. Or take a two-hour **tour** (meet at the VWS Discovery Center in Andrew Molera State Park, check www.ventanaws.org for upcoming tours, Sat.-Sun. Memorial Day-Nov., $75/pp) with the Ventana Wildlife Society, which uses radio telemetry to track the released birds. You can also visit the **Ventana Wildlife Society's Discovery Center** (Andrew Molera State Park, CA-1, 22 mi/35 km south of Carmel, 831/620-0702, www.ventanaws.org, 10am-4pm Sat.-Sun. Memorial Day-Labor Day), where there's an exhibit that details the near extinction of the condor and the attempts to restore its population. Or check out the condors in the wild virtually by tuning into VWS's Condor Cams, which stream at www.ventanaws.org.

right here, and storms tear clumps of jade out of the cliffs and into the sea. Much of it settles just off the shore of the tiny cove, and divers hope to find jewelry-quality stones to sell for a huge profit.

For a guided scuba dive, contact **Adventure Sports Unlimited** (303 Potrero St., Santa Cruz, 831/458-3648, www.asudoit.com, $200-1,018).

BIRD-WATCHING

Many visitors come to Big Sur just to see the birds. The Big Sur coast is home to innumerable species, from the tiniest bushtits up to grand pelicans and beyond. The most famous avian residents of this area are no doubt the rare and endangered California condors. Once upon a time, condors were all but extinct, with only a few left alive in captivity and conservationists struggling to help them breed. Today, more than 90 of these birds soar above the trails and beaches of Big Sur. You may even see one swooping down low over your car as you drive down CA-1!

The **Ventana Wildlife Society** (VWS, www.ventanaws.org) watches over many of the endangered and protected avian species in Big Sur. As part of their mission to raise awareness of the condors and many other birds, the VWS offers bird-watching expeditions. Check its website for schedules and prices.

SPAS

Spa Alila at Ventana Big Sur (28 mi/45 km south of Carmel, 800/628-6500, www.ventanabigsur.com, 10am-6:30pm daily, massages $175-615) offers a large menu of spa treatments to both hotel guests and visitors. Indulge in a soothing massage, purifying body treatment, or rejuvenating or beautifying facial. Take your spa experience a step further in true Big Sur fashion with an astrological reading or an essence portrait. Hotel guests can choose to have a spa treatment in the comfort of their own room or out on a private deck.

Across the highway from the Ventana, the **Post Ranch Inn's Spa** (Post Ranch Inn, 30 mi/48 km south of Carmel, 831/667-2200, www.postranchinn.com, 10am-7pm daily, massages $165-495) is an ultra-high-end resort spa only open to those who are spending the evening at the luxurious resort. Shaded by redwoods, the relaxing spa offers massages and facials along with more unique treatments, including an aromatherapy massage and a lymphatic massage. The spa also offers sessions inspired by Native American shamanism ($315-515) that include a shaman session, fire ceremony, and drum journey.

TUBING

Cool off during a hot day by floating in the Big Sur River on an inner tube. During the summer and fall, when the river has lower water levels, you'll be floating in deep pools (rather than traveling along the river) and most likely have to portage around river rocks and shallow areas. **Fernwood Camp Store** (47200 CA-1, 26 mi/42 km south of Carmel, 3.7 mi/6 km south of Andrew Molera State Park, 831/667-2422, 8am-10pm daily), the **Ripplewood Store** (47047 CA-1, 24 mi/39 km south of Carmel, 831/667-2242, www.ripplewoodresort.com, 8am-8pm daily), and **Riverside Campgrounds & Cabin Store** (CA-1, 24 mi/39 km south of Carmel, 831/667-2414, www.riversidecampground.com, 8am-9pm daily) all sell tubes during the summer months. You can put your tube in the river at any public access point below Pfeiffer Big Sur State Park's gorge and head toward Andrew Molera State Park, where the waterway spills into the ocean.

Big Sur Campgrounds & Cabins (47000 CA-1, 25 mi/40 km south of Carmel, 831/667-2322, www.bigsurcamp.com) rents tubes to their guests for $1 an hour with a $10 deposit. Walk along the stretch of river on their property to end at a sweet swimming hole under a bridge.

JADE HUNTING

Spend significant time in Big Sur and you'll notice locals wearing sea-polished jade jewelry, which is also for sale in many gift shops. Big Sur jade, which is a naturally occurring mineral, can be found on the beaches of Big Sur's south coast. The best places to find jade are at **Willow Creek** (CA-1, 62 mi/100 km south of Carmel, 2.4 mi/3.9 km south of Jade Cove, http://campone.com, 10am-6pm daily, $10/vehicle) and **Jade Cove** (60 mi/97 km south of Carmel, 0.7 mi/1.1 km south of Sand Dollar Beach). Ideal times for jade hunting are after big winter storms. It's not easy to tell jade apart from serpentine, a similar-looking mineral. One way is to get the rock wet and hold it up into the sunlight. If it is somewhat translucent, you may have a piece of jade in your hand. Another way is to scrape a pocketknife across the suspected jade. Serpentine will be scratched easily, while it is difficult to mark jade with a knife. Jade can only be taken from below the high-tide line.

Entertainment

LIVE MUSIC

Big Sur River Inn (46480 CA-1, 24 mi/39 km south of Carmel, 2.5 mi/4 km south of Andrew Molera State Park, 831/667-2700, www.bigsurriverinn.com, concerts 1pm-5pm Sun. late Apr.-mid Oct.) has been doing Sunday afternoon concerts on its back deck since the 1960s with famed local act Jack Stock and the Abalone Stompers. Now it's mostly local jazz bands that play on the restaurant's sunny deck, while a barbecue is set up on the large green lawn. It's a great way to end a weekend.

Over the last few years, Big Sur has become an unexpected hotbed of big music concerts. More than just a place to down a beer and observe the local characters, **Fernwood Tavern** (47200 CA-1, 26 mi/42 km south of Carmel, 3.7 mi/6 km south of Andrew Molera State Park, 831/667-2422, www.fernwoodbigsur. com, 11am-11pm Sun.-Thurs., 11am-1am Fri.-Sat.) also has live music. Most of the big-name acts swing through Big Sur in the summer and fall. Even when it isn't hosting nationally known touring bands, Fernwood has a wide range of regional acts on Saturday nights. You may hear country, folk, or even indie rock from the small stage. Most live music happens on weekends, especially Saturday nights, starting at 9:30pm.

The **Henry Miller Memorial Library** (48603 CA-1, 30 mi/48 km south of Carmel, 0.25 mi/0.4 km south of Nepenthe, 831/667-2574, www.henrymiller.org) has had some internationally known acts perform on its stage, including The Flaming Lips, Philip Glass, and Angel Olsen, who typically fill far bigger venues. Check the website for upcoming events.

BARS

The **Big Sur River Inn Restaurant** (46840 CA-1, 24 mi/39 km south of Carmel, 2.5 mi/4 km south of Andrew Molera State Park, 831/667-2700, www.bigsurriverinn.com, 8am-9pm daily) is a fine place for a cocktail or beer any time of day. During daylight hours, you can take your drink to the nearby Big Sur River and plop down on a chair in the stream to enjoy it. In the late afternoon and early evening, the intimate bar area gets a fun local crowd.

Fernwood Tavern (47200 CA-1, 26 mi/42 km south of Carmel, 3.7 mi/6 km south of Andrew Molera State Park, 831/667-2422, www. fernwoodbigsur.com, 11am-11pm Sun.-Thurs., 11am-1am Fri.-Sat.) is Big Sur's living room. It's a classic tavern with redwood timbers and a fireplace that warms the place up in the chilly months. Inside, it's a great place to watch sports or listen to live bands, especially on Saturday nights. Outside, a large deck sits under the redwoods with heat lamps, fire tables, and a ping-pong table. The full bar serves nine beers on tap along with handmade Bloody Marys and margaritas. On any summer evening Fernwood can be an intriguing mix of longtime locals, international tourists, and everyone in between. The bar also has free Internet for customers, a prized commodity in Big Sur.

The **Big Sur Taphouse** (47250 CA-1, 28 mi/45 km south of Carmel, 2.7 mi/4.3 km south of Pfeiffer Big Sur State Park, 831/667-2225, www.bigsurtaphouse.com, noon-9pm Mon.-Fri., 8am-9pm Sat.-Sun.) is a great place to treat yourself to a beer after a long hike. The establishment, which is located in a little business strip by the Big Sur Deli, has 10 rotating beers on tap with a heavy emphasis on West Coast microbrews. The cozy interior has wood tables, a gas fireplace, and board games. With two big-screen TVs, the Taphouse is also a good place to catch your favorite sports team in action. Out back is a large patio with picnic tables and plenty of sun. They also serve better-than-average bar food, including tacos and pork sliders.

To have a cocktail with a stunning view, head to **The Sur House** at Ventana Big Sur

Big Sur Playlist

Big Sur has been a popular subject of many songwriters. The following songs make a great playlist while cruising down Highway 1.

- **Alanis Morissette's "Big Sur":** The Jagged Little Pill artist softens up for the Big Sur coast in this song that proclaims: "All roads lead to Big Sur/ All roads home to Big Sur."

- **Beach Boys' "California Saga (Big Sur)":** The surf-rock band goes country-tinged in this knowing look at Big Sur's natural treasures.

- **Buckethead's "Big Sur Moon":** This instrumental from the KFC bucket-wearing musician would be an ideal soundtrack for a moonlit drive down Highway 1.

- **Death Cab for Cutie's "Bixby Canyon Road":** Inspired by frontman Ben Gibbard's trip to the canyon where Beat writer Jack Kerouac wrote his dark novel *Big Sur*, this is a highlight of the indie rock group's 2008 album *Narrow Stairs*.

- **Jack Johnson's "Big Sur":** Mellow pop-rocker Jack Johnson seems to be inspired by a Big Sur camping experience on this acoustic, island-flavored ditty.

- **Jason Aldean's "Texas Was You":** Country artist Jason Aldean recounts experiences across the country, including a drive down Big Sur's coastline, in this song.

- **Jay Farrar and Ben Gibbard's "Big Sur":** The Son Volt frontman and the Death Cab for Cutie frontman team up for this acoustic song that soundtracked the 2008 documentary *One Fast Move or I'm Gone: Kerouac's Big Sur*.

- **Johnny Rivers's "Going Back to Big Sur":** The man behind "Secret Agent Man" sings: "I'm going back to Big Sur/This time I might just stay." He kept his word and is now a Big Sur resident.

- **Judy Collins's "Big Sur":** The folk singer and songwriter puts her big voice into an ode to Big Sur on this track from 2011's *Bohemian*.

- **Mason Jennings's "Big Sur":** The folky singer-songwriter uses Big Sur in this tune with the refrain: "This is a song to bring you hope" from his 1997 self-titled debut.

- **Ramblin' Jack Elliott's "South Coast":** With lyrics from Big Sur novelist Lillian Bos Ross, this superb acoustic story song capped Elliott's Grammy-winning 1995 album of the same name.

- **Red Hot Chili Peppers' "Road Trippin'":** This acoustic orchestral track shouts out the region with the line: "In Big Sur, we take some time to linger on."

- **Siskiyou's "Big Sur":** Canadian indie folk act Siskiyou whispers "Let's party all night long," like they are playing in a tent within a campground of sleeping campers, in this seven-minute, 40-second track.

- **The Thrills' "Big Sur":** The Irish indie-pop group's debut-album single warns "just don't go back to Big Sur" in a catchy way that suggests they may go against their better judgment.

(48123 CA-1, Ventana Big Sur, 29 mi/47 km south of Carmel, 4 mi/6.4 km south of Pfeiffer Big Sur State Park, 831/667-4242, www.ventanainn.com, 11:30am-4pm and 6pm-9pm daily). Order a drink at the bar and take it out on the sprawling outdoor deck with a view down the coast. Sur House has their own takes on classic cocktails including martinis and old fashioneds, plus a wine cellar featuring 10,000 bottles of regional wines.

FESTIVALS AND EVENTS

Tasty things grow in Big Sur's woods—including chanterelle mushrooms. The **Big Sur Foragers Festival** (various locations, 831/667-2580, www.bigsurforagersfestival.org, Jan.) celebrates found foods with a dinner, foraging hikes, and a cooking competition. Proceeds benefit the Big Sur Health Center.

The **Big Sur International Marathon** (831/625-6226, www.bigsurmarathon.org, entry $175-350, Apr.) is one of the most popular marathons in the world, due in no small part to the scenery encountered on the 26-mile (42-km) course. The race begins at Big Sur Station and then winds, climbs, and descends again on the way to Carmel's Rio Road. The April race weekend also includes 21-mile (34-km) runs, 9-mile (14.5-km) runs, 5K walks, relay runs, and a 3K kids' fun run.

Every Memorial Day weekend, the Monterey County Free Libraries' Big Sur branch takes advantage of the crowds for their annual **Big Sur Book and Bake Sale** (lawn adjacent to the Big Sur branch of the Monterey County Free Libraries, CA-1 at Ripplewood, 25 mi/40 km south of Carmel, 831/667-2537, Memorial Day weekend). There are always some used-book treasures and some tasty baked goods at this benefit, where all of the proceeds go to the library.

Each year, the Pacific Valley School hosts the fund-raising **Big Sur Jade Festival** (Pacific Valley School, 69325 CA-1, 59 mi/95 km south of Carmel, 805/924-1725, http://bigsurjadefest.com, Oct.). Come out to see the artists, craftspeople, jewelry makers, and rock hunters displaying their wares at this early-fall festival. The school is located across CA-1 from Sand Dollar Beach. You can munch snacks as you tap your feet to the live music. Check the website for the exact dates and information about this year's festival.

The **Big Sur Food & Wine Festival** (various locations, 831/596-8105, www.bigsurfoodandwine.org, Nov.) combines fine wines and cuisine with Big Sur's stunning views. Events include hiking with stemware, along with tastings and dinners. A big part of the money made from the event goes to local nonprofits.

Shopping

On the same grounds as the ultra-popular Nepenthe restaurant, **The Phoenix Shop** (48510 CA-1, 29 mi/47 km south of Carmel, 4 mi/6.4 km south of Pfeiffer Big Sur State Park, 831/667-2347, www.nepenthe.com, 10:30am-6pm daily) sells jade jewelry, boutique clothing, musical instruments, garden supplies, and books on Big Sur and beyond.

Across the highway from Nepenthe, the building that houses the **Hawthorne Gallery** (48485 CA-1, 29 mi/47 km south of Carmel, 4 mi/6.4 km south of Pfeiffer Big Sur State Park, 831/667-3200, www.hawthornegallery.com, 10am-5pm daily) is a piece of art itself. The glass and metal structure was created in collaboration with Post Ranch Inn architect Mickey Muenning. Inside are paintings, sculptures, and glass items created by the Hawthorne family and their artist friends.

Forgot to bring a book for your vacation? The **Henry Miller Memorial Library** (48603 CA-1, 30 mi/48 km south of Carmel, 0.25 mi/0.4 km south of Nepenthe, 831/667-2574, http://henrymiller.org, 11am-6pm Wed.-Mon.) is here to help with a wonderfully intuitive selection of books for sale, everything from local titles to Beat writers and French surrealists.

The **Big Sur Coast Gallery** (49901 CA-1, 32 mi/52 km south of Carmel, 7 mi/11.3 km south of Pfeiffer Big Sur State Park, 831/667-2301, www.bigsurcoastgallery.com, 10am-5pm daily) is in a pair of buildings that resemble giant wooden wine barrels. The gallery shows works by Henry Miller, Marc Chagall, and local artists. They also have a café with outdoor seating on the roof.

One of the major attractions at Lucia's New Camaldoli Hermitage is the **New Camaldoli Hermitage Bookstore** (62475 CA-1, Lucia, 52 mi/84 km south of Carmel, 16 mi/26 km south of Julia Pfeiffer Burns State Park, 831/667-2456, http://contemplation.com, 1:30pm-4:30pm daily). This quiet-as-a-library shop is known for its brandy-dipped fruitcakes and Father Arthur Poulin's art, striking landscape paintings composed of dots of paint. It also has holy medals, incense, crucifixes, candles, and religious books by everyone from C. S. Lewis to Thich Nhat Hanh.

Food

As you traverse the famed CA-1 through Big Sur, you'll quickly realize that a ready meal isn't something to take for granted. You'll see no In-N-Out Burgers, Starbucks, or Safeways lining the road here. While you can find groceries, they tend to appear in small markets attached to motels. To avoid paying premiums at the mini-marts, pick up staple supplies in Cambria or Carmel before you enter the area if you don't plan to leave again for a few days.

PUB FOOD

The **Fernwood Tavern** (47200 CA-1, 26 mi/42 km south of Carmel, 3.7 mi/6 km south of Andrew Molera State Park, 831/667-2129, www.fernwoodbigsur.com, 11am-10pm daily, $10-25) at Fernwood Resort looks and feels like a grill in the woods ought to look and feel. Even in the middle of a summer afternoon, the aging, wood-paneled interior is dimly lit and provides a good place to avoid the heat. It offers classic pub fare that includes burgers, tacos, pizzas, and a cheeseburger burrito.

The ★ **Big Sur Taphouse** (47250 CA-1, 28 mi/45 km south of Carmel, 2.5 mi/4 km south of Pfeiffer Big Sur State Park, 831/667-2197, www.bigsurtaphouse.com, noon-9pm Mon.-Fri., 8am-9pm Sat.-Sun., $5-17) is a casual place for a beer and an unfussy but tasty meal. Snack on chicken wings or marinated olives, or get something more substantial like a sandwich, taco plate, or nachos. On Taco Tuesdays, you can get two tasty tacos for just $6, one of Big Sur's best deals. On weekends, the Taphouse offers brunch with items like house-made corned beef and eggs.

CASUAL DINING

If it's a warm afternoon, get a table on the sunny back deck of the ★ **Big Sur River Inn Restaurant** (46840 CA-1, 24 mi/39 km south of Carmel, 2.5 mi/4 km south of Andrew Molera State Park, 831/667-2700, http://bigsurriverinn.com, 8am-9pm daily, $12-32). On summer Sundays, bands perform on the crowded deck, and you can take your libation out back to one of the chairs situated right in the middle of the cool Big Sur River. If it's chillier out, warm up by the large stone fireplace and then eat in the wood-beamed main dining room. This restaurant serves sandwiches, burgers, and fish-and-chips for lunch along with steak, ribs, and seafood at dinner. Noelle's salad (mixed greens with candied walnuts, blue cheese, apple slices, and a raspberry dressing) is always good and you can top it with meat. For dessert, the restaurant still makes the famous apple pie that put it on the map in the 1930s. The bar is known for its popular spicy Bloody Mary cocktails. The cozy atmosphere, outdoor deck, and seats placed in the river make this a worthy stop for a meal.

Don't overlook the **Ripplewood Café** (47047 CA-1, 25 mi/40 km south of Carmel, 3 mi/4.8 km south of Andrew Molera State Park, 831/667-2242, www.ripplewoodresort.com, 8am-2pm daily, $9-16) for breakfast or lunch. This unassuming spot may save the day on summer weekends when Deetjen's is flooded. Dine inside on the classic breakfast counter or on the outside brick patio among flowering plants. The breakfast menu includes pancakes, three-egg omelets, and a worthwhile chorizo and eggs. Be sure to order the grilled potato gratin with any breakfast dish; it may be the highlight of your meal. Ripplewood shifts to lunch at 11:30am, although it keeps a few breakfast items available past this time. Lunch offerings include sandwiches, Mexican food items, and salads. If you're missing the outside world, Ripplewood offers free Wi-Fi to its customers.

The **Big Sur Roadhouse** (47080 CA-1, 25 mi/40 km south of Carmel, 3 mi/4.8 km south of Andrew Molera State Park, 831/667-2370, www.glenoaksbigsur.com, 8am-2:30pm daily, $10-16) is an underrated option for breakfast and lunch. The decor inside and out has been dubbed "homegrown modernism," with contemporary artwork hanging on the walls and a comfortable feel. The simple menu includes items like a breakfast burrito and a roast turkey BLT.

Dine with views of Pfeiffer Big Sur State Park's redwoods at the Big Sur Lodge's **Homestead Restaurant** (47225 CA-1, inside Pfeiffer Big Sur State Park, 27 mi/43 km south of Carmel, 5.5 mi/8.9 km south of Andrew Molera State Park, 800/238-6950, www.bigsurlodge.com, 8am-8pm daily). The open dining room lacks ambience but has plenty of windows peering out into the woods and a fireplace at one end to warm things up on cool mornings and evenings. There's also an outdoor deck with heating lamps, dining setups, a small bar area, and a view of the Big Sur River. The restaurant serves a breakfast menu (cereal, pancakes, egg dishes) and transitions at noon to a casual lunch and dinner menu with salads, sandwiches, burgers, and pizzas made with house-made thin crusts.

The **Big Sur Bakery** (47540 CA-1, 28 mi/45 km south of Carmel, 3 mi/4.8 km south of Pfeiffer Big Sur State Park, 831/667-0520, www.bigsurbakery.com, bakery: 9am-until sold out daily, restaurant: lunch 11:30am-2:30pm daily, dinner: 5:30pm-8:30pm Wed.-Sun., $18-32) might sound like a casual, walk-up eating establishment, and the bakery part of it is. You can stop in beginning at 9am every day to grab a fresh-baked scone, a homemade jelly donut, or a flaky croissant sandwich to save for lunch. But on the dining room side, an elegant surprise awaits diners who have spent the day hiking the redwoods and strolling the beaches. Make reservations or you could miss out on the creative wood-fired pizzas, wood-grilled meats, and seafood. At brunch, they serve their unique wood-fired bacon and three-egg breakfast pizza.

The **Big Sur Smokehouse** (48123 CA-1, 29 mi/47 km south of Carmel, 4 mi/6.4 km south of Pfeiffer Big Sur State Park, 831/667-2419, www.bigsursmokehouse.com, 8am-8pm daily summer, noon-8pm Fri.-Sun. winter, $13-26) is located in the old Post family (of the Post Ranch Inn) homestead, a distinct red building right off Highway 1 that dates to 1867. The casual barbecue joint serves the classics, including brisket, pulled pork, and smoked chicken, served as part of hearty platters or in sandwiches. The barbecue sandwiches are huge and one of the better values in Big Sur at $13. Make it even better with a cold draft beer or well-crafted margarita.

One of Big Sur's most popular attractions is ★ **Nepenthe** (48510 CA-1, 29 mi/47 km south of Carmel, 4 mi/6.4 km south of Pfeiffer Big Sur State Park, 831/667-2345, www.nepenthebigsur.com, 11:30am-10pm daily, $20-55), a restaurant built on the site where Rita Hayworth and Orson Welles owned a cabin until 1947. The deck offers views on par with some of those you might attain on one of Big Sur's great hikes. Sit under multicolored umbrellas on bar-like long tables with stunning south-facing views. At sunset, order a basket of fries with Nepenthe's signature Ambrosia dipping sauce and wash them down with a potent South Coast margarita. Dinner entrées are pricey (you pay for the view here), but the best bet is the restaurant's most popular item: the Ambrosia burger, a ground steak burger drenched in tasty Ambrosia sauce. When Nepenthe has a line for tables, consider dining at **Café Kevah** (weather permitting, 9am-4pm daily mid-Feb.-Jan. 1, $10-22), an outdoor deck below the main restaurant that serves brunch, salads, and paninis.

Easing into the day is easy at ★ **Deetjen's** (48865 CA-1, 30 mi/48 km south of Carmel, 5 mi/8 km south of Pfeiffer Big Sur State Park, 831/667-2378, www.deetjens.com, 8am-noon and 6pm-9pm daily, $10-32), which plays classical music on speakers. The locals know Deetjen's for its breakfast, and it is an almost required experience for visitors to the area. Among fanciful knickknacks, framed photos of inn founder "Grandpa" Deetjen, and cabinets displaying fine china, diners can fill up on popular eggs Benedict dishes or the equally worthy Deetjen's dip, a turkey and avocado sandwich that comes with hollandaise dipping sauce. In the evening, things get darker and more romantic as home-cooked meals featuring fresh ingredients arrive at your candle-lit table.

Inside Coast Gallery, which is housed in three redwood water tanks along Highway 1, **COAST** (49901 CA-1, 32 mi/55 km south of Carmel, 7 mi/11.2 km south of Pfeiffer Big Sur State Park, 831/667-2301, http://coastbigsur.com, 11am-4pm Thurs.-Mon., $12-19) offers café fare. Order a filling sourdough focaccia pizza or artfully done salad and take it to scenic dining deck atop one of the redwood tanks for a superb view of the ocean. COAST also serves cold draft beer, wine, and soft serve ice cream, which hit the spot on warm days.

The best options for south coast dining are available at the Treebones Resort. The **Wild Coast Restaurant** (Treebones Resort, 71895 CA-1, 62 mi/100 km south of Carmel, 19 mi/31 km south of Limekiln State Park, 805/927-2390, www.treebonesresort.com, noon-2pm and 5:30pm-8:30pm daily, $19-52) is in the main lodge building of the resort by the check-in counter and gift store. Dine under a high, wooden, yurt-like ceiling on indulgent entrées including duck lasagna and lobster mac-and-cheese.

Treebones Resort's **Oceanview Sushi Bar** (Treebones Resort, 71895 CA-1, 62 mi/100 km south of Carmel, 19 mi/31 km south of Limekiln State Park, 805/927-2390, www.treebonesresort.com, by reservation only 4:30pm, 6pm, and 7pm Wed.-Sun. Mar.-Nov., $120 pp) offers an intimate place to eat artfully prepared raw fish. Just 10 seats are available at a redwood sushi bar located within a tent-like structure. Dining here is an intimate experience. The menu is "omakase," similar to a chef's tasting menu.

FINE DINING

Post Ranch Inn's **Sierra Mar** (47900 CA-1, Post Ranch Inn, 29 mi/47 km south of Carmel, 4 mi/6.4 km south of Pfeiffer Big Sur State Park 831/667-2800, www.postranchinn.com, 12:15pm-3pm and 5:30pm-9pm daily, lunch $75, dinner $125 pp) offers a decadent four-course prix fixe dinner menu nightly ($125). There's also a less formal lunch daily. With floor-to-ceiling glass windows overlooking the plunging ridgeline and the Pacific below, it's a good idea to make dinner reservations during sunset.

You don't need to be a guest at the gorgeous Ventana to enjoy a fine gourmet dinner at **The Sur House** (48123 CA-1, Ventana Big Sur, 29 mi/47 km south of Carmel, 4 mi/6.4 km south of Pfeiffer Big Sur State Park, 800/628-6500, www.ventanabigsur.com, 7:30am-10:30am, 11:30am-4:30pm, and 6pm-9pm daily, $20-50), which has a spacious dining room that boasts a warm wood fire, an open kitchen, and lodge-like wood beams. The underrated outdoor deck has views of the coast that rival nearby Nepenthe. Even in such a setting, the real star at this restaurant is the cuisine, with entrées like a Skuna Bay salmon and New York strip loin. Dinner frequently showcases ingredients from Ventana's on-site organic garden.

MARKETS

The **River Inn Big Sur General Store** (46840 CA-1, 24 mi/39 km south of Carmel, 2.5 mi/4 km south of Andrew Molera State

Park, 831/667-2700, www.bigsurriverinn.com, 7:30am-9pm daily summer, 7:30am-8pm daily winter, $7-10) has basic supplies, along with beer and a nice selection of California wines. Even better, it has a wonderful burrito bar and smoothie counter (8am-8pm daily summer, 8am-7pm daily winter) in the back. The burritos range from breakfast burritos to roasted veggie wraps and classic carnitas. These large burritos are some of Big Sur's best deals for the price. The freshly made fruit smoothies hit the spot after a long hike. There are also simple premade turkey and ham sandwiches in a nearby fridge for taking out on a hike or picnic.

With no supermarkets or chain mini-marts in the entire Big Sur region, the local markets do a booming business. The best of these is the ★ Big Sur Deli (47520 CA-1, 28 mi/45 km south of Rio Road in Carmel, 3 mi/4.8 km south of Pfeiffer Big Sur State Park, 831/667-2225, www.bigsurdeli.com, 7am-8pm daily, $3.50-7). Very popular with the locals, the deli has large, made-to-order sandwiches, burritos, tamales, tacos, and pasta salads. If the line is long at the counter, opt for a premade sandwich for a quicker exit. The deli also has cold drinks, wine, beer, and some basic supplies. This is the best place to stock up on treats for a day hike or beach picnic.

Accommodations

$150-250

A night in a cabin is a great way to spend an evening under the Big Sur stars. The **Ripplewood Resort** (47047 CA-1, 25 mi/40 km south of Carmel, 3 mi/4.8 km south of Andrew Molera State Park, 831/667-2242 or 800/575-1735, www.ripplewoodresort.com, $120-300) has you covered with 15 cabins and a duplex available for a night's stay. This was one of Big Sur's first resorts, operating before the Bixby Bridge was finished in 1932, allowing visitors to more easily access the area. A lot of the cabins are spread out along the Big Sur River and have decks with river views. Cabin features can include kitchens and/or fireplaces.

Budget travelers should be thankful a place like **Fernwood Resort** (47200 CA-1, 26 mi/42 km south of Carmel, 3.7 mi/6 km south of Andrew Molera State Park, 831/667-2422, www.fernwoodbigsur.com, motel rooms $180-235, cabins $290-340) still exists. It is refreshing to see a range of Big Sur lodging options for under $250 per night. Basic motel rooms flank either side of the bar, and the prices go up for amenities like gas fireplaces and hot

tubs. Down near the Big Sur River are cabins with fully equipped kitchens and a refrigerator, a good deal for groups of two to six people. Fernwood also offers coin-operated washers and driers in the campground.

Your guest room at ★ **Deetjen's Big Sur Inn** (CA-1, 30 mi/48 km south of Carmel, 5 mi/8 km south of Pfeiffer Big Sur State Park, 831/667-2377, www.deetjens.com, $130-435) will be unique, decorated with the art and collectibles chosen and arranged by Grandpa Deetjen. The historic inn prides itself on its rustic construction, so expect thin, weathered walls, funky cabin construction, and no outdoor locks on the doors. Five rooms have shared baths, but you can request a room with private bath when you make reservations. There is a small room called Petite Cuisine that can accommodate a single individual for $100 a night. Deetjen's prefers a serene environment, and so it does not permit children under eight unless you rent both rooms of a two-room building. Deetjen's has no TVs or stereos, no phones in rooms, and no cell phone service, but you can have a night's worth of entertainment and reflection by reading a book from the on-site library or your room's guest journals, which have been written about in

---

1: Nepenthe 2: Deetjen's Big Sur Inn

The New York Times. Since Deetjen's is a non-profit, the rates here are not as pricey as other area accommodations.

To truly soak in Big Sur's solitude, the **New Camaldoli Hermitage** (62475 CA-1, 52 mi/84 km south of Carmel, 0.5 mi/0.8 km south of Lucia, 831/667-2456, www.contemplation, $135-335, two-night minimum) offers a quiet stay in the mountains above Lucia. The Hermitage is home to a group of Roman Catholic monks, who offer various overnight accommodations for travelers of any or no religious denomination who want to "experience the precious gift of time for a contemplative life." Radios and musical instruments are not permitted here. The many benches on the property offer opportunities to take in the natural beauty at night, from the shining stars freckling the sky to the distant Piedras Blancas Light Station waving its light over the sea. The five private hermitages available to guests are basically trailers with porches. The trailers are decorated with religious iconography and outfitted with a bed, desk, bathroom, and kitchen with a gas-burning countertop stove. There are also nine private rooms, each with a half bath and a garden, located in the retreat house. Men can opt to stay overnight in a monk's cell within the monastic enclosure, while there are also a few units outside the enclosure that accommodate two guests. All rates include breakfast, lunch, and dinner. Staying at the Hermitage is one of the region's best deals. The accommodations can be rustic, but they are worth it if it's solitude you're after.

OVER $250

The **Big Sur River Inn** (46480 CA-1, 24 mi/39 km south of Carmel, 2.5 mi/4 km south of Andrew Molera State Park, 831/667-2700 or 800/548-3610, www.bigsurriverinn.com, $310-475) has been lodging guests in Big Sur since 1934. It was formerly the Apple Pie Inn and Rogers Redwood Camp before becoming the River Inn in 1943. The River Inn has 14 rooms on the east side of Highway 1 and six suites on the west side of the road. Units are

soundproofed (a big plus given their proximity to the highway) and have flat-screen TVs. (There are almost no lodging options in Big Sur with TVs.) The east-side rooms are cozy (read: fairly small) with knotty pine walls and small porch areas out front. The west-side suites each have two rooms, one with a king bed and the other with a trundle bed, good for families and small groups. The suites also have decks overlooking the property's grassy lawn and the Big Sur River. Also on site is a seasonally heated outdoor pool. All rooms are close to the Big Sur River Inn Restaurant.

Filled with creative touches and thoughtful amenities, ★ **Glen Oaks Big Sur** (47080 CA-1, 25 mi/40 km south of Carmel, 3 mi/4.8 km south of Andrew Molera State Park, 831/667-2105, www.glenoaksbigsur.com, $310-860) offers the region's best lodging for the price. Its 16 units bring the motor lodge into the new millennium with heated stone bathroom floors, in-room yoga mats, spacious two-person showers, and gas fireplaces that double as art pieces. These combine seamlessly with the classic adobe walls and wood rafters. The king rooms have nice enclosed outdoor courtyards, while all the units have fun items to entertain guests, from board games and a card deck of yoga poses to a copy of Henry Miller's *Big Sur and the Oranges of Hieronymus Bosch.* For those who would rather spend an evening in a standalone structure, Glen Oaks has two cottages amid the oak trees and 10 cabins in an impressive redwood grove by the Big Sur River. The cabins are clean with a modern rustic feel and have kitchenettes along with outdoor fire pits that are already set up with kindling and firewood. All guests have access to two on-site beaches situated on scenic sections of the Big Sur River. Glen Oaks' redwood grove is home to the Big Sur Valley's second-largest redwood, the Grandmother Pfeiffer Tree. Glen Oaks even has its own electric car charging station. For an upscale option, rent the **Bridge**

1: overnight retreat at the New Camaldoli Hermitage 2: Lucia Lodge

House ($2,200), which is reached by walking across the Big Sur River on a suspension bridge. The architectural marvel has a fully equipped kitchen and two master bedrooms with private bathrooms.

The best part about staying at the **Big Sur Lodge** (47225 CA-1, 27 mi/43 km south of Carmel, 5.5 mi/8.9 km south of Andrew Molera State Park, 855/238-6950, www.bigsurlodge.com, $329-449), inside Pfeiffer Big Sur State Park, is that you can leave your room and hit the trail. In the early 1900s, the park was a resort owned by the pioneering Pfeiffer family. Although the amenities have been updated somewhat, the Big Sur Lodge still evokes the classic woodsy vacation cabin. Set on a sunny knoll, the lodge has 62 units with the majority being family- and group-friendly two-bedroom options. Twelve units also have kitchenettes. The rooms could use a bit of a remodel, but everyone has a front or back deck for spending time outdoors. There are no TVs and access to the Internet requires an extra fee, but all stays come with a pass that allows you entrance into all of Big Sur's state parks, including Pfeiffer Big Sur State Park, Andrew Molera State Park, and Julia Pfeiffer Burns State Park. There are several amenities just a short walk down the hill from the rooms, including the **Homestead Restaurant, Espresso Bar,** and **Gift Shop & General Store.** Be sure to take advantage of the lodge's pool (9am-9pm Mar.-Oct.) during your stay and watch for the semi-wild turkeys that roam the property.

Although a night at **Post Ranch Inn** (47900 CA-1, 29 mi/47 km south of Carmel, 4 mi/6.4 km south of Pfeiffer Big Sur State Park, 800/527-2200 or 831/667-2200, www.postranchinn.com, $1,275-3,100) can total more than some people's monthly paycheck, an evening staring at the smear of stars over the vast blue Pacific from one of the stainless steel hot soaking tubs on the deck of Post Ranch's ocean-facing rooms can temporarily cause all life's worries to ebb away. It may be difficult to leave the resort's well-appointed units, but it's a singular experience to soak in the Infinity Jade Pool, an ocean-facing warm pool made from chunks of the green ornamental stone. Situated on a 1,200-foot-high (366-m) ridgeline, all the rooms at this luxury resort have striking views, whether it's of the ocean or the jagged peaks of the nearby Ventana Wilderness. The units also blend in well with the natural environment, including the seven tree houses, which are perched 10 feet (3 m) off the ground. Each one has a king bed, an old-fashioned wood-burning fireplace, a spa tub, and a private deck. In addition, the mini-bars are stocked with complimentary snacks, wine, and cold drinks. During your stay, take advantage of the resort's complimentary activities, including yoga classes, nature hikes, garden tours, and stargazing. A night at Post Ranch also includes an impressive breakfast with made-to-order omelets and French toast as well as a spread of pastries, fruit, and yogurt served in the Sierra Mar restaurant with its stellar ocean views.

Ventana Big Sur (48123 CA-1, 29 mi/47 km south of Carmel, 4 mi/6.4 km south of Pfeiffer Big Sur State Park, 800/628-6500 or 831/667-2331, www.ventanabigsur.com, $1,200-4,000) has a rustic design in its 59 rooms, each of which has a private balcony or patio. Room rates may be prohibitive, but note that pricing includes meals, wellness classes, gratuities, and more. Don your plush spa robe and rubber slippers and head for the Japanese bathhouses (there are two, one at each end of the property). Both are clothing-optional and gender segregated; the upper bathhouse has glass and open-air windows that let you look out over the ocean. Two swimming pools offer a cool respite from your busy life; the Mountain Pool is clothing-optional and the Meadow Pool perches on a high spot for enthralling views. Even daily complimentary yoga classes can be yours for the asking. The Social House is a communal space with a stone fireplace, a record player, a pool table, and a coffee lounge.

The **Lucia Lodge** (62400 CA-1, 50 mi/81 km south of Carmel, 13 mi/20.9 km south of

A New Age California Experience

The **Esalen Institute** (55000 CA-1, 41 mi/66 km south of Carmel, 4 mi/6.4 km south of Julia Pfeiffer Burns State Park, 831/667-3000, www.esalen.org) is known throughout California as the home of Esalen massage technique, a forerunner and cutting-edge player in ecological living, and a space to retreat from the world and build a new and better sense of self. Visitors journey from all over the state and beyond to sink into the haven that's sometimes called "The New Age Harvard."

One of the institute's biggest draws, the bathhouse, sits down a rocky path right on the edge of the cliffs overlooking the ocean. It includes a motley collection of mineral-fed hot tubs looking out over the waves—choose either the Quiet Side or the indoors Silent Side, and then sink into the water and contemplate the Pacific Ocean's limitless expanse, meditate on a perfect sunset or arrangement of stars, or (on the Quiet Side) get to know your fellow bathers—who will be nude.

Esalen's bathhouse area is "clothing optional"; its philosophy puts the essence of nature above the sovereignty of humanity, and it encourages openness and sharing among its guests—to the point of chatting nude with total strangers in a smallish hot tub. You'll also find a distinct lack of attendants to help you find your way around. Once you've parked and been given directions, it's up to you to find your way down to the cliffs. You'll have to find your own towel, ferret out a cubby for your clothes in the changing rooms, grab a shower, and then wander out to find your favorite of the hot tubs. Be sure you go all the way outside past the individual claw-foot tubs to the glorious shallow cement tubs that sit right out on the edge of the cliff with the surf crashing just below.

In addition to the nudity and new-age culture of Esalen, you'll learn that this isn't a day spa. You'll need to make an appointment for a **massage** (at $185 a pop), which grants you access to the hot tubs for an hour before and an hour after your 75-minute treatment session. If you just want to sit in the mineral water, you'll need to stay up late. Very late. Inexpensive ($35) open access to the Esalen **hot tubs** is from 1am to 3am. To secure a space, go online to www.esalen. org at 9am on the morning of the evening you hope to visit. Many locals consider the sleep deprivation well worth it to get the chance to enjoy the healing mineral waters and the stunning astronomical shows.

If you're not comfortable with your own nudity or that of others, you're uninterested in the all-inclusive spiritual philosophy, or you're unable to enjoy silence, Esalen is not for you. But if this description of a California experience sounds just fabulous to you, make your reservations now. The Esalen Institute accepts reservations by phone if necessary. Go to the website for more information.

Julia Pfeiffer Burns State Park, 866/424-4787, www.lucialodge.com, $300-450) has just 10 rooms, eight of which have a superb view of Big Sur's south coast. The original lodge was built in the 1930s as freestanding cabins, and now they feature gas fireplaces and four-poster beds. The other units are more modern but lack telephones and TVs. The lodge was featured in the 1999 film *The Limey* and the Netflix series *Ratched*. The main reason to stay here is the sweeping ocean views.

There are not many lodging choices on Big Sur's south coast. One of the only options is the **Gorda Springs Resort** (CA-1, 65 mi/105 km south of Carmel, 26 mi/42 km south of Julia Pfeiffer Burns State Park, 805/927-3918, www.gordaspringsresort.com, $200-650). Studio suites, cottages, and small house-like structures are available. The Gorda complex includes a restaurant, espresso bar, gift shop, and a gas station (known for a while as selling the most expensive gas in the country). The studio suites all have fireplaces, while some of the cottages and houses have kitchens.

The **Ragged Point Inn and Resort** (19019 CA-1, 85 mi/137 km south of Carmel, 805/927-4502, http://raggedpointinn.com, $250-400) is on the south end of Big Sur, right before the mountains level out and give way to the landscape surrounding San Simeon. The inn has 39 rooms that take advantage of their position on a seaside cliff. The most expensive units have superb views of the sea and sheltered balconies or decks. They also have gas fireplaces and hot tubs. Other rooms are set farther back from the edge. One worthwhile feature of the grounds is a steep 0.6-mile (1-km) round-trip trail to a black sand beach that is open to guests and nonguests alike. The property also is home to a gift shop, jewelry store, coffee bar, mini-mart, and the **Ragged Point Restaurant.**

CAMPING

Many visitors to Big Sur want to experience the unspoiled beauty of the landscape daily. To accommodate true outdoors lovers, many of the parks and lodges have overnight campgrounds. You'll find all types of camping, from full-service, RV-accessible areas to environmental tent campsites to wilderness backpacking. You can camp in a state park or out behind one of the small resort motels near a restaurant and a store and possibly the cool, refreshing Big Sur River. Pick the option that best suits you and your family's needs. Avoid camping in non-designated camping areas. (The 2016 Soberanes Fire was started by an illegal campfire in a day-use only section of Garrapata State Park.)

After being closed following a major flood in 2017, the campground at **Andrew Molera State Park** (CA-1, 22 mi/35 km south of Carmel, 3.1 mi/5 km south of Point Sur Light Station, 800/444-7275, www.parks.ca.gov, www.reservecalifornia.com) is set to reopen on the reservation system. The rustic campsites will be in a grassy meadow that is a 0.3-mile (0.5-km) walk from the parking lot. The price per site is yet to be determined.

The privately owned **Big Sur Campgrounds & Cabins** (47000 CA-1, 25 mi/40 km south of Carmel, 3 mi/4.8 km south of Andrew Molera State Park, 831/667-2322, www.bigsurcamp.com, tent sites $65-75, RV sites $75-85, camping cabins $175, cabins $240-430) offers space to pitch a tent beside the redwoods and river. The tent sites come with a fire pit and picnic table, while the RV sites can accommodate vehicles up to 40 feet

(12.2 m) with electrical and water hookups. A slight step up are the camping cabins, which have a queen bed with linens and blankets but no indoor plumbing or heating. There are also more equipped cabins ranging from one-room units to A-frames to two-bedroom options. They each have a gas or wood-burning fireplace for keeping warm. The on-site facilities include a camp store, a playground, and laundry facilities. Right next door, **Riverside Campground & Cabins** (47020 CA-1, 25 mi/40 km south of Carmel, 3 mi/4.8 km south of Andrew Molera State Park, 831/667-2414, www.riversidecampground.com, tent sites $70-80, RV sites $75-85, cabins $160-275) has 22 tent sites and 12 RV sites on 12 redwood-shaded acres (4.9 ha) by the Big Sur River. The tent sites include the requisite fire pits and picnic tables. The RV sites have water and electrical hookups. Or, opt for one of the cabins, which range from a small unit with a shared bathhouse to larger ones with a queen bed, bathroom, and kitchenette. The cabins (except for the studio cabin) are dog-friendly for a $30 fee.

The **Fernwood Resort** (47200 CA-1, 26 mi/42 km south of Carmel, 3.7 mi/6 km south of Andrew Molera State Park, 831/667-2422, www.fernwoodbigsur.com, tent site $70-100, campsite with electrical hookup $85-95, tent cabin $130-190, adventure tent $175-195) offers a range of camping options. There are 66 campsites located around the Big Sur River, some with electrical hookups for RVs. Fernwood also has tent cabins, which are small canvas-constructed spaces with room for four in a double and two twins. You can pull your car right up to the back of your cabin. Bring your own linens or sleeping bags, pillows, and towels to make up the inside of your tent cabin. Splitting the difference between camping and a motel room are the rustic "Adventure Tents," canvas tents draped over a solid floor whose biggest comforts are the fully made queen beds and electricity courtesy of an extension cord run into the tent. All camping options have easy access to the river, where you can swim, inner tube, and hike. Hot showers and restrooms are a short walk away. There's a volleyball court in the campground if you're feeling competitive. Also, you will be stumbling distance from Big Sur's most popular watering hole, the Fernwood Tavern.

The biggest and most developed campground in Big Sur is at ★ **Pfeiffer Big Sur State Park** (CA-1, 27 mi/43 km south of Carmel, 5.5 mi/8.9 km south of Andrew Molera State Park, 800/444-7275, www. parks.ca.gov, www.reservecalifornia.com, standard campsite $35, riverside campsite $50, hike-in/bike-in campsite site $5). With more than 150 individual sites, each of which can handle two vehicles and eight people or an RV (maximum 32 ft/9.8 m, trailers maximum 27 ft/8.2 m, dump station on site), there's enough room for almost everybody, except during a crowded summer weekend. During those times, a grocery store and laundry facility operate within the campground for those who don't want to hike down to the lodge, and plenty of flush toilets and hot showers are scattered throughout the campground. In the evenings, walk down to the Campfire Center for entertaining and educational programs. Pfeiffer Big Sur fills up fast in the summertime, especially

on weekends. **Reservations are essential during summer.** Self-contained RVs can try to stay for one night with en-route overnight parking ($45) if arriving without a reservation when the campground is full. There's also a single ADA-accessible cabin available for $75 a night.

Far from roughing it, Ventana Big Sur's **Redwood Canyon Glampsites** (48123 CA-1, 29 mi/47 km south of Carmel, 4 mi/6.4 km south of Pfeiffer Big Sur State Park, 800/628-6500, www.ventanabigsur. com, $300-600) are canvas tents perched on wooden platforms in a 20-acre (8.1-ha) redwood canyon. The tents shelter king beds with heated blankets, and have electric lamps and outlets. Comfy Adirondack chairs are situated around a propane fire pit on the deck.

★ **Julia Pfeiffer Burns State Park** (CA-1, 37 mi/60 km south of Carmel, 12 mi/19.3 km south of Pfeiffer Big Sur State Park, 800/444-7275, www.parks.ca.gov, www. reservecalifornia.com, $30) has two walk-in environmental campsites perched over the ocean behind stunning McWay Falls. It's a short 0.3-mile (0.5-km) walk to these two sites, which have fire pits, picnic tables, and a shared pit toilet, but there is no running water. More importantly, they have some of the best

campground at Julia Pfeiffer Burns State Park

views of the California coast that you can find in a developed state park campground. At night, fall asleep to the sound of waves crashing into the rocks below. Saddle Rock is the better of the two sites, but you can't go wrong with either one. These two sites book up far in advance, particularly in summer. Reservations can be made seven months in advance.

Limekiln State Park (63025 CA-1, 52 mi/84 km south of Carmel, 15 mi/24 km south of Julia Pfeiffer Burns State Park, 800/444-7275, www.reservecalifornia.com, $35) can satisfy your desire to sleep in a redwood grove or near Big Sur's crashing sea. The 32 sites include 12 in the beach area—some with coastal views—while the rest are creekside or in the redwoods. The campground has the standard state park setup in which all sites have a picnic table and fire pit. There are also shared hot showers and flush toilets. Of the sites, 29 can be reserved in advance, while three are overflow sites with no parking. One of the best sites is an overflow site with an ocean view tucked under the towering bridge. It's located behind campsite four.

A popular U.S. Forest Service campground on the south coast, **Kirk Creek Campground** (CA-1, 54 mi/87 km south of Carmel, 1.7 mi/2.7 km south of Limekiln State Park, U.S. reservations 877/444-6777, international reservations 606/515-6777, www.recreation.gov, $35) has a great location on a bluff above the ocean. Right across the highway is the trailhead for the Vicente Flat Trail and the scenic Nacimiento-Fergusson Road. The sites have picnic tables and campfire rings with grills, while the grounds have toilets and drinking water.

★ **Plaskett Creek Campground** (CA-1, 59 mi/95 km south of Carmel, 7 mi/11.3 km south of Limekiln State Park, U.S. reservations 877/444-6777, international reservations 606/515-6777, www.recreation.gov, $35) is located right across the highway from Sand Dollar Beach. The sites are in a grassy area under Monterey pine and cypress trees. There are picnic tables and a campfire ring with a grill at every site, along with a flush toilet and drinking water in the campground.

Camping on the Big Sur coast is very popular during the summer. If you haven't made reservations months in advance, it's going to be difficult to find a place to pitch your tent. **Nacimiento Campground** (Nacimiento-Fergusson Rd., 11 mi/17.7 km east of CA-1, 831/385-5434, www.fs.usda.gov, first-come, first-served, $20) is 10 miles (16.1 km) inland, but it does offer a place to stay when the coast is inundated with campers. There are eight first-come, first-served sites, all located by the Nacimiento River.

Two miles (3.2 km) east of Nacimiento Campground, and far more spacious, **Ponderosa Campground** (Nacimiento-Fergusson Rd., 13 mi/20.9 km east of CA-1, reservations 877/444-6777, international reservations 606/515-6777, www.recreation.gov, $25) has 23 sites along the Nacimiento River. All of the sites have picnic tables, fire pits, and raised grills. Reservations must be made more than eight days in advance. Fewer than that, you can test your luck by trying to secure a site in person. Be aware that it will be hot and bug-filled during the summer.

For the ultimate high-end California, green lodging-cum-camping experience, book a yurt (from $340)—a circular structure made with a wood frame covered by cloth—at the **Treebones Resort** (71895 CA-1, 62 mi/100 km south of Carmel, 18 mi/29 km south of Limekiln State Park, 877/424-4787, www.treebonesresort.com). The yurts at Treebones tend to be spacious and charming, with polished wood floors, queen beds, seating areas, and outdoor decks for lounging. They are really cool structures, but they are not soundproofed. There are also five walk-in campsites ($105 for two people, breakfast and use of the facilities included). For a truly different experience, camp in the human nest ($225), a bundle of wood off the ground outfitted with a futon mattress, the two-story twig hut ($235), or the 500-square-foot (46.5-sq-m) autonomous tent ($645) with a gas fireplace and bathroom. A stay in any of the facilities includes a complimentary breakfast with make-your-own waffles. In the central lodge, you'll find hot showers and usually clean restroom facilities. There is also a heated pool with an ocean view and a hot tub on the grounds. Treebones has a couple of on-site dining options: The **Wild Coast Restaurant** and the **Oceanview Sushi Bar.**

Transportation

Big Sur is not a town but rather the name for the lightly developed coastline stretching from San Simeon to Carmel. It can only be reached via CA-1. The drive north from San Simeon into Big Sur is where the Pacific Coast Highway gets really interesting, twisting and turning along with the coastline. The largest concentration of businesses is located within the Big Sur Valley, 61 miles (98 km) north of San Simeon.

CAR

The drive north from San Simeon to the Big Sur Valley usually takes around 1.5 hours, but it can be slow going, especially if you are behind an RV. You may want to stop every few miles to snap a photo of the stunning coastline. If traffic is backing up behind you, pull into a turnoff to let other cars pass; the local drivers can be impatient with tourist traffic.

CA-1 can have one or both lanes closed at times, especially in the winter months when rockslides occur. Check the **Caltrans** website (www.dot.ca.gov) or the **Big Sur California Blog** (www.thebigsurblog.com) for current road conditions. A favorite local resource for road conditions and updates during wildfires is **Big Sur Kate's Blog** (http://bigsurkate. blog).

BUS

It is difficult to get around Big Sur without a car. However, **Monterey-Salinas Transit** (888/678-2871, www.mst.org, $3.50, daily Memorial Day-Labor Day; hours vary Sat.-Sun.) runs a seasonal bus route through Big Sur that stops at Nepenthe, Pfeiffer Big Sur State Park, Big Sur River Inn, and Andrew Molera State Park as it heads to Carmel and Monterey.

SERVICES

There is no comprehensive visitors center in Big Sur, but the website for the **Big Sur Chamber of Commerce** (www. bigsurcalifornia.org) includes up-to-date information about hikes as well as links to lodging and restaurants. Pick up the *Big Sur Information Guide,* a publication of the Big Sur Chamber of Commerce that includes a map and guide to local businesses.

Big Sur Station 47555 CA-1, 27 mi/43 km south of Carmel, 0.6 mi/1 km south of Pfeiffer Big Sur State Park, 831/667-2315, 9am-4pm daily) is the closest thing to a visitors center. The staffed building offers maps and brochures for all the major parks and trails of Big Sur, plus a bookshop.

Big Sur has its own **post office** (47500 CA-1, 831/667-2305, 28 mi/45 km south of Carmel, 3 miles (4.8 km) south of Pfeiffer Big Sur State Park, www.usps.com, 8:30am-10am and 1pm-4pm Mon.-Fri.). Pick up a postcard at Big Sur Station or the adjacent Big Sur Deli and send it to a friend to make them jealous of the stunning natural beauty you are seeing.

Your **cell phone** may not work anywhere in Big Sur, but especially out in the undeveloped reaches of forest and on CA-1 away from the valley. The best places to get cell service are around Andrew Molera State Park and Point Sur, along with the large dirt pullout a 0.25 mile (0.4 km) south of Big Sur Station on Highway 1. Likewise, GPS units may struggle in this region. It's best to have a map in your vehicle, or pick up a free *Big Sur Guide,* which has a general map of the region.

The **Big Sur Health Center** (46896 CA-1, Big Sur, 25 mi/40 km south of Carmel, 2.5 mi/4 km south of Andrew Molera State Park, 831/667-2580, http://bigsurhealthcenter.org, 10am-1pm and 2pm-5pm Mon.-Fri.) can take care of minor medical needs and provides an ambulance service and limited emergency care.

The nearest full-service hospital is the **Community Hospital of the Monterey Peninsula** (23625 Holman Hwy., Monterey, 831/624-5311 or 888/452-4667, www.chomp.org).

Cambria, San Simeon, and Morro Bay

The rugged coastline twists and turns through

Cambria and San Simeon and onward to Morro Bay. The hills to the east contain this small coastal region, keeping it distinct both naturally and culturally.

These towns have remained relatively unspoiled, not only in their natural beauty but in the old-fashioned simplicity of the homes and businesses that adorn their streets. Morro Bay still looks much like it did decades ago, a small beach community that fronts the Pacific Ocean, its namesake Morro Rock standing guard at the mouth of the bay. Within the bay is an active fishing fleet as well as a rebounding local sea otter population. Cayucos is an unassuming little beach town with a popular beach and a pier that dates back to the 1800s. Just north

Highlights

Look for ★ to find recommended sights, activities, dining, and lodging.

★ **Hearst Castle:** Opulent, erratic, and ultimately all-American, this massive, lavish compound built on a remote hill for media mogul William Randolph Hearst is the closest thing to a true castle in California (page 246).

★ **Nitt Witt Ridge:** This small, rambling ode to one man's eccentricity is made of abalone shells, car rims, toilet seats, and what others might call garbage (page 248).

★ **Moonstone Beach:** This stretch of beach exemplifies the beauty of this rugged area. It's named for the semi-clear stones that you can find on the sand (page 249).

★ **Piedras Blancas Elephant Seal Rookery:** Every winter elephant seals show up north of San Simeon to birth their pups. The males spar, the females wean their newborns, and the people get a free show (page 250).

★ **Morro Rock:** Primal, austere, and endlessly photogenic, this ancient dormant volcano is a refuge for endangered falcons, a home to Native American lore, and a traveler's delight (page 266).

★ **Montaña de Oro State Park:** With 7 miles (11.3 km) of coastline and almost 50 miles (81 km) of trails, the park is a great place for wildlife lovers and outdoor recreation enthusiasts (page 266).

Piedras Blancas Elephant Seal Rookery ✪
✪ **Hearst Castle**
San Simeon
Nitt Witt Ridge ✪
Cambria
Moonstone Beach ✪
46
PACIFIC OCEAN
1
Morro Rock ✪
Morro Bay
Kayaking and Stand-Up Paddleboarding in Morro Bay ✪
✪ **Montaña de Oro State Park**
© MOON.COM

★ **Kayaking and Stand-Up Paddleboarding in Morro Bay:** Get on the water for the best chance to see wildlife up close, including resident otters (page 269).

of Cayucos, Cambria still has many 1880s storefronts and a feel of yesteryear.

But when it comes to this area, there is only one true sight: palatial Hearst Castle, located about 7 miles (11.3 km) north of Cambria in San Simeon. Once functioning mainly to service the palatial estate's inhabitant, millionaire William Randolph Hearst, San Simeon hasn't grown much since the beginning of the 20th century.

PLANNING YOUR TIME

These beachside communities are all located along Highway 1. The big draw in this region—and one of the most visited attractions in California—is Hearst Castle. Most visitors plan their itineraries around touring the immense mansion, including visits to its gateway towns, Cambria and Morro Bay. There's no advantage to planning to spend the night specifically in Morro Bay or Cambria, since they are only 15 miles (24 km) apart. Heading south, stop in Cambria and work your way down the coast, finding accommodations in Morro Bay.

You can stop off at Hearst Castle for the day as part of a longer road trip, but seeing all the area has to offer requires a weekend. One day and a night is enough time to get a feel for Cambria and San Simeon. Similarly, one day and a night can be perfect for just Morro Bay. The village of Cambria can be scouted out in a day, and you'll leave with an appreciation for the area, although you'll undoubtedly want to return. Morro Bay and nearby Cayucos can also be explored relatively well in a day and a night. But these places beg for leisure time: the ability to wander the beaches, the hillsides, and the streets with no agenda, which makes for a restful weekend getaway.

Cambria and San Simeon

Cambria, originally known as Slabtown, retains nothing of its original if uninspired moniker. Divided into east and west villages, it is a charming, easily walkable area of low storefronts, with moss-covered pine trees as a backdrop. Typically you'll see visitors meandering in and out of the local stores, browsing art galleries, or combing Moonstone Beach for souvenir moonstone rocks. The really great thing about Cambria is that, aside from the gas stations, you won't find any chain stores—not one—in town, and Cambrians, and most visitors, like it that way. It truly is an idyllic spot, even during bustling summer months when the crowds swell dramatically. Many of the buildings are original, dating to the 1880s.

Cambria owes much of its prosperity to the immense mansion on the hill, Hearst Castle.

Located about 7 miles (11.3 km) north in San Simeon, Hearst Castle, quite frankly, *is* San Simeon; the town grew up around it to support the overwhelming needs of its megalomaniacal owner and never-ending construction. The town dock provided a place for ships to unload tons of marble, piles of antiques, and dozens of workers. Today, San Simeon is less a town and more a stopping point for visitors heading to Hearst Castle. Stores, hotels, and restaurants flank both sides of Highway 1. If there's any strolling to be done, it's along the bluffs or on the rocky beaches. Set amid incredible open space between the hills and the ocean, San Simeon is truly a paradise of natural beauty, with stunning coastlines and gorgeous sunsets casting warm tones of amber light on the craggy rocks at the surf line.

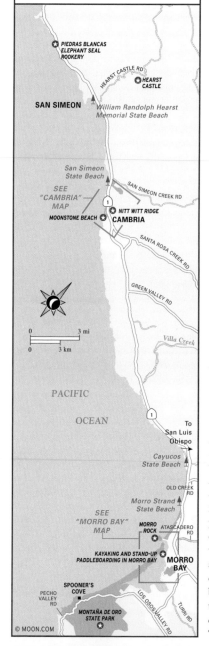

Cambria and San Simeon

PIEDRAS BLANCAS ELEPHANT SEAL ROOKERY

HEARST CASTLE RD

HEARST CASTLE

SAN SIMEON

William Randolph Hearst Memorial State Beach

San Simeon State Beach

SEE "CAMBRIA" MAP

SAN SIMEON CREEK RD

MOONSTONE BEACH

NITT WITT RIDGE

CAMBRIA

SANTA ROSA CREEK RD

GREEN VALLEY RD

0   3 mi
0   3 km

Villa Creek

PACIFIC

OCEAN

1

To San Luis Obispo

Cayucos State Beach

OLD CREEK RD

Morro Strand State Beach

SEE "MORRO BAY" MAP

MORRO ROCK   ATASCADERO RD

KAYAKING AND STAND-UP PADDLEBOARDING IN MORRO BAY   **MORRO BAY**

SPOONER'S COVE

PECHO VALLEY RD

MONTAÑA DE ORO STATE PARK

LOS OSOS VALLEY RD   TURRI RD

© MOON.COM

SIGHTS

★ Hearst Castle

There's nothing else in California quite like **Hearst Castle** (Hwy. 1 and Hearst Castle Rd., 800/444-4445, www.hearstcastle.org, tours 8:20am-3:20pm daily). Newspaper magnate William Randolph Hearst conceived the idea of a grand mansion in the Mediterranean style on land his parents bought along the central California coast. His memories of camping on the hills above the Pacific led him to choose the spot where the castle now stands. He hired Julia Morgan, the first female civil engineering graduate from the University of California, Berkeley, to design and build the house for him. She did a brilliant job with every detail, despite the ever-changing wishes of her employer. By way of decoration, Hearst purchased hundreds of European and Renaissance antiquities, from tiny tchotchkes to whole gilded ceilings. Hearst also adored exotic animals, and he created one of the largest private zoos in the nation on his thousands of Central Coast acres. Most of the zoo is gone now, but you can still see the occasional zebra grazing peacefully along Highway 1 south of the castle, heralding the exotic nature of Hearst Castle ahead.

The visitors center is a lavish affair with a gift shop, restaurant, café, ticket booth, and movie theater. Here you can see the much-touted film *Hearst Castle—Building the Dream,* which will give you an overview of the construction and history of the marvelous edifice, and of William Randolph Hearst's empire. (Only daytime tours offer free showings of the movie. During evening tours, a movie ticket is $6 for adults and $4 for children. To see the movie without going on a tour, tickets cost $10 for adults and $8 for children.) After buying your ticket, board the shuttle that takes you up the hill to your tour. No private cars are allowed on the roads up to the castle. There are several tours to choose from, and each focuses on the different spaces and aspects of the castle.

THE TOURS

Expect to walk for at least an hour on whichever tour you choose, and to climb up and down many stairs. Even the most jaded traveler can't help but be amazed by the beauty and opulence that drips from every room in the house. Lovers of European art and antiques will want to stay forever.

The **Grand Rooms Tour** (45 minutes, 106 stairs, 0.6 mi/1 km, adults $25, children age 5-12 $12) is recommended for first-time visitors. It begins in the castle's assembly room, which is draped in Flemish tapestries, before heading into the dining room, the billiard room, and the impressive movie theater, where you'll watch a few old Hearst newsreels. The guide then lets you loose to take in the swimming pools: the indoor pool, decorated in gold and blue, and the stunning outdoor Neptune Pool.

For a further glimpse into Hearst's personal life, take the **Upstairs Suites Tour** (60 minutes, 273 stairs, 0.75 mi/1.2 km, adults $25, children age 5-12 $12). Among the highlights are a stop within Hearst's private suite and a visit to his library, which holds more than 4,000 books and 150 ancient Greek vases. At the end of this tour, you can explore the grounds, including the Neptune Pool, on your own.

Epicureans should opt for the **Cottages & Kitchen Tour** (60 minutes, 176 stairs, 0.75 mi/1.2 km, adults $25, children age 5-12 $12). Visit the wine cellar first, where there are still bottles of wine, gin, rum, beer, and vermouth lining the walls. (After a visit here, actor David Niven once said that "the wine flowed like glue.") Then take in the ornate guest cottages Casa del Monte and Casa del Mar, where Hearst spent the final two years of his life. The tour concludes in the massive castle kitchen, with its steam-heated metal counters, before leaving you to explore the grounds on your own.

The **Designing the Dream Tour** (75 minutes, 320 stairs, 1.2 mi/1.9 km, adults $30, children age 5-12 $15) highlights the estate's three-decade evolution in architectural design. This option includes visits to the estate's biggest guesthouse and the north wing of the main house. The guided tour wraps up at the indoor Roman Pool and its dressing rooms. The price of this tour also includes a viewing of the 40-minute film *Hearst Castle—Building the Dream.*

entrance to the Hearst Castle

Cambria

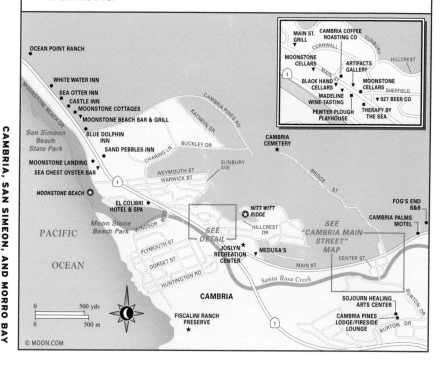

The seasonal **Evening Tour** (100 minutes, 308 stairs, 0.75 mi/1.2 km, adults $36, children age 5-12 $18) is only given in spring and fall. Volunteers dress in 1930s fashions and welcome guests as if they are arriving at one of Hearst's legendary parties.

The **Art of San Simeon Tour** (120 minutes, 750 stairs, adults and children age 5-12 $100) takes in the amazing art pieces in the castle and how Hearst acquired them.

Hollywood legends including Charlie Chaplin, Greta Garbo, Clark Gable, and more visited Hearst Castle. The **Hearst and Hollywood Tour** (120 minutes, 750 stairs, adults and children age 5-12 $100) looks at Hearst's connection to Hollywood.

Reserve tour tickets at least a few days in advance, and even farther ahead on summer weekends. Wheelchair-accessible Grand Rooms and Evening Tours are available for visitors with limited mobility. Strollers are not permitted. The restrooms and food concessions are all in the visitors center. No food, drink, or chewing gum is allowed on any tour.

★ Nitt Witt Ridge

While William Randolph Hearst built one of the most expensive homes ever seen in California, local eccentric Arthur Harold Beal (aka Captain Nit Wit or Der Tinkerpaw) got busy building the cheapest "castle" he could. **Nitt Witt Ridge** (881 Hillcrest Dr., 805/927-2690, http://nit-wit-ridge.business.site, tours on the hour 10am-4pm daily, adults $10, children $5) is the result of five decades of scavenging trash and using it as building supplies to create a multistory home like no other on the coast. The rambling structure is made of abalone shells, used car rims, and toilet seats, among other found materials. Features like

Julia Morgan: Pioneering California Architect

Best known for designing and building Hearst Castle over a 21-year period, architect Julia Morgan designed more than 700 buildings in an illustrious career that spanned nearly 50 years. On a cool spring morning in 1919, William Randolph Hearst swaggered into Morgan's office in San Francisco. "Miss Morgan, we are tired of camping out in the open at the ranch in San Simeon, and I would like to build a little something," Hearst said in his high-pitched voice. And that set in motion events that would catapult her into architectural history.

Julia Morgan was the first woman to graduate from the prestigious École des Beaux-Arts in Paris and was one of the first graduates, male or female, from the University of California, Berkeley, with a degree in civil engineering. Her notable California projects include not only the enduring Hearst Castle, but also the Bavarian-style Wyntoon, also for William Randolph Hearst; Asilomar, located in Pacific Grove; the Los Angeles Herald Examiner Building in Los Angeles; the Margaret Baylor Inn in Santa Barbara; and a plethora of commercial buildings, YWCAs, private residences, apartments, churches, and educational facilities.

Today the Julia Morgan School for Girls, an all-girls middle school in Berkeley, works to educate and empower females. Morgan died in 1958 at the age of 85. In 1957 she granted her one and only press interview, stating simply and succinctly: "My buildings will be my legacy. They will speak for me long after I am gone."

the cobblestone archways reveal a true artist's touch. Today, you can make an appointment with owner Mike O'Malley to take a tour of the property, but don't just drop in. O'Malley is a quirky spirit himself who relishes the chance to spread the gospel about this one-of-a-kind sight. It's weird, it's funky, and it's fun—an oddly iconic experience of the Central Coast.

To find Nitt Witt Ridge, drive on Cambria's Main Street toward Moonstone Beach and make a right onto Cornwall Street. Take the second right onto Hillcrest Avenue and look for the unique structure.

Cambria Cemetery

Artsy isn't a word that's usually associated with graveyards, but in Cambria it fits. The Cambria Cemetery (6005 Bridge St., 805/927-5158, www.cambriacemetery.com, 9am-4pm daily) reflects the artistic bent of the town's residents in its tombstone decor. Unlike many cemeteries, at Cambria the family and friends of the deceased are allowed to place all manner of personal objects at their loved ones' graves. You'll see painted tombstones, beautiful panes of stained glass, unusual wind

chimes, and many other unique expressions of love, devotion, and art as you wander the 12 wooded acres (49 ha).

★ Moonstone Beach

Known for its namesake shimmering stone, Moonstone Beach (Moonstone Beach Dr.) is a scenic, pebbly slice of coastline with craggy rocks offshore. Cambria's moonstones are bright, translucent pebbles that can be easiest to find at low tides and when the sun shines, highlighting their features. They are fairly easy to collect, especially after winter storms. The moonstones on Moonstone Beach are not gem quality, but they make a fun souvenir. If you can't find any, many Cambria boutiques and galleries carry moonstone jewelry.

Huts constructed from driftwood can be found on some sections of the beach, and there is plenty more than just moonstones on the shoreline. A wooden boardwalk runs along the top of the bluffs above the beach. From here, you can take in the scenery and watch moonstone collectors with buckets wander below in the tide line. Access is at Leffingwell Landing, Moonstone Beach Drive, and Santa Rosa Creek.

Cambria Main Street

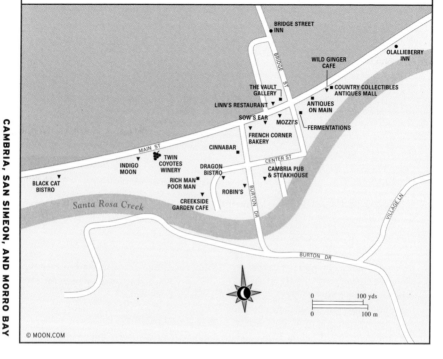

BRIDGE STREET INN

WILD GINGER CAFE

OLALLIEBERRY INN

THE VAULT GALLERY

COUNTRY COLLECTIBLES ANTIQUES MALL

LINN'S RESTAURANT

ANTIQUES ON MAIN

SOW'S EAR

MOZZI'S

FERMENTATIONS

FRENCH CORNER BAKERY

MAIN ST

CINNABAR

INDIGO MOON

TWIN COYOTES WINERY

DRAGON BISTRO

CENTER ST

CAMBRIA PUB & STEAKHOUSE

BLACK CAT BISTRO

RICH MAN POOR MAN

ROBIN'S

BURTON DR

CREEKSIDE GARDEN CAFE

Santa Rosa Creek

VILLAGE LN

BURTON DR

| 0 | | 100 yds |
| 0 | | 100 m |

© MOON.COM

Piedras Blancas Light Station

First illuminated in 1875, the **Piedras Blancas Light Station** (tours meet at the Piedras Blancas Motel, 1.5 mi/2.4 km north of the light station on Hwy. 1, 805/927-7361, www.piedrasblancas.org, tours 9:45am Mon.-Sat. mid-June-Sept., 9:45am Tues., Thurs., and Sat. Sept.-mid-June, adults $10, ages 6-17 $5, under age 5 free) and its adjacent grounds can be accessed on a two-hour **tour** (www.recreation.gov). In 1948, a nearby earthquake caused a crack in the lighthouse tower and the removal of a first-order Fresnel lens, which was replaced with an automatic aero beacon. Since 2001, the lighthouse has been run by the federal Bureau of Land Management. *Piedras blancas* means "white rocks" in Spanish.

★ Piedras Blancas Elephant Seal Rookery

Stopping at the **Piedras Blancas Elephant Seal Rookery** (Hwy. 1, 7 mi/11.3 km north of San Simeon, 805/924-1628, www. elephantseal.org, free) is like watching a nature documentary in real time. On this sliver of beach, up to 17,000 elephant seals rest, breed, give birth, or fight one another. The rookery is right along Highway 1; turn into the large gravel parking lot and follow the boardwalks north or south to viewing areas where informative plaques give background on the elephant seals. Volunteer docents are available to answer questions (10am-4pm daily). The beaches themselves are off-limits to humans, since they're covered in the large marine mammals. But thanks to the wheelchair-accessible boardwalks built above the beach, visitors can get just a matter of feet away from the giant creatures. In the fall, most adult seals head out to sea, returning in early to mid-December. Most of the seal births occur between the end of December and the middle of February.

Fiscalini Ranch Preserve

A terrific place to take in Cambria's natural assets, the Fiscalini Ranch Preserve (805/927-2856, www.ffrpcambria.org, dawn-dusk daily, free) is home to abundant plants and animals, including one of the last three remaining native Monterey pine forests and 25 special-status species such as American peregrine falcons, western snowy plovers, and California red-legged frogs. Birdwatchers have spotted at least 182 bird species here. The preserve is actually two parcels of land on both the east and west side of Highway 1; head for the 364-acre (147-ha) western portion. There are a few entry points, so to avoid confusion, download the map from the ranch's website or stop in at the Friends of Fiscalini Ranch Preserve Office (604 Main St., 11am-2pm Thurs.-Fri., 11am-3pm Sat.).

The preserve is named for the Fiscalini family, who started a cattle ranch and dairy farm on the land back in the mid-1850s. A housing development was planned here in the 1980s until an organization was formed to maintain the ranch as public open space. The land was finally purchased and preserved in 2000. The Friends of Fiscalini Ranch Preserve (www.cambriaranchwalks.com) also offers free monthly docent-guided walks.

William Randolph Hearst Memorial State Beach

Down the hill from Hearst Castle is William Randolph Hearst Memorial State Beach (750 Hearst Castle Rd., 805/927-2035, www.parks.ca.gov, dawn-dusk daily, free), a stretch of kelp-strewn sand along a protected cove. The beach's 795-foot-long (242-m) pier is great for fishing and strolling, and the Coastal Discovery Center (805/927-2145, 805/927-6575, http://montereybay.noaa.gov, 11am-5pm Fri.-Sun., free), run by California State Parks and Monterey Bay National Marine Sanctuary, warrants a stop. It focuses on local natural history and culture, with exhibits on shipwrecks, a display on elephant seals, and an interactive tidepool. This beach is also an ideal place to try kayaking.

elephant seals at the Piedras Blancas Elephant Seal Rookery

WINE-TASTING

Cambria has a handful of tasting rooms showcasing wines made here and in nearby Paso Robles.

Moonstone Cellars

Moonstone Cellars (812 Cornwall St., 805/927-9466, www.moonstonecellars.com, by reservation 11am-4pm daily, tasting $10) is an appropriate name for this little Cambria winery: Father and son Muril and Todd Clift began their winemaking careers producing wine in a basement near Moonstone Beach. They showcase their passion in the tasting room by pouring two chardonnays, a viognier, a cabernet sauvignon, a merlot, and a zinfandel.

Black Hand Cellars

Although the tasting room of **Black Hand Cellars** (766 Main St., Ste. B, 805/927-9463, www.blackhandcellars.com, noon-5pm daily, tasting $10) is in Cambria's west village, the vineyard is located northwest of Paso Robles. The focus is on Syrahs, but they also do Rhône-style blends, Bordeaux-style blends, a Grenache, and a dessert wine.

Hearst Ranch Winery

The **Hearst Ranch Winery** (442 SLO San Simeon Rd., 805/927-4100, www. hearstranchwinery.com, 11am-4pm daily, tasting $15) occupies a cliffside building in tiny San Simeon. The tasting room pours a range of wines, including the award-winning Pico Creek Merlot and the Glacier Ridge Chardonnay.

RECREATION

Surfing

Cambria is not a popular surfing destination, but there can be waves to ride if you have a board with you. The north end of the strip of businesses in San Simeon is where you'll find **Pico Creek,** a reef break off the spot where Pico Creek enters the ocean. Just south of the creek is a beach where there can be peaky beach break waves. Park in the cul-de-sac at the western end of Pico Avenue. Another option is **Santa Rosa Creek,** at the southern end of Cambria's Moonstone Beach. This is a beach break littered with a few rocks. To get here, turn left into the public parking lot off Moonstone Beach Drive.

Lawn Bowling

The **Joslyn Recreation Center** (950 Main St., 805/927-3364, www.joslynrec.org, club hours 10am-2pm Mon.-Fri., donation) has a large artificial turf field for lawn bowling. Lawn bowling is similar to bocce, in which you try to roll balls closest to a target ball. If you don't know how to play, someone at the recreation center will be able to show you the basics during club hours. Groups can reserve the green during non-club hours.

Hiking

Fiscalini Ranch Preserve (www. ffrpcambria.org, dawn-dusk daily, free) is a wonderful place to take a walk. Hike the **Bluff Trail** (trailheads at the end of S. Windsor Blvd. and N. Windsor Blvd, 2 mi/3.2 km round-trip, easy) to view wildflower-colored bluffs and rocky shoreline, which includes tidepools and attracts relaxing sea lions. Monterey pines crown the ridgeline above. Multiple spur trails branch out to the bluffs' edges. A wooden boardwalk protects some sensitive areas, while arty driftwood benches provide places to sit and enjoy the scenery. The Bluff Trail can become a 2-mi/3.2-km loop by taking the **Marine Terrace Trail** back. This wider trail is higher up on the hill. When you return to the south side of the preserve, you'll have to walk a block down on Wedgewood Street to return to the South Windsor Boulevard parking area. Trail maps are available for download on the preserve's website, or stop into the **Friends of the Fiscalini Ranch Preserve Office** (604 Main St., 11am-2pm Thurs.-Fri., 11am-3pm Sat.).

In **Hearst San Simeon State Park** (500 San Simeon Creek Rd.,805/772-6101, www. parks.ca.gov, dawn-dusk daily, free), the **San**

Simeon Creek Trail (3.5 mi/5.6 km round-trip, moderate) goes through the park's wetlands, up to a grassy ridge studded with Monterey pines. To reach the trailhead, park in the Washburn Day Use Area. Walk east on the service road, and take the trail on the right.

Spas

Therapy by the Sea (816 Main St., 805/927-2956, http://therapybythesea.com, 8am-8pm Sun.-Thurs., 8am-9pm Fri.-Sat., massages $90-135) offers a range of massages including Swedish, Reiki, warm stone, and prenatal. They also provide facials and other relaxation packages.

ENTERTAINMENT
Nightlife

If touring Hearst Castle leaves you thirsty for a beer, Cambria has a few different options. Mozzi's (2262 Main St., 805/927-4767, http://mozzissaloon.com, 1pm-midnight Mon.-Fri., 11am-2am Sat., noon-midnight Sun.) is a classic old California saloon—there's been a bar on this site since 1866. Old artifacts like lanterns and farm equipment hang from the ceiling above the long redwood bar, jukebox, and pool tables in this historic watering hole.

Cambria Pines Lodge Fireside Lounge (Cambria Pines Lodge, 2905 Burton Dr., 805/927-4200, www.cambriapineslodge.com, 2pm-midnight daily) has live music nightly, performed on a stage to the right of a big stone fireplace. Enjoy a cocktail, beer, or wine seated at one of the couches or small tables.

Local craft brewery the 927 Beer Company (821 Cornwall St., 805/203-5265, www.927beer.com, noon-7pm Mon.-Sat., noon-6pm Sun.) has anywhere from 6 to 11 beers on tap, with unique offerings including an olallieberry sour, orange wheat, vanilla bourbon porter, and chocolate mole stout. The most popular is the Old Number 23 Porter. Get a taster flight with four samples for $7. The tasting room feels like a small cottage, with local art and vintage Pearl Jam posters on the walls.

Festivals and Events

Sample wines from more than 35 local wineries, as well as wine and food pairings, at the Cambria Art and Wine Festival (various venues, 805/927-3624, http://cambriaartwine.org, Jan.). The popular three-day event has been known to sell out. It also includes an art show and silent auction.

The Pinedorado Grounds, next to the Veterans Memorial building, are home to Pinedorado Days (Pinedorado Grounds, Main St., www.cambrialions.org, Labor Day weekend), a community celebration that's occurred here since 1949. Expect a parade and a car show along with barbecues, live music, kids' games, art shows, and food booths.

The Cambria Historical Society sponsors the Cambria Scarecrow Festival (various venues, 805/395-2399, http://cambriascarecrows.com, Oct.), with creative scarecrows lining the streets of town.

SHOPPING

This is a town chock-full of unique shops. Antiques, local art, and funky gift and specialty food shops are where Cambria shines.

For antiques lovers, there are multiple options. The three floors of Antiques on Main (2338 Main St., 805/927-4292, 10am-5pm daily) have everything from fossils to furniture. In the Redwood Center shopping strip, Rich Man Poor Man Antiques Mall (2110 Main St., 805/203-5350, www.richmanpoormanantiques.com, 10am-5pm daily) has two floors of high-quality antiques and collectibles from more than 30 dealers, selling everything from furniture to estate jewelry. They have so much stuff that they also have an annex store (2084 Main St., 805/927-7724, 10am-5pm daily).

Examine the local art scene at The Vault Gallery (2289 Main St., 805/927-0300, www.vaultgallery.com, 10:30am-6pm daily), which displays the work of Central Coast photographers, painters, and sculptors, as well as a large collection of plein air paintings. A large bronze sculpture out front welcomes visitors to the Artifacts Gallery (775 Main

St., 805/927-7335, www.artifactsgallery.com, 10am-5pm Sun.-Thurs., 10am-6pm Fri.-Sat.), where oil paintings, more bronzes, and fine-art reproductions fill the space. The two-story building includes an in-house framing studio.

The **Lucia Apothecary** (746 Main St., 805/927-1831, www.luciacompany.com, 11am-5pm Mon.-Fri., 10am-5pm Sat., 10am-4pm Sun.) has body oils, scrubs, creams, washes, and mists in 19 scents inspired by California locales. Located in a beautiful old building that was a blacksmith shop in the 1800s, **Cinnabar** (4121 Burton Dr., 805/395-4111, http://cinnabaronline.com, 11am-6pm Sun.-Thurs., 11am-9pm Fri., 11am-10pm Sat.) has unique folk art pieces, home decor, and furnishings, including pieces made from reclaimed wood and even lamps made out of tree leaves.

Fermentations (2306 Main St., 805/927-7141, www.fermentations.com, 10am-8pm daily) has a large selection of gourmet food and wines, with a focus on the products of nearby Paso Robles vineyards.

FOOD
Seafood
If the smell of the salt air on Moonstone Beach leaves you longing for a seafood dinner, head for the ★ **Sea Chest Oyster Bar** (6216 Moonstone Beach Dr., 805/927-4514, http://seachestoysterbar.com, 5:30pm-9pm daily, $20-30, cash only). No reservations are accepted, so expect a long line out the door at opening time, and prepare to get here early (or wait a long while) for one of the window-side tables. The wait is worth it. The restaurant is located in a wooden cottage with great ocean views. Framed photographs on the walls and books on the shelves add to the homey feel of the place. Sit at the bar to watch the cooks prepare impressive dishes such as halibut, salmon, and cioppino, served in the pot in which it was cooked. The menu of oyster and clam appetizers includes the indulgent Devils on Horseback, a decadent dish of sautéed oysters drenched in wine, garlic, and butter, and topped with crispy bacon on two slabs of toast.

The lightly breaded calamari strips are superb as well.

An unassuming steak and seafood restaurant attached to San Simeon's Quality Inn, the family-owned **Manta Rey Restaurant** (9240 Castillo Dr., 805/924-1032, www.mantareyrestaurant.com, 5pm-9pm daily, $17-50) pleasantly surprises with its artfully done and tasty seafood dishes. Items like sand dabs, salmon, oysters, and sea bass come from nearby Morro Bay when in season. The decor here is basic—white tablecloths, flowers on the table—and there is a view of the highway and the ocean in the distance from the porthole-like windows. Being near Hearst Castle, there is frequently an international clientele.

At the very least, the **Moonstone Beach Bar & Grill** (6550 Moonstone Beach Dr., 805/927-3859, www.moonstonebeach.com, 11am-9pm Mon.-Sat., 9am-9pm Sun., $20-59) is a great place for a drink. The deck out front—always crowded on summer days—has a nice view of the beach. It's ideal for a late-afternoon beer, local wine, or specialty cocktail. The dinner menu is heavy on grilled seafood, while lunch has a wide variety of sandwiches.

New American
The eclectic menu at ★ **Robin's** (4095 Burton Dr., 805/927-5007, www.robinsrestaurant.com, 4:30pm-8pm Mon.-Tues., 11:30am-2:30pm and 4:30pm-8pm Wed.-Thurs., 11am-3pm and 4:30pm-9pm Fri.-Sat., 11am-3pm and 4:30-8pm Sun., $21-38) has cuisine from around the world, including Thailand (Thai green chicken), India (a selection of curries), Mexico (chicken mole enchiladas), and the old US of A (burgers), as well as a number of vegetarian and gluten-free dishes. What makes this so impressive is that the restaurant does it all so well. No matter what you order, start with the signature salmon bisque. The setting is a historic building that was erected by Hearst Castle's construction foreman and used as his own residence. It has a large dining room and an outdoor deck decorated with hanging vines.

Olallieberries

You'll see the name olallieberry around Cambria, perhaps spelled differently each time. Part lo-ganberry, part raspberry, this berry grows in and around Cambria, but it was actually created in a laboratory. The original cross was made as early as 1935 as a joint project between Oregon State University and the U.S. Department of Agriculture. Selected in 1937 and tested in Oregon, Washington, and California and referred to as Oregon 609, it was eventually named Olallie and released in 1950. (The name means "berry" in Native American languages.) While developed in Oregon and planted there, it has never been very productive in that environment and is primarily grown in California. It has usually been marketed as olallieberry, just as Marion is sold as marionberry. The taste, as well as the structure, is similar to a blackberry but a little milder. Make sure you try it while you're in town, or pick up a jar of jam to take with you as a souvenir for people back home, who probably haven't heard of it before.

One of the most popular restaurants in Cambria is the **Black Cat Bistro** (1602 Main St., 805/927-1600, www.blackcatbistro.com, 5pm-9pm daily, $22-42), serving creative sea-food, vegetarian, meat, and poultry entrées. The interior is homey, with a fireplace and wood floors. Reservations are recommended at this small spot.

Part of an expansive local family business, **Linn's Restaurant** (2277 Main St., 805/927-0371, www.linnsfruitbin.com, 8am-10pm Fri.-Sat., 8am-9:30pm Sun.-Thurs. summer, 8am-9pm daily winter, $18-36) serves tasty, unpretentious favorites in a casual family-friendly atmosphere. Think potpies, stro-ganoff, and pot roast. Save room for the olallieberry pie—or purchase a ready-to-bake pie, jam, or even vinegar to take home.

Madeline's Restaurant and Wine Shop (788 Main St., 805/927-4175, www.madelinescambria.com, 11:30am-3pm and 5pm-9pm daily, $25-55) pours local wines by day (tasting room 805/927-0990, 11am-5pm daily) and serves French-influenced din-ner fare by night, with entrées like seafood gumbo, pan-seared duck, and vegetarian po-lenta, plus a fresh fish dish.

The Sow's Ear Café (2248 Main St., 805/927-4865, http://thesowsear.com, 5pm-close daily, $18-36) breathes new life into comfort-food classics. The potpies are stuffed with lobster, while the macaroni and cheese is spiked with sausage and smoked chicken. The chicken-fried steak and chicken and dump-lings hew to classic rib-sticking recipes.

Indigo Moon (1980 Main St., 805/927-2911, www.indigomooncafe.com, 11am-3pm and 5pm-9pm Tues.-Sat., 10am-9pm Sun., $16-44) is a worthy dining destination. The menu is a fusion of American, European, and Asian influences, with entrées like the per-fectly breaded calamari *piccata* with a tasty red curry sauce. Dine inside the historic cottage or out on the covered garden patio. Indigo Moon also sells artisanal cheeses and bottles of wine, so it's a good place to stop for picnic supplies.

Mexican
Every town in California has a taqueria, and Cambria is no different. **Medusa's** (1053 Main St., 805/927-0135, 7am-8pm Mon.-Sat., $6-12) offers the usual tacos, burritos, and enchiladas as well as an extensive breakfast menu that includes chilaquiles, huevos ran-cheros, and chorizo and eggs. Get it to go or dine inside under a mural of a jungle pyramid.

Asian
One of the best bargains in town is **Wild Ginger** (2380 Main St., 805/927-1001, www.wildgingercambria.com, 11am-2:30pm and 5pm-9pm Mon.-Wed. and Fri.-Sat., 5pm-9pm Sun., $15-22). This tiny pan-Asian café serves delicious fresh food like Vietnamese caramel-ized prawns and eggplant curry. There's also

an array of take-out fare. Come early for the best selection.

Breakfast and Brunch

The ★ **Main Street Grill** (603 Main St., 805/927-3194, www.firestonegrill.com, 11am-9pm daily June-Aug., 11am-8pm daily Sept.-May, $5-22) is a popular eatery housed in a cavernous building located on the way into Cambria. The tri-tip steak sandwich—served drenched in barbecue sauce and placed on a French roll dipped in butter—is the favorite, although the ABC burger, with avocado, bacon, and cheese, puts most burger joints to shame. The giant Cobb salad comes with lots of diced-up bacon and your choice of chicken or steak.

Take in a hearty breakfast or lunch on the outdoor patio at the family-owned **Creekside Garden Café** (2114 Main St., 805/927-8646, www.creeksidegardencafe.com, 7am-2pm Mon.-Sat., 7am-1pm Sun., $5-10). Fuel up with omelets, scrambles, or pancakes. Lunch showcases burgers, sandwiches, salads, and south-of-the-border items.

Coffee and Bakeries

The **Cambria Coffee Roasting Company** (761 Main St., 805/927-0670, www.cambriacoffee.com, 7am-5:30pm daily) roasts their own beans. Head upstairs to stretch out and enjoy the free Wi-Fi.

The French Corner Bakery (2214 Main St., 805/927-8227, www.frenchcornerbakery.com, 6:30am-6pm daily, $7) offers a selection of fresh-made bread and pastries behind a glass counter, overseen by a large mural of Paris. There's also a small menu of lunch options, including cold deli sandwiches, Mexican tortas, and hot offerings like an Italian meatball sandwich.

Farmers Markets

Stock up on produce, fruit, and honey at the food-only **Cambria Farmer's Market**

1: the ABC burger at Cambria's Main Street Grill
2: Robin's restaurant **3:** the Sea Chest Oyster Bar

(Veterans Hall parking lot, 1000 Main St., www.cambriafarmersmarket.com, 2:30pm-5:30pm Fri. Apr.-Sept., 2:30pm-5pm Fri. Oct.-Mar.).

ACCOMMODATIONS

Many of the accommodations in Cambria are along the small town's Hotel Row, aka Moonstone Beach Drive. San Simeon has a small strip of hotels on either side of the highway south of Hearst Castle.

Under $150

Her Castle Homestay Bed and Breakfast Inn (1978 Londonderry Ln., 805/924-1719, http://hercastle.com, $140-170) is a bit different from your average B&B, with only two guest rooms available and lots of personal attention from the owners. When you make your reservations, ask about a half-day wine tour or dinner reservations. Her Castle can be the perfect hideaway for two couples traveling together who desire the privacy of "their own house."

Although it was established in 1957, **Cambria Palms Motel** (2662 Main St., 805/927-4485, www.cambriapalmsmotel.com, $129-190) has been remodeled and modernized; the 18 guest rooms have free Wi-Fi and cable TV. Some guest rooms also have private patios, and pet-friendly rooms are available.

One of San Simeon's best lodging options, **The Morgan** (9135 Hearst Dr., 800/451-9900, www.hotel-morgan.com, $138-249) is named for Hearst Castle architect Julia Morgan, paying tribute to her with reproductions of her architectural drawings in all of the guest rooms. The rooms are clean and well appointed, and some have partial ocean views; eight rooms come with soaking tubs and gas fireplaces. The Morgan also has a wind-sheltered pool and deck. A complimentary continental breakfast is served every morning.

$150-250

A pebble's throw from Moonstone Beach, the ★ **Sand Pebbles Inn** (6252 Moonstone Beach Dr., 805/927-5600, www.cambriainns.

com, $164-364) is a two-story gray building where most guest rooms have glimpses of the ocean through bay windows. The clean, tastefully decorated rooms have comfortable beds, mini-fridges, and microwaves. The six west-facing rooms have full ocean views, while the bottom three have patios. Expect nice little amenities such as welcome cookies and a lending library of DVDs.

For a great selection of anything from economical standard rooms up to rustic cabins with king beds and a fireplace, pick the **Cambria Pines Lodge** (2905 Burton Dr., 805/927-4200 or 800/927-4200, www. cambriapineslodge.com, $165-365). All guest rooms have plenty of creature comforts, including TVs, private baths, and, in some cases, fireplaces. There's also a nice garden area with flowering plants, benches, and sculptures.

The family-friendly **Castle Inn** (6620 Moonstone Beach Dr., 805/927-8605, www. cambriainns.com, $150-244) has a great location, right across the road from Moonstone Beach, offering excellent ocean views. Guest rooms are unassuming, with wooden bed frames, coffee pots, fridges, and flat-screen TVs. The heated pool and hot tub are sheltered from the coastal winds.

Located on the north end of Moonstone Beach, the **White Water Inn** (6790 Moonstone Beach Dr., 805/927-1066, www. whitewaterinn.com, $189-339) is a small family-run hotel. The distinct yellow building looks like a collection of connected cottages, with 15 guest rooms and two mini-suites. All of the guest rooms have gas fireplaces; the mini-suites have spas on private patios. The service is notable and includes coffee service.

The **Best Western Cavalier Oceanfront Resort** (9415 Hearst Dr., San Simeon, 805/927-4688, www.cavalierresort.com, $179-339) occupies a prime piece of real estate in San Simeon on a bluff above the ocean just south of Pico Creek. The highest-priced rooms are oceanfront offerings with wood-burning fireplaces, soaking tubs, and private patios. The grounds include a pool, an exercise room, a day spa, and a restaurant.

Oceanpoint Ranch (7200 Moonstone Beach Dr., 805/927-4648, www. oceanpointranch.com, $190-350) brings a ranch chic to the area with leather-accented rooms on a 9-acre (3.6-ha) property. Play croquet, shuffleboard, cornhole, or lawn bowling on-site with your new cowpoke pals or take a private trail down to the beach at Leffingwell Landing. If there's some rustling in your belly, mosey on over to **The Canteen** for breakfast and dinner.

Moonstone Landing (6240 Moonstone Beach Dr., 805/927-0012, www. moonstonelanding.com, $200-400) provides inexpensive partial-view guest rooms with the decor and amenities of a mid-tier chain motel, as well as oceanfront luxury guest rooms featuring porches with ocean views, soaking tubs, and gas fireplaces.

Over $250

The adults-only ★ **Blue Dolphin Inn** (6470 Moonstone Beach Dr., 805/927-3300, www. cambriainns.com, $200-400) has six ocean-view rooms with fireplaces, Keurig coffee-makers, robes, and slippers. Breakfast is delivered to your room every morning.

One of the cuter and more interesting options on Moonstone Beach Drive, **Moonstone Cottages** (6580 Moonstone Beach Dr., 805/927-1366, http:// moonstonecottages.com, $319-389) offers peace and luxury along the sea. Each of the three cottages includes a fireplace, a marble bath with a whirlpool tub, a flat-screen TV with a DVD player, Internet access, and a view of the ocean. Breakfast is delivered to your cottage each morning.

Camping

At **Hearst San Simeon State Park** (500 San Simeon Creek Rd., Cambria, 800/444-7275, www.reservecalifornia.com, $20-25), you can experience the opulence of Hearst Castle on a budget. The **San Simeon Creek Campground** ($25) is the more developed option here, with 115 campsites for tents and RVs. All have fire pits and picnic tables. At the time of publication all of the toilets and showers were closed due to the state's water shortage. The **Washburn Campground** ($20) is a primitive campground 1 mi (1.6 km) inland. There are views of the Santa Lucia Mountains and the Pacific Ocean from Washburn's sites.

TRANSPORTATION AND SERVICES

Car

Cambria and San Simeon are located directly along Highway 1 and are only accessible by this road, whether you're coming from the north or the south. You can access Highway 1 from US-101 via scenic Highway 46, which connects to Highway 1 just south of Cambria. If you use Cambria as a base to explore the Paso Robles wine area, or even for excursions to Morro Bay (15 mi/24 km), a car will be necessary. The only available taxi service is **Cambria Cab** (4363 Bridge St., 805/927-4357).

Bus

The regional bus system, the **RTA** (805/541-2228, www.slorta.org, $1.75-3.25), connects San Luis Obispo, Morro Bay, Cayucos, Cambria, and San Simeon.

Train

There is no rail service to Cambria or San Simeon; the nearest Amtrak train station is located in San Luis Obispo, 35 miles (56 km) south of Cambria.

Air

There are scheduled flights from Los Angeles, San Francisco, Phoenix, Seattle, Dallas, and Denver to the **San Luis Obispo County Regional Airport** (SBP, 975 Airport Dr., San Luis Obispo, 805/781-5205, www.sloairport. com), which is 35 miles (56 km) south of Cambria.

Services

MAPS AND VISITOR INFORMATION

The **Cambria Chamber of Commerce** (767 Main St., 805/927-3624, www. cambriachamber.org, 9am-5pm Mon.-Fri., noon-4pm Sat.-Sun.) is probably the best resource for information on the area. It also provides a free annual publication that lists many of the local stores, restaurants, and lodgings. Be sure to pick up a trail guide for additional hikes and walks—Cambria has great places to roam. The **Cambria Public Library** (1043 Main St., 805/927-4336, www.slolibrary.org, 9am-5pm Tues.-Wed., 10am-6pm Thurs., 10am-5pm Fri.-Sat.) offers additional information and local history, including a map for a self-guided historical walking tour.

EMERGENCY SERVICES

Cambria is served by three facilities: **Twin Cities Hospital** (1100 Las Tablas Rd., Templeton, 805/434-3500, www. tenethealthcentralcoast.com), 25 miles (40 km) inland, and **Sierra Vista Regional Medical Center** (1010 Murray Ave., 805/546-7600, www.tenethealthcentralcoast.com) and **French Hospital** (1911 Johnson Ave., 805/543-5353, www.dignityhealth.org), both in San Luis Obispo, which is 37 miles (60 km) south. Cambria and San Simeon are policed by the **San Luis Obispo Sheriff's Department** (805/781-4550, www.slosheriff. org). If you have an emergency, dial 911.

NEWSPAPERS AND MEDIA

The Cambrian (www.sanluisobispo.com, $0.50) is the local paper, published each Thursday. **KTEA** (103.5 FM, http://1035ktea. com) is the local radio station.

POSTAL SERVICES

There is a **post office** (4100 Bridge St., 805/927-8610, www.usps.com, 9am-4:30pm Mon.-Fri.) in Cambria.

Cayucos

Just 13 miles (20.9 km) south of Cambria along Highway 1, Cayucos is one of California's best little beach towns. There are no real attractions here except for the small strip of a beach between open hillsides and the Pacific, but there are a good number of nice restaurants and places to stay, so it makes a nice, less touristy place to spend the night while visiting the area's attractions, including Hearst Castle, 30 miles (48 km) north.

Cayucos is named after the Chumash people's word for kayak or canoe. One of the early proponents of the town was Captain James Cass, who, with a business partner, built the pier, a store, and a warehouse in the late 1800s. Today, the long, narrow pier still stands, while the warehouse is the town's community center and home of the Cayucos Art Society Gallery.

RECREATION
Beaches
The major attraction in Cayucos is **Cayucos State Beach** (Cayucos Dr., 805/781-5930, www.parks.ca.gov, sunrise-sunset daily) and the pier, which was built in 1875 by Captain James Cass. The beach has volleyball courts, swing sets, and lifeguard stands, which are staffed during the summer months. The pier is lit at night for fishing. Cayucos is not known for consistent surf, but rideable waves can occur on the south side of the pier. This is a usually mellow beach-break spot good for beginners. The relatively calm waters off Cayucos Beach are a good place to try kayaking or stand-up paddleboarding.

Just a few feet from the beach, **Good Clean Fun** (136 Ocean Front Ln., 805/995-1993, www.goodcleanfunusa.com, 9am-6pm daily) rents out surfboards ($10/hour), wetsuits ($8/hour), body boards ($5/hour), stand-up paddleboards ($15/hour), and kayaks ($30-40/hour). They also have surf lessons, a surf camp, kayak tours, and kayak fishing outings. Another place to pick up

beach equipment is the **Cayucos Surf Company** (95 Cayucos Dr., 805/995-1000, www.cayucossurfcompany.com, 10am-6pm daily summer, 10am-5pm daily winter). They have wetsuits ($15/day), surfboards ($29/day), body boards ($11/day), and stand-up paddleboards ($40/day) for rent. They also offer private and group surfing lessons.

Hiking
The oceanfront land between Cayucos and Cambria is mostly undeveloped because it's preserved as part of the state park system. The 355-acre (144-ha) **Estero Bluffs State Park** (west of Hwy. 1 from N. Ocean St. to Villa Creek, 805/772-6101, www.parks.ca.gov, 6am-sunset daily, free) is a coastal terrace that offers trails into intertidal areas. It includes a pocket cove and a beach at Villa Creek, which is also an important habitat for the endangered snowy plover.

The 784-acre (317-ha) **Harmony Headlands State Park** (Hwy. 1, 5 mi/8 km north of Cayucos, 805/772-6101, www.parks. ca.gov, 6am-sunset daily, $3/vehicle) was ranch and dairy land until the mid-1960s, and it opened as a state park in 2008. The only real way to experience this park is the 1.5-mile (2.4-km) hike from the small 10-car parking lot out to the coast. The trail is a mostly flat dirt road. As it begins, it passes over a bridge where you may be able to look down and spot southwestern pond turtles. The trail continues through grasslands and hugs the side of a scenic ravine, then runs north along a marine terrace. It ends at a small finger that juts out between rocks and tidepools. In the spring, wildflowers such as morning glories, California buttercups, and lupine color the grasslands. Keep your eyes peeled for endangered California red-legged frogs and rare southwestern pond turtles. There are no facilities except for a portable toilet located next to a ranch house just a few

Living in Harmony

Harmony sign

In the mid-1800s the hilly land around the present-day community of **Harmony** (http://harmonytown.com), between Cambria and Cayucos, was settled by Swiss immigrants interested in dairy farming. The first cheese factory was established in the area in 1869. After that, this portion of San Luis Obispo County became known for its cheese and butter, becoming home to companies like the Excelsior Cheese Factory and the Diamond Creamery. William Randolph Hearst traveled to Harmony to get his milk. Eventually, tensions grew between competing dairy farmers, which led to a feud and a murder. After peace was restored and a truce was made, the farmers decided to name the town Harmony in 1907 to reflect their newly adopted situation.

In 1958, Harmony ceased its cheese and butter making. The population of the town dropped until the 1970s, when some of the old dairy buildings were occupied by artist studios, galleries, and shops. The new influx of residents didn't quite restore Harmony to its former glory of the dairy days.

Today, Harmony is primarily known for **Harmony Cellars** (3255 Harmony Valley Rd., 805/927-1625, www.harmonycellars.com, 10am-5:30pm daily summer, 10am-5pm daily fall-spring, tasting $15), a winery that makes reds and whites, and **Harmony Glassworks** (2180 Old Creamery Rd., 805/927-4248, http://harmonyglassworks.com, 9am-6pm daily summer, 9am-5pm daily winter), a glass-art gallery, studio, and school. Harmony is also home to the **Harmony Chapel** (805/927-1028, www.harmonychapelca.com), a recording studio and café.

minutes into the trail, on a short side-spur trail to the right.

Spas

After a tough day of relaxing on Cayucos Beach, you deserve a massage. The **Cayucos Aloha Spa** (196 S. Ocean Ave., 805/995-2222, www.cayucosalohaspa.com, by appointment) has you covered with massages ($65 per hour),

pedicures, manicures, and "bacials" (a facial treatment for your back).

Wine-Tasting

Cayucos Cellars (2020 Main St., 805/935-9050, www.cayucoscellars.com, noon-5pm Thurs.-Mon., tasting $10) is a true family affair. All the employees are members of the Selkirk family. Cayucos Cellars produces only

500 to 800 cases of wine per year, including zinfandels and cabernet sauvignons.

ENTERTAINMENT AND EVENTS

The **Old Cayucos Tavern** (130 N. Ocean Ave., 805/995-3209, www.oldcayucostavern. com, 10am-2am daily) is a classic Western saloon, with a poker room in the back and a bar up front. In the barroom, more than 10 beers are available on tap, and topless cowgirl paintings adorn the walls. There are also two pool tables and a shuffleboard table for those who want to play games without the fear of losing their money in the card room. Western scenes decorate the walls and wooden barrels serve as tables.

On New Year's Day, join the locals for the **Carlin Soule Memorial Polar Bear Dip** (Cayucos Pier, www.cayucoschamber.com, noon on New Year's Day). It began with just seven brave souls (including founder Carlin Soule) hopping into the frigid Pacific without wetsuits. Bravery must be contagious: Today there are more than 1,000 participants.

The **Independence Day Celebration** (various venues, 805/995-1200, www. cayucoschamber.com, July 4) is a big deal, with a serious sand sculpture contest on the beach, a parade, a barbecue, and a fireworks show from the pier.

SHOPPING

Located in a red two-story building on Cayucos's main drag, **Brown Butter Cookie Company** (98 N. Ocean Ave., 805/995-2076, www.brownbuttercookies.com, 9am-6pm daily) bakes and sells original cookie creations, including their original brown butter sea salt cookie and more recent recipes such as coconut lime and cocoa mint. Witness the delectable creative process as it takes place right behind the counter. **Remember When** (152 N. Ocean Ave., 805/995-1232, www.rememberwhenantiquemalls.com, 10am-5pm daily) is home to antiques and collectibles.

FOOD
Seafood

Cayucos is a place for seafood, and there is probably nothing in town as revered as ★ **Rudell's Smokehouse** (101 D St., 805/995-5028, www.smokerjim.com, 11am-6pm Wed.-Mon., $4-20). Rudell's is nothing more than a little shack near the beach, but this place serves some of the tastiest fish tacos you'll ever eat, including salmon and albacore variations. The seafood is smoked, and the unexpected but welcome presence of chopped apples gives the fixings a sweet crunch. The seating options are limited to a few outdoor tables, so plan on taking your taco to the nearby beach.

Living up to its name, **Schooners Wharf** (171 N. Ocean Ave., 805/995-3883, www. schoonerswharf.com, 11am-9pm daily, $12-38) has a serious nautical theme going: It's a two-story compound of corrugated metal and wood decorated heavily with marine flotsam and jetsam. The menu here is seafood-heavy, with a range of items from hearty cioppino to seared ahi. But the burgers, made with local Hearst Ranch beef, are also worthy of your attention. If you are looking for somewhere to eat in Cayucos later at night, Schooners will probably be the only option.

At **Duckies Chowder House** (55 Cayucos Dr., 805/995-2245, www.duckieschowder. com, 11am-8pm daily, $7-14), you can get your chowder New England or Manhattan style and served in a cup, bowl, or bread bowl. Other seafood options are mostly fried; there are also salads and sandwiches on the menu. Pitchers of beer and the company of friends make it all go down easy.

The **Sea Shanty** (296 S. Ocean Ave., 805/995-3272, www.billandcarolseashanty. com, 8am-10pm daily summer, 8am-9pm daily winter, $10-25) serves gut-busting portions for breakfast, lunch, and dinner. The carb-loaded Cayucos Breakfast is biscuits drenched in eggs and gravy alongside a small mound of diced Swiss sausage. Lunches focus on charbroiled and fried seafood. Noteworthy desserts include a range of pies and cobblers. Dine inside under hundreds of hanging baseball caps—or better yet, sit outside on the covered wooden deck.

Mexican and Italian

If you can't decide between Mexican and Italian food, head to **Martin's Restaurant** (49 S. Ocean St., 805/995-2626, www.martinsrestaurantcayucos.com, 8am-9pm daily, $9-20); they do both. Fish tacos, shrimp enchiladas, tostadas, and burritos appear on the menu alongside pizza, calzones, and full entrées like chicken parmesan and salmon fettuccine.

Pizza

A blue building just a few feet from Cayucos Beach, **Ocean Front Pizza** (156 1/2 Ocean Front Ave., 805/995-2979, www.oceanfrontpizza.com, 11am-8pm Thurs.-Mon., $11-23) offers classic pizza combos, build-your-own pies, specialty pizzas like pesto and Thai, and barbecued chicken. All feature hand-tossed dough and homemade sauce.

Farmers Markets

Cayucos has its own **farmers market**

(Cayucos Veterans Hall parking lot, 10 Cayucos Dr., 805/296-2056, 10am-12:30pm Fri. summer).

ACCOMMODATIONS
Under $150

The **Seaside Motel** (42 S. Ocean Ave., 805/995-3809 or 800/549-0900, www.seasidemotel.com, $130-190) has brightly colored and uniquely decorated guest rooms with names like "Birdhouse Bungalow" and "Sunflower Surprise." Some guest rooms have kitchenettes; all have flat-screen TVs and Internet access. Suites are available for larger groups. All guests have access to the on-site garden.

$150-250

The **Cayucos Motel** (20 S. Ocean Ave., 805/995-3670 or 800/965-2699, www.cayucosmotel.com, $165-325) is also all about the beach, with beach access, an outdoor shower, and bodyboards and beach towels that guests can check out to further enjoy the surf and sand. Each of the eight guest rooms is different; some have private patios. The outdoor deck includes a barbecue grill and a ping-pong table.

The modern rooms at **On the Beach Bed**

The Saltbox

& Breakfast (181 N. Ocean Ave., 805/995-3200, www.californiaonthebeach.com, $219-369) have gas fireplaces, private balconies, and jetted tubs. The rooftop hot tub offers views of the ocean and pier. Enjoy homemade cookies and wake up to complimentary breakfast in the morning.

Over $250

Located right behind the Brown Butter Cookie Company, ★ The Saltbox (150 D St., 800/995-2322, www.thesaltbox.com, $390-887) makes a superb home base while exploring the coast. The historic blue building, constructed by a ship's captain in the 1880s, is split into three units, each with a fully equipped kitchen, private entrance, and a deck or patio. The ground-floor Captain's Quarters can accommodate six to eight people with three bedrooms, two bathrooms, and an enclosed brick patio area. It's a perfect fit for three couples or a big family. The Crow's Nest is an upstairs apartment with two bedrooms that can accommodate four people and has a nice view of the sea and the pier. The Carriage House is a small studio in the shade of the main house.

True to its name, the Shoreline Inn (1 N. Ocean Ave., 805/995-3681 or 800/549-2244, www.cayucosshorelineinn.com, $239-329)

is right on the beach. All of the guest rooms have impressive beach and pier views as well as access to the beach and beachside showers. Everyone also gets a mini-fridge, a microwave, free Wi-Fi, and a flat-screen TV with a DVD player. There's a DVD library in the office, where you can borrow films.

SERVICES

Before visiting, the website Cayucos by the Sea (www.cayucosbythesea.com) has information on everything from the town's history to its current lodging and restaurant options. Visit the brick-and-mortar location or the website of the Cayucos Chamber of Commerce (41 S. Ocean Ave., 805/995-8552, www.cayucoschamber.com, 11am-4pm Fri.-Mon.).

Cayucos has a few basic services, including a post office (97 Ash Ave., 805/995-3479, www.usps.com, 9am-4pm Mon.-Fri.). The Cayucos Super Market (301 S. Ocean Ave., 805/995-3929, 8am-7pm daily) has all the basic supplies you'll need. For something to grill, head to the Cayucos Sausage Company (12 N. Ocean Ave., 805/900-5377, www.cayucossausagecompany.com, 11am-5pm Wed.-Mon.), which has an array of homemade sausages and meats, as well as deli sandwiches.

Morro Bay

The picturesque fishing village of Morro Bay is dominated by Morro Rock, a 576-foot-high (176-m) volcanic plug that looms over the harbor. In 1542, Juan Rodríguez Cabrillo, the first European explorer to navigate the California coast, named the landmark Morro Rock because he thought it resembled a moor's turban.

With a view of the rock, the small city's Embarcadero is a string of tourist shops, restaurants, and hotels strung along Morro Bay, a large estuary that includes the harbor, the Morro Bay State Marine Recreational

Management Area, and the Morro Bay State Marine Reserve. Uphill from the water, more restaurants, bars, and stores are located in Morro Bay's Olde Towne section.

With the town's waterfront setting, not to mention resident otters that can regularly be spotted at the T-dock behind the Great American Fish Company restaurant, and natural attractions like the stunning Montaña de Oro State Park just miles away, Morro Bay is a worthy destination or detour for a weekend. A lot of the area's lodgings fill up during high-season weekends.

Morro Bay

To
Cambria

Morro Strand
State Beach

OLD U.S. ROUTE 466

MAIN ST

MAIN ST

Morro Creek

1

MORRO
ROCK

TOGNAZZINI'S
DOCKSIDE
RESTAURANT

MASTERPIECE
HOTEL

SEE
"MORRO BAY
TOWN"
MAP

MORRO BAY BLVD

MAIN ST

To
San Luis
Obispo

QUINTANA RD

Morro Bay

Sandspit

Tidelands
Park

MORRO BAY STATE
PARK GOLF COURSE

Wednesday
Island

MORRO BAY STATE PARK RD

Churro Creek

SOUTH BAY BLVD

MORRO BAY MUSEUM
OF NATURAL HISTORY

A KAYAK
SHACK

BAYSIDE
CAFE

Morro Bay

State Park

PACIFIC OCEAN

Morro Bay

State Park

Morro

Bay

KAYAKING AND STAND-UP
PADDLEBOARDING IN MORRO BAY

Morro Bay

Marine Reserve

Los Osos
Creek

NOI'S LITTLE
THAI TAKEOUT

SANTA YSABEL AVE

2ND ST

BACK
BAY INN

EL MORRO AVE

PASO ROBLES AVE

0   300 yds

0   300 m

© MOON.COM

Morro Bay Town

FRANKIE AND LOLA'S

FRONT STREET INN & SPA

BAY BEAUTY SPA

WEST ST

SCOTT ST

STAX WINE BAR & BISTRO

BEACH ST

CARLA'S COUNTRY KITCHEN

THE COFFEE POT RESTAURANT

EMBARCADERO

MARKET AVENUE

BEACH BUNGALOW INN & SUITES

GIOVANNI'S FISH MARKET AND GALLEY

WAVELENGTHS SURF SHOP

FRONT ST

DUNES ST

MONTEREY AVE

ANCHOR MEMORIAL PARK

MAGILSE DR

HOFBRAU

THE GALLERY SEAFOOD BAR & GRILL

HARBOR ST

ANDERSON INN

LEGENDS BAR

MORRO AVE

SPA BY THE BAY

OTTER ROCK CAFE

BLUE SAIL INN

TOP DOG COFFEE BAR

MAIN ST

SHINE CAFE

THE LIBERTINE PUB

DORN'S ORIGINAL BREAKERS CAFE

GIANT CHESSBOARD

EMBARCADERO

MORRO BAY BLVD

BAY THEATRE

ASCOT INN

To → Hwy CA-1

SUB SEA TOURS

PACIFIC ST

WINDOWS ON THE WATER

MORRO BAY SKATEBOARD MUSEUM

GARDEN GALLERY

SUNDOWN INN

MORRO BAY NATIONAL ESTUARY PROGRAM

MARINA STREET INN

MORRO BAY WINE SELLER

MARINA ST

GALLERY AT MARINA SQUARE

THE SHELL SHOP

KAYAK HORIZONS

THAI BOUNTY

0   100 yds

0   100 m

DRIFTWOOD ST

© MOON.COM

SIGHTS

★ Morro Rock

It would be difficult to come to the town of Morro Bay and not see **Morro Rock** (www.morro-bay.ca.us). The 576-foot-high (176-m) volcanic plug, which has been called the "Gibraltar of the Pacific," dominates the town's scenery, whether you are walking along the bayside Embarcadero or beachcombing on the sandy coastline just north of the prominent geologic feature. The rock was an island until the 1930s, when a road was built connecting it to the mainland. The area around the rock is accessible, but the rock itself is off-limits because it is home to a group of endangered peregrine falcons. Indeed, multitudes of birds always seems to be swirling around the rock they call home.

★ Montaña de Oro State Park

Montaña de Oro State Park (Pecho Rd., 7 mi/11.3 km south of Los Osos, 805/772-6101, www.parks.ca.gov, 6am-10pm daily, free) is for those seeking a serious nature fix on the Central Coast. This sprawling 8,000-acre (3,237-ha) park with 7 miles (11.3 km) of

1: Morro Rock **2:** Montaña de Oro State Park

coastline has coves, tidepools, sand dunes, and almost 50 miles (81 km) of hiking trails.

A great way to get a feel for the park's immense size is to hike up the out-and-back **Valencia Peak Trail** (4 mi/6.4 km round-trip, moderate). In springtime the sides of the trail are decorated with blooming wildflowers, and the 1,347-foot-high (411-m) summit offers commanding views of Montaña de Oro's pocked coastline and Morro Rock jutting out in the distance. From this vantage point in spring, the park's sticky monkey flower, wild mustard, and California poppies dust the hillsides in gold. The hike is steep and exposed, so make sure to bring plenty of water on warm days.

For a feel of the coast, park right in front of **Spooner's Cove** and walk out on its wide coarse-grained beach. On the cove's north end, Islay Creek drains into the ocean. There's also a picturesque arch across the creek in the rock face on the north side. The **Spooner Ranch House Museum** informs visitors about early inhabitants of the park's land, the Spooner family. There are also displays about the area's plants, mountain lions, and raptors in the small facility.

Morro Bay State Park

Morro Bay State Park (Morro Bay State Park Rd., 805/772-6101, www.parks.ca.gov, $8/vehicle) is not a typical state park. It has hiking trails, a campground, and recreational opportunities, but this park also has its own natural history museum, a golf course, and a marina. Located just south of town, the park is situated on the shores of Morro Bay. One way to get a feel for the park is to hike the **Black Hill Trail** (3 mi/4.8 km round-trip, moderate).

A unique aspect of Morro Bay State Park is the **Morro Bay Museum of Natural History** (Morro Bay State Park Rd., 805/772-2694, www.ccnha.org, 10am-5pm daily, adults $3, under age 16 free). Small but informative, the museum has displays that explain the habitats of the Central Coast and some interactive exhibits for kids. An observation deck

hanging off the museum allows for a great view of Morro Bay. Beside the museum is a garden that shows how the area's original inhabitants, the Chumash people, utilized the region's plants.

Play a round of golf at the **Morro Bay State Park Golf Course** (201 State Park Rd., 805/772-1923, www.slocountyparks.com, Mon.-Fri. $45, Sat.-Sun. $54), or head out on the water in a kayak, a canoe, or a stand-up paddleboard rented from the **Kayak Shack** (10 State Park Rd., 805/772-8796, www.morrobaykayakrental.com, 9am-5pm daily summer, 9am-4pm Fri.-Sun. winter, kayak rentals $16-20/hour, canoe rentals $20/hour, SUP rentals $16/hour).

Morro Bay Harbor Walk

The **Morro Bay Harbor Walk** (0.5 mi/0.8, easy) is a great way to take in Morro Bay's harbor. Beginning at the north end of the Embarcadero, the boardwalk and bike trail runs along the harbor to towering Morro Rock. The harbor views are nice, and you can get some scenic photos of the picturesque town and the hills behind it. You may also spot some sea otters in the water. Along the way, the walk passes through **Coleman Park** (101 Coleman Dr., 805/772-6200, www.morro-bay.ca.us, dawn-dusk daily), a small city park with a picnic area, a basketball court, and a swing set for kids.

One way to complete the Morro Bay Harbor Walk is by pedal power. Located near the start of the trail is **Beachfront Kites, Surreys, and More** (1108 Front St., 805/772-0113, 10am-6pm Mon., 10am-5pm Tues.-Sun.). This store rents beach cruisers ($10/hour) along with two-person and four-person surrey bikes ($20-30/hour).

Giant Chessboard

Morro Bay's most unusual sight is the 16-by-16-foot (4.9-by-4.9-m) **Giant Chessboard** (Centennial Pkwy., 805/772-6278). The waist-high chess pieces used in the game weigh as much as 30 pounds (13 kg). Four picnic tables adjoin the Giant Chessboard; each has a chessboard where the local chess fiends play. You can reserve the board for a small fee (8am-5pm Mon.-Fri.). Or join the Morro Bay Chess Club when they play on Saturdays starting at noon.

Morro Bay Estuary Nature Center

Run by the Morro Bay National Estuary Program, the **Morro Bay Estuary Nature Center** (601 Embarcadero, Ste. 11, 805/772-3834, www.mbnep.org, 10am-6pm daily) explains the significance of the 2,300-acre (931-ha) estuary that is a focal point of the town. A watershed exhibit shows where rainfall goes, while an aquarium has live steelhead trout. Another aquarium houses eelgrass along with hermit crabs and anemones. There are also windows looking out on the estuary, where you may be able to spot sea otters, harbor seals, and sea lions in the water.

RECREATION

Beaches

There are several beaches in and around Morro Bay. Popular with surfers and beachcombers, **Morro Rock Beach** (west end of Embarcadero, 805/772-6200, www.morro-bay.ca.us) lies within the city limits, just north of Morro Rock. Two lifeguard towers are staffed from Memorial Day to Labor Day (10am-6pm).

Just north of town is **Morro Strand State Beach** (2 mi/3.2 km south of Cayucos, CA-1, 805/772-8812, www.parks.ca.gov). The 3-mile (4.8-km) strand of sand is popular with anglers, windsurfers, and kite fliers. **North Point** (Hwy. 1 at Toro Ln., 805/772-6200, www.morro-bay.ca.us) is a bluff-top city park with a stairway to the beach and great tidepools. From here, you can also walk north all the way to Cayucos or head south toward looming Morro Rock. The wetlands at **Cloisters Park** (San Jacinto St. and Coral St., 805/772-6200, www.morro-bay.ca.us) are home to fish and birds. This city park also offers access to the beach.

Surfing

Morro Rock Beach (west end of Embarcadero, 805/772-6200, www.morro-bay.ca.us) has a consistent beach break. It's a unique experience to be able to stare up at a giant rock while waiting for waves. **Wavelengths Surf Shop** (998 Embarcadero, 805/772-3904, 9:30am-6pm daily, board rentals $20/day, wetsuit $10/day), on the Embarcadero on the way to the beach, rents boards and wetsuits.

★ Kayaking and Stand-Up Paddleboarding

Paddling the protected scenic waters of Morro Bay, whether you're in a kayak or on a stand-up paddleboard, is a great way to see wildlife up close. You may see otters lazily backstroking in the estuary or clouds of birds gliding just above the surface of the water. On the bay with a view of the rock, **Rock Kayak** (845 Embarcadero, 805/772-2906, http://rockkayak.com, 9:30am-5pm daily summer, 9:30am-3:30pm daily winter, kayak rentals $15-25/hour, SUP rentals $15/hour) offers gear rentals for your aquatic adventure. In Morro Bay State Park, you can secure a canoe or kayak from **A Kayak Shack** (10 State Park Rd., 805/772-8796, www.morrobaykayakrental.com, 9am-5pm daily summer, 9am-4pm Fri.-Sun. winter, kayak rentals $16-20/hour, canoe rentals $20/hour, SUP rentals $16/hour).

Boat Tours

Sub Sea Tours (699 Embarcadero, 805/772-9463, www.subseatours.com, adults $17, seniors and students $13, children $8) is like snorkeling without getting wet. The yellow 27-foot (8.2-m) semisubmersible vessel has a cabin outfitted with windows below the water. The 45-minute tour takes you around the harbor in search of wildlife. Expect to see sea lions sunning on a floating dock and sea otters playing in the water. At a much-touted secret spot, fish congregate for feeding. You'll typically see smelt, appearing like silver splinters, but you may also catch a glimpse of salmon, lingcod, perch, and sunfish. The captain may even cue up the Beatles' "Yellow Submarine" on the sound system. Kids will love it.

Sub Sea Tours also schedules 2- to 3.5-hour whale-watching excursions (adults $50, seniors and students $45, children under age 12 $35) to see California gray whales and humpback whales.

Bird-Watching

Morro Bay is one of California's great birding spots. **Morro Bay State Park** is home to a **heron rookery,** located just north of the Museum of Natural History. At **Morro Rock,** you'll see endangered peregrine falcons, ever-present gulls, and the occasional canyon wren. On the northwest end of **Morro Bay State Park Marina Area** (off State Park Dr.), birders can spot loons, grebes, brants, and ducks; you may also see American pipits and Nelson's sparrows. The cypress trees host roosting black-crowned night herons. The **Morro Coast Audubon Society** (805/772-1991, www.morrocoastaudubon.org) conducts birding field trips to local hotspots; check its website for information on upcoming trips.

Hiking

Morro Bay State Park (Morro Bay State Park Rd., 805/772-6101, www.parks.ca.gov) has 13 miles (20.9 km) of hiking trails. One of the most popular is the **Black Hill Trail** (3 mi/4.8 km round-trip, moderate), which begins from the campground road. This climb gains 600 vertical feet and passes through chaparral and eucalyptus on the way to the 640-foot-high (195-m) Black Hill, part of the same system of volcanic plugs that produced nearby Morro Rock.

Montaña de Oro State Park (Pecho Rd., 7 mi/11.3 km south of Los Osos, 805/772-6101, www.parks.ca.gov) has almost 50 miles (81 km) of hiking trails. Take in the park's coastline along the **Montaña de Oro Bluffs Trail** (4 mi/6.4 km round-trip, easy). The trailhead begins about 100 yards (91.4 m) south of the visitors center and campground entrance and runs along a marine terrace to the park's

southern boundary. On the way it passes **Corallina Cove,** where you may see harbor seals and sea otters. Starting at the parking area just south of the visitors center, **Valencia Peak Trail** (4 mi/6.4 km round-trip, moderate) leads to its namesake 1,347-foot-high (411-m) peak, which offers a nice view of the coastline spread out below. The **Hazard Peak Trail** (6 mi/9.7 km round-trip, moderate-strenuous) starts at Pecho Valley Road and climbs to the summit of 1,076-foot (328-m) Hazard Peak, with unobstructed 360-degree views. The **Islay Canyon Trail** (6 mi/9.7 km round-trip, moderate) takes you through the park's inland creek beds and canyons. Starting at the bottom of Islay Creek Canyon, this wide dirt path is popular with birders because of the 25 to 40 different bird species that frequent the area. An abandoned barn makes a good marker to turn back toward the trailhead.

Just south of Montaña de Oro State Park, the **Point Buchon Trail** (3.5 mi/5.6 km round-trip, easy; 8am-5pm Thurs.-Mon. Apr.-Oct., 8am-4pm Thurs.-Mon. Nov.-Mar.) leads along pristine shoreline, passing a natural sinkhole and jagged sea-sculpted cliffs. The trail begins at Montaña de Oro State Park's Coon Creek Parking Lot. It's located on a parcel of land owned by utility company PG&E.

Located in nearby Los Osos, the **Elfin Forest Boardwalk Trail** (www.elfin-forest.org, dawn-dusk daily, 0.75 mi/1.2 km round-trip, easy) offers a boardwalk trail through 90 acres (36.4 ha) of marsh, dune scrub, and pygmy oak woodland. While some California live oaks reach heights of 50 feet, the persistent winds and poor soil keep these tiny specimens just 4-20 feet tall. Parking is off any street from 11th to 17th, which end at the edge of the forest. The 16th Street entrance offers the best access for people using wheelchairs or strollers.

City Parks

A couple of small city parks appeal to families or those who want a break from browsing in the Embarcadero's shops. Tiny **Anchor Memorial Park** (931 Embarcadero,

805/772-6278, www.morro-bay.ca.us) is dedicated to local people who have been lost at sea on fishing boats. This bayfront space has a statue of an anchor and nifty benches that resemble boat cleats. **Tidelands Park** (300-394 Embarcadero, 805/772-6278, www.morro-bay.ca.us) has a kids' play area with a pirate ship and some seal statues. A staircase leads to the mudflats below. There's also a fish-cleaning station.

Golf

How many state parks have their own golf course? People call the **Morro Bay Golf Course** (201 State Park Rd., 805/772-1923, www.golfmorrobay.com, greens fees Mon.-Fri. $45, Sat.-Sun. $54) the "poor man's Pebble Beach," probably because of the hilly terrain and great ocean views. It also has a driving range, rental clubs, a pro shop, and a bar and grill.

ENTERTAINMENT
Bars

Across the street, **Legends Bar** (899 Main St., 805/772-2525, 10am-2am daily) has a red pool table and a giant moose head poking out from behind the bar. Grab a drink and look at the framed historic photos covering the walls.

Down on the Embarcadero, **The Libertine Pub** (801 Embarcadero, 805/772-0700, http://libertinebrewing.com, 11am-10pm Mon.-Thurs., 11am-11pm Fri.-Sat., 10am-10pm Sun.) is the place for the discerning beer drinker. It began as a craft beer bar before moving into brewing its own wild ales. The pub features more than 30 rotating craft beers on tap. One of the beers will always be a sour. Pub food, including seafood tacos, burgers, and gourmet tater tots, are available to accompany your suds.

Stax Wine Bar & Bistro (1099 Embarcadero, 805/772-5055, http://staxwinebar.com, noon-8pm Sun.-Thurs., noon-10pm Fri.-Sat.) has a nice sidelong view of the harbor. Sit at the long, black granite bar or at the handful of tables to try some of the selection of more than 100 wines, many from local wineries. The small food menu includes crostinis, charcuterie, salads, and pizzas.

A place to sip wine is the **Waves Wine Bar** (845 Embarcadero, Ste. H, 805/225-1628, http://waveswinebar.wix.com/waves, 2pm-8pm Mon. and Wed.-Thurs., 2pm-10pm Fri., noon-10pm Sat., noon-8pm Sun.), where the focus is on Paso Robles reds. There's also a limited food menu that includes a couple of pizzas and cheese plates.

Cinema

There's only one movie house in town, the **Bay Theatre** (464 Morro Bay Blvd., 805/772-2444, www.morrobaymovie.com), and it has only one screen, so you're pretty limited unless you drive 20 minutes south to San Luis Obispo. This small-town theater has been screening films since the 1940s.

Festivals and Events

Bird-watchers flock to the **Morro Bay Winter Bird Festival** (various venues, 805/234-1170, http://morrobaybirdfestival.org, Jan.). Some 200 species are typically spotted during the three-day event, which includes birding classes and tours of local birding spots.

Strong winds kick up on the Central Coast in the spring. The **Morro Bay Kite Festival** (Morro Bay Beach, 200 Coleman Dr., 805/305-0579, www.morrobaykitefestival.org, last weekend in Apr.) takes advantage of these gales with pro kite fliers twirling and flipping their kites in the sky. The festival also offers kite-flying lessons.

For more than 30 years, the **Morro Bay Harbor Festival** (Embarcadero between Marina St. and Harbor St., 800/772-1155, www.mbhf.com, Oct.) has showcased the best of the region, including wines, seafood, live music, and a clam chowder contest.

SHOPPING

The Embarcadero is a fine place to stroll and pop into shops. One of the best is **The Shell Shop** (590 Embarcadero, 805/772-8014, 9:30am-7pm daily summer, 9:30am-5:30pm daily winter), which has imported shells from more than 22 countries. Beautiful marine items on sale include nautilus shells, abalone shells, and decorative pieces of coral as well as seashell jewelry.

Run by a community of artists, the **Gallery at Marina Square** (601 Embarcadero, Ste. 10, 805/772-1068, www.galleryatmarinasquare. com, 10am-6pm daily) showcases local art, including the work of sculptors, photographers, jewelry makers, glassworkers, and woodworkers. A public reception on the second Friday of every month (5pm-8pm) celebrates a member artist and a guest artist.

The Garden Gallery (680 Embarcadero, 805/772-4044, www.thegardengalleryinc. com, 10am-5pm daily) occupies a two-story building designed and built by one of its owners. The indoor and outdoor areas are filled with cacti and other succulents, along with garden decorations like fountains and pottery and indoor items like clocks and candles.

Wavelengths Surf Shop (998 Embarcadero, 805/772-3904, www. wavelengthssbi.com, 9:30am-6pm daily) has a good selection of new surfboards, skateboards, wetsuits, and surf wear, including hoodies and T-shirts. Browse the outlet store located right across the street to find deals on used boards and wetsuits. It's also where you can rent a surfboard or wetsuit.

FOOD
Seafood

Seafood is the way to go when dining in the fishing village of Morro Bay. An unassuming fish house with views of the fishing boats and the bay, ★ **Tognazzini's Dockside Restaurant** (1245 Embarcadero, 805/772-8100, www.morrobaydockside.com, 11am-9pm daily, $18-27) has an extensive seafood menu as well as art depicting sultry mermaids hanging on the wall. Entrées include albacore kebabs and wild salmon in a unique tequila marinade. If you're an oyster lover, you simply can't go wrong with Dockside's barbecued oysters appetizer, which features the shellfish swimming in garlic butter studded with scallions. Behind the main restaurant is

the **Dockside Too Fish Market** (10am-8pm Fri.-Sat., 10am-7pm Sun.-Thurs. summer, 10am-6pm Sun.-Thurs., 10am-8pm Fri.-Sat. winter), a local favorite with beer, seafood, and live music.

Located on a hill above the Embarcadero, ★ **Dorn's Original Breakers Café** (801 Market St., 805/772-4415, www.dornscafe. com, 7am-9pm daily, $14-44) offers a great view of Morro Rock from its dining room. It has been family owned and operated since 1942. Dinner begins with bread and a dish of garlic, olive oil, vinegar, and cheese. The large menu of seafood and steak includes fresh daily specials like snapper, petrale sole, salmon, and halibut from local waters.

Giovanni's Fish Market & Galley (1001 Front St., 805/772-2123, www. giovannisfishmarket.com, market 9am-6pm daily, restaurant 11am-6pm daily, $6-15) is a real working market, with live abalone and sushi-grade fish pulled right out of the bay. The fish-and-chips wins raves, and the clam chowder wins awards. Try the barbecued oysters in garlic or sriracha butter, or Rockefeller-style with bacon and jalapeños. During summer months, expect long lines to dine on the outdoor patio.

Elegant **Windows on the Water** (699 Embarcadero, Ste. 7, 805/772-0677, www. windowsmb.com, 5pm-close Tues.-Sat., $17-44) showcases local seafood like abalone, oysters, halibut, and sand dabs. The wine list is heavy with local vintages.

The upscale **Galley Seafood Bar & Grill** (899 Embarcadero, 805/772-7777, http:// galleymorrobay.com, 11:30am-8pm daily, $18-52) is popular for items like pan-seared scallops. The menu changes daily depending on the fresh catch.

Classic American

The giant parking lot outside **Carla's Country Kitchen** (213 Beach St., 805/772-9051, www.carlaskitchenmb.com, 6:30am-2pm daily, $6-12) attests to the popularity of this breakfast and lunch spot. With blue-and-white checkered tablecloths, Carla's

Water Farms

Aquaculture is the practice of farming aquatic organisms. The Cambria and Morro Bay area has two fine examples of aquaculture operations. The **Morro Bay Oyster Company** (1287 Embarcadero, 805/234-7102, www.morrobayoysters.com, store 11am-5pm Fri.-Sun.) uses environmentally sustainable techniques to raise Pacific Gold oysters in the cold, nutrient-rich waters of Morro Bay. The oysters start off as small as a pencil eraser, encased in mesh nets, and are "farmed" for 12 to 24 months until they have developed into tasty bivalve mollusks with a shell.

Farther up the road in Cayucos, **The Abalone Farm** (805/995-2495, www.abalonefarm.com) is the largest aquaculture facility in the nation. It produces an impressive 100 tons of California red abalone per year. The natural California red abalone population was decimated by years of overharvesting, so the Abalone Farm is a way for seafood lovers to once again dine on the large edible sea snail. Seafood enthusiasts can seek out these tasty, sustainably farmed products while dining at local restaurants.

serves heaping portions of breakfast classics, including scrambles and omelets, along with sandwiches and burgers. The Pooney scramble is a tasty mess of spinach, cheeses, eggs, bacon, and mushrooms. The biscuits can be on the dry side.

Within Morro Bay State Park, the **Bayside Café** (10 State Park Rd., 805/772-1465, www.baysidecafe.com, 11am-3pm Mon.-Wed., 11am-8:30pm Thurs. and Sun., 11am-9pm Fri.-Sat., $10-27), true to its name, is right by the bay. The lunch menu skews toward burgers and fish-and-chips, while dinner features fancier fare such as lobster scampi.

In the mood for a darn fine hamburger? In nearby Los Osos, **Sylvester's Burgers** (1099 Santa Ynez Ave., Los Osos, 805/528-0779, www.sylvestersburgers.com, 11am-9pm daily, $7-15) attracts carnivores with juicy beef slathered in signature sauce. The yellow shack has a range of juicy, tasty, never-frozen beef burgers, including The Sylvester Burger, a pound of beef topped with cheddar cheese, onion rings, bacon—and of course, Sylvester's sauce. Four beers are available on tap to wash it down. Eat on the outdoor deck or inside, where the walls are decorated with photos of the regulars.

Mexican

People worship the crab cake and fish tacos at ★ **Taco Temple** (2680 N. Main St., 805/772-4965, http://tacotemple.com, 11am-8pm Sun.-Thurs., 11am-8:30pm Fri.-Sat., $7-22). Housed in a big multicolored building east of Highway 1, where colorful surfboards hang on the walls, this is not the standard taqueria. Its California take on classic Mexican dishes includes sweet potato enchiladas and tacos filled with soft-shell crab or calamari. The tacos are served like salads, with the meat and greens piled on tortillas. The chips and salsa are terrific.

Thai

Thai Bounty (560 Embarcadero, 805/772-2500, http://thethaibounty.com, 11am-2:30pm and 5pm-9pm Mon.-Fri., 11am-9pm Sat.-Sun., $11-14) has won second place for its oyster entry in the Central Coast Oyster Festival, so the chefs know seafood. They take advantage of the local bounty—both fresh seafood and vegetables and herbs from their own garden—to create daily specials with preparations like panang curry, garlic pepper, and spicy stir-fry. Dine indoors or out on the patio.

German

The roast beef brings people back to the **Hofbrau** (901 Embarcadero, 805/772-2411, www.hofbraumorrobay.com, 11am-9pm daily, $7-15). It has been serving up popular half-pound hand-carved roast beef sandwiches au jus since 1971. The informal waterfront

eatery also cooks up clam chowder, burgers, and fish-and-chips alongside German fare like bratwurst and sauerkraut. There's also a salad bar to balance your meat intake.

Vegetarian

Run by the folks who own the adjacent Sunshine Health Foods store, the Shine Café (427 Morro Bay Blvd., 805/771-8344, www.sunshinehealthfoods-shinecafe.com, 11am-5pm Mon.-Fri., 9am-5pm Sat., 10am-4pm Sun., $4.50-11) is a vegetarian's dream, focusing on local and organic ingredients in their smoothies, sandwiches, and salads. The BLT uses bacon-flavored tempeh, and the namesake hummus wrap is big enough to sate even a carnivore's appetite. Gluten-free tempeh tacos are a house specialty. Order at the inside kitchen counter, then dine indoors under local art or out at sidewalk tables.

Breakfast and Brunch

★ Frankie and Lola's (1154 Front St., 805/771-9306, www.frankieandlolas.com, 6:30am-2pm daily, $4-13) does breakfast right. Creative savory dishes include the fried green tomato Benedict topped with creole hollandaise sauce and tasty, colorful chilaquiles with red chorizo, avocado, and tomatillo salsa. Lunch focuses on salads and sandwiches, while dinner is a little heartier, with options like a bacon-wrapped meatloaf or chorizo-stuffed chicken.

On the road toward Montaña de Oro State Park, Celia's Garden Café (1188 Los Osos Valley Rd., Los Osos, 805/528-5711, http://celiasgardencafe.com, 7:30am-2pm Mon.-Fri., 7:30am-2:30pm Sat.-Sun., $9-12) is an ideal place to fuel up for a day of hiking. Fill up on a pork chop and eggs or the chicken-fried steak. Other options include omelets, benedicts, and hotcakes. Located in a plant nursery, the café has an indoor dining room and a dog-friendly outdoor patio.

1: Taco Temple 2: Frankie and Lola's

Coffee Shops

Popular Top Dog Coffee (875 Main St., 805/772-9225, www.topdogcoffeebar.com, 7am-5pm daily) is the place to get caffeinated, with all of the usual options as well as a few creative beverages like mango chai and Mexican mocha. The coffee beans are roasted right here. For lunch (6:30am-4pm), they also serve café fare: bagels, burritos, paninis, and sandwiches. There are tables inside and out front on the sidewalk.

Farmers Market

Morro Bay has two weekly farmers markets: the Thursday farmers market (Spencer's Fresh Markets parking lot, 2650 Main St., 805/544-9570, www.slocountyfarmers.org, 2:30pm-4:30pm Thurs.) and the Saturday farmers market (Main St. and Morro Bay Blvd., 805/602-1009, 2:30pm-5:30pm Sat.).

ACCOMMODATIONS
Under $150

The Sundown Inn (640 Main St., 805/772-3229 or 800/696-6928, http://sundowninn.com, $109-229) is a well-priced motel within walking distance of Morro Bay's downtown and waterfront areas. Guest rooms have fridges, microwaves, and—here's something different—coin-operated vibrating beds.

$150-250

The ★ Masterpiece Hotel (1206 Main St., 805/772-5633 or 800/527-6782, www.masterpiecehotel.com, $109-339) is a great place to stay for art enthusiasts and lovers of quirky motels. Each guest room is decorated with framed prints from master painters, and the hallways also have prints of paintings by Henri Matisse, Vincent Van Gogh, and Norman Rockwell. A large indoor spa pool decorated like a Roman bathhouse further differentiates this motel from other cookie-cutter lodging options. Expect a deluxe breakfast in the morning and a wine-and-cheese serving in early evening.

Built in 1939, the bright ★ Beach Bungalow Inn & Suites (1050 Morro

Ave., 805/772-9700, www.morrobaybeach bungalow.com, $129-309) has been extensively renovated. The 12 clean, spacious, and modern guest rooms have hardwood floors, local art on the walls, and flat-screen TVs. Eleven of the guest rooms have gas fireplaces. Family suites accommodate four people, while king deluxe suites have full kitchens. Two bicycles are available for cruising around town.

The owners of the **Marina Street Inn** (305 Marina St., 805/772-4016, www.marinastreetinn.com, $150-170) honeymooned here, so they know what visitors want. The four suites are individually decorated; one has a nautical theme, while another features a willow-limb bedpost and a birdhouse table. Each suite shares a balcony or porch with the adjoining room.

From the outside, the **Ascot Suites** (260 Morro Bay Blvd., 805/772-4437 or 800/887-6454, www.ascotsuites.com, $159-359) resembles an English country inn. The theme continues in the guest rooms, with English country fabrics and fireplaces. A rooftop garden showcases views of Morro Rock and the bay. Deluxe guest rooms include jetted tubs.

The **Estero Inn** (501 Embarcadero, 805/772-1500, www.esteroinn.com, $219-399) is located right on the waterfront. All eight guest rooms are suites with microwaves and fridges. They each have a balcony or ocean view.

Over $250

The family-run **Anderson Inn** (897 Embarcadero, 805/772-3434, www.andersoninnmorrobay.com, $279-429) is an eight-room boutique hotel located right on Morro Bay's busy Embarcadero. Three of the guest rooms are perched right over the estuary with stunning views of the nearby rock. Those premium guest rooms also include fireplaces and jetted tubs.

The unique **Front Street Inn and Spa** (1140 Embarcadero, 805/772-5038, www.frontstreetinn.net, $249-289) offers just two

large guest rooms that share a floor with a spa. The high-ceilinged rooms are oriented around large windows, with superb views of the harbor and the rock. Both have deep soaking tubs, fridges, and gas fireplaces. Expect to wake to the aroma of the bakery on the first floor.

Camping

Located a couple of miles outside downtown Morro Bay, the **Morro Bay State Park Campground** (Morro Bay State Park Rd., 800/444-7275, www.reservecalifornia.com, tents $35, RVs $50) has 140 campsites, many shaded by eucalyptus and pine trees; right across the street is the Morro Bay estuary. Six miles (9.7 km) southwest of Morro Bay, **Montaña de Oro State Park** (Pecho Rd., 7 mi/11.3 km south of Los Osos, 800/444-7275, www.reservecalifornia.com, $25) has more primitive camping facilities. There are walk-in environmental campsites and a primitive campground behind the Spooner Ranch House that has pit toilets.

One mile (1.6 km) north of Morro Rock, **Morro Strand State Beach** (Yerba Buena St. and CA-1, 800/444-7275, www.reservecalifornia.com, $35) has more than 80 sites within spitting distance of the beach.

TRANSPORTATION AND SERVICES

Car

As with most towns on the Central Coast, CA-1 cuts through Morro Bay. If you're traveling south from San Francisco, take US-101 south to Atascadero, take Highway 41 west, and then head south on Highway 1. Exit at Main Street in Morro Bay. If you're traveling from Los Angeles, the best route is US-101 north to San Luis Obispo, and then north on Highway 1 to Morro Bay; take the Morro Bay Boulevard exit into town.

Morro Bay is 30 miles (48 km) south of Hearst Castle on CA-1. Simply look for the Main Street exit to get to downtown Morro Bay.

Bus

There is no direct bus service to Morro Bay, although **Greyhound** (805/238-1242, www.greyhound.com) travels along US-101 and stops at 1460 Calle Joaquin Street in San Luis Obispo. From there you'll need to connect with **Regional Transit Authority** (805/781-4472, www.slorta.org, $1.75-5.50) buses to get to Morro Bay. There are various weekday and weekend routes.

Trolley

The **Morro Bay Trolley** (595 Harbor Way, 805/772-2744, 11am-5pm Mon., 11am-7pm Fri.-Sat., 11am-6pm Sun. Memorial Day weekend-first weekend in Oct., $1 per ride, children under 5 free) operates three routes. The **Waterfront Route** runs the length of the Embarcadero, including out to Morro Rock. The **Downtown Route** runs through the downtown (as in uptown) area all the way out to Morro Bay State Park. The **North Morro Bay Route** runs from uptown through the northern part of Morro Bay, north of the rock, along Highway 1. An all-day pass (not a bad idea if you plan on seeing a lot of sights) is $3.

Services

The **Morro Bay Chamber of Commerce** (845 Embarcadero, Ste. D, 800/225-1633, www.morrobay.org, 9am-5pm daily) has a wonderful visitors center overlooking the bay at the end of a small boardwalk. It has a vast array of printed material you can take with you.

French Hospital Medical Center (1911 Johnson Ave., San Luis Obispo, 805/543-5353, www.dignityhealth.org) and **Sierra Vista Regional Medical Center** (1010 Murray Ave., San Luis Obispo, 805/546-7600, /www.tenethealthcentralcoast.com) are the closest hospitals. Both are in San Luis Obispo, 13 miles (20.9 km) from Morro Bay. If you have an emergency, dial 911. The local police are the **Morro Bay Police Department** (850 Morro Bay Blvd., 805/772-6225).

To access the **post office** (898 Napa Ave., 805/772-0839, 9am-5pm Mon.-Fri., 9am-1pm Sat.), you'll need to leave the Embarcadero area and head uptown.

Background

The Landscape

The Monterey Bay region and Central Coast were formed by tectonic events occurring over the past 30 million years. The inland section of Monterey County is on the very active San Andreas Fault, the boundary between the Pacific Plate and North American Plate. The fault line frequently causes earthquakes in the historic town of San Juan Bautista. Santa Cruz was the epicenter of the Loma Prieta Earthquake, a magnitude 6.9 event that rocked the region in 1989.

The area's coastal mountain ranges were also formed by tectonic activity. Both the Santa Lucia Mountains and Santa Cruz Mountains

parallel the coastline and help contribute to the area's stunning scenery and many recreation opportunities. The Santa Cruz Mountains begin on the San Francisco Peninsula and run south into the Salinas Valley. Their highest point is 3,786-foot (1,154-m) Loma Prieta Peak.

The dramatic Santa Lucia Mountains form the backdrop for Big Sur. They traverse Monterey County and the northern portion of San Luis Obispo County. The highest point in the range is 5,857-foot (1,785-m) Junípero Serra Peak on the eastern flank of the mountains, while 5,155-foot (1,571-m) Cone Peak has the most dramatic rise from sea to summit.

Rivers and streams bisect the area on their way to the sea. The San Lorenzo River begins in the Santa Cruz Mountains and spills into the sea just south of the Santa Cruz Beach Boardwalk. The largest river in the region is the Salinas River, which runs through the Salinas Valley before turning its course to the ocean south of Moss Landing. The Carmel River originates in the Santa Lucia Mountains and hits the Pacific just a shade south of Carmel-by-the-Sea.

The entire section of the Pacific Ocean offshore of this region is part of Monterey Bay National Marine Sanctuary, which stretches from Marin County above San Francisco down to Cambria. Monterey Bay is a Pacific Ocean bay between Santa Cruz and Monterey. It is known for its abundant kelp forests and the Monterey Submarine Canyon, an underwater valley off Moss Landing in the middle of the bay. The canyon plunges to a depth of 2 miles (3.2 km), twice as deep as Arizona's Grand Canyon.

CLIMATE

Like most of coastal California, the Monterey Bay area is known for its mostly mild Mediterranean climate. This means that summer and fall are warm and dry, while winter and spring are chillier and see more rainfall. Precipitation is rare in the region from May to October, while pretty much all of the rain falls between November and April. Unfortunately, the last few years have seen minimal rainfall throughout the year, a phenomenon that is contributing to California's drought.

Summers on the coast can be chillier than expected due to fog. This effect is caused by hot inland air that meets with cool air coming off the Pacific Ocean. The best places to get out of the fog are the inland sections of Monterey County, including Carmel Valley and Salinas Valley. Big Sur Valley also offers sunny relief when the coast is socked in with fog. On many summer days, the Monterey Peninsula is obscured by fog, while Santa Cruz across the bay is sunny and a few degrees warmer.

ENVIRONMENTAL ISSUES

Californians face several major environmental issues. The state battles drought, and water for crops, farms, and human consumption is always in short supply. Monterey Bay is not immune to this problem and is even considering desalination plants that transform seawater into drinking water. Water conservation measures can include limiting development and urban sprawl, restricting water usage, and designating set periods for personal and recreational use, such as watering lawns.

Water pollution is also an issue. Most tap water is safe to drink, but swimming in bays, lakes, and rivers, as well as the Pacific Ocean, requires more caution. Pollution may cause *E. coli* outbreaks at beaches, affecting wildlife and beachgoers alike. Santa Cruz's Cowell's Beach and Capitola Beach have been known to have bacteria in their waters after winter rains.

Many of the state's grand oak trees have succumbed to sudden oak death, a disease that spreads through spores to eventually kill live oaks, black oaks, and tan oaks. To control its spread, travelers are advised to clean all camping equipment thoroughly and to buy and burn local firewood rather than importing it from elsewhere.

Plants and Animals

PLANTS
Redwoods

The **coast redwood** (*Sequoia sempervirens*) grows as far south as Big Sur. Coast redwoods are characterized by their towering height, flaky red bark, and moist understory. Among the tallest trees on earth, they are also some of the oldest, with some individual trees almost 2,000 years old. Because they collect moisture from the ocean and fog, coast redwoods occupy only a narrow strip of coastal California; they grow no more than 50 miles (81 km) inland. Their tannin-rich bark is crucial to their ability to survive wildfires and regenerate afterward. Big Basin Redwoods State Park, Henry Cowell Redwoods State Park, and Big Sur's state parks are the region's best places to marvel at the giants.

Oaks

California is home to many native oaks. The most common are the **valley oak, black oak, live oak,** and **coastal live oak.** The deciduous black oak grows throughout the foothills of the Coast Range; the coastal live oak occupies the Coast Range itself. The acorns of all these oaks were an important food supply for California's Native American populations and continue to be an important food source for wildlife.

Wildflowers

The state flower is the **California poppy** (*Eschscholzia californica*). The pretty little perennial grows just about everywhere, even on the sides of the busiest highways. The flowers of most California poppies are bright orange, but they also appear occasionally in white, cream, and an even deeper red-orange.

ANIMALS
Mountain Lions

Mountain lions (*Felis concolor*) are an example of powerful and potentially deadly beauty. Their solitary territorial hunting habits make them elusive, but human contact has increased as more homes are built in mountain lion habitat throughout California. Many parks in or near mountain lion territory post signs with warnings and advice: Do not run if you come across a mountain lion; instead make noise and raise and wave your arms so that you look bigger. The California Department of Fish and Wildlife (www.dfg.ca.gov) offers a downloadable brochure on encounters and other tips.

Whales

The massive, majestic **gray whale** (*Eschrichtius robustus*) was once endangered, but its numbers have rebounded with international protection. The gray whale measures about 40 feet (12.2 km) long and has mottled shades of gray with black fins; its habitat is inshore ocean waters, so there is a chance to get a glimpse of them from headlands up and down the coast. Gray whales generally migrate south along the coast November-January and closer to shore February-June, when they return northward.

Perhaps a more recognizable behemoth is the **humpback whale** (*Megaptera novaeangliae*). At 45-55 feet (13.7-16.8 m) long, the humpback is the only large whale to breach regularly; it then rolls and crashes back into the water, providing one of the best shows in nature. The whale also rolls from side to side on the surface, slapping its long flippers. Humpbacks generally stay a little farther from shore, so it may be necessary to take a whale-watching cruise to catch a glimpse of them, but their 20-foot (6.1-m) spouts can help landlubbers spot them from shore. Look for humpbacks April-early December off the coast near Big Sur, particularly at Julia Pfeiffer Burns State Park.

The blue whale (Balaenoptera musculus) is the largest animal on earth. At 70-90 feet (21.3-27.4 m) long, the blue whale even exceeds most dinosaurs in size. Sporting a blue-gray top and a yellowish bottom, the blue whale has a heart the size of a small car—and two blowholes—but, alas, does not breach. They can be seen June-November off the California coast, especially at Monterey.

California Sea Lions

Watching a beach full of California sea lions (Zalophus californianus) sunning themselves and noisily honking away can be a pleasure. Sea lions are migratory, so they come and go at will, especially in the fall when they head to Southern California for breeding.

Sea Otters

Even higher on the cuteness scale is the sea otter (Enhydra lutris), which can be spotted just offshore in shallow kelp beds. Once near extinction, the endearing and playful sea otter has survived; now there are more than 2,000 in California waters. It can be a bit mesmerizing to witness a sea otter roll on its back in the water and use a rock to break open mollusks for lunch. Sea otter habitat runs from Monterey Bay to Big Sur.

Birds

California has a wide range of habitat with accessible food and water that makes it perfect for hundreds of bird species to nest, raise their young, or just stop over and rest during long migrations. Nearly 600 species have been spotted in California.

Among the most regal of California's bird species are raptors. The red-tailed hawk (Buteo jamaicensis) is found throughout California and is frequently sighted perched in trees along highways and even in urban areas. The red-tailed hawk features a light underbelly with a dark band and a distinctive red tail that gives the bird its name.

Although not as common as it once was, Swainson's hawk (Buteo swainsoni) has been an indicator species in California's environment. The Swainson's hawk population has declined due to loss of habitat and excessive pesticide use in agricultural lands; its main diet consists of the locusts and grasshoppers that feed on these crops, passing the contaminants on to the birds. These hawks are smaller than the red-tailed hawk, with dark brown coloring and some white underparts either on the chest or under the tail.

With wings spanning 10 feet (3 m) from tip to tip, the California condor (Gymnogyps californianus) is the largest flying bird in North America. In the recent past, the condors' population had plummeted due to its susceptibility to lead poisoning, along with deaths caused by electric power lines, habitat loss, and gunshots from indiscriminate humans. In 1987, there was only one California condor left in the wild; it was taken into captivity as part of a breeding program. In 1997, a Monterey County-based nonprofit, the Ventana Wildlife Society (VWS), began releasing the giant birds back into the wild. As of 2021, 90 wild condors soar above California's Central Coast. The species' recovery is one of conservation's great success stories.

Reptiles

Several varieties of rattlesnakes are indigenous to the state. If you spot California's most infamous native reptile, keep your distance. All rattlesnakes are venomous, although death by snakebite is extremely rare in California. Most parks with known rattlesnake populations post signs alerting hikers to their presence; hikers should stay on marked trails and avoid tromping off into meadows or brush. Pay attention when hiking, especially when negotiating rocks and woodpiles, and never put a foot or a hand down in a spot you can't see first. Wear long pants and heavy hiking boots for protection from snakes as well as insects, other critters, and unfriendly plants you might encounter.

Butterflies

California's vast population of wildflowers attracts an array of gorgeous butterflies. The **monarch butterfly** *(Danaus plexippus)* is emblematic of the state. These large orange-and-black butterflies have a migratory pattern that's reminiscent of birds. Starting in August, they begin migrating south to cluster in groves of eucalyptus trees. As they crowd together and close up their wings to hibernate, their dull outer wing color camouflages them as clumps of dried leaves, thus protecting them from predators. In spring, the butterflies begin to wake up, fluttering lazily in the groves for a while before flying north to seek out milkweed on which to lay their eggs. Pacific Grove and Santa Cruz are great places to visit these "butterfly trees."

History

THE FIRST RESIDENTS

The diverse ecology of California allowed Native Americans to adapt to the land in various ways. These groups included the Ohlone. More than 100 Native American languages were spoken in California, and each language had several dialects, all of which were identified with geographic areas.

Ohlone

The Ohlone people once occupied what is now Santa Cruz, Monterey, and the lower Salinas Valley, as well as land to the north. The Ohlone lived in permanent villages, only moving temporarily to gather seasonal foods such as acorns and berries. The Ohlone formed an association of about 50 different communities with an average of 200 members each. The villages interacted through trade, marriages, and ceremonies. Basket weaving, ceremonial dancing, piercings and tattoos, and general ornamentation indicated status within the community and were all part of Ohlone life. Like other Native Americans in the region, the Ohlone depended on hunting, fishing, gathering, and agrarian skills such as burning off old growth each year to get a better yield from seeds.

The Ohlone culture remained fairly stable until the first Spanish missionaries arrived to spread Christianity and to expand Spanish territorial claims. Spanish explorer Sebastián Vizcaíno reached what is now Monterey in December 1602, and the Rumsen group of Ohlone were the first Indigenous people he encountered. Father Junípero Serra's missionaries built seven missions on Ohlone land, and most of the Ohlone people were brought to the missions to live and work. For the next 60 years, the Ohlone suffered, as did most Indigenous people at the missions. Along with the culture shock of subjugation came the diseases for which they had no immunity—measles, smallpox, syphilis, and others. It wasn't until 1834 that the California missions were abolished and the Mexican government redistributed the mission land holdings.

The Ohlone lost the vast majority of their population between 1780 and 1850 because of disease, social upheaval from European incursion, and low birth rates. Estimates are that there were 7,000-26,000 Ohlone when Spanish soldiers and missionaries arrived, and about 3,000 in 1800 and 864-1,000 by 1852. There are 1,500-2,000 Ohlone people today.

THE MISSION PERIOD

In the mid-1700s, Spain pushed for colonization of Alta California, rushing to occupy North America before the British beat them to it. The effort was overly ambitious and underfunded, but missionaries started to sweep into present-day California.

The priest Junípero Serra is credited with influencing the early development of California. A Franciscan monk, Serra took an active role in bringing both Christianity and European diseases to Native American people from San Diego north to Sonoma County. The Franciscan order built a string of missions; each was intended to act as a self-sufficient parish that would grow its own food, maintain its own buildings, and take care of its own people. However, mission structures were limited by a lack of suitable building materials and skilled labor. Later, the forced labor of Native Americans was used to cut and haul timbers and to make adobe bricks. By the time the missions were operating, they claimed about 15 percent of the land in California, or about one million acres (404,686 ha) per mission.

Missions in this region include Santa Cruz Mission, San Juan Bautista Mission, San Carlos Borromeo de Carmelo Mission (better known as the Carmel Mission), Soledad's Mission Nuestra Senora de la Soledad, and inland Monterey County's Mission San Antonio de Padua.

Spanish soldiers used subjugation to control Indigenous people, pulling them from their villages and lands to the missions. Presidios (royal forts) were built near some of the missions to establish land claims, intimidate Indigenous people, and carry out the overall goal of finding wealth in the New World. The presidios housed the Spanish soldiers that accompanied the missionaries.

The city of Monterey was founded in 1770 with the establishment of the Presidio of Monterey and Mission San Carlos. At this time, Monterey became the capital of Spain's Alta California territory. Junípero Serra moved the mission to Carmel in 1771 to be closer to a better water supply.

In 1821, Mexico gained independence from Spain along with control of Alta California and the missions. The Franciscans resisted giving up the land and free labor, and continued to enslave Native Americans. From 1824 to 1834 the Mexican government handed out 51 land grants to colonists for land that had belonged to Native Americans and was held by nearby missions. From 1834 to 1836 the Mexican government revoked the power of the Franciscans to use Native American labor, and it began to redistribute the vast mission land holdings.

STATEHOOD

The first U.S. flag officially raised in California was hoisted up by the Custom House in 1846, although it was the Treaty of Guadalupe Hidalgo, which ended the Mexican-American War in 1848, that officially sold the land for the future state to the U.S. for a nominal fee. The dramatic population boom caused by the Gold Rush that began in 1848 ensured that California would be on the fast track to admission into the United States, bypassing the territorial phase. Monterey was integral to California's burgeoning statehood and hosted California's first constitutional convention at Colton Hall in 1849. The next year, California became a state. It had gone from a Mexican province to the 31st U.S. state in little more than four years. Monterey is known for having many of the state's firsts, from its first government building to its first theater to its first newspaper.

THE RISE OF THE TOURISM INDUSTRY

In 1880, a sprawling seaside resort called the Hotel Del Monte opened in Monterey, establishing the peninsula's reputation as a vacation destination. Its on-site features included a polo field, a horse track, a hedge maze, and a golf course. The buildings and grounds would be leased by the U.S. government in 1942 before becoming the still-operating Naval Postgraduate School.

THE GREAT DEPRESSION

The stock market crash of 1929 led to the Great Depression. Many property owners lost their farms and homes, and unemployment in California hit 28 percent in 1932; by 1935, about 20 percent of all Californians were on public relief.

Monterey Movies

The Monterey region has long had a starring role in films and TV, beginning in 1897 when the Thomas Edison Company shot the short films *Surf at Monterey* and *Hotel Del Monte*. More recent cameos for the stunning setting include HBO's *Big Little Lies* and as the series finale of AMC's *Mad Men*. Following is a list of a few of the movies shot in Monterey.

- *Rebecca:* Director Alfred Hitchcock filmed scenes at Point Lobos as a stand-in for Cornwall in this 1940 release.

- *East of Eden:* The 1955 film adaptation of John Steinbeck's novel, starring James Dean, filmed in the Salinas Valley and the city of Salinas.

- *The Parent Trap:* The original 1961 movie was shot around the Monterey Peninsula, including scenes at the Monterey Peninsula Airport and The Lodge at Pebble Beach.

- *Play Misty for Me:* Clint Eastwood's 1971 directorial debut was truly a Monterey Peninsula film. His character frequents a local bar (Monterey's Sardine Factory) and includes a scene at the Monterey Jazz Festival on the Monterey County Fairgrounds.

- *Star Trek IV: The Voyage Home:* The Cetacean Institute in the 1986 movie is actually the Monterey Bay Aquarium.

- *Turner & Hooch:* A good portion of this 1989 Tom Hanks film was filmed in downtown Pacific Grove.

- *Basic Instinct:* The 1992 thriller starring Michael Douglas and Sharon Stone utilized the coastal beauty of Carmel and Carmel Highlands. In the film, Stinson Beach is actually Big Sur's Garrapata Beach.

- *Bandits:* This 2001 film includes scenes of a bank heist at what is now Giorgio's restaurant in Salinas.

The Great Depression transformed the nation. Beyond the economic agony was an optimism that moved people to migrate to California. Many migrants from the Midwest settled in California, preserving their ways and retaining identities separate from other Californians. The Midwestern migrants' plight was captured in John Steinbeck's 1939 novel *The Grapes of Wrath.* Steinbeck, a Salinas native, gathered information by viewing firsthand the deplorable living and labor conditions under which Okie families existed. The novel was widely read and was turned into a movie in 1940. Government agencies banned the book from public schools, and libraries and large landowners campaigned to have it banned elsewhere. That effort lost steam, however, when Steinbeck won the 1940 Pulitzer Prize.

SARDINE CAPITAL OF THE WORLD

The first half of the 1900s found Monterey Bay's fishing industry flourishing. The center of the activity was Cannery Row, a road in Monterey lined with sardine-canning factories. The fishermen and canneries were extremely busy in the 1930s and early 1940s, gaining Monterey the title "Sardine Capital of the World." The catch began decreasing in 1945 and never recovered. The time and place were immortalized that same year with the publication of John Steinbeck's *Cannery Row.* The street is now a popular tourist attraction due in large part to the Monterey Bay Aquarium, which opened there in 1984.

Government and Economy

GOVERNMENT

California is home to what many consider liberal views: support of political protests and free speech, legalized marijuana use, environmental activism, and gay and lesbian rights. These beliefs are not incorporated as a whole throughout the state, however. Major metropolitan and coastal areas have become havens for artists, musicians, and those seeking alternatives to mainstream America. Inland populations, however, often show more conservative leanings at the polls.

California is overwhelmingly Democratic. The 2016 presidential election found just 32 percent of the state voted for President Donald Trump.

ECONOMY

California boasts the fifth-largest economy in the world. California's contribution to the United States outpaces even its immense size and population, and it continues to be the country's number-one economy.

California's number-one economic sector is farming. Sweet strawberries and spiky artichokes grow in abundance in the cooler Central Coast region. The Salinas Valley is a world-renowned agricultural region. Agriculture, including fruit, vegetables, nuts, dairy, and wine production, helps make California the world's fifth-largest supplier of food and agriculture commodities.

Today, organic farms and ranches are proliferating across the state. An increasing number of small farms and ranches growing crops use organic, sustainable, and even biodynamic practices. Most of these farmers sell directly to consumers by way of farmers markets and farm stands—almost every town or county in California has a weekly farmers market in the summer, and many are held year-round.

And then there's the wine. It seems like every square inch of free agricultural land has a grapevine growing on it. The vineyards that were once seen primarily in Napa and Sonoma can now be found in Monterey, Carmel Valley, and the Santa Cruz Mountains. It's actually the wine industry that's leading the charge beyond mere organic techniques and into biodynamic growing practices.

Essentials

Transportation

AIR
Monterey
The **Monterey Regional Airport** (MRY, 200 Fred Kane Dr., 831/648-7000, www.montereyairport.com) is the easiest way to travel to the Monterey Bay area. Five airlines (Alaska Airlines, American Airlines, Allegiant, United, U.S. Airways) fly commuter flights to and from San Francisco, San Diego, Los Angeles, Dallas, Portland, Seattle, Phoenix, Las Vegas, and Denver. The airport is just 3.5 miles (5.6 km) from downtown. Most of the time you can get better deals flying into San

Jose or San Francisco, but it is worth looking at Monterey Regional Airport, as there are occasionally good deals.

San Jose

The largest and closest airport to the Monterey region is **Mineta San Jose International Airport** (SJC, 1701 Airport Blvd., San Jose, 408/392-3600, www.flysanjose.com). This is a large, easily navigable airport that's a 75-minute drive from downtown Monterey. **Monterey Airbus** (831/373-7777, www.montereyairbus.com, $37-42) is a shuttle service that takes travelers from San Jose Airport to downtown Monterey. You can save five dollars by booking online.

San Francisco

San Francisco International Airport (SFO, 650/821-8211, www.flysfo.com) is a major airport that's an under-two-hour drive from downtown Monterey if traffic goes in your favor. The **Monterey Airbus** (831/373-7777, www.montereyairbus.com, $47-52) is a shuttle service that takes travelers from San Francisco Airport to downtown Monterey. You can save five dollars by booking online.

TRAIN

One **Amtrak** (www.amtrak.com) train route serves the region: The *Coast Starlight* travels down the West Coast, but stops only as close as **Salinas** (11 Station Pl.) before cutting inland. Amtrak has Thruway stations and stops in Santa Cruz, Monterey, and Carmel that bus passengers to the nearest Amtrak station.

BUS

Greyhound (800/231-2222, www.greyhound.com) has stations in Santa Cruz (920 Pacific Ave., 831/423-4082) and Salinas (3 Station Pl., 831/424-4418). Greyhound routes generally follow the major highways, traveling US-101.

CAR

CA-1, which is also known as **Highway 1,** is the major highway that runs along the coast from Santa Cruz through Monterey, Carmel, and Big Sur down to Cambria and Morro Bay. **US-101** runs through the inland areas of Monterey, including Salinas, before heading out to the coast south of Morro Bay at San Luis Obispo.

The easiest route to get to the Monterey Peninsula is to take US-101 south from the San Francisco or San Jose airport and then take CA-156 east to CA-1. Head south on CA-1 for Monterey, Carmel, and all communities to the south. **CA-17** is a mountainous highway that can be used as a shortcut to get from San Jose to Santa Cruz.

Road closures are not uncommon in winter. CA-1 along the coast and CA-17 can shut down due to flooding or landslides. Traffic jams, accidents, mudslides, fires, and snow can affect highways and interstates at any time. Before heading out on your adventure, check road conditions online at the **California Department of Transportation** (Caltrans, www.dot.ca.gov). One of the best local resources for Big Sur road information is the **BigSurKate blog** (http://bigsurkate.blog). The **Thomas Guide Road Atlas** (www.thomasguidebooks.com, $20-130) is a reliable and detailed map and road guide and a great insurance policy against getting lost.

Car and RV Rental

Most car-rental companies are located at the airports. To reserve a car in advance, contact **Budget Rent A Car** (800/268-8900, www.budget.com), **Dollar Rent A Car** (800/800-4000, www.dollar.com), **Enterprise** (855/266-9289, www.enterprise.com), or **Hertz** (inside U.S. and Canada 800/654-3131, outside U.S. 800/654-3001, www.hertz.com).

To rent a car, drivers in California must be at least 21 years of age and have a valid driver's license. California law also requires that all vehicles carry liability insurance. You can purchase insurance with your rental car, but it generally costs an additional $10 per day, which can add up quickly. Most private auto insurance will also cover rental cars. Before buying rental insurance, check your car insurance policy to see if rental car coverage is included.

The average cost of a rental car is $40 per day or $210 per week; however, rates vary greatly based on the time of year and distance traveled. Weekend and summer rentals cost significantly more. Generally, it is more expensive to rent from car rental agencies at an airport. To avoid excessive rates, first plan travel to areas where a car is not required, then rent a car from an agency branch in town to further explore more rural areas. Rental agencies occasionally allow vehicle drop-off at a different location from where it was picked up for an additional fee.

Another option is to rent an RV. You won't have to worry about camping or lodging options, and many facilities, particularly farther north, accommodate RVs. However, RVs are difficult to maneuver and park, limiting your access to metropolitan areas. They are also expensive, both in terms of gas and the rental rates. Rates during the summer average $1,300 per week and $570 for three days, the standard minimum rental. **Cruise America** (800/671-8042, www.cruiseamerica.com) has branches in San Francisco, San Mateo, and San Jose. **El Monte RV** (888/337-2214, www.elmonterv. com) operates out of San Francisco, San Jose, and Santa Cruz.

Jucy Rentals (800/650-4180, www. jucyusa.com) rents minivans with pop-up tops. The colorful vehicles are smaller and easier to manage than large RVs, but still come equipped with a fridge, gas cooker, sink, DVD player, and two double beds. Rent one just south of San Francisco (1620 Doolittle Dr., San Leandro, 9am-4pm Mon.-Fri., 9am-noon Sat.) and cruise down the coast.

Visas and Officialdom

PASSPORTS AND VISAS

Visiting from another country, you must have a valid passport and a visa to enter the United States. However, under the Visa Waiver Program, citizens of some countries do not need a visa for travel to the United States, provided they are staying for less than 90 days. You can find the list of eligible countries online (http://travel.state. gov). Holders of Canadian passports don't need visas or visa waivers. In most other countries, the local U.S. embassy should be able to provide a tourist visa. The average fee for a visa is US$160. While a visa may be processed as quickly as 24 hours on request, plan at least a couple of weeks, as there can be unexpected delays, particularly during the busy summer season (June-Aug.).

CUSTOMS

Before you enter the United States from another country by sea or by air, you'll be required to fill out a customs form. Check with the U.S. embassy in your country or **Customs and Border Protection** (inside the U.S. 877/227-5511, outside the U.S. 202/325-8000, www.cbp.gov) for an updated list of items you must declare.

If you require medication administered by injection, you must pack your syringes in a checked bag; syringes are not permitted in carry-ons coming into the United States.

Also, pack documentation describing your need for any narcotic medications you've brought with you. Failure to produce documentation for narcotics on request can result in severe penalties in the United States.

If you're driving into California along I-5 or another major highway, prepare to stop at Agricultural Inspection Stations a few miles inside the state line. You don't need to present a passport, a visa, or even a driver's license; instead, you must be prepared to present all your fruits and vegetables. California's largest economic sector is agriculture, and a number of the major crops grown here are sensitive to pests and diseases. In an effort to prevent known pests from entering the state and endangering crops, travelers are asked to identify all produce they're carrying in from other states or from Mexico. If you've got produce, especially homegrown or from a farm stand, it could be infected by a known problem pest or disease. Expect it to be confiscated on the spot.

You'll also be asked about fruits and veggies on your U.S. Customs form, which you'll be asked to fill out on the airplane or ship before you reach the United States.

Travel Tips

MONEY

Most businesses accept the major credit cards Visa, MasterCard, Discover, and American Express. ATM and debit cards work at many stores and restaurants, and ATMs are available throughout the region. In more remote areas, some businesses may only accept cash, so don't depend entirely on your plastic.

You can change currency at any international airport. Currency-exchange points also crop up in some of the major business hotels in urban areas.

Banks

As with anywhere, traveling with a huge amount of cash is not recommended, which may make frequent trips to the bank necessary. Fortunately, most destinations have at least one major bank. Usually Bank of America or Wells Fargo can be found on the main drags through towns. Banking hours tend to be 8am-5pm Monday-Friday and 9am-noon on Saturday. Never count on a bank being open on Sundays or on federal holidays. If you need cash when the banks are closed, there is generally a 24-hour ATM available. Furthermore, many cash-only businesses have an on-site ATM for those who don't have enough cash ready in their wallets. The unfortunate downside to this convenience is a fee of $2-4 per transaction. This also applies to ATMs at banks at which you don't have an account.

Tax

Sales tax in California varies by city and county, but the average rate is around 7.5 percent. All goods are taxable with the exception of food not eaten on the premises. For example, your bill at a restaurant will include tax, but your bill at a grocery store will not. The hotel tax is another unexpected added expense to traveling. Most cities have enacted a tax on hotel rooms largely to make up for budget shortfalls. As you would expect, these taxes are higher in areas more popular with visitors.

Tipping

Tipping is expected and appreciated, and a 15 percent tip for restaurants is about the norm. When ordering in bars, tip the bartender or wait staff $1 per drink. For taxis, plan to tip 15-20 percent of the fare, or simply round up the cost to the nearest dollar. Cafés and coffee shops often have tip jars out. There is no consensus on what is appropriate when purchasing a $3 beverage. Often $0.50 is enough, depending on the quality and service.

COMMUNICATIONS

With the exception of rural and wilderness areas, California is fairly well connected. Cell phone reception is good except in places far from any large town, such as Big Sur. Likewise, you can find Internet access just about anywhere. The bigger cities are well wired, but even in small towns you can log on either at a library or in a café with a computer in the back. Be prepared to pay a per-minute usage fee or purchase a drink.

Because of California's size both geographically and in terms of population, you will have to contend with multiple area codes—the numbers that prefix the seven-digit phone number—throughout the state. The 800 or 866 area codes are toll-free numbers. Any time you are dialing out of the area, you must dial a 1 plus the area code followed by the seven-digit number.

To mail a letter, find a blue post office box, which are found on the main streets of any town. Postage rates vary by destination. You can purchase stamps at the local post office, where you can also mail packages. Stamps can also be bought at some ATMs and online at www.usps.com, which can also give you the location and hours of the nearest post office. Post offices are generally open Monday-Friday, with limited hours on Saturday. They are always closed on Sunday and federal holidays.

MAPS AND TOURIST INFORMATION

If you are looking for maps, almost all gas stations and drugstores sell maps both of the place you're in and of the whole state. **California State Automobile Association** (CSAA, http://calstate.aaa.com) offers free maps to auto club members.

Many local and regional visitors centers also offer maps, but you'll need to pay a few dollars for the bigger and better ones. But if all you need is a wine-tasting map in a known wine region, you can probably get one for free along with a few tasting coupons at the nearest regional visitors center. Basic national park maps come with your admission payment. State park maps can be free or cost a few dollars at the visitors centers.

The state's **California Travel and Tourism Commission** (916/444-4429, www.

visitcalifornia.com) also provides helpful and free tips, information, and downloadable maps and guides. The **Monterey County Convention & Visitors Bureau** (www. seemonterey.com) has a superb website for travel information about attractions, lodging, and restaurants along with insider tips, a great blog, and a comprehensive events calendar.

California is in the Pacific time zone (PST and PDT) and observes daylight saving time March-November.

CONDUCT AND CUSTOMS

The legal **drinking age** in California is 21. Expect to have your ID checked if you look under age 30, especially in bars and clubs, but also in restaurants and wineries.

Smoking has been banned in many places throughout California. Don't expect to find a smoking section in any restaurant or an ashtray in any bar. Smoking is illegal in all bars and clubs, but your new favorite watering hole might have an outdoor patio where smokers can huddle. Taking the ban one step further, many hotels, motels, and inns throughout California are strictly nonsmoking, and you'll be subject to fees of hundreds of dollars if your room smells of smoke when you leave.

There's no smoking in any public building, and even some of the state parks don't allow cigarettes. There's often good reason for this; the fire danger in California is extreme in the summer, and one carelessly thrown butt can cause a genuine catastrophe.

In 2018, sales of **recreational marijuana** became legal in California, although cities are able to decide if they want to prohibit selling of the drug. In Monterey County, Monterey, Carmel, and Pacific Grove decided to ban recreational marijuana sales. Meanwhile, the cities of Seaside and Del Rey Oaks decided to allow it. There's also Big Sur Canna & Botanicals in The Barnyard Shopping Center, but it is legal because it's right outside Carmel-by-the-Sea city limits. Santa Cruz and nearby Soquel also sell recreational marijuana.

Coasting California with the Kids

- Families flock to **Monterey Bay Aquarium** (page 40) to see cute sea otters and scary sharks up close.

- If your kids just want to play, you can't beat Monterey's **Dennis the Menace Park** (page 50), which has all sorts of slides, bridges, and swing sets.

- The **Santa Cruz Beach Boardwalk** (page 162) offers nonstop amusement in the form of rides and arcades.

- To see underwater sea life without donning snorkeling gear, hitch a ride with Morro Bay's **Sub Sea Tours** (page 269), where you ride in a mini-submarine.

ACCESS FOR TRAVELERS WITH DISABILITIES

Most attractions, hotels, and restaurants are accessible for travelers with disabilities. State law requires that public transportation must accommodate the special needs of travelers with disabilities and that public spaces and businesses have adequate restroom facilities and equal access. This includes national parks and historic structures, many of which have been refitted with ramps and wider doors. Many hiking trails are also accessible to wheelchairs, and most campgrounds designate specific campsites that meet the Americans with Disabilities Act standards. The state of California also provides a free telephone TDD-to-voice relay service; just dial 711.

If you are a traveler with a disability, there are many resources to help you plan your trip. **Access Northern California** (http://accessnca.org) is a nonprofit organization that offers general travel tips, including recommendations on accommodations, parks and trails, transportation, and travel equipment. **Gimp-on-the-Go** (www.gimponthego.com) is a travel resource. The message board on the **American Foundation for the Blind** (www.afb.org) website is a good forum to discuss travel strategies for the visually impaired. For a comprehensive guide to wheelchair-accessible beaches, rivers, and shorelines on the Central Coast, contact the **California**

Coastal Conservancy (510/286-1015, www.scc.ca.gov), which publishes a free and downloadable guide (www.wheelingcalscoast.org). **Accessible Vans** in San Francisco (866/224-1750, www.accessiblevans.com) rents wheelchair-accessible vans and offers pick-up and drop-off service from airports.

TRAVELING WITH CHILDREN

Many places in this region are ideal destinations for families with children of all ages. Amusement parks, interactive museums, zoos, parks, beaches, and playgrounds all make for family-friendly fun. On the other hand, there are a few spots that beckon more to adults than to children. Before you book a room at a B&B that you expect to share with your kids, check to be sure that the inn can accommodate extra people in the guest rooms and whether guests under age 16 are allowed.

SENIOR TRAVELERS

You'll find senior discounts nearly every place you go, including restaurants, golf courses, major attractions, and even some hotels, although the minimum age can range 50-65. Just ask, and be prepared to produce ID if you look young or are requesting a senior discount. You can often get additional discounts on rental cars, hotels, and tour packages as a member of **AARP** (888/687-2277, www.aarp.org). If you're not a member, its website can also offer helpful travel tips and advice. **Road**

Scholar (800/454-5768, www.roadscholar. org) is another great resource for senior travelers. Dedicated to providing educational opportunities for older travelers, Road Scholar provides package trips to beautiful and interesting destinations. Called "Educational Adventures," these trips are generally 3-9 days long and emphasize history, natural history, art, music, or a combination thereof.

GAY AND LESBIAN TRAVELERS

Santa Cruz is a quirky town specially known for its lesbian-friendly culture. A relaxed vibe informs everything from underground clubs to unofficial nude beaches to live-action role-playing games in the middle of downtown. Even the lingerie and adult toyshops tend to be woman-owned and -operated.

As with much of the country, the farther you venture into rural and agricultural regions, the less likely you are to experience the liberal acceptance for which California is known. The **International Gay and Lesbian Travel Association** (954/630-1637, www.iglta.org) has a directory of gay- and lesbian-friendly tour operators, accommodations, and destinations.

Health and Safety

MEDICAL SERVICES

For an emergency, **dial 911.** Inside hotels and resorts, check your emergency number as soon as you get to your guest room. In urban and suburban areas, full-service hospitals and medical centers abound, but in more remote regions, help can be more than an hour away.

If you're planning a **backcountry expedition,** follow all rules and guidelines for obtaining **wilderness permits** and for self-registration at trailheads. These are for your safety, letting the rangers know roughly where you plan to be and when to expect you back. National and state park visitors centers can advise in more detail on any health or wilderness alerts in the area. It is also advisable to let someone outside your party know your route and expected date of return.

Being out in the elements can present its own set of challenges. Despite California's relatively mild climate, **heat exhaustion** and **heat stroke** can affect anyone during the hot summer months, particularly during a long, strenuous hike in the sun. Common symptoms include nausea, lightheadedness, headache, or muscle cramps. **Dehydration** and loss of electrolytes are the common causes of heat exhaustion. If you or anyone in your group develops any of these symptoms, get out of the sun immediately, stop all physical activity, and drink plenty of water. Heat exhaustion can be severe, and if untreated can lead to heat stroke, in which the body's core temperature reaches 105°F (41°C). Fainting, seizures, confusion, and rapid heartbeat and breathing can indicate the situation has moved beyond heat exhaustion. If you suspect this, call 911 immediately.

Similar precautions hold true for **hypothermia,** which is caused by prolonged exposure to cold water or weather. For many in California, this can happen on a hike or backpacking trip without sufficient rain gear, or by staying too long in the ocean or another cold body of water without a wetsuit. Symptoms include shivering, weak pulse, drowsiness, confusion, slurred speech, or stumbling. To treat hypothermia, immediately remove the wet clothing, cover the person with blankets, and feed him or her hot liquids. If symptoms don't improve, call 911.

WILDERNESS SAFETY

Many places are still wild, making it important to use precautions with regard to wildlife. **Mountain lions** can be found in the Coast Range, as well as grasslands and forests. Because of their solitary nature, it is unlikely

Coronavirus in Monterey & Carmel

At the time of writing in summer 2021, California—including the areas covered in this book—were recovering from the significant effects of the coronavirus, but the situation was constantly evolving. Monterey County, especially Salinas and the Salinas Valley, were hit very hard by the pandemic.

Now more than ever, Moon encourages its readers to be courteous and ethical in their travel. We ask travelers to be respectful to residents, and mindful of the evolving situation in their chosen destination when planning their trip.

BEFORE YOU GO

- Check regional websites (listed below) for local restrictions and the overall health status of the destination and your point of origin. If you're traveling to or from an area that is currently a COVID-19 hotspot, you may want to reconsider your trip.

- Moon encourages travelers to get vaccinated if their health status allows, and to take a coronavirus test with enough time to receive results before departure if possible. Some destinations may require proof of vaccination or a negative COVID test result before arrival. Check local requirements and factor these into your plans.

- If you plan to fly, check with your airline and the destination's health authority for updated travel requirements. Some airlines may be taking more steps than others to help you travel safely, such as limiting occupancy; check their websites for more information before buying your ticket, and consider a very early or very late flight, to limit exposure. Flights may be more infrequent, with increased cancellations.

- Check the website of any parks, wineries, museums, and other venues you wish to patronize to confirm that they're open, if their hours have been adjusted, and to learn about any specific visitation requirements, such as mandatory reservations or limited occupancy.

- Pack plenty of face masks, hand sanitizer, and a thermometer. Consider packing snacks, bottled water, a cooler, or anything else you might need to limit the number of stops along your route, and to be prepared for possible closures and reduced services over the course of your travels.

- Assess the risk of entering crowded spaces, joining tours, and taking public transit.

- Expect general disruptions. Events may be postponed or cancelled, and some tours, wineries, and venues may require reservations, enforce limits on the number of guests, be operating during different hours than the ones listed, or be closed entirely.

RESOURCES

- **Monterey County Health Department** (www.co.monterey.ca.us)

- **Public Health Department of Santa Cruz County** (www.santacruzhealth.org)

- **Monterey County Convention & Visitors Bureau** (www.seemonterey.com)

- **Centers for Disease Control and Prevention** (www.cdc.gov)

you will see one, even on long trips in the backcountry. Still, there are a couple things to remember. If you come across a kill, probably a large partly eaten deer, leave immediately. And if you see a mountain lion and it sees you, identify yourself as human, making your body appear as big as possible, just as with a bear. And remember: Never run. As with any cat, large or small, running triggers its hunting instincts. If a mountain lion should attack, fight back; cats don't like to get hurt.

The other treacherous critter in the back-country is the **rattlesnake.** It can be found in summer in generally hot and dry areas. When hiking in this type of terrain—many parks will indicate if rattlesnakes are a problem in the area—keep your eyes on the ground and an ear out for the telltale rattle. Snakes like to warn you to keep away. The only time this is not the case is with baby rattlesnakes that have not yet developed their rattles. Unfortunately, they have developed their fangs and venom, which is particularly potent. If you're bitten by a rattlesnake, seek immediate medical attention.

Mosquitoes can be found throughout the state. At higher elevations they can be worse, prompting many hikers and backpackers to don head nets and apply potent repellents, usually DEET. The high season for mosquitoes is late spring-early summer.

Ticks live in many of the forests and grasslands throughout the state, except at higher elevations. Tick season generally runs late fall-early summer. If you are hiking through brushy areas, wear pants and long-sleeved shirts. Ticks like to crawl to warm, moist places (armpits are a favorite) on their host. If a tick is engorged, it can be difficult to remove. There are two main types of ticks found in California: dog ticks and deer ticks. Dog ticks are larger, brown, and have a gold spot on their backs, while deer ticks are small, tear-shaped, and black. Deer ticks are known to carry Lyme disease. While Lyme disease is relatively rare in California—there are more cases in the northernmost part of the state—it is very serious. If you get bitten by a deer tick

and the bite leaves a red ring, seek medical attention. Lyme disease can be successfully treated with early rounds of antibiotics.

There is only one major variety of plant in California that can cause an adverse reaction in humans if you touch the leaves or stems: **poison oak,** a common shrub that inhabits forests throughout the state. Poison oak has a characteristic three-leaf configuration, with scalloped leaves that are shiny green in the spring and then turn yellow, orange, and red in late summer-fall. In fall, the leaves drop, leaving a cluster of innocuous-looking branches. The oil in poison oak is present year-round in both the leaves and branches. Your best protection is to wear long sleeves and long pants when hiking, no matter how hot it is. A product called Tecnu is available at most California drugstores—slather it on before you go hiking to protect yourself from poison oak. If your skin comes into contact with poison oak, expect a nasty rash known for its itchiness and irritation. Poison oak is also extremely transferable, so avoid touching your eyes, face, or other parts of your body to prevent spreading the rash. Calamine lotion can help, and in extreme cases a doctor can administer cortisone to help decrease the inflammation.

CRIME AND SAFETY PRECAUTIONS

The outdoors is not the only place that harbors danger. In both rural and urban areas, theft can be a problem. When parking at a trailhead or in a park or at a beach, don't leave any valuables in the car. If you must, place them out of sight, either in a locked glove box or in the trunk. The same holds true for urban areas. Furthermore, avoid keeping your wallet, camera, and other expensive items, including lots of cash, easily accessible in backpacks; keep them within your sight at all times. Certain neighborhoods are best avoided at night. Consider taking a cab to avoid walking blocks and blocks to get to your car or to wait for public transportation. In case of a theft or any other emergency, call 911.

Resources

Suggested Reading

Monterey County has been home to some of the world's most revered writers, including John Steinbeck, Henry Miller, and Robinson Jeffers. Other writers like Robert Louis Stevenson, Jack Kerouac, and Richard Brautigan were inspired after spending a little time in the area. The Monterey Bay region has also been the focus of works on the natural world and human history.

LITERATURE

Jeffers, Robinson. *Selected Poems.* New York: Vintage Books, 1965. The superb nature poems in this collection include "The Place For No Story," set in present-day Garrapata State Park; "The Purse-Seine," about a boat off the Santa Cruz coast; and "Tor House," named for the author's self-constructed residence on Carmel Point.

Kerouac, Jack. *Big Sur.* New York: Penguin Books, reprint 2013. The Beat writer made famous by *On the Road* goes dark in this 1962 novel about a man's mental deterioration and struggle with alcoholism that takes place mostly at a cabin in Big Sur.

Miller, Henry. *Big Sur and the Oranges of Hieronymus Bosch.* New York: Pocket Books, reprint 1975. The controversial author spent 18 years residing in Big Sur and wrote this 1957 portrait about the rural region and his life there.

Steinbeck, John. *Cannery Row.* New York: Penguin Books, reprint 2014. Pulitzer Prize-winning writer John Steinbeck set many of his novels in Monterey County, but *Cannery Row,* originally published in 1945, is a favorite among many for its depiction of a marine biologist and the other colorful inhabitants of Monterey's old fish-canning neighborhood.

CULTURAL AND NATURAL HISTORY

Bignell, Steven, and Susan Brujines. *228 Interesting, Odd, Beautiful and Historic Things to See in Santa Cruz County.* Santa Cruz, CA: Journeyworks Publishing, 2013. A fun book that covers major Santa Cruz sights, including the Santa Cruz Mission and the Giant Dipper Roller Coaster, along with lesser-known gems like the Bigfoot Discovery Museum and Kitchen's Temple, a West Side lot filled with detailed minarets and walls.

Henson, Paul, Donald J. Unser, and Valerie A. Kells. *The Natural History of Big Sur.* Oakland: University of California Press, 1996. The in-depth book covers Big Sur's plants, animal species, geology, significant places, and human history.

Lundy, A. L. "Scrap." *Real Life on Cannery Row: Real People, Places and Events that Inspired John Steinbeck.* Santa Monica, CA: Angel City Press, 2008. A thin volume packed with historic photos and anecdotes about the people and places that shaped John Steinbeck's novel *Cannery Row.*

Margolin, Malcolm. *The Ohlone Way: Indian Life in the San Francisco-Monterey Bay Area.* Berkeley, CA: Heydey Books, 1997. This book details the Ohlone lifestyle and how it was irrevocably destroyed by the arrival of the Spanish.

Norman, Jeff. *Big Sur: Images of America.* Mount Pleasant, SC: Arcadia Publishing, 2004. Big Sur historian and biologist Jeff Norman wrote this photo-heavy book about the rugged region.

Palumbi, Stephen R., and Carolyn Sotka. *The Death and Life of Monterey Bay: A Story of Revival.* Washington DC: Island Press, 2012. The director of Pacific Grove's Hopkins Marine Station tells the story of Monterey Bay, from its pristine past to its overfished days to its eventual renewal.

Stevenson, Robert Louis. "Old Pacific Capital." First published in *Fraser's Magazine,* Vol. XXII, 1880. This essay by the famed author of *Treasure Island* and *Kidnapped* describes what Monterey was like when Stevenson resided here in 1879. It's available online for free.

Internet Resources

The California travel industry leads the way in the use of the Internet as a marketing, communications, and sales tool. The overwhelming majority of destinations have their own websites—even tiny towns in the middle of nowhere proudly tout their attractions on the Web.

Big Sur Chamber of Commerce
www.bigsurcalifornia.org
This website has visitors information and a blog about highway and emergency conditions.

California Department of Transportation
www.dot.ca.gov
Check here for a state map and highway information before planning a coastal road trip.

California State Parks
www.parks.ca.gov
The official website lists hours, accessibility, activities, camping areas, fees, and more information for all parks in the state system.

Cambria Chamber of Commerce
www.cambriachamber.org
It's a good idea to visit this site before a trip for information about Cambria's lodging, shops, attractions, and restaurants.

CarmelCalifornia.com
www.carmelcalifornia.com
This website has information on restaurants, shopping, art galleries, spas, and more along with exclusive offers, including reduced-rate accommodations and two-for-one wine-tastings.

Good Times
http://goodtimes.sc
Santa Cruz's alternative weekly offers lots of information on local events, including concerts.

Monterey County Convention & Visitors Bureau
www.seemonterey.com
This fantastic website has the usual visitor information (lodging, attractions, and

restaurants) and other creative components, including videos, a blog, insider tips, and a comprehensive calendar of events.

Monterey County Weekly
www.montereycountyweekly.com
Monterey County's alternative weekly has lots of information on local events and dining.

Monterey Herald
www.montereyherald.com
This is the website for Monterey's daily newspaper.

Santa Cruz County Conference and Visitors Council
www.santacruz.org
The Santa Cruz County Conference and Visitors Council puts their comprehensive Santa Cruz Traveler's Guide online at this site.

State of California
www.ca.gov
This website offers outdoor resources for California state and government organizations. Check for information about fishing and hunting licenses, backcountry permits, boating regulations, and more.

Ventana Wilderness Alliance
www.ventanawild.org
This website provides the best and most up-to-date details on conditions in Big Sur's Ventana Wilderness.

Visit California
www.visitcalifornia.com
Before your visit, check out the official tourism site of the state of California.

Index

List of Maps

Photo Credits

All photos © Stuart Thornton except page 3 © Nalukai | Dreamstime.com; page 6 © (top right) Aaron West | Dreamstime.com; page 7 © (top) Sbeketov | Dreamstime.com; (bottom left) Stuart Thornton; (bottom right) Gloria Moeller | Dreamstime.com; page 8 © Rdubose52 | Dreamstime.com; page 10 © (bottom) Adeliepenguin | Dreamstime.com; page 12 © Digital94086 | Dreamstime.com; page 13 © (top) Nalukai | Dreamstime.com; page 17 © (bottom) timla/123rf.com; page 18 © (top) Armyblues83 | Dreamstime.com; page 19 © (bottom) Cupertino10 | Dreamstime.com; page 23 © (bottom) Serge Novitsky | Dreamstime. com; page 25 © (top) Yuval Helfman | Dreamstime.com; page 26 © (bottom) Robertbohrer | Dreamstime. com; page 28 © (top) Pansa Sunavee | Dreamstime.com; page 31 © (top) Larry Gevert | Dreamstime. com; page 36 © (top left) Chase Dekker | Dreamstime.com; page 45 © (bottom) Juliscalzi | Dreamstime. com; page 56 © (top left) Sbeketov | Dreamstime.com; (top right) Wirestock | Dreamstime.com; (bottom) Moisesserrato | Dreamstime.com; page 80 © Yuval Helfman | Dreamstime.com; page 100 © (top left) Andrei Gabriel Stanescu | Dreamstime.com; page 137 © (top left) Msurdin | Dreamstime.com; (top right) Cheri Alguire | Dreamstime.com; page 149 © (top) Cheri Alguire | Dreamstime.com; page 158 © Paul Topp | Dreamstime.com; page 159 © (top right) Malbright | Dreamstime.com; page 169 © (top) Pikappa | Dreamstime.com; (bottom) Xiaoyong | Dreamstime.com; page 207 © (left middle) Vampy1 | Dreamstime. com; (right middle) Toms Auzins | Dreamstime.com; (bottom) Anderm | Dreamstime.com; page 212 © (top right) Tupungato | Dreamstime.com; page 243 © Randy Vavra | Dreamstime.com; page 247 © Joe Sohm | Dreamstime.com; page 267 © (top) Paul Brady | Dreamstime.com; (bottom) Bjulien03 | Dreamstime.com

Acknowledgments

I would like to dedicate this book to my loving, supportive, and beautiful partner for life, Sarah Kenoyer. In addition, I'd like to give a virtual pat on the head to Max, my canine companion.

There's no doubt that Monterey County's greatest resource is its people, so I would like to thank all of my local and regional friends for all of their love and support over the years. A special shout-out to Mark C. Anderson for the restaurant and foodie tips.

As always, thanks to my family for all they have given me throughout life.

Finally, thank you to all of the folks at Moon Travel Guides who have helped make my dream of writing travel guidebooks a reality. For this edition, a special shout-out to production coordinator Darren Alessi, map editor Albert Angulo, and editor Kristi Mitsuda, who had great ideas and was very understanding while I navigated the challenges of working on a travel guide during a worldwide pandemic.

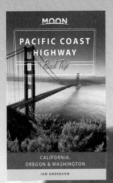
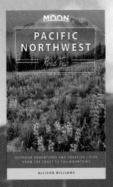

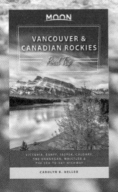

COASTAL CALIFORNIA

MOON

MONTEREY & CARMEL

WITH SANTA CRUZ AND BIG SUR

MOON

SAN DIEGO

IAN ANDERSON

MOON

TAHOE & RENO

LOCAL SPOTS • GETAWAY IDEAS • HIKING & SKIING

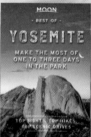

MOON

- BEST OF -

YOSEMITE

MAKE THE MOST OF ONE TO THREE DAYS IN THE PARK

TOP SIGHTS, TOP HIKES, TOP SCENIC DRIVES

ANN MARIE BROWN

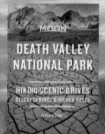

MOON

DEATH VALLEY NATIONAL PARK

HIKING SCENIC DRIVES
DESERT SPRINGS & HIDDEN OASES

MOON

JOSHUA TREE & PALM SPRINGS

MOON

SEQUOIA & KINGS CANYON

HIKING CAMPING
WATERFALLS & BIG TREES

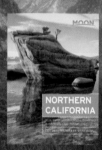

MOON

NORTHERN CALIFORNIA

MOON

PACIFIC COAST HIGHWAY Road Trip

CALIFORNIA, OREGON & WASHINGTON

IAN ANDERSON

MOON

SOUTHERN CALIFORNIA Road Trip

DRIVES ALONG THE BEACHES, MOUNTAINS, AND DESERTS, WITH THE BEST STOPS ALONG THE WAY

IAN ANDERSON

Getaways
or the great
outdoors:
See more
California
with Moon

MOON

52 WEEKEND ADVENTURES IN NORTHERN CALIFORNIA

TOM STIENSTRA

MY FAVORITE OUTDOOR GETAWAYS

MOON

CALIFORNIA CAMPING

The Complete Guide to More Than 1,400 Tent and RV Campgrounds

TOM STIENSTRA

MOON

CALIFORNIA HIKING

THE COMPLETE GUIDE TO 1,000 of the BEST HIKES in the GOLDEN STATE

TOM STIENSTRA • ANN MARIE BROWN

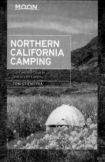

MOON

NORTHERN CALIFORNIA CAMPING

The Complete Guide to Tent and RV Camping

TOM STIENSTRA

#TravelWithMoon

MAP SYMBOLS

▰▰▰ Expressway	○ City/Town	✗ Airport	⌁ Golf Course
▰▰ Primary Road	◉ State Capital	✗ Airfield	℗ Parking Area
▬ Secondary Road	⊛ National Capital	▲ Mountain	⬟ Archaeological Site
═ ═ ═ Unpaved Road	◉ Highlight	✚ Unique Natural Feature	♦ Church
- - - Trail	★ Point of Interest		⬗ Gas Station
·········· Ferry	• Accommodation	⚐ Waterfall	⬭ Glacier
►-►-► Railroad	▼ Restaurant/Bar	⚑ Park	Mangrove
▰▰ Pedestrian Walkway	■ Other Location	TH Trailhead	Reef
▥▥▥ Stairs	Λ Campground	⛷ Skiing Area	Swamp

CONVERSION TABLES

°C = (°F - 32) / 1.8
°F = (°C x 1.8) + 32
1 inch = 2.54 centimeters (cm)
1 foot = 0.304 meters (m)
1 yard = 0.914 meters
1 mile = 1.6093 kilometers (km)
1 km = 0.6214 miles
1 fathom = 1.8288 m
1 chain = 20.1168 m
1 furlong = 201.168 m
1 acre = 0.4047 hectares
1 sq km = 100 hectares
1 sq mile = 2.59 square km
1 ounce = 28.35 grams
1 pound = 0.4536 kilograms
1 short ton = 0.90718 metric ton
1 short ton = 2,000 pounds
1 long ton = 1.016 metric tons
1 long ton = 2,240 pounds
1 metric ton = 1,000 kilograms
1 quart = 0.94635 liters
1 US gallon = 3.7854 liters
1 Imperial gallon = 4.5459 liters
1 nautical mile = 1.852 km

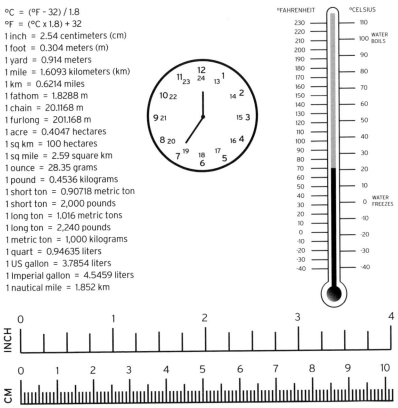

MOON MONTEREY & CARMEL

Avalon Travel
Hachette Book Group
1700 Fourth Street
Berkeley, CA 94710, USA
www.moon.com

Editor: Kristi Mitsuda
Series Manager: Kathryn Ettinger
Graphics and Production Coordinator: Darren Alessi
Cover Design: Faceout Studios, Charles Brock
Interior Design: Domini Dragoone
Moon Logo: Tim McGrath
Map Editor: Albert Angulo
Cartographer: Karin Dahl

ISBN-13: 9781640495418
Printing History
1st Edition — 2002
7th Edition — January 2022
5 4 3 2 1

Text © 2021 by Stuart Thornton.
Maps © 2021 by Avalon Travel.

Front cover photo: A humpback whale breaches in Monterey Bay © Della Huff / Alamy Stock Photo
Back cover photo: People sunbathing at beach in Carmel-by-the-Sea © Sergiy Beketov | Dreamstime.com

Printed in Malaysia for Imago